Studies in the History of Medieval Religion

VOLUME XXX

THE CULTURE OF MEDIEVAL ENGLISH MONASTICISM

Studies in the History of Medieval Religion

ISSN 0955-2480

General Editor
Christopher Harper-Bill

Previously published titles in the series
are listed at the back of this volume

THE CULTURE OF MEDIEVAL
ENGLISH MONASTICISM

Edited by
JAMES G. CLARK

THE BOYDELL PRESS

First published 2007
The Boydell Press, Woodbridge

ISBN 978–1–84383–321–5

The Boydell Press is an imprint of Boydell & Brewer Ltd
PO Box 9, Woodbridge, Suffolk IP12 3DF, UK
and of Boydell & Brewer Inc.
668 Mt Hope Avenue, Rochester, NY 14620, USA
website: www.boydellandbrewer.com

A catalogue record of this publication is available
from the British Library

This publication is printed on acid-free paper

Printed in Great Britain by
Antony Rowe Ltd, Chippenham, Wiltshire

Contents

The Culture of the Community

Illustrations

10. [Richard Fox, bishop of Winchester], *Here Begynneth the rule of seynt Benet,*
    R. Pynson [London, 1516]. Title page. Oxford, Bodl. Arch. A. d. 15, title
    page. © The Bodleian Library.
11. The formula of profession from the text of the *Regula Benedicti* given to
    the nuns of Wherwell by Bishop Richard Fox of Winchester. The formula
    confirms the identification, since the dedication of the house is given as of St.
    Cross and St. Peter. Fox presented copies of the Rule to the four nunneries
    of his diocese, Nunnaminster (St Mary's Winchester), Romsey, Wherwell
    and Wintney. The Nunnaminster book also survives, as Cambridge, Univer-
    sity Library, MS Mm. 3. 13. Oxford, Bodl., Barlow MS 11, fol. 13r. © The
    Bodleian Library.
12. The commonplace book of William Glastynbury, monk of Christ Church,
    Canterbury; here a leaf containing epistolary salutations. Oxford, Corpus
    Christi College, MS 256, fol. 171v/176v. © President and Fellows of Corpus
    Christi College, Oxford.
13. The opening lines of Anselm of Canterbury's *Epistolae*, from an English
    manuscript of the twelfth-century of unknown provenance. London, BL
    Royal MS 5 F IX, fol. 109r. © The British Library.
14. The opening lines of Aelred of Rievaulx's *De spiritali amicitia*, from a manu-
    script of *c.*1200 which belonged to Revesby Abbey, where Aelred had held
    the abbacy (1143?–46). London, BL, Royal MS 8 F I, fol. 4r. © The British
    Library.
15. Detail of a portrait of the fourteenth-century horologer, Richard of Wall-
    ingford, abbot of St Albans, showing the pioneering clock for which he was
    widely celebrated. Taken from the St Albans, *Liber benefactorum,* a codex
    first compiled in 1380. London, BL Cotton MS Nero D VII, fol. 20r. © The
    British Library.

Acknowledgements

The origin of this collection was a conference, sponsored by the British Academy, under the title 'Monastic Culture in Medieval England' which took place at Robinson College, Cambridge, in September 2002. The majority of the essays are derived from papers delivered at the conference; additional contributions have come subsequently from David Bell, who was sadly unable to attend the conference itself, and from Joan Greatrex. Joan was co-organiser of the Cambridge conference and together with her late husband, Warren, worked tirelessly not only on the programme but also on matters of financial and domestic management before, during and after the event: its success was very much their joint achievement. To them both I owe a great debt of gratitude. Joan has also proved a source of wise counsel throughout the preparation of this collection and for this I am also very grateful. I would like to acknowledge the assistance of the University of Bristol Arts Faculty Research Fund whose generous grant made it possible to include the plates. I should also like to thank Caroline Palmer for her advice, assistance and support in seeing this project through to publication.

James G. Clark
Maiden Bradley
September 2006

List of Contributors

James G. Clark is Senior Lecturer in Late Medieval History at the University of Bristol. His previous publications include *The Religious Orders in Pre-Reformation England* (2002) and *A Monastic Renaissance at St Albans: Thomas Walsingham and his Circle, c.1350–c.1440* (2004). He is currently completing a study of the dissolution of the monasteries for Yale University Press.

David N. Bell is Research Professor in the Department of Religious Studies at the Memorial University of Newfoundland. His previous publications include *The Libraries of the Cistercians, Gilbertines and Premonstratensians* (1992), *What Nuns Read* (1995), and *Par mille chemins: développement et diversité de la théologie médiévale* (2000).

Roger Bowers is Emeritus Reader in Medieval and Renaissance Music in the University of Cambridge, and Emeritus Fellow of Jesus College, Cambridge. He has research interests in the composition and theory of music in England between the fourteenth and the seventeenth centuries and has published widely on the music of the monasteries and secular cathedrals in medieval and pre-Reformation England.

Barry Collett is Senior Fellow in the Department of History at the University of Melbourne and also Research Fellow at Corpus Christi College, Oxford. His previous publications include *Italian Benedictine Scholars and the Reformation: The Congregation of St Giustina of Padua* (1985), *Female Monastic Life in Early Tudor England: An Edition of Richard Fox's Translation of the Benedictine Rule for Women, 1517*, with an introductory monograph, *The Early Modern Englishwoman, 1500–1750* (2002), and *The Early Modern Englishwoman: A Facsimile Library of Essential Works, Series 1 Printed Writings, 1500–1640: Part 4 Volume 3. Late Medieval Englishwomen: Julian of Norwich, Margaret Kempe and Juliana Berners* (2007).

Mary Erler is Professor of English at Fordham University, New York. She has research interests in medieval drama, devotional literature and the book culture of medieval women. Recent publications include *Women, Reading and Piety in Late Medieval England* (2002), and (with M. Kavaleski) *Gendering the Master Narrative* (2003).

G. R. Evans is Professor Emeritus of Medieval Theology and Intellectual History in the University of Cambridge. She has published many works on medieval theology. Recent books include *Bernard of Clairvaux* (2000), (as editor) *Mediaeval Commentaries on Peter Lombard's Sentences* (2001) and *Law and Theology in the Middle Ages* (2002).

Miriam Gill is Slide Curator in the Department of History of Art and Film, University of Leicester. She has published widely on wall paintings and other aspects of medieval English religious art.

Joan Greatrex was Associate Professor of History at Carleton University, Ottawa, until her retirement in 1984. She subsequently held the Bye Fellowship at Robinson College, Cambridge. She has published widely on the life and learning of the Benedictine monks of the English cathedral priories. Her most recent book is A Biographical Register of the English Cathedral Priories of the Province of Canterbury, c. 1066–1540 (1997). She is currently completing a history of the cathedral priories for Oxford University Press.

Julian Haseldine is Senior Lecturer in Medieval History at the University of Hull. His research focuses on friendship in monastic culture and politics in the eleventh and twelfth centuries. He has edited the letters of Peter of Celle for Oxford Medieval Texts (2001), and published a number of articles on friendship in monastic letters.

A. J. Piper is Keeper of Cathedral Muniments in the Special Collections Department of Durham University Library. He is the author of many articles on the medieval monks of Durham and is the co-editor of The Durham Liber Vitae and its Context (2004). His biographical register of the Durham monks will form a substantial element in the forthcoming edition, by David and Lynda Rollason, of the Durham Liber vitae.

J. D. North was, until 1999, Professor of the History of Philosophy and the Exact Sciences at the University of Groningen. His many books include Richard of Wallingford (1976), The Ambassadors' Secret: Holbein and the World of the Renaissance (2002) and God's Clockmaker: Richard of Wallingford and the Invention of Time (2005). His next book, Cosmos: An Illustrated History of Astronomy, will be published shortly by Chicago University Press.

R. M. Thomson is Professor of Medieval History in the School of History and Classics at the University of Tasmania. He is the author of many works on medieval intellectual history, the editor of a number of medieval Latin texts, and the cataloguer of several collections of medieval manuscripts. Recent publications include The Bury Bible (2003), A Descriptive Catalogue of the Medieval Manuscripts in Worcester Cathedral Library (2001), and with M. Winterbottom the Oxford Medieval Texts edition of William of Malmesbury's Gesta regum Anglorum (1998).

List of Abbreviations

ABR	*American Benedictine Review*
AJ	*Antiquaries Journal*
ArchJ	*Archaeological Journal*
Annales	*Annales Monasterii S. Albani, a Johanne Amundesham*
Amundesham	*Monacho, ut videtur, conscripti (A.D. 1421–1440)*, ed. H. T. Riley, 2 vols., RS 28 (1870–71)
BAACT	British Archaeological Association Conference Transactions
BAST	*Birmingham Archaeological Society Transactions*
BIHR	*Bulletin of the Institute of Historical Research*
BJRL	*Bulletin of the John Rylands Library*
BL	London, British Library
BM	*Burlington Magazine*
BRECP	See Greatrex (below)
BRUO	See Emden (below)
CAS	Cambridge Antiquarian Society
CBMLC	Corpus of British Medieval Library Catalogues
CCAL	Canterbury Cathedral Archives and Library
CCCC	Cambridge, Corpus Christi College
CCCR, CCP	Canterbury Cathedral Chapter Records, Christ Church Priory
CCM	Corpus Consuetudinum Monasticarum
CGCC	Cambridge, Gonville and Caius College
Chapters, ed. Pantin	*Documents Illustrating the Activities of the General and Provincial Chapters of the English Black Monks, 1215–1540*, ed. W. A. Pantin, 3 vols., Camden Society, 3rd series, 45, 47, 54 (1931–37)
CHJ	*Cambridge Historical Journal*
CKC	Cambridge, King's College
CMM	Corpus Mensurabilis Musicae
Concilia, ed. Wilkins	*Concilia Magnae Britanniae et Hiberniae, a Synodo Verolamiensi, AD CCCCXLVI ad Londinensem AD MDCCXVII accedunt constitutiones et alia ad historiam Ecclesiæ Anglicanæ spectantia*, ed. D. Wilkins, 4 vols. (London, 1737)
CSJC	Cambridge, St John's College
CSQ	*Cistercian Studies Quarterly*
CTC	Cambridge, Trinity College
CUL	Cambridge, University Library
DCA	Durham Cathedral Archives
DR	*Downside Review*

EBL	*English Benedictine Libraries: The Shorter Catalogues*, ed. R. Sharpe, *et al.*, CBMLC, 4 (1996)
EECM	Early English Church Music
EETS ES	Early English Text Society, Extra Series
EETS OS	Early English Texts Society, Original Series
EHR	*English Historical Review*
EM	*Early Music*
Emden, *BRUO*	A. B. Emden, *A Biographical Register of the University of Oxford to AD 1500*, 3 vols. (Oxford, 1957–59)
EMH	*Early Music History*
Greatrex, *BRECP*	J. Greatrex, *Biographical Register of the English Cathedral Priories of the Province of Canterbury, c. 1066–1540* (Oxford, 1997)
GRO	Gloucestershire Record Office
HBS	Henry Bradshaw Society
HJ	*Historical Journal*
HRO	Hampshire Record Office
James, *Ancient Libraries*	M. R. James, *The Ancient Libraries of Canterbury and Dover* (Cambridge, 1903)
JBAA	*Journal of the British Archaeological Association*
JBS	*Journal of British Studies*
JEH	*Journal of Ecclesiastical History*
JHS	*Journal of Historical Sociology*
JMH	*Journal of Medieval History*
Knowles, *Monastic Order*	D. Knowles, *The Monastic Order in England* (Cambridge, 1940)
Knowles, *Religious Orders*	D. Knowles, *The Religious Orders in England*, 3 vols. (Cambridge, 1948–59)
Leclercq, *Love of Learning*	J. Leclercq, *The Love of Learning and the Desire for God. A Study of Monastic Culture*, tr. C. Misrahi (New York, 1961)
Lee, *Nunneries*	P. Lee, *Nunneries, Learning and Spirituality in Late Medieval English Society: The Dominican Priory of Dartford* (York, 2001)
LGL	London, Guildhall Library
LP	*Letters and Papers Foreign and Domestic of the Reign of Henry VIII*, ed. J. S. Brewer, J. Gairdner, and R. H. Brodie, 22 vols. in 35 (London, 1862–1932)
LPL	Lambeth Palace Library
MA	*Monasticon Anglicanum*, ed. W. Dugdale, new edn by J. Caley, H. Ellis and B. Bandinel, 6 vols. in 8 (London, 1817–30)
MRB	*Monastic Research Bulletin*
MQ	*The Musical Quarterly*
NA	National Archives (formerly PRO)
New Grove	*The New Grove Dictionary of Music and Musicians*, ed. S. Sadie and J. Tyrrell, 29 vols. (London, 2001)
NCDCA	Norwich Cathedral, Dean and Chapter Archives

NRS	Norfolk Record Society
ODNB	*Oxford Dictionary of National Biography*, ed. C. Matthew and B. Harrison, 60 vols. (Oxford, 2004)
OHS	Oxford Historical Society
OMT	Oxford Medieval Texts
Oxford, Bodl.	Oxford, Bodleian Library
PMLA	*Publications of the Modern Language Association*
PL	*Patrologia Latina*
PCC	Prerogative Court of Canterbury
Power, *Nunneries*	E. Power, *Medieval English Nunneries, c. 1275–1535* (Cambridge, 1922)
PRMA	*Proceedings of the Royal Musical Association*
PRO	Public Record Office (now The National Archives)
RB	*La règle de saint Benoît*, ed. A. de Vogüé and J. Neufville 7 vols. (Paris, 1971–2)
RB: 1980	*RB 1980: The Rule of St Benedict in Latin and English with notes*, ed. T. Fry (Collegeville, Minnesota, 1981)
Religious Orders, ed. Clark	*The Religious Orders in Pre-Reformation England*, ed. J. G. Clark, Studies in Medieval Religion, XVIII (Woodbridge, 2002)
RS	Rolls Series
SCA	Salisbury Cathedral Archives
SCH	Studies in Church History
Sharpe, *Latin writers*	R. W. Sharpe, *A Handlist of the Latin Writers of Great Britain and Ireland before 1540* (Turnhout, 1997)
SRSP	Suffolk Record Society Publications
SS	Surtees Society
STC	*A Short-Title Catalogue of Books Printed in England, Scotland and Ireland and of English Books printed abroad, 1475–1640*, ed. A. W. Pollard and G. R. Redgrave, rev. W. A. Jackson, F. S. Ferguson, and K. F. Pantzer and P. R. Rider, 3 vols. (London, 1976–91)
TBGAS	*Transactions of the Bristol and Gloucestershire Archaeological Society*
TEAS	*Transactions of the Essex Archaeological Society*
VCH	*Victoria County History*
VE	*Valor Ecclesiasticus*, ed. J. Caley and J. Hunter, 6 vols., Record Commission ([London], 1810–34)
Visitations, ed. Thompson	*Visitations of Religious Houses in the Diocese of Lincoln*, ed. A. H. Thompson, 2 vols. in 3, CYS, 17, 24, 33 (1915–27)
Visitations, 1517–31, ed. Thompson	*Visitations in the Diocese of Lincoln, 1517–31*, ed. A. H. Thompson, 3 vols., Lincoln Record Society, 33, 35, 37 (1940–7)
WAM	Westminster Abbey Muniments
WAS	*Worcester Archaeological Society*
WCL	Worcester Cathedral Library

WHS	Worcester Historical Society
WRS	Wiltshire Record Society
YAJ	*Yorkshire Archaeological Journal*
YAS	Yorkshire Archaeological Society

Introduction:
The Culture of Medieval English Monasticism

JAMES G. CLARK

The cultural remains of the medieval English monasteries have always been a source of scholarly fascination. Even at the Dissolution when their personnel were dispersed and their physical structures dismantled there were vigorous efforts to preserve the greatest of their treasures, their decorative objects, their vestments, their illuminated manuscripts and those whose contents were held to be of historical importance.[1] The enthusiasm for collecting and conserving former monastic fragments intensified in the seventeenth and eighteenth centuries and, with the inauguration of the Rolls and other record series in the middle years of the nineteenth century, monastic culture emerged at the very heart of the national historical enterprise.[2] In recent times the research agenda has expanded and it is the culture, and cultural remains, of the laity (so long eclipsed by the clergy) that now preoccupy many medievalists, but new discoveries,

---

[1] In fact as early as the 1520s crown agent John Leland had combed monastic book collections collecting manuscripts for the nascent royal collection. For the most authoritative account of this process see J. P. Carley, *The Libraries of Henry VIII*, CBMLC, 6 (2001), pp. xxvii–xlvi. A decade later the dissolution commissioners demonstrated a degree of curiosity about the cultural artefacts of the surrendered convents. See *Three Chapters of Letters relating to the Dissolution of the Monasteries*, ed. T. Wright, Camden Society, 26 (1843), pp. 90–1, 120, 144. The saving and safe-keeping of books, vestments and other monastic artefacts by former religious and their supporters has been documented in the case of Christ Church Cathedral Priory, Canterbury and Reading and St Albans Abbeys. See C. F. R. de Hamel, 'The Dispersal of the Library of Christ Church, Canterbury, from the Fourteenth to the Sixteenth century' in *Books and Collectors, 1200–1700: Essays Presented to Andrew Watson*, ed. J. P. Carley and C. G. C. Tite, British Library Studies in the History of the Book (London, 1996), pp. 263–79; A. Coates, *Medieval English Books: The Reading Abbey Book Collections from Foundation to Dispersal* (Oxford, 1999), pp. 122–42; J. G. Clark, 'Reformation and Reaction at St Albans Abbey, c.1530–58', *EHR*, 115 (2000), 297–328. See also J. P. Carley, 'Monastic Collections and their Disposal' in *The Cambridge History of the Book in Britain 4, 1557–1695*, ed. J. Barnard, D. F. McKenzie and M. Bell (Cambridge, 2002), pp. 339–47.

[2] 'Since the days of Spelman and Cotton', wrote David Knowles, the monasteries of England were regarded as 'a beneficent source of light': D. Knowles, 'The Cultural Influence of English Medieval Monasticism', *CHJ*, 7/3 (1943), 146–59 at 146. For a lively account of the inauguration of the Rolls Series and the monastic material which it made its own see D. Knowles 'The Rolls Series' in *id., Great Historical Enterprises* (Cambridge, 1960), pp. 101–34. For the background to this work see also J. W. Burrow, *A Liberal Descent: Victorian Historians and the English Past* (Cambridge, 1981), pp. 126–51.

displays, and reproductions of monastic art, manuscripts and music continue to command academic and – perhaps increasingly – public attention.[3]

The appreciation of monastic culture has always tended to treat the surviving fragments – whether they are manuscripts, vestments or wall paintings – in separation from the monastic community whose beliefs and values had first given them form. For the first generation of antiquarians this was undoubtedly a political imperative: the monasteries' manuscripts and other remains were to be stripped, just as their former churches had been, of every trace of the old monastic 'mumpsimus'.[4] Such prejudices may not be shared by medievalists of the modern era but they have still tended to treat monastic art, book production and scholarship in isolation from the patterns and preoccupations of conventual life itself. The architectural and other artistic remains of English monasteries have been studied in depth and served as the basis for new interpretations of insular trends and for new typologies, but only rarely for a new understanding of the communities that created them.[5] The books and book learning of English

[3]   The greatest discovery or recovery of recent years has been the chapter house fragments from the excavated ruins of Coventry Cathedral Priory. For a preliminary account of the artefacts recovered see M. Gill and R. Morris, 'A Wall Painting of the Apocalypse in Coventry rediscovered', BM, 143 (2001), 467–73; R. K. Morris, 'Monastic architecture: Destruction and Reconstruction' in The Archaeology of Reformation c. 1480–1580, ed. R. Gilchrist, Society for Post-Medieval Archaeology Monograph, 1 (Leeds, 2003), pp. 235–51 and Miriam Gill's essay below, pp. 55–6, 63–71. Architectural fragments, decorative objects and illuminated manuscripts from English monasteries have featured prominently in public exhibitions: Gothic Art for England, 1400–1547, ed. R. Marks and P. Binski with E. Townsend (London, 2003), pp. 238, 349, 352; The Cambridge Illuminations: Ten Centuries of Book Production in the Medieval West, ed. P. Binski and S. Panayotova (Cambridge, 2005), especially pp. 39–162. A number of exceptional codices connected with English monasteries have recently been digitised or reproduced in colour facsimile, notably The Bury Bible, ed. R. M. Thomson (Cambridge, 2003) and The Sherborne Missal, ed. J. Backhouse (2003). The music of the monasteries has also been recently reconstructed and recorded including the work of the composers (under monastic patronage) John Dunstable and Robert Fayrfax. See, for example, John Dunstable, Masses and Motets (Naxos: 2005); Robert Fayrfax, Missa et Magnificat (ASV: 1998); The Rose and the Ostrich Feather (Coro: 2004).

[4]   For the treatment of monastic manuscripts by Elizabethan antiquarians see The Recovery of the Past in Early Elizabethan England: Documents from the Circle of John Bale and John Joscelyn, ed. T. Graham and A. Watson, Cambridge Bibliographical Society Monographs, 13 (1998); John Stow and the Making of the English Past: Studies in Early Modern Culture and the History of the Book, ed. I. Gadd and A. Gillespie (London, 2004). See also M. McKisack, Medieval History in the Tudor Age (Oxford, 1961).

[5]   A notable exception to this trend is the series of symposia organised by the British Archaeological Association that have examined the artistic, intellectual and material culture of a succession of greater abbeys and priories. See, for example, Yorkshire Monasticism, Archaeology, Art and Architecture from the 7th to 16th centuries, ed. L. R. Hoey, BAACT, xv (1995); Bury St Edmunds: Medieval Art, Architecture, Archaeology, and Economy, ed. A. Gransden, BAACT, xx (1998); Alban and St Albans: Roman and Medieval Architecture, Art and Archaeology, ed. M. Henig and P. Lindley, BAACT, xxiv (2001); Medieval Art, Architecture and Archaeology at Rochester, ed. T. Ayers and T. Tatton-Brown, BAACT, xxviii (2006). In a study of the artistic and architectural enterprises undertaken by or for the Benedictine monasteries of south-west England Julian Luxford has sought similarly to analyse material culture against the background of the 'patterns of history' – the dynamics of English ecclesiastical (if not specifically monastic) life – that influenced its creation:

monks have formed the focus of much research and (re)interpretation, but for the most part the emphasis has been upon the insights they offer into the development of scholarly disciplines and cultural trends – history, theology, science, and humanism, for example – or on the development of the canons of celebrated monastic authors, Anselm of Canterbury, William of Malmesbury, and Matthew Paris.[6] Only latterly have historians turned to these manuscripts for the light they might shed on the place of learning in the monastic community as a whole. Towards the end of his career Sir Richard Southern signalled a shift in his approach to monastic material by returning to his portrait of St Anselm not only to retouch it but also to paint in the landscape that surrounded him.[7]

This approach to monastic art, manuscripts and scholarship reflects certain assumptions about the nature of monastic culture itself. There is no doubt that for some scholars the monastic environment has represented in cultural terms only a microcosm – albeit one dynamic and well documented – of wider medieval society. 'From the coming of Augustine till c.1150', declared one of the most distinguished authorities on medieval monasticism, 'the intellectual and cultural life of England was often at its purest and most intense within the monasteries. ... They were the cultural heart of England'.[8] The monasteries were prominent as patrons and producers, and in particular fields – architecture, book production – their influence was palpable, but as such they were exponents of (essentially) a common set of cultural values.[9] Others have argued for a fundamental distinction between the culture of the cloister and the secular world, recognising the capacity of monastic *regulae*, codes and customs to create an exclusive environment – which some historians have characterised as *Gegenkultur* – unencumbered by the beliefs and values of the world beyond.[10] If the essence of monastic culture was established in the rules that remained the *raison d'être* of monastic life throughout the medieval centuries then surely it is a matter beyond conventional historical analysis? For Dom Jean Leclercq there was only one history of monastic culture that could be written, one which traced the development of the cenobitic programme of *Opus Dei* and *Opus manuum* from its origins in the time of Benedict of Nursia to its fruition in the age of Anselm and Bernard of

J. M. Luxford, *The Art and Architecture of English Benedictine Monasteries, 1300–1540. A Patronage History*, Studies in the History of Medieval Religion, XXV (The Boydell Press: Woodbridge, 2005), p. xviii.

6   See, for example, G. R. Evans, *Anselm and Talking About God* (Oxford, 1978); *id.*, *Anselm and a New Generation* (Oxford, 1980); G. E. M. Gasper, *Anselm of Canterbury and his Theological Inheritance* (Aldershot, 2004); *The Cambridge Companion to Anselm*, ed. B. Davis and B. Leftow (Cambridge, 2005). See also R. Vaughan, *Matthew Paris* (Cambridge, 1956); R. M. Thomson, *William of Malmesbury* (Woodbridge, 1987).

7   R. W. Southern, *Anselm: Portrait in a Landscape* (Cambridge, 1990).

8   Knowles, 'Cultural Influence', pp. 147, 151.

9   *Monasticism and the Arts*, ed. T. G. Verdon with J. Dally and J. W. Cook (Syracuse, 1984). Verdon (p. 8) characterises the relationship of monastery to Christian society as one of 'exemplary microcosm to macrocosm'. Friedrich Prinz has characterised the monastic community of the early Middle Ages as a filter through which cultural traditions were transmitted to the wider world: F. Prinz, *Askese und Kultur. Vor- und frühbenediktinisches Mönchtum an der Wiege Europas* (Munich, 1985), p. 10.

10   Prinz, *Askese und Kultur*, p. 11.

Clairvaux.[11] Those who have challenged the notion of a cultural continuum and have admitted the tendency of the monastic tradition to be distorted or diverted over time and allowed the possibility of the emergence of particular epochs in European monastic culture, have nonetheless doubted that it is a subject that can be studied in any depth. Dom David Knowles concluded in the case of England that it was impossible to 'recapture the … atmosphere of the monastery' or 'reconstruct the mentality of the monk', not only because the 'traditional monastic *ascèse* has never lent itself to analysis or reduction to method' but also because available sources were so limited, there was no 'autobiography, [or body of] spiritual doctrine or even so much as a treatise, or collection of conferences or letters on [these] matters'.[12]

The research of recent decades, however, has offered a fresh approach to these conceptual and practical difficulties. While they acknowledge the significance of certain universal values, many studies now draw attention to the distinct cultural environments which coexisted in medieval society whether shaped by institutional structures (as in the case of the monastic order), gender, economic conditions or social status.[13] A new generation of monastic historians have challenged the notion of a continuum in medieval monastic observance outlining the fundamental differences in institutional, intellectual, spiritual and social life that separate the Carolingian and Gregorian periods, the twelfth century and later Middle Ages.[14] At the same time the recent discovery and recovery of material and manuscript sources – the cataloguing of the manuscripts of Worcester Cathedral Library, for example, and the excavation of the site of Coventry Cathedral Priory, both of which feature here – have served to supply some of

---

[11] Leclercq, *Love of Learning*, pp. 250–1.

[12] Knowles, *Monastic Order*, p. 691.

[13] A. Musson, 'Legal Culture: Medieval Lawyers' Aspirations and Pretensions' in *Fourteenth- Century England*, III, ed. W. M. Ormrod (Woodbridge, 2004), pp. 17–30; M. C. Erler, *Women, Reading and Piety in Late Medieval England* (Cambridge, 2002); C. M. Barron, 'Chivalry, Pageantry and Merchant Culture in Medieval London' in *Heraldry, Pageantry, and Social Display in Medieval England*, ed. P. Coss and M. Keen (Woodbridge, 2002), pp. 219–41; M. Connolly, *John Shirley: Book Production and the Noble Household in Fifteenth-Century England* (Aldershot, 1998); N. Orme, 'The Culture of Children in Medieval England', *PP*, 148 (1995), 48–88; P. W. Fleming, 'The Hautes and their "Circle": Culture and the English Gentry' in *England in the Fifteenth-Century: Proceedings of the 1986 Harlaxton Symposium*, ed. D. Williams (Woodbridge, 1987), pp. 85–102.

[14] See, for example, *Carolingian Culture: Emulation and Innovation*, ed. R. McKitterick (Cambridge, 1994); R. B. Dobson, 'English Cathedral Priories in the Fifteenth Century', *TRHS*, (1995), pp. 151–72; J. Burton, *The Monastic and Religious Orders in Britain, 1100–1300* (Cambridge, 1994); id., *The Monastic Order in Yorkshire, 1069–1215* (Cambridge, 1999); G. Constable, *The Reformation of the Twelfth Century* (Cambridge, 1996); *Monasteries and Society in Medieval Britain: Proceedings of the 1994 Harlaxton Symposium*, ed. B. J. Thompson (Stamford, 1999); S. Foot, *Veiled Women, 871–1066*, 2 vols., Studies in Early Medieval Britain, (Aldershot, 2000); J. G. Clark, 'The Religious Orders in Pre-Reformation England', in *The Religious Orders in Pre-Reformation England*, ed. id. (Woodbridge, 2002), pp. 1–33; S. Boynton, *Shaping a Monastic Identity: Liturgy and History at the Imperial Abbey of Farfa, 1000–1125* (Ithaca, 2006); *From Dead of Night to End of Day: The Medieval Customs of Cluny*, ed. S. Boynton and I. Cochelin (Turnhout, 2006).

the evidence that David Knowles regarded as essential for the reconstruction of monastic mentalities.[15]

In the light of these discussions and discoveries, researchers are beginning to explore the cultural dynamics of English monasteries in greater depth. There have been several significant studies of female monasticism which have sought to characterise not only their spiritual culture but also – after centuries of disparagement – their culture of reading and independent study.[16] The study of male monastic culture has languished somewhat in their shadow, but a number of recently published monographs have shown just how far the culture of a particular convent might be recovered from its material fragments and manuscript remains.[17] The essays in this collection aim to extend this enterprise to explore the culture of English monasticism in the six centuries between the Conquest and Dissolution. They address monasteries of men and women, of the Benedictines, the Cistercians, the regular canons and the reformed orders, not only the greater abbeys and cathedral priories but also those of lesser status and meagre endowment. They consider the observant life of the cloistered religious in this period, their performance of the liturgy (and liturgical music), their practice of prayer, reading and their pursuit of study, and their occupation in the practical arts, and also their conception of community, fraternity (and specifically friendship) and of the monastic vocation itself. They also touch on those dynamics of life in the cloister which are less well documented, the struggle between shared experience and private space, for example, and the monastic conception (and measurement) of the passage of time. The contributors have been directly involved in the new discoveries of recent decades, both archaeological and codicological, and there are manuscripts, wall paintings and original writings described here in depth for the first time.

The culture of English monasticism evolved over a millennium but it was founded on the rules, constitutions and customs established in its earliest centuries and in particular upon the rule of St Benedict. The culture of cenobitic life envisaged by the author of the rule differed in significant ways from the mode of life

---

[15] For the manuscripts of Worcester Cathedral Priory see R. M. Thomson, *Descriptive Catalogue of the Medieval Manuscripts of Worcester Cathedral Library* (Cambridge, 2001). For the excavation of Coventry Cathedral Priory see above note 3. For another recent (re)discovery see S. Keynes, 'The Cartulary of Athelney Abbey Rediscovered', MRB, vii (2001), 2–5.

[16] C. Cross, 'The Religious Life of Women in Sixteenth-Century Yorkshire', in *Women in the Church. Papers read at the 1989 Summer Meeting and the 1990 Winter Meeting of the Ecclesiastical History Society*, ed. W. J. Sheils and D. Wood, SCH, 27 (Oxford, 1990), pp. 307–24; R. Gilchrist and M. Oliva, *Religious Women in Medieval East Anglia: History and Archaeology, c. 1100–1540* (Studies in East Anglian History, 1; Norwich, 1993); *Women, the Book and the Godly*, ed. L. Smith and J. H. M. Taylor (Cambridge, 1995); D. N. Bell, *What Nuns Read: Books and Libraries in Medieval English Nunneries* (Kalamazoo, 1995); Erler, *Women, Reading and Piety*; Lee, *Nunneries*.

[17] Coates, *Medieval English Books; Bury St Edmunds: Medieval Art, Architecture, Archaeology and Economy*, ed. A. Gransden (Leeds, 1998); J. G. Clark, *A Monastic Renaissance at St Albans: Thomas Walsingham and his Circle, c.1350–1440* (Oxford, 2004).

that later was seen to epitomise the older monastic order.[18] There was no place in Benedict's programme either for the pursuit of learning or for the production of books or other decorative or devotional objects. The essential dynamic of his *cenobium* was the daily *Opus Dei*. It was the service of the Lord (*Constituenda est ergo nobis dominici schola servitii: RB*, prologue) to which every monk was called under his vocation and for which he and his fellows came together to form – in the words of the founder – a school (*schola: RB*, prologue). It was also the embodiment of the community ethic which was Benedict's unique contribution to European monasticism. It underlined their separation from the secular world (in contrast to the Sarabaites who 'still conform to the ways of the world') and their stability (in contrast to the Girovagues: *RB*, i). Not only did the demands of the *Opus Dei* direct the active and contemplative lives of the monks, it also dominated their mental horizons. Ardo, the biographer and contemporary of Benedict of Aniane (d. 821), recalled that while labouring in the fields the monastic community could still be heard to murmur the psalter under their breath.[19] The counterpoint to the *Opus Dei*, and its principal support, was the *Opus manuum*, the physical and practical labour required to sustain the community in material terms combined with the mental labour of sacred reading (*lectio divina: RB*, xlviii), a practice conceived not as intellectual endeavour as such but as a physical and spiritual exercise to prepare the community for their performance in the *Opus Dei*.[20]

This was the culture of Benedict's *cenobium* and it was a reflection of the extraordinary power of the *Regula* right across Europe that it remained the primary influence on monastic life and observance to the very end of the Middle Ages. The *Opus Dei* was never displaced from the *horarium* – in fact under the *Consuetudines Lanfranciae* its forms were extended – although it later became crowded with a host of new (and often unmonastic) obligations.[21] There were changes over the centuries made to the liturgy of the principal offices but there was no significant reduction in the power that 'the magnificent treasure of the Roman liturgy' (as David Knowles described it) exercised over the monks who performed them.[22] As Roger Bowers describes in his essay below, in the shadow

---

18 For early Benedictinism see M. Dunn, *The Emergence of Monasticism: From the Desert Fathers to the Early Middle Ages* (Oxford, 2000), pp. 111–37; See also G. Penco, *Storia del Monachesimo in Italia dalla origini fine del Medio Evo* (Rome, 1961), pp. 47–84; M. Dell'omo, *Monte Cassino, un abbazia nella storia* (Monte Cassino, 1999), especially pp. 233–5. For the process by which Benedict's blueprint 'und den Planern aus den Händen gleiten' see also V. Dammertz, 'Benediktner-Kultur, 750–1050' in *Benedictine Culture*, ed. W. Lourdazux and D. Verhelst (Leuven, 1983), p. x.

19 A. Cabaniss, 'Ardo, The Life of St Benedict, Abbot of Aniane and of Inde' in *Soldiers of Christ. Saints and Saints' Lives from Late Antiquity and the Early Middle Ages*, ed. T. F. X. Noble and T. Head (London, 1995), pp. 213–54 at 233. See also *Vita Benedicti abbatis Anianensis et Indensis*, ed. W. Wattenbach, MGH 15/1 (1900), pp. 200–20.

20 See also Dammertz, 'Benediktiner-Kultur, 750–1050', p. xi.

21 For an overview of liturgical developments in England see S. J. Roper, *English Benedictine Liturgy: Studies in the Formation, Structure and Content of the Monastic Votive Office, c. 950–1540* (New York, 1993). For the changes made first by the *Consuetudines Lanfranciae* and subsequently by capitular canons see *The Monastic Constitutions of Lanfranc*, ed. Knowles, p. xviii; *Chapters*, ed. Pantin, vol. 1, pp. 68–71.

22 Knowles, *Monastic Order*, p. 691.

of the Dissolution the monks of the greater English abbeys and priories still invested their time and community resources in the embellishment of the *Opus Dei*. Modish polyphonic music was introduced first into their Lady Chapels and later into the monks' quire.[23] In this period the performance of the liturgy was professionalised and if a monastery could not secure the services of stipendiary musicians it saw to it that selected brethren acquired the same level of expertise. Even so, it seems the daily observance of the offices still shaped the reflections and readings of the typical cloister monk.[24] The commonplace book of the Canterbury monk, William Glastynbury, whose contents are described here by Joan Greatrex, contained familiar phrases from scripture perhaps for the purpose of directing his meditation or private prayer.[25] The same was true of the women religious of the early Tudor period. As Barry Collett describes below, to the women of Winchester diocese the *regula sancti Benedicti* still represented the best expression of 'the crafte of religiose lyvinge'.[26]

The discipline of the *regula sancti Benedicti* remained the bedrock of monastic culture in medieval England but over the course of ten centuries many of the practices, patterns of behaviour and thought it demanded were transformed. The daily *Opus manuum* in farm and field disappeared from Benedictine monasteries even before the end of the eleventh century and re-emerged only in the formative decades of the reformed orders.[27] The community ethic so characteristic of Benedict's *cenobium* could be seen in the *exordia* of monastic diplomata in any period of the Middle Ages but, in practice, the administrative and physical separation of abbot (or prior) from the conventual community, the development of the obedientiary system, the increase in the patronal obligations (i.e. masses, suffrages etc.) of individual monks and the introduction of salaries (the *peculium*) encouraged only the progressive privatisation of the monastic experience.[28]

Of course, it was not only the institutional developments that affected the observance of the rule over the course of the medieval centuries. English convents were also transformed through their exposure to the shifting currents of continental monasticism. The cultural consequences of, in the first instance, the coming of the Norman monks – both before and after the Conquest – and, subsequently, the involvement of English monks in the monastic and secular politics of the papal schism and the conciliar period should not be underestimated.[29]

---

23 See below, pp. 21–54.
24 See below, pp. 169–76 at 172.
25 See below, pp. 172–3.
26 See below, pp. 147–65 at 156.
27 Knowles, *Monastic Order*, pp. 211–12, 214–16, 467.
28 For these developments see Knowles, *Monastic Order*, pp. 404–6; *id.*, *Religious Orders*, vol. 1, pp. 25–7; vol. 2, pp. 3–8; Dobson, *Durham Priory, 1400–50* (Cambridge, 1973), pp. 51–80; B. F. Harvey, *Westminster Abbey and its Estates in the Middle Ages* (Oxford, 1977), pp. 85–90; *Monastery and Society in Later Medieval England: Selected Account Rolls of Selby Abbey, 1387–1534*, ed. J. H. Tillotson (Woodbridge, 1988), pp. 56–7, 72–4, 77, 134–5, 165–6; Clark, *Monastic Renaissance*, pp. 10–41, especially 26–41.
29 For the influence of Norman monasticism in England see especially M. Gibson, *Lanfranc of Bec* (Oxford, 1978); J. Burton, *The Monastic Order in Yorkshire, 1069–1215* (Cambridge,

The communal character of the cloistered life may have receded over time, but the fraternal bond between the brethren remained a constant feature both of formal and informal monastic writing. In her essay below, Gillian Evans finds fraternal bonds expressed with the same force in the age of Anselm as they had been in the age of Ardo of Aniane.[30] As Julian Haseldine describes below, the twelfth-century monastic writers cultivated the language of Classical *amicitia* in their correspondence with colleagues.[31] These monastic expressions of friendship owed much to epistolographical practice beyond the convent walls and, like their secular counterparts, the monastic letters of this period served to secure not only personal but also political relationships. But as Haseldine argues, they also bore the imprint of purely monastic concepts of community and confraternity and as such they inspired the formation of intense individual bonds. The 'ardent even erotic' language of particular letters from this period has led some scholars to suggest the practice of monastic friendship was a symptom of the underlying homosexual culture of the cloister.[32] Haseldine remains unconvinced by present-minded reading of these sensitive texts, but he concedes there are examples that evoke a real 'emotional attachment'.[33]

The decline of the communal day did not necessarily undermine the monastic traditions of observance, spiritual reading and scholarship. On the contrary, the inconographic evidence from Coventry, St Albans and Westminster which Miriam Gill examines in her essay would indicate that if the *lectio* had passed out of the cloister it was continued elsewhere by other means.[34] As A. J. Piper also demonstrates here in his survey of the Durham Priory manuscripts, the increasing independence of the fifteenth- and sixteenth-century monks served as a positive stimulus to their studies.[35] It seems unlikely that a monk such as Dr Thomas Swalwell would have enjoyed the freedom to purchase his books and pursue his studies in any other period of medieval history.[36] There is also no doubt that the influence of the secular world upon monastic practice and patterns of thought was more pervasive in subsequent centuries than was permitted in the *regula sancti Benedicti*. It is a truism that the artistic and intellectual achievements of English monks in the high and later Middle Ages were informed and enriched by their interaction with the world beyond the convent walls.[37] It would be a mistake, however, to claim that at the same time the very essence of monastic

1999); Southern, *Anselm*; M. Chibnall, *The World of Orderic Vitalis* (Oxford, 1984). For the impact of English monks' involvement in the schism and the early councils see M. Harvey, *Solutions to the Schism: A Study of Some English Attitudes, 1378 to 1409* (St Ottilien, 1983); id., *The English in Rome, 1362–1420: Portrait of an Expatriate Community* (Cambridge, 1999).

30 See below, pp. 78–80.
31 See below, pp. 181–2.
32 See below, pp. 180, 187–94.
33 See below, pp. 188–9, 201.
34 See below, pp. 62–3, 70–1.
35 See below, pp. 101–3.
36 For Swalwell see below, pp. 101–3.
37 See, for example, S. Lewis, *The Art of Matthew Paris* (Aldershot, 1994); *Westminster Abbey and the Plantagenets: Kingship and the Representation of Power, 1200–1400*, ed. P. Binski (New Haven and London, 1995).

culture was overwritten with secular concerns. It has been suggested that when Benedictine monks saw the world beyond their walls 'they paid it the compliment of imitation'.[38] This may have been true of their taste in food and fashion but it appears not to have governed other aspects of community life. The culture of friendship cultivated in twelfth-century cloisters (as described here by Julian Haseldine) was undoubtedly informed by secular political and social practice but it was refracted in the prism of monastic preoccupations.[39] As the essays by Piper, Thomson and North also demonstrate, the monastic scholars of the fourteenth, fifteenth and sixteenth centuries engaged directly with secular trends but not to the exclusion of their own established patterns of study in the liberal arts and the scriptures. Moreover, new research suggests that in certain scholarly fields – Classical studies, the theory and practice of music – the monks of this period were not in thrall to but in advance of the preoccupations of their secular counterparts.[40]

Without doubt the most significant departure from the *regula sancti Benedicti* in subsequent centuries was the importance attached – both by monastic authorities and those who maintained jurisdiction over them – to intellectual activities. Even as the rule spread from the first Roman foundations, its proponents made greater provision for education than Benedict himself had envisaged.[41] In England the tenth-century reformers were the first to place a premium on learning and although the *Regularis Concordia* itself made no additions to the reading time, its publication inaugurated a tradition of education, book production and private study which survived the Norman Conquest.[42] From this artistic and intellectual ferment emerged 'masterpieces of supreme beauty' from the Winchester psalter to the Bury Bible.[43] The place of books and learning in the eleventh- and twelfth-century cloister stands in sharp contrast to the

---

[38] B. F. Harvey, *Living and Dying in Medieval England: The Monastic Experience, 1100–1540* (Oxford, 1993), p. 210.

[39] See below, pp. 179–202, esp. 182.

[40] For Classical studies see S. Wenzel, 'The Classics in Late Medieval Preaching', *Medieval Antiquity*, ed. A. Welkenhuysen, H. Braet and W. Verbeke, Mediaevalia Lovaniensia Series 1, Studia 24 (Leuven, 1995), pp. 127–43; Clark, *Monastic Renaissance*, pp. 209–38. For monastic musical practice see Roger Bowers's essay below, pp. 21–54.

[41] Dunn, *Emergence of Monasticism*, pp. 111–37; Penco, *Storia del Monachesimo*, pp. 47–84; Dammertz, 'Benediktiner-Kultur, 750–1050', p. x.

[42] *Aelfric's Letter to the Monks of Eynsham*, ed. C. A. Jones (Cambridge, 1998), pp. 126–7, 138–9, 148–9. See also *Regularis Concordia Anglicae Nationis Monachorum Sanctionialiumque. The Monastic Agreement of the Monks and Nuns of the English Nation*, ed. T. Symons, Nelsons Medieval Texts (London, 1953), p. xxxiv. Mechtold Gretsch traces the emergence of English monastic studies in this period through the transmission of Aethelwold's Old English translation of the *regula sancti Benedicti*: M. Gretsch, *The Intellectual Foundations of the English Benedictine Reform* (Cambridge, 1999).

[43] The quotation is from Knowles, 'Cultural Influence', p. 151. For the Winchester psalter see F. Wormald, *The Winchester Psalter* (London, 1973). For the Bury Bible see R. M. Thomson, *The Bury Bible* (Woodbridge, 2001); id., 'Early Romanesque Book-Illustration in England: the Dates of the Pierport Morgan *Vitae Sancti Edmundi* and the Bury Bible', *Viator*, 2 (1971), 211–25; T. A. Heslop, 'The Production and Artistry of the Bury Bible' in *Bury St Edmunds, Art, Architecture and Economy*, ed. Gransden, pp. 172–85.

cenobium of the sixth century but it should also be distinguished from the fundamental reorganisation that occurred in the later Middle Ages. It is now generally recognised that the monastic reforms of the thirteenth and fourteenth centuries – promulgated in the statutes of the General and Provincial Chapters of the Benedictine Order in England (1277, 1343) and confirmed in the canon *Summi magistri* of Benedict XII (1336) – represent a watershed in the history of English monasticism.[44] Among many other changes, the canons presented English monks with a new educational programme. A proportion of the men from every monastery were now to study at university, a dramatic departure from tradition designed to bring about the revival of the order by creating a cadre of accomplished, graduate monks. The provision of education in the cloister was to be extended to underpin this ambitious strategy, establishing a syllabus of studies in grammar, logic and philosophy (the so-called 'primitive sciences') and theology lectures to be delivered if necessary by a secular master.[45] The reform canons also made small but significant changes to the traditional rubric governing cloister reading, Benedict's *lectio divina*. The statutes of 1277 (revised in 1343) made specific reference to the art of book production, calling upon those brethren not occupied in reading to busy themselves in the copying, decorating, limning or binding of books.[46]

The canons created a new climate in the cloisters of the fourteenth and fifteenth centuries one which – since the capitular statutes had no parallel in Europe – served to set English convents apart from their continental counterparts. Under the terms of the canons it was possible that as many as half the monastic community in any given convent were now occupied with some form of study, whether as novices and juniors preparing for university, or senior scholar monks preparing for their work as preachers and teachers.[47] Anecdotal evidence suggests that at Winchcombe, under the supervision of Abbot Kidderminster, the monastic community recreated the atmosphere of the academic *studium* complete with their own sequence of lectures on the Sentences of Peter Lombard.[48] This was exceptional, but even if the academic exercises were not replicated in other houses the evidence examined here by Piper and Thomson would suggest that reading patterns were as wide-ranging as in any of the univer-

---

[44] For a general account of this reform process see Knowles, *Religious Orders*, vol. 1, pp. 25–7; vol. 2, pp. 3–8; W. A. Pantin, *The English Church in the Fourteenth Century* (Cambridge, 1955), pp. 117–19. The statutes of the General and Provincial Chapters were printed in *Chapters*, ed. Pantin. For the text of *Summi magistri* see *Concilia*, ed. Wilkins, vol. 2, pp. 585–613.

[45] *Chapters*, ed. Pantin, vol. 1, pp. 27–8, 64–92 at 75; *Concilia*, ed., Wilkins, vol. 2, pp. 585–613.

[46] *Chapters*, ed. Pantin, vol. 1, p. 74: 'abbates vero monachos suos claustrales loco operis manualis secundum suam habilitatem ceteris occupacionibus deputent in studendo libros scribendo, corrigendo, illuminando, ligando vel aliter secundum quod viderint eorum saluti convenire'.

[47] The renewed intellectual vigour stimulated by these reforms has been studied in respect of several greater abbeys and priories. See especially J. Greatrex, 'Monk Students from Norwich Cathedral Priory at Oxford and Cambridge, c.1300 to 1530', *EHR*, 106 (1991), 555–83; *id.*, 'The English Cathedral Priories and the Pursuit of Learning in the Later Middle Ages', *JEH*, 45 (1994), 396–411.

[48] W. A. Pantin, 'Abbot Kidderminster and Monastic Studies', *DR*, 47 (1929), 198–211.

sity schools.[49] As J. D. North suggests below, it was also a scholarly climate which seems to have favoured even ground-breaking scientific studies.[50]

There were many convents that after a hiatus of more than a century were also compelled to restock their libraries.[51] The production of books resumed in a number of greater abbeys and priories, stimulated not only by the needs of the students and their teachers but also perhaps by the promotion in the statutes of the *ars scribendi*.[52] It is the channelling of conventual resources to the cause of education that R. M. Thomson traces here in the manuscripts of Worcester Cathedral Priory that survive from the fourteenth and fifteenth centuries.[53] This evidence challenges directly David Knowles's conclusion that in the later Middle Ages the monks 'ceased to be either directly or indirectly educators'.[54]

The impression is often given that the advent of an academic syllabus and the arrival of university monks served to efface any trace of the early traditions of monastic learning.[55] There is no doubt that, as Thomson and A. J. Piper find in connection with Worcester and Durham Priories, academic authorities were the dominant feature of new accessions to the conventual library.[56] But this did not mean that academic controversies eclipsed all other patterns of thought. A. J. Piper discovers at Durham an enduring interest in earlier traditional scriptural exegesis.[57] Miriam Gill suggests that the schemes of wall paintings produced at Coventry, St Albans, Westminster and a number of other greater abbeys and priories represented a paradigm of scriptural exegesis that was essentially monastic.[58] Gill's study also offers another example of the monastic adaptation of a secular artistic trend.

Glastynbury was not the only monk of this period to profess an attachment to what David Knowles described as the traditional monastic 'ascèse'.[59] A number of monastic authors of the later fourteenth and fifteenth centuries produced new meditations in traditional form. The *Meditatio deuota* of the Durham monk and prior of Finchale, John Uthred of Boldon, attracted monastic readers in the northern and southern province.[60] A contemporary of Brother Glastynbury, John

---

49 See below, pp. 86–110.
50 See below, pp. 206, 209–11.
51 There were significant new acquisitions recorded at several monasteries in the middle years of the fourteenth century, such as Glastonbury, Norwich, Ramsey, St Albans and Westminster. See *EBL*, pp. 220–32 (B43); 300–4 (B58); 350–415 (B68); 611–29 (B104–7). See also Clark, *Monastic Renaissance*, pp. 79–123.
52 There is evidence of a return to at least sporadic book production at Bury St Edmunds, Durham, Norwich and apparently a more systematic programme at St Albans. See Dobson, *Durham Priory*, pp. 376–78; Clark, *Monastic Renaissance*, pp. 79–123.
53 See below, pp. 104–10.
54 Knowles, 'Cultural Influence', p. 159.
55 See, for example, W. A. Pantin, *The English Church in the Fourteenth Century* (Cambridge, 1955), pp. 117–19 and even Knowles in his estimation of John Uthred of Boldon as the 'representative monk-scholar of his age': *Religious Orders*, vol. 2, p. 48.
56 See below, pp. 91–110.
57 See below, pp. 97–8.
58 See below, pp. 55–71 at 70.
59 Knowles, *Monastic Order*, p. 691.
60 H. Farmer, 'The *Meditacio devota* of Uthred of Boldon', *Analecta Monastica: Textes et Études sur la vie des Moines au Moyen Âge*, 5th series (1958), pp. 187–206. See also W. A. Pantin

Matthew, of Glastonbury Abbey, revised a twelfth-century *De professione mona-chorum* which may have commanded a comparable readership.[61] The fragments reviewed here by Miriam Gill suggest this revival of the old 'ascèse' extended to the iconography of the monastic enclosure. [62]

The culture of female monasteries passed through a parallel process of evolution over the course of the medieval centuries. The evidence of the earliest English convents is scant indeed but the impression is of an observant existence comparable in its essentials to that of the men.[63] The *Regularis Concordia* was presented to women religious in the same way as to men, and in the pre-Conquest period their lives were likely dominated by the *Opus Dei* in the extended form the reformers had demanded.[64] The *Consuetudines Lanfranciae*, and the earliest Norman customaries, made only minor changes to this mode and until the end of the twelfth century the focus of female monastic life was still the daily observance of the choir supported by the discipline of the cloister and chapter house.[65] It has been suggested that in spite of the burden of the offices there was perhaps greater scope in this period than in subsequent centuries for women religious to pursue wider intellectual and spiritual interests.[66] A number of nuns of this period are known to have been learned (and perhaps Latinate), to have composed works of their own and to have served as spiritual counsellors within their community and even outside.[67] These roles were not promoted by the supervisors (abbots, bishops) of women religious and no general provision was

---

'Two Treatises of Uthred of Boldon on the Monastic Life' in *Studies in Medieval History presented to Frederick Maurice Powicke*, ed. R. W. Hunt, W. A. Pantin, R. W. Southern (Oxford, 1948), pp. 363–85.

[61] The unique copy of the *Speculum monachorum* survives in Oxford, Bodl. Bodley MS 496. See also Sharpe, *Latin writers*, p. 282.

[62] See below, pp. 55–71.

[63] For early English nunneries see S. Foot, *Veiled Women, 871–1066*, 2 vols., Studies in Early Medieval Britain, (Aldershot, 2000). See also B. Mitchell, 'Anglo-Saxon Double Monasteries' *History Today*, 45/10 (1995), 33–9; B. Yorke, 'Sisters Under the Skin? Anglo-Saxon Nuns and Nunneries in Southern England' *Reading Medieval Studies*, 15 (1989), pp. 95–117.

[64] As the prooemium expressed, the code was presented to men and women religious, 'Prooemium regularis concordiae anglicae nationis monachorum sanctimonialiumque orditur': *Regularis Concordia*, ed. Symons, pp. 1, xxiii.

[65] *Monastic Constitutions*, ed. Knowles, pp. 1–132. For early Norman observance see also Roper, *Medieval English Benedictine Liturgy*, pp. 44–54.

[66] B. L. Venarde, *Women's Monasticism in Medieval Society: Nunneries in France and England, c.850–1215* (Cornell, 1997), especially pp. 53–4: Venarde challenges the contention that the effect of the Gregorian reform was to constrain female spirituality and that the expansion of foundations and orders was driven by an impulse essentially hostile to women. See also in this regard B. L. Kerr, *Religious Life for Women: Fontevraud in England, c. 1100–1350* (Oxford, 1999).

[67] Of course, the best-known nun of this period was Christina, Abbess of Markyate, a nunnery under the jurisdiction of St Albans Abbey. She was the subject of a near contemporary *vita* which survives in a mid-fourteenth-century copy: *The Life of Christina of Markyate*, ed. and trans. C. H. Talbot (rev. edn., Oxford, 1987) and now *Christina of Markyate: A Twelfth-Century Holy Woman*, ed. S. Fanous and H. Leyser (London, 2005). For other notable nuns of this period see Power, *Nunneries*, pp. 237–9, 243; Venarde, *Women's Monasticism*, pp. 116–17.

made for the education of novices or the establishment of conventual libraries, but nonetheless a place was made for learning within the precinct walls.

The later Middle Ages saw significant changes in the culture of female convents. The communal ethic was compromised, not, of course, by the expanding obligations for private masses and other suffrages that undermined the common life of the male monasteries, but by the burdens of conventual administration, the adoption of the *peculium* (stipend), and certain other domestic comforts.[68] As Mary Erler demonstrates in her essay below, however, the private character of convent life did not stifle the intellectual and spiritual pursuits of the nuns. The new-found privacy of the dormitory provided the opportunity for private reading and the possibility of a personal library.[69] As Erler observes, the supervisors of women religious and the prescriptive manuals which they produced or promoted, were persuaded to welcome these changes since they seemed to stimulate and support personal spiritual instruction.[70] It is possible that women religious of this period also experienced a greater exposure to – and perhaps also sought a closer participation in – the cultural activities of secular society than their counterparts of earlier centuries. The recruiting ground of English nunneries appears to have narrowed in the fourteenth and fifteenth centuries and many of the women whose careers are well documented appear to have been drawn from the same cultural, social, and in some cases metropolitan milieus.[71] The manuscript sources reviewed here by David Bell and Mary Erler suggest these cultural connections continued and prospered even after profession.[72] Erler infers the nuns' inclination to read may have been in imitation of lay society.[73] Barry Collett's analysis of Richard Fox's translation of the *regula sancti Benedicti* shows how the bishop employed the idiomatic usage and imagery of the social elite to ensure the nuns of his diocese would engage fully with the text.[74]

There were also new patterns in the culture of female convents in this period for which there was no parallel in the monasteries of men. Women religious were not subject to the process of reform that transformed the monasteries at the turn of the thirteenth century but they were exposed to new and sustained pressure over the principle of enclosure. The papal decree *Periculoso* (1298) sought to enforce the strict separation that – as Roberta Gilchrist has suggested – was already implicit in the situation and physical structure of many female foundations.[75] Recent studies have suggested that in England the decree was never

---

68 See, for example, the dynamics of conventual life described by Marilyn Oliva in respect of East Anglian nunneries, M. Oliva, *The Convent and the Community in Late Medieval England: Female Monasteries in the Diocese of Norwich, c.1350–1540* (Woodbridge, 1998), pp. 37–74, 102–5.

69 See below, pp. 139–42.

70 See below, pp. 144–6.

71 See, for example, Erler, *Women, Reading and Piety*, especially pp. 48–67; Lee, *Nunneries*, pp. 57–67; Oliva, *The Convent and the Community*, pp. 52–61.

72 See below, pp. 126–7, 138, 143–4.

73 See below, pp. 140–1.

74 See below, pp. 152–3.

75 For *Periculoso* see E. Makowski, *Canon Law and Cloistered Women: Periculoso and its Commentators, 1298–1545* (Washington DC., 1997). See also R. Gilchrist, *Contemplation and Action: The Other Monasticism* (London, 1995), p. 6.

effectively enforced and in the event it neither restricted the mobility of the nuns, nor the extent of their exchanges either with the secular clergy or with the wider lay community.[76] The transmission of books in, and occasionally out, of nunneries in the fifteenth and sixteenth centuries as traced by David Bell and Mary Erler, among others, bears witness to the still permeable nature of the precinct walls.[77] But *Periculoso* did leave its imprint on the formative literature of the period, on the commentaries and translations of rules and other spiritual manuals intended for the consumption of professed women. The *formulae* of profession from this period placed particular emphasis on the separation of the professed sister from secular (and male) society, entering as she was upon an inviolable union with Christ.[78] The use of this rhetoric was not confined to the texts of the reformed religious orders such as the Brigittines but was also to be found in the *Furme how a novice sall be made* of a moderate Benedictine convent.[79]

In fact it could be argued that contemporary currents of reform and spiritual renewal reached a greater number of female convents in England far more rapidly than they did the monasteries of men. The manuscripts and printed books examined here by David Bell, Mary Erler and Barry Collett bear witness to wide-ranging reading in the expanding corpus of spiritual literature, not only the insular representatives – Walter Hilton, Nicholas Love – but also those already influential in mainland Europe.[80] With the exception of the larger Carthusian libraries, and the extraordinary resources of the exceptional scholars of Syon Abbey, there is little trace of these interests and influences in the convents of men.[81] As A. J. Piper's analysis of the Durham manuscripts suggests, the scriptural and theological studies of English monks were increasingly informed by contemporary academic authorities but made little reference to other trends.[82]

The level of interest in contemporary spiritual literature among women religious of this period is one measure of the new (if not renewed) importance attached to the pursuit of learning in these communities. It is this perhaps more than any other pattern of life of thought that separates the nuns of the later Middle Ages from their predecessors. Of course, the full extent of learning and literacy in English convents of the early and high Middle Ages is far from conclusive but the evidence of surviving books, book-lists, and in a handful of cases, of original compositions, does point towards a significant expansion of both in the period after 1300.[83] Even in the later period it has been argued that anything more than pragmatic literacy remained the preserve of a small

[76] N. B. Warren, *Spiritual Economies: Female Monasticism in Later Medieval England* (Princeton, 1998), pp. 5–6.
[77] For Bell and Erler see below, pp. 117–18, 128, 131–2, 143–4. See also the transmission of books at Dartford Priory as documented by Lee, *Nunneries*, pp. 167–216.
[78] Warren, *Spiritual Economies*, pp. 4–14.
[79] Warren, *Spiritual Economies*, p. 4.
[80] See below, pp. 113–65, espec. 117, 123, 129, 135, 137, 144.
[81] For the Carthusians and the monks of Syon Abbey see *Syon Abbey*, ed. V. Gillespie and A. I. Doyle, CBMLC, 9 (2001).
[82] See below, pp. 86–103.
[83] Bell, *What Nuns Read*, pp. 33–96; Oliva, *Convent and the Community*, pp. 64–72; Erler, *Women, Reading and Piety*, pp. 38, 116; Lee, *Nunneries*, pp. 136–38, 149–65.

number of privileged and well born women; but David Bell suggests below that cognitive literacy was commonplace in many convents and was the mainstay of their successful administration.[84] The geographical range of the evidence suggests this was more than a regional phenomenon, although the exceptional circumstances surrounding a handful of convents in the purview of the metropolis – Barking, Dartford, Syon – should never be underestimated.[85] Moreover, the chronological spread of the surviving books, some of which, as Bell and Erler show, were printed, suggests it was an expansion that was sustained even into the shadow of the dissolution itself.[86] It cannot be correlated to a conscious, countrywide programme of reform. There were prelates who showed more than passing interest in the welfare of the women religious under their jurisdiction, but Richard Fox's provisions for the women of Winchester diocese were exceptional.[87] The work of David Bell, Barry Collett, and Mary Erler, presented here, would suggest that the primary stimulus for the pursuit of learning in the female convents of this period came from the lively and literate religious culture of the (especially metropolitan) laity from which the women were recruited.[88]

It was once thought that in cultural terms the English monasteries were more or less moribund in the later Middle Ages, their artistic, intellectual and spiritual energies dissipated by the pressures of administration and the pervasive problems of internal indiscipline. David Knowles hesitated to pass judgement on the houses of this period: 'they retained that aura of sanctity' although 'what became of it all, who could say?'[89] However, there was little doubt where his suspicions lay. His own description of the male and female monasteries of the fifteenth and sixteenth centuries was founded on the *comperta* of contemporary visitations and the major indiscipline and minor infringements of the rule they reported.[90]

The essays in this volume present a contrasting picture of the period, one of cultural vitality when not only were old themes renewed – such as scriptural exegesis, meditative and even mystical literature – but also new trends were taken up in philosophy (Worcester), theology (Durham), and even in music.[91] In

---

84 See below, pp. 120–2, 127–8, 131–2.

85 Erler, *Women, Reading and Piety*, pp. 12–13, 17–18, 42–5, 86–7; Lee, *Nunneries*, pp. 81–3, 173–88.

86 See below, pp. 127–9, 138, 144.

87 See for example the efforts of Thomas de la Mare, mid-fourteenth-century abbot of St Albans, to enforce a minimum level of literacy on the nuns of his abbey of St Mary de Pré: *Gesta abbatum sancti Albani*, ed. H. T. Riley, 3 vols., RS 28 (1864–66), vol. 2, pp. 410–12, and the injunctions issued to the nunneries of his diocese by Bishop William Alnwick of Lincoln (1436–49): *Visitations*, ed. Thompson, vol. 2, pp. 9, 115, 125; vol. 3, pp. 230, 350; Power, *Nunneries*, pp. 244–5, 483–98.

88 See below, pp. 120–2, 128, 143–4, 150–2, 163–5. The same impression is cast by the surviving books of Dartford Priory examined by Lee, *Nunneries*, pp. 167–216, especially 177–83.

89 Knowles, *Religious Orders*, vol. 2, p. 363. In his short survey of English monastic culture Knowles was more openly critical, 'the monastic order [of the later Middle Ages] ceased to exert any specific influence outside their own body ... and with the opening of the sixteenth century [they were] as an intellectual and cultural force, all but negligible in the life of England': Knowles, 'Cultural Influence', p. 159.

90 Knowles, *Religious Orders*, vol. 3, pp. 62–86.

91 See below, pp. 21–54, 101–2, 105, 107–8.

respect of women religious this was not so much a process of recovery as one of progression. The evidence examined below by David Bell, Mary Erler and Barry Collett suggests a number of English nunneries in the fifteenth and sixteenth centuries maintained a higher standard of observant and spiritual life than they had managed in earlier times. Bell argues that the balance of the book-evidence points to a higher level of literacy among a higher number of nuns.[92] Mary Erler shows how place, space and time were made for the practice of private reading and Barry Collett how the progressive Bishop Fox was persuaded to promote it through his translation of the rule.[93]

It would be wrong, of course, to translate the evidence of a particular monastery too readily into a general trend. The reforms and statutes of the thirteenth and fourteenth centuries had lent a degree of homogeneity to the lives of men and women religious in England but there remained pronounced differences – both institutional and regional – in their experiences. There is no doubt the process of cultural renewal or revival perceived in this period took on different forms in different convents. The dominant trend at Durham Priory was for the study of scripture.[94] At Worcester there was an emphasis on education.[95] While the patterns of reading in female convents shared many common features, there appears to have been considerable variety in the choice of texts.[96] There are grounds for suggesting that some of the greater abbeys and priories – Christ Church Canterbury, Durham, St Albans, Westminster – should be treated in this period as a distinct cultural environment in their own right with their own self-determined traditions of intellectual endeavour, artistic and musical expression.[97] There were also male and female convents which witnessed no cultural renewal or revival at all.[98]

It has been objected that these signs of life in the late medieval monastery were

---

[92] See below, pp. 120–3, 127–8.
[93] See below, pp. 134–46, 148–51.
[94] See below, pp. 86–103. Undoubtedly there is some truth in David Knowles's judgement 'Durham is *facile princeps*': Knowles, 'Cultural Influence', p. 156.
[95] See below, pp. 104–10.
[96] See below, pp. 116–19.
[97] See R. B. Dobson, 'The Monks of Canterbury in the Later Middle Ages, 1220–1540', in *A History of Canterbury Cathedral*, ed. P. Collinson, N. Ramsey, and M. Sparks (Oxford, 1995), pp. 69–153. For Durham see Dobson, *Durham Priory*; *The Durham Liber Vitae and its Context*, ed. D. Rollason, A. J. Piper, M. Harvey and L. Rollason, Regions and Regionalism in History, 1 (Woodbridge, 2004). For St Albans see Clark, *Monastic Renaissance*; J. D. North, *God's Clockmaker: Richard of Wallingford and the Invention of Time* (London, 2005). For Westminster see P. Binski, *Westminster Abbey and the Plantagenets: Kingship and the Representation of Power, 1200–1400* (New Haven and London, 1995); B. F. Harvey, 'A Novice's Life at Westminster Abbey in the Century before the Dissolution' in *The Religious Orders in Pre-Reformation England*, Studies in the History of Medieval Religion, 18 (Woodbridge, 2002), pp. 51–73. See also now J. F. Merritt, *The Social World of Early Modern Westminster: Abbey, Court, and Community, 1525–1640* (Manchester, 2005).
[98] For example a number of ancient convents known for their cultural vitality in the earliest centuries of English monasticism, such as Abingdon, Ramsey, Shaftesbury and Winchester Cathedral Priory showed no signs of a renewal or revival in the century and a half before the dissolution. See also Knowles, *Religious Orders*, vol. 3, pp. 80, 65–6, 354.

only signs of its subjection to the patterns and preoccupations of secular society.[99] However, as the contributors argue below, it is more accurate to characterise the cultural exchanges between the cloister and the world in this period in terms of a process of critical engagement.[100] The scholarly monks of Durham admitted academic texts into their programme of teaching and private study but did not allow them to displace earlier traditions.[101] When they covered the walls of their chapter house and church with paintings, the monks of Coventry, St Albans and Westminster were mindful of contemporary trends but also profoundly conscious of their own tradition of *lectio divina*.[102] The nuns of Barking, Campsey, Dartford and elsewhere may have read in the manner of their unprofessed mothers and sisters, choosing something of the same material, but their reading was to deepen their vocation and direct their devotion in the *Opus Dei*.[103] Polyphonic music was not the invention of pre-Reformation monasteries and there is no doubt their cantors cultivated it with lay worshippers in mind, but its selective adoption reflects the priority they attached to their own traditions of observance.[104] In the case of polyphony, Roger Bowers suggests, the monks were not merely passive consumers but played a major role in the promotion of a new cultural trend. Perhaps the most celebrated composer of the Reformation period, Thomas Tallis, honed his craft in a monastic house.[105] The same may be true of the monasteries' role in the transmission of other pre-Reformation trends. It is well known that there were monks, and whole communities, where there was an early interest in the work of the Italian humanists.[106] It has also been suggested that the greater abbeys and priories in England were pioneers of the new technology of printing. [107]

The emergence of these trends is a measure of how far the culture of English monasticism had evolved in the centuries since its first foundation. The discipline of daily observance survived to the Dissolution but it came to be surrounded by a complex of other cultural patterns. In the light of the research presented here it appears this process of cultural renewal and reinvention continued even

---

[99] See, for example, B. J. Thompson, 'Monasteries, Society and Reform in Late Medieval England' in *The Religious Orders in Pre-Reformation England*, ed. J. G. Clark, (Woodbridge, 2002), pp. 165–95.

[100] See below, pp. 52–4, 85, 99–102, 171–3, 180–2.

[101] See below, pp. 86–103.

[102] See below, pp. 70–1.

[103] See below, pp. 137–9, 145–6, 148.

[104] See below, pp. 21–54 at 24–6.

[105] See below, p. 32.

[106] Humanist works were read and reproduced at Christ Church, Canterbury, as early as the middle years of the fifteenth century, as witnessed by the compilations of Henry Cranbrook. Humanist interests in the convent intensified in the priorate of William Sellyng. See R. Weiss, *Humanism in England during the Fifteenth Century* (2nd edn., Oxford, 1957), pp. 128–40, 153–9. Another circle of monks with interests in classical and Christian humanism is documented at Evesham Abbey in the 1510s and 1520s. See *The Letter Book of Robert Joseph, Monk-Scholar of Evesham and Gloucester College, Oxford, 1530–3*, ed. H. Aveling and W. A. Pantin, OHS, New Series, 19 (1967).

[107] See J. G. Clark, 'Print and Pre-Reformation Religion: The Benedictines and Printing in England, *c.*1470–1540' in *The Uses of Script and Print, 1300–1700*, ed. J. Crick and A. Walsham (Cambridge, 2004), pp. 71–92.

in the shadow of the Reformation. There can now be no doubt that the treasures recovered from the ruins of the religious houses after 1540 were not the fossils of a long forgotten world but fragments of a cultural tradition that – at the time of its destruction – was still very much alive.

Observant Culture

An Early Tudor Monastic Enterprise: Choral Polyphony for the Liturgical Service

ROGER BOWERS

Among at least the better-favoured of the English monasteries, their first half-century under the Tudor regime appears to have been a period not at all unpropitious. In these houses, numbers of monks or canons appear to have been predominantly stable, sources of revenue were secure, and provision was made for higher education in the universities for the younger monks able to benefit thereby.[1] This prevailing level of stability and even vitality sufficed to generate and sustain certain instances of the promotion of real intellectual and artistic enterprise. One which hitherto has been somewhat overlooked was the recognition at many houses of the value of making provision for incorporating within the liturgical service the performance of a newly invented body of virtuoso polyphonic music, generated for the purpose and executed by teams of expert singers specially trained.[2] The greatest houses led the way in accomplishing this, subjecting from about 1480 onwards small-scale provision already made during the preceding 100 years or so (for the execution of a less demanding repertory) to major transformation and expansion. Hereby they established an example soon to be emulated eagerly at other houses great, middling, and even small.

---

[1]   See, for example, J. G. Clark, 'The Religious Orders in Pre-Reformation England', in *Religious Orders*, ed. Clark, 3–33, at pp. 6–7, 12–15, 20–1, 32, and sources and studies there quoted; J. Greatrex, 'After Knowles: Recent Perspectives in Monastic History', *ibid.*, 35–47, at pp. 39, 40–1; B. F. Harvey, 'A Novice's Life at Westminster Abbey in the Century Before the Dissolution', *ibid.*, 51–73 at pp. 61–2, 67–70; also R. Bowers, 'The Musicians of the Lady Chapel of Winchester Cathedral Priory, 1402–1539', *JEH*, 45 (1994), 210–37 at pp. 231–2 (repr. with corrections in *id.*, *English Church Polyphony: Singers and Sources from the 14th to the 17th Century* (Aldershot, 1999), Section V and Commentary, pp. 6–7).

[2]   This topic was considered briefly in Knowles, *Religious Orders*, vol. 3, pp. 15–21; however, although much of the source material and informed musicological comment upon it has long been available in print, the subject seems to have attracted little further attention. For studies of individual houses see R. Bowers, 'The Liturgy of the Cathedral and its Music, c.1075–1642', in *A History of Canterbury Cathedral*, ed. P. Collinson, N. Ramsey and M. Sparks (2nd edn, Oxford, 2002), pp. 408–50; *id.*, 'Musicians of the Lady Chapel', pp. 210–37; *id.*, 'The Musicians and Liturgy of the Lady Chapels of the Monastery Church', in *Westminster Abbey: The Lady Chapel of Henry VII*, ed. T. Tatton-Brown and R. Mortimer (Woodbridge, 2003), pp. 33–57. More generally, see also F. Ll. Harrison, *Music in Medieval Britain* (2nd edn, London, 1963), pp. 38–45, 185–97, and R. Bowers, 'The Almonry Schools of the English Monasteries, c.1265–1540', in *Monasteries and Society in Medieval Britain*, ed. B. Thompson, Harlaxton Medieval Studies, VI (Stamford, 1999), 177–222, esp. pp. 208–13, 217–22.

The grandeur of their liturgical service, most particularly on festivals and in honour of the Blessed Virgin, was something in which the monastics were by now electing to take a constructive and emphatic pride.

In respect of its artistic content this was not a departure inaugurated and developed on the initiative of the monastics themselves. Rather, they were adapting to their own circumstances an enterprise generated a little earlier by the musicians of the secular Church, and it was common (though not universal) for the monks to draw on and engage the expertise of professional lay musicians in their adoption of these developments within their own churches. By the 1530s this degree of enterprise had succeeded in producing a culture of liturgical and musical observance of genuine significance. In the case of the middling and smaller houses its adoption exhibited an eagerness to recognise and keep abreast of contemporaneous endeavour elsewhere in the Church, while at the most enterprising of the greater houses it sufficed to place them in a league inviting comparison with all but the grandest of the secular churches. Eventually such a degree of accomplishment achieved recognition at the highest level of state, for when dissolution finally overtook these greater houses in 1538–40 the king's government directed particularly that at those which were to continue as secularised churches the singers of polyphony, boys and men, were to be retained in service to become the nucleus of the newly established secular choir.[3]

No matter what the triumphs or vicissitudes through which the monastic ideal passed in England between the tenth century and the sixteenth, the performance of divine worship according to the liturgies authorised by the several Orders remained ever paramount. To the mind both of the monks themselves and of much of the populace, the ceaseless observance night and day of sacrifice and prayer in mass and office glorified God as He both demanded and deserved, sanctified the monks themselves, and reassured a gratified deity that, despite everything, humanity was still worth the bestowal of those many graces which He was pleased to confer and of which mankind was properly both conscious and appreciative.

It was during the third quarter of the fifteenth century that there was created one of the greatest glories of the late-medieval English church, namely a body of elaborate and virtuosic polyphonic music composed for performance by a small chorus of the voices of men and boys, applied to enhancement of the beauty and dignity of the liturgical service.[4] Prior to this, polyphonic music for the church service at large had normally been composed for the solo voices of just three or four men (altos and tenors), constrained within an overall compass not exceeding two octaves. It was in about the early 1450s that composers first began to expand upon this traditional ensemble by adding to it both boys' treble and adult bass voices, and by composing for performance not just by specialist soloists but by most or all of the members of a choral ensemble. By thus creating music engaging an overall compass extending to three octaves and a second, composed

---

3   PRO, E36/116, pp. 19–20 (LP, XIV part i, p. 530).
4   For broad surveys, see H. Benham, *Latin Church Music in England 1460–1575* (London, 1977); Harrison, *Music in Medieval Britain*, pp. 257–94, 302–415; D. Wulstan, *Tudor Music* (London, 1985), pp. 250–77.

for a five-part chorus employing the voices of both boys and men (treble, alto, two tenors, and bass), the composers were creating what has been considered ever since to be the unique and quintessential sound of English cathedral music. Though always cultivated alongside and never entirely replacing traditional composition for men's voices alone, by the early 1470s such music was becoming standard at those greater cathedrals, collegiate churches and household chapels of royalty and aristocracy by whose musicians it had first been developed.[5]

Unlike the monodic chant of the plainsong to which the entirety of the liturgical service had been sung for centuries (the learning of which, in the case of the monasteries, filled much of the noviciate of every well-trained monk), the multi-voiced virtuoso polyphony created by the composers of the period 1460–1540 was no ordinary music. Its composers were men of the stature of John Browne and the elder William Cornysh, Richard Davy and Walter Lambe, Robert Fayrfax and Hugh Aston, Nicholas Ludford, John Taverner and the young Thomas Tallis.[6] Its fundamental role was to serve as a means for giving distinction and prominence to feast day over ferial, and to more important devotion over less, and, unsupported by any accompaniment, its most conspicuous feature was the manner in which it made of its executants great and unprecedented demands in terms of refinement of technique and stamina of voice.

Music so extended and physically so taxing could be deployed at service only sparingly. This meant that in practice only a relatively small range of liturgical categories could be considered amenable for execution in this manner; however, such restraint also served to render the impact of its performance only all the greater. One form on which composers concentrated their efforts was the four movements of the ordinary of the mass, both in expansive settings for use at High Mass in quire on festivals, and also in other settings somewhat less grand. These latter were sung during votive masses performed out of quire in chapels specially designated for the purpose, such as the daily Lady Mass (for which the Kyrie and sequence might also be set) and the weekly Mass of the Name of Jesus. Further, for performance daily at a separate evening devotion conducted most commonly in the Lady Chapel, composers set in profusion antiphons ('anthems') votive to the Blessed Virgin. For the office they created many festal settings of the Magnificat and some also of the Te Deum, the canticles at, respectively, vespers and matins; by the end of this period, for these services they were also composing settings of certain of the responsories and hymns. Virtually all polyphonic composition fell into just these few categories, evidently judged to be those in which its capacity to enhance the spiritual and mental immersion of the participants in the divine mysteries would most effectively be realised.

In no sense whatever was this a music for amateurs. Any votive antiphon might consist of up to fifteen minutes of strenuous and highly demanding coloratura singing, the mass ordinary some twenty to thirty-five minutes, a Magnificat

---

5   R. Bowers, 'To Chorus from Quartet: the Performing Resource for English Church Polyphony, c.1390–1559', in English Choral Practice 1400–1650, ed. J. Morehen (Cambridge, 1995), 1–47, at pp. 20–31.

6   For all these composers the material in ODNB is fully up to date, if not quite so comprehensive in technical coverage as that in New Grove.

some seven to ten minutes. The demands made by such music could satisfactorily be met only by those who not only possessed a fine singing voice but also had undergone specialist training in vocal technique, and appropriate instruction in reading and singing from contemporary musical notation, commonly known as 'pricksong'.

It was from around 1480 that the more enterprising of the monastic houses began to commit themselves to a decisive effort to emulate their secular colleagues, and to address their attention to the incorporation of choral polyphony of this most recent and ambitious kind into their liturgical observance. By the 1530s they had achieved a great deal, and the practice of music of this character had become surprisingly widespread. The singers by whom it was performed were mostly laity, but it would be disingenuous to interpret the monks' employment of lay expertise to assist them in the accomplishment of these ends as evidence of some pernicious lethargy or indifference. Execution of the new elaborate polyphony demanded resources which the very nature of monasticism ensured they could not provide from among themselves. Performance required the unbroken voices of young boys, which were simply unobtainable among monastics operating a responsible minimum age of profession.[7] Moreover, the skills of singing such music, and of composing it and directing its performance, were by now specialised and arcane to an extent greater than that which it was reasonable to expect to be readily available among bodies of men characterised by adherence to a vocation wholly unrelated to advanced musicianship. What the monks could do for themselves in these respects, they did; to achieve what they themselves could not, they engaged external expertise.

The earliest monasteries to embark upon this enterprise were certain of those at which such a departure involved not the recruitment of a totally new performing resource and its organisation as a supplementary choir, but the thorough reordering and reassessment of the potential inherent in a resource which, albeit on a much smaller scale, they already possessed. These were the existing Lady Chapel choirs, bodies of secular singers created at any time from the 1380s onwards, primarily to ensure the provision of an egregious level of distinction for the daily observance of the Mass of the Blessed Virgin, or Lady Mass, celebrated out of quire in the Lady Chapel of the monastery church. This mass, whose celebration as a daily observance had commonly been introduced in the thirteenth century,[8] was performed by a select group generally of six to eight monks specially entabled for this duty. The celebrant and two others formed the altar party, and the remainder a chorus to sing the plainsong of the mass. The supplementary group of secular singers took one or other of two different forms.

At abbeys such as Bristol and Westminster the group was of part-time singingmen, numbering three or four; these singers appear all to have been of equal

---

7   For evidence that at this period the voices of English singing-boys were breaking at about the age of fourteen, see R. Bowers, 'The Music and Musical Establishment of St George's Chapel in the Fifteenth Century', in St George's Chapel, Windsor, in the Late Middle Ages, ed. C. Richmond and E. Scarff, Historical Monographs relating to St George's Chapel, Windsor Castle, 17 (Windsor, 2001), 171–214, at pp. 206–7, and other sources quoted there.

8   Knowles, Religious Orders, vol. 3, p. 16.

status, none being particularly designated as leader or master. Primarily, each of these groups formed an ensemble for the performance of polyphony daily at Lady Mass. However, on occasions identifiable as the greatest festivals of the year they might, as at Westminster Abbey, also be required to participate in the major services observed in the principal quire, performing, as a solo ensemble, polyphonic settings sung in festal enhancement of the monks' liturgy there.[9]

Elsewhere, and more commonly, provision of a kind entirely different had been developed. In these instances the monastery employed just a single professional musician, often for convenience called the Cantor. His principal function was to draw from among the younger of the resident pupils of the monastery's almonry grammar school a group of boys with unbroken voices, most commonly numbering four to six, for training as singers at the daily Lady Mass. This latter arrangement had been adopted at, for instance, the cathedral priories of Winchester in 1402, Ely by 1404, Durham in 1414 and Canterbury in 1438.[10] At this period boys' voices were not yet used in composed polyphony, and these singing-boys attended Lady Mass just to enhance the monks' rendering of its plainsong. Commonly, however, such enhancement extended also to the improvisation by individual boys of descant, a line of counterpoint complementing the plainsong and sung impromptu according to standard rules taught by the Cantor. At this period these secular boys participated only in services held in the Lady Chapel, and never in those of the monks' quire.

In these latter houses the Cantor's activity was not necessarily limited to teaching his singing-boys for Lady Mass; he was available also to coach any of the monks who were interested in acquiring the more elevated skills of music-making. Consequently, at these houses there could readily be established an ensemble consisting of three or four enthusiasts among the monks, who were coached by the Cantor and became accomplished in performing, with him, polyphonic settings at appropriate points in the course of the monastic observance in the principal quire. In the libraries of the cathedrals of Canterbury and Durham there still survive some fragments of the mid-fifteenth-century repertories of such teams of monk-executants of soloist polyphony.[11]

Arrangements such as these for the enhancement of daily Lady Mass and select components of the festal quire-service were relatively modest and self-

9   R. Bowers, 'Choral Institutions within the English Church: their Constitution and Development, 1340–1500', unpublished Ph.D. dissertation (University of East Anglia, 1975), pp. 4077–85; id., 'The Musicians and Liturgy of the Lady Chapels', pp. 37–43 (esp. p. 40), 47. The early history of the ensemble at Westminster was complex. Inaugurated in 1384 as a choir of the second type (a Cantor and four boys), briefly between 1393 and 1399 it was amplified with up to six further singing-men. However, the use of boys' voices was discontinued in c.1401, and thereafter until 1480 the ensemble consisted just of four men's voices (three, c.1400–c.1414).

10   Bowers, 'Musicians of the Lady Chapel', pp. 215–21; id., 'The Liturgy of the Cathedral and its Music', pp. 419–20; id., 'Some Observations on the Life and Career of Lionel Power', PRMA, 102 (1975–76), 103–27, at pp. 111–20; id., 'Choral Institutions', pp. 4091–6.

11   Bowers, 'The Liturgy of the Cathedral and its Music', pp. 420–1; N. Sandon, 'Fragments of Medieval Polyphony at Canterbury Cathedral', Musica Disciplina, 30 (1976), 37–53, at pp. 44–8. R. Bowers and A. Wathey, 'New Sources of English Fourteenth- and Fifteenth-Century Polyphony', EMH, 3 (1983), 123–73, at pp. 128–36.

effacing; however, at the time they sufficed to satisfy the aspirations of the then monastic authorities. It was in the 1480s that their successors were confronted with the challenge posed by the generation of a whole new repertory of full-range polyphony for chorus, developed in earnest during the previous fifteen years or so, and such music was speedily perceived at the most enterprising houses as constituting a development in devotional practice fully worthy of adoption and replication.[12]

Music of this character could be performed at any church able and willing to assemble the necessary resources; at the monasteries two procedures only were involved in its reception. The first was the appointment of a professional musician possessing all the skills now required to serve as director or Cantor; the second was the establishment of a full ensemble for him to direct.

The nature of the service which the monastic authorities expected to gain from their Cantors can most readily be discerned from the contracts of employment issued to them. Some twenty-six texts are known, twenty-three dating from the period following 1480; there are summaries of, or references to, a further four whose present whereabouts are unknown, while the gist of another can be recovered from the record of a law-suit. Also helpful are four contracts of professional singing-men. The incidence of these thirty-five indentures is somewhat uneven. Nine come from the cathedral priory of Durham, and six from Winchester Cathedral; two each come from Worcester, St. Albans, and Tavistock, and the remainder singly from fourteen further institutions. Somewhat less relevant, though still informative, are two contracts with men who served as organ-player in the monastic church, but were given no singers, either men or boys, to direct.[13] In the case of certain prominent monasteries from which no contracts survive (such as Westminster Abbey, Canterbury Cathedral), some information can be drawn from obedientiary accounts and kindred documents.

Some details of the surviving indentures appear in Table 1, which will also serve the remainder of this article as a source for bibliographic reference.[14]

The common objective sought by the monastic authorities was the establishment of an ensemble fully constituted of the voices of boys and men, all trained in the skills of performing polyphonic music. In practice, the required initiative could take a variety of forms, according to the nature of the provision already existing. Wherever there was no pre-existent provision, the monastic authorities had to start from scratch. At that minority of houses where there already existed a team just of the voices of lay singing-men, the need was for its amplification with a team of trained boys plus a qualified Cantor. Wherever there existed already a group of boys and a Cantor, the first need was for an upgrade in

---

12 Bowers, 'Almonry Schools', pp. 208–13.

13 These indentures arise from the priories of Maiden Bradley and Sempringham; see Table 1.

14 I am grateful to the staff of the Somerset Record Office for identifying the present location of the indenture of Ralph Drake (c.1520), and also to those of the National Register of Archives and of the Record Offices of Devonshire, Nottinghamshire, Derbyshire, and the City of Sheffield for their help in establishing that the indentures of Christopher Haslam (1490), Robert Derkeham (1522), anon. (Tavistock, 1523), and John Elyott (1529) cannot at present be located.

Table 1
Indentures of Employment Issued to Monastery Cantors, 1402–1538

Date	Institution	Name	MS source	Edition (or calendar, summary or reference)
1402	Winchester C.P.	John Tyes	Priory Reg. I, fol. 15v	B. Matthews, *The Music of Winchester Cathedral* (London, 1974), p. 9 [facsimile]; *The Register of the Common Seal of the Priory of St Swithun, Winchester, 1345–1497*, ed. J. Greatrex, HRS, 2 (1978), p. 19, no. 53 [calendar]
1430	Durham C.P.	John Stele	Priory Reg. III, fol. 157v	Bowers, 'Choral Institutions', pp. A056–7
1448	Durham C.P.	John Stele	Priory Reg. IV, fol. 60r; Locellus xxviii, nos. 15, 16, 16*	*Historiae Dunelmensis scriptores tres*, ed. J. Raine, SS, xviii (1839), p. cccxv
1482	Winchester C.P.	Edmund Pynbrygge	Priory Reg. I, fol. 106v	*Register of the Common Seal*, ed. Greatrex, p. 140, no. 402 [calendar]
1486	Worcester C.P.	John Hampton	MS A6(1), fol. 82r	*The Early Occupants of the Office of Organist and Master of the Choristers of the Cathedral Church of … Worcester*, ed. I. Atkins (Worcester, 1918), p. 12
1487	Durham C.P.	Alexander Bell	Priory Reg. V, fol. 3v	[none]
1490	Beauchief Ab.	Christopher Haslam	[not known]	S. O. Addy, *Historical Memorials of Beauchief Abbey* (Sheffield, 1878), pp. 128–9 [ref. only]
1496	Durham C.P.	Thomas Foderley	Priory Reg. V, fol. 37r	*Historiae Dunelmensis scriptores tres*, ed. J. Raine, p. ccclxxxvi
1496	Tutbury Pr.	Thomas Alenson	PRO, C1/603/1	[none]
1502	Durham C.P.	John Tildesley	Priory Reg. V, fol. 70r	*Historiae Dunelmensis scriptores tres*, ed. Raine, p. cccxcviii
1510	Winchester C.P.	§Edmund Pynbrygge	Priory Reg. II, fol. 44v	[none]
1510	Winchester C.P.	Thomas Goodman	Priory Reg. II, fol. 44r	[none]
1512	Durham C.P.	Robert Porret	Priory Reg. V, fol. 142r	[none]
1513	Durham C.P.	Thomas Ashwell	Priory Reg. V, fol. 152r	*Historiae Dunelmensis scriptores tres*, ed. Raine, p. ccccxiii
1513	Durham C.P.	Thomas Ashwell	Priory Reg. V, fol. 153r	[none]
1515	Coventry C.P.	*Guy Speke	PRO E315/93, fol. 25v	[none]
1515	Gloucester Ab.	John Tucke	Reg. D, fol. 24v	*Historia et Cartularium Monasterii Sancti Petri Gloucestrie*, ed. W. H. Hart, 3 vols., RS (London, 1863–67), vol. 3, pp. xlvii, 290; R. Woodley, *John Tucke: A Case Study in Early Tudor Music Theory* (Oxford, 1993), p. 133
1518	Chester Ab.	John Byrchley	PRO, E315/98, fol. 30v	[none]

c.1520 Muchelney Ab.	Ralph Drake	BL, Add.MS 43405, fol. xxiij v	*Adam de Domersham: Historia de rebus gestis Glastoniensibus*, ed. T. Hearne, 2 vols., Oxford, 1727), vol. 1, p. lxxx
1522 Buckland Ab.	Robert Derkeham	[not known]	G. Oliver, *Monasticon Diocesis Exoniensis* (Exeter, 1847), p. 380 [summary]
1522 Thurgarton Pr.	John Patenson	PRO E315/100, fo. 74r	[none]
1522 Tywardreath Pr.	Thomas Rayne	PRO, E315/100, fol. 233r	N. Orme, 'Music and Teaching at Tywardreath Priory, 1522–36', *Devon and Cornwall Notes and Queries*, xxxvi (1990), p. 279
1522 Worcester C.P.	Daniel Boyce	MS A6(2), fol. 127v	*The Early Occupants of the Office of Organist and Master of the Choristers of the Cathedral Church of ... Worcester*, ed. I. Atkins, p. 16
1523 Tavistock Ab.	[not known]	[not known]	H. P. R. Finberg, *Tavistock Abbey* (2nd edn., Cambridge, 1969), p. 224 [ref. only]
1524 Brecon Pr.	Geoffrey Ferrour alias Jones	PRO, E315/91, fol. 71r	[none]
1529 Tavistock Ab.	John Elyott	[not known]	G. Oliver, *Monasticon Diocesis Exoniensis*, p. 92 [summary]
1533 Llanthony II Pr.	John Hodges	PRO, E315/93, fol. 231v	*A Calendar of the Registers of the Priory of Llanthony by Gloucester 1457–1466, 1501–1525*, ed. J. Rhodes, Bristol and Gloucestershire Archaeological Society, Gloucestershire Record Series 15 (2002), pp. 195–7.
1533 St Albans Ab.	Thomas Monyngham	PRO, E315/93, fol. 175r	[none]
1534 Glastonbury Ab.	James Renynger	PRO, E135/2/31	*The Reliquary*, new series vol. 6 (1892), p. 176; A. Watkin, 'Last glimpses of Glastonbury', *Downside Review*, 67 (1948–49), p. 76
1534 Maiden Bradley Pr.	§Nicholas Hullande	PRO, E315/101, fol. 93v	[none]
1534 Sempringham Pr.	+John Smythe	PRO, SC6/Henry VIII/2030	J. Youings, *The Dissolution of the Monasteries* (London, 1971), p. 244
1537 Durham C.P.	John Brymley	Priory Reg. V, fol. 261v	[none]
1537 Winchester C.P.	*Henry Stempe	Priory Reg. III, fols. 35v, 69v	[none]
1538 Cirencester Ab.	Henry Edmunds	PRO, E315/94. fol. 159v	[none]
1538 St Albans Ab.	*Walter Burre	PRO, E315/97, fol. 40r	[none]
1538 Taunton Pr.	Thomas Foxe	PRO, E315/100, fol. 323v	[none]
1538 Winchester C.P.	Matthew Fuller	Priory Reg. III, fol. 73r	[none]

* singing-man (quire and Lady Chapel)
+ singing-man (quire only)
§ organ-player and singing-man only

Except where indicated otherwise, the manuscript sources cited remain in the library or archives of the church where they were produced.

the training of the boys, so as to include not simply plainsong and descant, but composed and notated polyphony as well. This qualified them to be joined by a team of men's voices similarly accomplished; at the choice of the authorities, this latter might consist either of monks of the house, or of professional singing-men recruited for the purpose, in an ensemble directed overall by the Cantor.

In a surge of enterprise evident between 1480 and the early sixteenth century, full ensembles of singers, men and boys under the direction of a Cantor were established at many of the better-managed of the monasteries. The initiative seems to have been taken earliest by that small number of houses which already possessed an ensemble consisting of a group of singing-men. Here unbroken boys' voices were readily available for recruitment from among the younger scholars of the monastery's almonry school. At Worcester, piecemeal between 1478 and 1486 and on the initiative of John Alcock as bishop, a group of eight boys under John Hampton as Cantor (appointed 1484) was added to the existing Lady Chapel singing-men. At Westminster Abbey the existing team of four singing-men was augmented in March 1480 by a group of six boys under the Cantor William Cornysh, while at Bristol Abbey, apparently during 1491/2, a group of six boys, under William Thorne as Cantor, was added to the existing ensemble of three men.[15]

Where, as more commonly was the case, there already existed a Cantor and an ensemble of boys' voices, two stages had to be undertaken. Firstly, the monastery had to resolve to upgrade its existing office of Cantor, appointing to it a practitioner possessing the skills of teaching to boys not only the long-established plainsong and descant, but also the far more refined and intellectual arts of singing from composed and notated polyphony. At Winchester Cathedral this step was taken in 1482 (and simultaneously the number of boys was raised from four to eight),[16] at Durham in 1487,[17] and at Ely apparently in 1490.[18] At Canterbury the transition to instruction in 'pricksong' for the boys probably was made during the occupation of the Cantor's office by John Nesbett, 1473/4–1487/8,[19] known as a composer of church polyphony requiring full choral forces in five parts, including boys.[20] Each such monastery now had a Cantor and a team of boys capable of tackling the new polyphony.

For the second element in this process, namely the provision of the voices of

15 Indenture: 1486 Hampton. Bowers, 'Musicians and Liturgy of the Lady Chapels' [Westminster Abbey], pp. 47–8; id, 'Choral Institutions', pp. 6044–55.

16 Indenture: 1482 Pynbrygge. Bowers, 'Musicians of the Lady Chapel', pp. 224–7.

17 Indenture: 1487 Bell. Bell succeeded John Stele, first appointed in 1430 as a Cantor of the original type (Indenture: 1430 Stele).

18 It was in this year that the long-established Lady Chapel choir of boys' voices was for the first time provided with a Cantor paid at a full professional rate (£9 2s 6d p.a.), indicating the appointment of a musician accomplished in adding the skills of singing composed polyphony to the achievement of his boys (confirmation of appointment of Richard Holme as Cantor: CUL, MS EDR G2/3, fol. 105r). The endowment sustaining this charge was furnished by John Alcock, now bishop of Ely and here replicating his earlier endeavours at Worcester.

19 Bowers, 'The Liturgy of the Cathedral and its Music', pp. 421–2.

20 Nesbett's setting of Magnificat: The Eton Choirbook, ed. F. Ll. Harrison, 2nd edn, 3 vols., Musica Britannica, 10–12 (London, 1967–73), vol. 3, pp. 63–8.

men to sing with the Cantor and boys, each monastery had two options. The first was to recruit a group of three or four professional singing-men. This expedient was expensive but was undertaken at certain of the wealthiest houses, such as at Winchester, where a team of three men (in addition to the Cantor) was created piecemeal between 1510 and 1529,[21] at Gloucester by 1515 (a Cantor, with three singing-men by 1515 at the latest),[22] and by the 1520s and 1530s at Glastonbury (a large group, of ten men)[23] and St Albans.[24] The result at these houses was the creation of a full and self-contained supplementary choir of lay singers, men and boys, small but complete.[25]

The second option was to engage the Cantor to generate and train, in sufficient numbers, an ensemble of men's voices from among the house's own monks or canons. This procedure was less grandiose than the alternative, but cost little or nothing to implement and was the option to which resort was generally made. It was undertaken at houses such as Chester, and the priories of Taunton and Llanthony Secunda.[26] In certain houses this might be a matter merely of continuing current provision. At Durham since at least 1430 the Cantor had been committed to teach and coach such monks of the house as were deemed suitable for training in the more advanced musical arts, including the singing of polyphony, and this duly continued.[27] In all these instances, the Cantor and his selected monks now possessed the capacity to constitute, with the boys, a full four- or five-part ensemble for polyphonic music.

Long after the first flush of early foundations, groups of singers were still being established in ways such as these almost to the very eve of the dissolutions,[28] and the number of monasteries at which it is known that there existed by the

---

[21] Bowers, 'Musicians of the Lady Chapel', pp. 227–32.

[22] Indenture: 1515 Tucke; *VE*, vol. 2, p. 418.

[23] During 1538/9 the Cantor James Renynger and his colleagues (*socii*) were paid 3s 0d for their attendance at the obit of Walter Monyngton and John Chynnock, abbots; when this sum was paid in 1532/3 the *socii* of his predecessor, one Mr Finch, were numbered at ten. Accounts of Pittancer: PRO, SC6/Henry VIII/3114, 3118 (17), *Anniversaria*. The manner in which, since the early fourteenth century, the Lady Chapel had appropriated and aggregated the various secular clerkships now occupied by singing-men is rather too complex to describe here.

[24] Indenture: 1538 Burre.

[25] Commonly the singing-men could be offered accommodation on site among the secular servants of the monastery, or in the town immediately adjacent to the boundary of the Close: Bowers, 'Musicians and Liturgy of the Lady Chapels', pp. 46, 52; F. Kisby, 'Music and Musicians of Early Tudor Westminster', *EM*, 23 (1995), 223–40, at pp. 232–4; *The Itinerary of John Leland*, ed. L. T. Smith, 5 vols. (London, 1907–10), vol. 1, pp. 289–90 (Glastonbury); Bowers, 'Musicians of the Lady Chapel', pp. 230–1.

[26] Indentures: 1518 Byrchley, 1538 Foxe, 1533 Hodges.

[27] Indentures: 1430 Stele, 1448 Stele, 1487 Bell, 1496 Foderley, 1502 Tildesley, 1512 Porret, 1513 Ashwell, 1513 Ashwell, 1537 Brymley.

[28] For instance, at Norwich Cathedral Priory a Lady Chapel choir of a Cantor and boys, first established in c.1441 but disbanded soon after 1469 (Bowers, 'Choral Institutions', Appendix 7, pp. A031–5), was revived early in the next century, apparently in 1506 (NCDCA, MS NR594: account of Almoner, 1506/7, *Stipendia*). At St Osyth's Abbey John Vintner, abbot, introduced a boys' choir under a Cantor for the Lady Chapel in about 1513 (deduction from numerous entries on abbey accounts: PRO, SC6/Henry VIII/939–40, SC6/Addenda 3479/13). At Winchcombe Abbey an endowment for the establishment of

1530s the professionally trained resources required to sing polyphonic music now stands at over fifty.[29] The list does not extend only to the greater houses; the degree of enterprise required to initiate such a venture may be found at monasteries of all descriptions, among the Benedictines, Cistercians, and the Regular Canons.[30] The list includes seven of the ten cathedral priories, namely Canterbury, Winchester, Durham, Worcester, Coventry,[31] Ely,[32] and Norwich;[33] the absence of Rochester, Carlisle and Bath is most probably best explained by the general lack of documentation surviving from these houses. It extends also to such greater abbeys as Westminster, Glastonbury,[34] Bury St Edmunds,[35] Gloucester,[36] Peterborough,[37] Ramsey,[38] Reading,[39] and St Albans.[40] It includes in particular middle-ranking houses such as Battle,[41] Tavistock,[42] Cerne (which in 1517 recruited a Cantor from Tavistock Abbey),[43] Chertsey,[44] Chester,[45]

a Cantor and six singing-boys was received in 1521: PRO, LR6/29/2, mm. 10v–12r; VE, vol. 2, pp. 459, 460.

[29] For a preliminary listing, see Bowers, 'Almonry Schools', pp. 221–2, adding Bury St Edmund's 1539(D) and Cerne (1517), and correcting the date of Brecon to 1524–37(D) and that of Tavistock to 1517–39(D).

[30] References will not be given below in the case of houses from which no actual indenture survives, but for which full references are given elsewhere in specific notes.

[31] Indenture: 1515 Speke.

[32] CUL, MS EDR G2/3, fol. 105r (see note 18 above). William Smith, first Master of the Choristers under the New Foundation, 1539 (CCCC, MS 120, p. 294), had previously been the last Cantor before the dissolution (CUL, MS EDR Account of Sacrist 33 (1535/6), Stipendia).

[33] NCDCA, MSS NR594–615: accounts of Almoner 1506–33, Stipendia; also epitaph of Osbert Parsley, singing-man or Cantor of the monastery, c.1535 to 1538 (dissolution), and lay clerk of the New Foundation, 1538–85: quoted in J. Morehen, 'Parsley, Osbert', New Grove, XIX, pp. 160–1.

[34] Indenture: 1534 Renynger.

[35] The secular musician and composer Robert Cowper, Mus.D., is known to have been employed (presumably as Cantor) at Bury St Edmunds Abbey (The Autobiography of Thomas Whythorne, ed. J. M. Osborn (Oxford, 1961), p. 300). Apparently it was the dissolution that ended his employment there, since on 25 September 1539 he attended (unsuccessfully) for interview and audition for engagement as a minor canon of St Paul's Cathedral (Chapter Acts, 1536–41: LGL, MS 25630/1, fol. 83v).

[36] Indenture: 1515 Tucke.

[37] Account Rolls of the Obedientiaries of Peterborough, ed. J. Greatrex, Northampton Record Society, 33 (1983), pp. 183, 197; also pp. 51, 210; 143, 178, 191, 206, 214.

[38] Account of Warden of Lady Chapel, 1480/1: BL, Add. Ch. 34682, Expense necessarie.

[39] Account of Warden of Lady Chapel, 1536/7: BL, Add. Ch. 19659, Expense necessarie.

[40] Indentures: 1533 Monyngham, 1538 Burre.

[41] Account of Abbot, 1498/9: PRO, SC6/Henry VIII/1874 fol. 18v, Empcio rerum pro noviciis et pueris capelle.

[42] Indentures: 1523 [name unknown], 1529 Elyott; and see Cerne Abbey, n. 43 below.

[43] Court of Chancery, 1521. William Preston (Cantor of Cerne, sometime of Tavistock) v. Robert, abbot of Cerne: PRO, C1/557, nos. 60–3.

[44] Account of Abbot, 1532/2: PRO, SC6/Henry VIII/3456, p. 79, Soluciones forinsece.

[45] Indenture: 1518 Byrchley.

Colchester,[46] Selby,[47] Winchcombe, Leicester,[48] Thetford,[49] Bristol, Cirencester,[50] Llanthony II,[51] Walsingham,[52] Waltham,[53] Oseney,[54] St Osyth, and Holy Trinity Priory, Aldgate, London.[55]

Among the smaller monasteries, even possession of only modest resources did not inhibit some from finding the drive and initiative to engage a Cantor and boys, and to inaugurate the deployment of polyphonic music. These included Dover Priory, which furnished the composer Thomas Tallis with his first known job in about 1530;[56] Tutbury Priory, already engaging a Cantor and boys as early as 1496;[57] Garendon and Ulverscroft in Leicestershire, which both maintained singing-boys in the 1530s;[58] and the unpretentious priories of Thurgarton in Leicestershire, Tywardreath in Cornwall, and Brecon in Wales.[59] Admittedly, at some of the smaller houses the Cantor's job was recognised as less than full-time. At Thurgarton, John Patenson also performed waiting service for the prior, while at Tywardreath, Thomas Rayne made himself useful as the prior's barber. Rayne also served among the prior's escort when he was riding on business away from the priory, as did Geoffrey Ferrour for his prior at Brecon.[60] At each of

---

[46] Account of Warden of Lady Chapel, 1524/5: PRO, SC6/Henry VIII/935, m. 7r, *Expense necessarie*; Account of Precentor, 1526/7: PRO, SC6/Henry VIII/936, *Allocaciones*.

[47] *Monastery and Society in the Late Middle Ages: Selected Account Rolls from Selby Abbey, Yorkshire, 1398–1537*, ed. J. H. Tillotson (Woodbridge, 1988), p. 234.

[48] Visitation of 1518: *Visitations, 1517–31*, ed. Thompson, vol. 2, p. 186. Accounts of abbey, 1536/7: PRO, E315/279, fol. 24v, *Soluciones facte in officio precentoris*.

[49] Volume of account of priors' disbursements, 1482–1540: *The Register of Thetford Priory*, ed. D. Dymond, 2 vols., NRS, 59–60 (1995–96), pp. 74, 414, 600, 653. During 1506–09 the Cantor was Robert Burton (pp. 222, 234, 253); Edmund Stroger, apparently one of the singing-boys in 1535/6 (p. 650), later became a minor composer of keyboard music.

[50] Indenture: 1538 Edmunds.

[51] Indenture: 1533 Hodges.

[52] 1483: *Household Books of John, Duke of Norfolk, and Thomas, Earl of Surrey*, ed. J. P. Collier, Roxburghe Club (1848), p. 438. 1514: *Visitations in the Diocese of Norwich AD 1492–1532*, ed. A. Jessopp, Camden Society, New Series 43 (1888), pp. 114, 119. c.1515: Cambridge, King's College, MS Inventory without ref. (contains lists of members of college, c.1444–1523), fol. 77r.

[53] Dissolution inventory, 1540: PRO, E117/11/24, fols. 9v, 20v, 21r.

[54] *The Cartulary of Oseney Abbey*, ed. H. E. Salter, 6 vols., OHS, 89–91, 97–8, 101 (1929–36), vol. 6, pp. 212, 221.

[55] Often known as Christ Church priory: a Cantor (Thomas Clerk), at least one singing-man (Thomas Rufford), and at least five boys. Accounts of Prior, 1513/14: PRO E36/108, fols. 27r, *Expense Elimosinarii*; 35r, *Expense ecclesie*; 35v, *Seyntkatatryn Crycherch*; 36r, *For the Resurreccion* (i.e., the Easter procession and pageant); 41r–44r, *Stipendia famulorum*; 49v, *Expense forinsece*.

[56] *Dover Priory*, ed. C. R. Haines (Cambridge, 1930), p. 448. VE, vol. 1, p. 54. Dissolution inventory, 1536: PRO, E36/154, pp. 196, 224.

[57] Court of Chancery, 1530/1. Thomas Alenson (Cantor) v. Richard, prior of Tutbury: PRO, C1/603, no. 1.

[58] See p. 49 and note 160 below. Royal visitation 1535: PRO, E36/154, pp. 106–7, 110–11 (*LP*, X, p. 496).

[59] N. Orme, 'Music and Teaching at Tywardreath Priory, 1522–1536', *Devon and Cornwall Notes and Queries*, 36 (1990), 277–80; Indentures: 1522 Patenson; 1522 Rayne; 1524 Ferrour.

[60] Something of the conditions prevailing in this part of Wales in the 1520s may be grasped from the manner in which Ferrour's indenture made provision for two levels of compensa-

Thurgarton and Tywardreath the Cantor was given only two boys to train, and at Brecon only an undefined number; expectations in the case of some of the smaller houses may not have been of the highest, but that did not stop them trying.

The terms of the indentures, amply corroborated by entries on obedientiary accounts, demonstrate clearly that the primary objective informing the decision by any monastery to engage a Cantor was the teaching, cultivation and performance of polyphonic music at divine service.[61] In general the function of the Cantor, with his singers, was to enhance on a daily basis the Lady Mass and commonly also the Marian antiphon; on festivals certain of the principal services in the monks' quire; and, at many institutions, on Fridays the mass and antiphon of the Name of Jesus observed in the Jesus Chapel. For fulfilment of this role, the Cantor needed to be both pedagogue and performer.

At monasteries where much was expected of the brethren, provision was made for certain of them to be among the Cantor's pupils so that he might elicit and develop their latent talents. One example was Durham, where from 1487 onwards the Cantor's tutees included all such monks of the priory as the prior or his deputy saw fit to identify and to assign to him for this purpose.[62] To these the Cantor was to teach the total range of contemporary musical science required for ecclesiastical purposes: organ-playing, singing polyphony from notation, including 'squarenote',[63] and singing both plainsong itself and all the techniques then current for improvising at sight a vocal counterpoint to a plainsong melody; these were faburden, descant, and counter.[64] The Cantor was kept busy; he taught on all ferial days, for two sessions in the morning and two in the afternoon.

Similar provisions obtained at Chester, where in 1518 John Byrchley was

tion payable in the event of mishap befalling him when performing escort duty, one to himself in the event of his being merely 'maymed in any parte of his bodye', another to his widow in the event of his actually being killed. Indenture: 1524 Ferrour. Further on Ferrour, see Sally Harper, *Music in Welsh Culture before 1560* (Aldershot, 2007), pp. 285–6 and n. 19, 286–8 and n. 24.

[61] At Glastonbury, James Renynger was expected also to entertain the abbot and his household at Christmas and other festival seasons of the year 'with songis and playng yn Instruments of musyke': Indenture, 1534 Renynger. In all likelihood this was a regular feature of the functions of Cantors in monastic service.

[62] Indentures: 1487 Bell, 1496 Foderley, 1502 Tildesley, 1512 Porret, 1513 Ashwell, 1513 Ashwell, 1537 Brymley.

[63] 'Squarenote' was added to this list with effect from 1496 (Indenture: 1496 Tildesley). The meaning of 'squarenote' is not entirely clear, but may relate to the performance of polyphony from a simplified notation using only square note-shapes appropriated for the purpose from plainsong. For an example actually of Durham provenance, see the facsimile of DCA, MS Endpapers and Bindings 25, in Bowers and Wathey, 'New Sources of English Fourteenth- and Fifteenth-Century Polyphony', pp. 130–1.

[64] The technique of 'Counter' appears to have been akin to that of descant (see p. 25 above), except that the counterpoint was improvised below the given melody. In 'Faburden' the duplication of the plainsong by voices both above (by an interval of a fourth) and below (by a third, but a fifth at the start and end of phrases) produced a simple three-part improvised harmony consisting of strings of six-three chords articulated at each end of the phrase by an eight-five, performed to rules so strict that the technique could be executed by ensembles larger than soloists. For faburden, see also below, p. 51 and n. 166.

required to teach all those monks who of their own volition came to him for instruction in music.[65] He undertook to convey a similarly comprehensive list of accomplishments, including singing from notated polyphony, organ-playing, and singing plainsong, faburden, descant and counter; to those monks who 'be disposed to learne the same' he would also teach composition.[66] At Buckland, Robert Derkeham taught music and organ-playing to any monks of the house who wished to learn; at Muchelney the same was required of Ralph Drake and at Taunton of Thomas Foxe, while at Llanthony II, John Hodges was required to instruct in musical skills any of the canons whom the prior selected.[67]

It is likely that such teaching was commonplace even when not expressly stipulated in the Cantor's indenture. At Cirencester, in 1538, Henry Edmunds undertook to attend certain festal services in the canons' quire 'with singing of prickid song and playing at the organs'. He could not sing polyphonic music on his own, and consequently it appears he was expected to work informally with talented canons, coaching them appropriately.[68] Such teaching could raise logistical problems; in 1507 at St Mary Overy, Southwark, the canons had to be found some special premises to practise their 'pricksong', since their doing so in the cloister was disturbing their colleagues.[69]

The development of a culture fully supportive of music duly produced successive generations of monks well accomplished in musical skills. Such experts were found at Westminster, where in 1489 the abbot was pleased to commend one of his monks, Edward Botiller, as possessing 'competent lernyng and understondyng, and can syng bothe playn songe and prikked song'.[70] For the first time since the fourteenth century, monks appear among the named composers of their day. They include Robert Holyngborne, monk of Christ Church, Canterbury, and William Stratford, monk of Stratford-at-Bow (Essex); of the work of the former

---

65 Indenture: 1518 Byrchley.

66 No music by Byrchley is known to survive.

67 Indentures: 1522 Derkeham, c.1520 Drake, 1538 Foxe, 1533 Hodges.

68 Indenture: 1538 Edmunds. Indeed, the expectation that the Cantor would coach monks or canons to form with him an ensemble for the performance of polyphony at festal service in the monastic quire was all but universal. Brecon Priory, however, may have been an exception. The contract of Geoffrey Ferrour as Cantor required him to be in attendance at the monastic service on feast days at High Mass and vespers, and on certain greater feasts at matins and lauds also, but limited his duties there to merely playing the organ. It seems safe to draw an inference that such eschewment of stipulation that he participate in performances of 'pricksong' or other forms of polyphony indicates a general absence among the monks of interest in forming with him an ensemble to sing polyphony. His playing at the canticles of matins and lauds (respectively, Te Deum and Benedictus) was specifically mentioned, no doubt in performances alternating organ interludes with vocal plainsong, in a manner manifest by all the surviving Te Deum organ settings (see e.g. *Early Tudor Organ Music, I. Music for the Office*, ed. J. Caldwell, EECM, 6 (1966), nos. 1–3, pp. 1–22; *The Mulliner Book*, ed. D. Stevens, Musica Britannica, 1 (2nd edn., 1954), no. 77, pp. 55–8).

69 HRO, MS Ep. Reg. Foxe, fol. 85r. In 1442 at Durham, the monks practising their polyphony had to be moved out of the chapter house and found somewhere more secluded, for the same reason: DCA, MSS 1.8.Pont.2 (§31); 1.8.Pont.3 (§31); Locellus xxvii, no. 39; Misc. Charters 2658 (§6).

70 WAM, Register A, fol. 30v, quoted in J. Armitage Robinson and M. R. James, *The Manuscripts of Westminster Abbey* (Cambridge, 1908), p. 12.

there remains a four-part Marian antiphon 'Gaude virgo salutata', and of the latter a four-part setting of the Magnificat.[71] Most conspicuous of all was John Dygon, monk and prior of St Augustine's Abbey, Canterbury, an all-round intellectual and fine composer awarded the degree of Bachelor of Music at Oxford in 1512. Among his many accomplishments was the preparation of a condensation of Book IV of *Practica Musice*, a standard treatise on music published in 1496 by the Italian theorist Franchino Gaffurius; Dygon ventured to improve upon it by replacing all of Gaffurius's music examples with others newly composed by himself.[72] Indeed, the lamentably little of his work that survives indicates that he was an assured composer of the expansive and non-imitative melismatic polyphony of the 1510s and 1520s.[73]

At less exalted levels, competence and skill in music and participation in its performance may safely be presumed also on the part of those monks who appear as copyists of polyphonic settings for use in the liturgical service. These include William Wolverley of Worcester, who in 1532 copied out no fewer than eight five-part settings of the Magnificat;[74] William London *alias* Allen of Winchester, who may also be identifiable with the composer of that name;[75] and the unnamed monk of Abingdon by whom music was copied for the use of the chapel singers of Corpus Christi College, Oxford, in 1535.[76] Monks could also become capable organists. For instance, at a large monastery such as Canterbury Cathedral Priory the employment of a Cantor since 1438 had long ensured that there was always a steady stream of monks sufficiently knowledgeable to be able to play the principal organ in the monks' quire. As one among many these included Thomas Chart, lamented on his death in 1493 as 'very learned in music and upon the organ, and most devout'.[77] At Durham there was always at least one monk capable of playing the organ in quire at service on ferial days when the Cantor was absent.[78]

In addition to his work with the monks or canons of the house, the Cantor was universally obliged to instruct a team of boy singers. These teams were never large. Eight singing-boys were committed to the Cantor's teaching at each of

---

71 *Eton Choirbook*, ed. Harrison, vol. 3, pp. 154–60, 104–11. For the identification of Holyngborne, see Bowers, 'The Liturgy of the Cathedral and its Music', pp. 422, 424–5.

72 CTC, MS O.3.38.

73 R. Bowers, 'Dygon, John', *ODNB*, vol. 17, p. 495. In 1506/7 Richard Ede, an Augustinian canon, likewise supplicated for conferment of the Oxford degree of Bachelor of Music; he, however, evidently obtained leave to make a living outside his home monastery, at least briefly, in the city of Westminster: Kisby, 'Music and Musicians of Early Tudor Westminster', pp. 227, 228, 235.

74 WCL, MS A XI, fols. 134v, 135v, printed as *The Journal of Prior William More*, ed. E. S. Fagan (Worcester, 1914), pp. 347, 350.

75 Bowers, 'Musicians of the Lady Chapel', p. 229, n. 57.

76 J. R. Liddell, 'The Library of Corpus Christi College, Oxford, in the Sixteenth Century', *The Library*, 4th series xviii (1938), 385–416, at p. 400 n. 2.

77 *Christ Church, Canterbury: 1. The Chronicle of John Stone*, ed. W. G. Searle, CAS, 34 (1902), p. 189; Bowers, 'Liturgy of the Cathedral and its Music', p. 423.

78 *The Rites of Durham*, ed. J. T. Fowler, SS, 107 (1902), pp. 62–3.

the cathedral priories of Canterbury,[79] Durham,[80] Worcester,[81] and Winchester (though ten at Winchester during the 1510s);[82] at Glastonbury Abbey six contractually, though ten in practice;[83] six at Battle,[84] Bristol,[85] Chester,[86] Tutbury,[87] St Albans,[88] Ramsay,[89] and Westminster;[90] five or six at Gloucester,[91] Tavistock,[92] Peterborough,[93] St Osyth,[94] and Holy Trinity Priory, London;[95] four at Chertsey,[96] Buckland, Llanthony II, and Muchelney;[97] and two at Thurgarton and Tywardreath.[98] Numbers of this order are also likely for the groups of singing-boys who are known to have been maintained elsewhere.[99]

Universal also was the requirement that the boys be trained to sing polyphonic music from notation, while certain contracts specified particularly fully the content of the boys' education. At Chester and Durham this was to be no less full than that offered to the monks, extending to plainsong, 'pricksong', and all the techniques of improvising counterpoint to plainsong.[100] At Llanthony II, a small house wherein perhaps no more than two canons were found suitable with the Cantor to supply the broken voices, the boys were specifically to be taught in both the treble and alto parts of composed polyphony.[101] Such

79   Bowers, 'Liturgy of the Cathedral and its Music', p. 420; id., 'Some Observations on the Life and Career of Lionel Power', pp. 114–17.
80   Indentures: 1430 Stele, 1448 Stele, 1487 Bell, 1496 Foderley, 1502 Tildesley, 1512 Porret, 1513 Ashwell, 1513 Ashwell, 1537 Brymley.
81   Indentures: 1486 Hampton, 1522 Boyce.
82   Indentures: 1482 Pynbrygge (eight boys), 1510 Goodman (ten boys), 1538 Fuller (eight boys); Bowers, 'Musicians of the Lady Chapel', pp. 225, 228, 230, 232–3.
83   Indenture: 1534 Renynger (six boys); Accounts of Anniversarian, 1532/3, 1538/9: PRO, SC6/Henry VIII/3115, 3118(17), *Anniversaria* (ten boys).
84   Account of Abbot, 1498/9: PRO, SC6/Henry VII/1874, *Empcio rerum pro noviciis et pueris capelle.*
85   GRO, MS D674a/Z3: abbey accounts 1503/4, account of Almoner, *Empcio victualium.*
86   Indenture: 1518 Byrchley.
87   PRO, C1/603, no. 1.
88   Indenture: 1533 Monyngham.
89   VE, vol. 4, p. 275.
90   Bowers, 'Musicians and Liturgy of the Lady Chapels', pp. 48, 54.
91   Indenture: 1515 Tucke. VE, vol. 2, p. 418.
92   Indentures: 1523 [unnamed], 1529 Elyott.
93   *Account Rolls*, ed. Greatrex, pp. 183, 197.
94   Abbey accounts 1521/2, account of Almoner: PRO, SC6/Henry VIII/942, fol. 16v: *Exhibucio puerorum*; account of Almoner 1526/7: PRO, SC6/Henry VIII/939, *Salaria et Vadia*; abbey accounts 1530/1, account of Almoner: PRO, SC6/Henry VIII/943, fol. 15r, *Exhibucio vj puerorum.*
95   Priory accounts 1513/14: PRO, E36/108, fol. 27r, *Expense Elimosinarii* (four boys named; 'great Richard' supposes the existence also of a 'little Richard').
96   Account of Abbot, 1532/2: PRO, SC6/Henry VIII/3456, p. 79, *Soluciones forinsece.*
97   Indentures: 1522 Derkeham, 1533 Hodges, c.1520 Drake.
98   Indentures: 1522 Patenson, 1522 Rayne.
99   E.g. at Barnwell Priory, Cambridge: Item to syngyng boys vjs viijd (gratuities at dissolution, 1538: PRO, E315/172, p. 95). For Garendon Abbey and Ulverscroft Priory see n. 160 below.
100 Indentures, 1518 Byrchley (Chester); 1430 Stele, 1448 Stele, 1487 Bell, 1496 Foderley, 1502 Tildesley, 1512 Porret, 1513 Ashwell, 1513 Ashwell, 1537 Brymley (Durham).
101 Indenture: 1533 Hodges. For a further instance, see also note 151 below.

specificity, however, was not universal; more commonly, the lawyers by whom the contracts were formulated were content to eschew technical terms, each convent relying on the professional integrity of its Cantor to know what was intended by an obligation expressed simply as a requirement to teach the boys in 'plainsong and polyphony' (in cantu et discantu), 'in playnsong, pricksong and descant', or simply just 'in pricksong', plainsong being taken for granted.

Commonly it was also instructed that the Cantor teach the boys to play the organ, which indeed was but a natural extension of their training as singers. Although by this period the organ in church was ubiquitous in England, there yet existed little music specifically composed for it to play. Most organ-playing consisted of improvisation, the player executing with his fingers elaborations of techniques the same as those which he had learnt for improvising vocal counterpoint to plainsong. At Durham, Chester and Llanthony, the Cantor routinely taught his boys to play the organ, and at Buckland, Robert Derkeham taught organ-playing to those who specifically sought it. Probably simple practicality was the motive for the manner in which the contract of the last Cantor at Durham, John Brymley (1537), required him to have only one or two boys as organ pupils at any one time. At Glastonbury, James Renynger undertook to teach organ-playing to any two of the boys at once; each such boy was to bind himself, on completion of two years' instruction, to remain at the abbey's disposal for a further six years, to be available to play when required at the services.[102] The abbey authorities supplied Renynger with a pair of clavichords for each of these pupils, to expedite their practice and learning; doubtless it was for the same purpose that at Westminster the subalmoner, as housemaster to the singing-boys, acquired a clavichord in 1512.[103] At all the institutions mentioned above, such teaching was free; elsewhere, however, it might be regarded as supplementary. In 1522 Daniel Boyce at Worcester undertook to teach the organ to those boys who sought it, but was empowered to ask a fee of 12d per quarter.[104]

It may be noted that, unlike the boys and untrained monks, the secular singing-men were never listed among those whom the Cantor was directed to instruct or coach. These were regarded as skilled craftsmen; evidently they were expected, simply as part of their professional calling and integrity, to learn their music and to arrive at their job each day fully capable of executing it without particular coaching.

All this volume of teaching and coaching for both singing-boys and monks or canons had of course a very practical objective. It served the Cantor and his singers with the groundwork necessary for the execution of those of their duties which were actually visible and audible at service in the monastery church. The overall shape of the monastic liturgy was, except to experts, all but indistinguishable from the secular, and it is no surprise to note that the services to be elevated with the provision of elaborate polyphony were precisely the same as those for

[102] Indentures, 1430 Stele, 1448 Stele, 1487 Bell, 1496 Foderley, 1502 Tildesley, 1512 Porret, 1513 Ashwell, 1513 Ashwell, 1537 Brymley (Durham); 1518 Byrchley (Chester); 1533 Hodges (Llanthony); 1522 Derkeham (Buckland); 1534 Renynger (Glastonbury).
[103] Bowers, 'Musicians and Liturgy of the Lady Chapels', p. 54.
[104] Indenture: 1522 Boyce.

whose distinction it was employed also at the principal secular churches and chapels.

The duties expected of their Cantor and singers by the several monasteries exhibited much commonality in principle, though plenty of diversity in detail. At all the services at which they were present, the singers were routinely expected to support the monks' performance of the plainsong. More particularly, the Cantor was also to deliver to divine worship the rendering of polyphonic music both vocal and sounded by the organ. Considered very broadly, the singing duties of the Cantor and his colleagues, men and boys, fell into two principal categories. One consisted of routine and standard work, conducted daily in side chapels; the other was comprised of intermittent but more spectacular work, undertaken on feast days at the monks' service in the principal quire.

Perpetuating their historic function, one item of routine daily work always required of these ensembles was attendance each morning at the Lady Mass cele-brated in the Lady Chapel. The monks by whom the mass was celebrated were attended by the Cantor and the full team of boys, with the secular singing-men where these were employed. Here their function was to sing the ordinary in a polyphonic setting, often amplified with the Kyrie and sequence of the proper.

Thus at Winchester, Lady Mass was sung by a full team of Cantor, three singing-men and eight boys, and at Westminster from 1480 onwards by the full choir of Cantor, four singing-men and six boys. At St Albans, the Cantor was required to be present daily with his six boys trained in singing polyphony; so also was the singing-man Walter Burre, indicating that all the singing-men routinely attended to participate in the polyphony. At Coventry, likewise, daily attend-ance at Lady Mass was required of the singing-man Guy Speke.[105] The daily Lady Mass was one of the devotions for participation in which, at Gloucester in 1515, John Tucke was required explicitly to instruct his boys, and for which, at Glas-tonbury, John Renynger taught his boys 'pricke songe and descaunte' and organ-playing. At both Gloucester and Glastonbury singing-men were employed as well as a Cantor and boys, so that in each case the Lady Mass was attended by the full chorus of secular singers.

Where no team of professional singing-men was maintained, the musical conduct of Lady Mass continued generally to be enhanced as of old, by Cantor and boys alone. In the period concerned here, the singing of such groups could extend to formal polyphony composed in three parts for divided boys' voices and the adult voice of the Cantor.[106] Thus at Llanthony II, John Hodges was required to 'kepe our lady masse and antheym dayly', 'synging and playng at Organs' 'wyth foure childerne well and suffycyently enstructed that is to say too meanys and too trebles' – coached, that is, in singing the alto as well as the treble parts in composed polyphony. At Chester, John Byrchley was to teach his boys specifically 'for the saide Chapell' (i.e., the Lady Chapel), where he and

[105] Indentures: 1533 Monyngham, 1538 Burre; 1515 Tucke; 1534 Renynger; 1515 Speke.
[106] For a complete weekly cycle of seven settings of Lady Mass for such an ensemble, see *Nicholas Ludford: Opera omnia*, ed. J. Bergsagel, 3 vols., CMM, xxvii (Rome, 1963–i.p.), vol. 1. The music, preserved in a set of four part-books, supplies an explicit role for the organ-player; he alternated phrases with the choir, improvising on the plainsong supplied by the fourth book.

they were to keep both Lady Mass and votive antiphon daily 'with prycksonge and organs'. At Tavistock in 1529 John Elyott was required to teach his five boys in the settings used in the Lady Chapel at both daily Lady Mass and the Marian antiphon, and it was specifically to serve in the Lady Chapel that at Taunton Thomas Foxe undertook to teach his boys the arts of singing.[107]

Also universal as an occasion for the attendance of secular singers was the evening Marian votive antiphon, sung daily as an extra-liturgical devotion. Towards the end of the working day the participants gathered in the Lady Chapel, at a lectern placed adjacent to the principal image of St Mary, and began their devotion with the singing of a setting, in particularly elaborate polyphony when-ever possible, of a text (such as 'Salve regina') votive to the Blessed Virgin. The attendance of Cantor and boys appears to have been universal, as at Llanthony II, Chester, and Tavistock, mentioned above; at churches such as the cathedral priories of Canterbury, Durham, Worcester, and Winchester, where the office and duties of the Cantor had long been established, the practice whereby he and his singing-boys attended the Marian antiphon daily continued as before, and it is known to have been observed also at houses such as Tutbury, Gloucester, and Cirencester.[108] It is in the nature of the extant documentation that little material survives to indicate the extent of the participation of the adult voices. However, the singing-men of Coventry and (apparently) St Albans attended this observ-ance, as also did John Byrchley's trained monks at Chester,[109] and the common choice for the Marian antiphon of texts carrying substantial indulgences may well have ensured an enthusiastic attendance of religious and (where employed) singing-men for these occasions.

Commonly, the monastic authorities also required their Cantor and singers to attend the weekly Mass of the Name of Jesus, celebrated on Friday mornings in the Jesus chapel of the monastery church, and at the votive antiphon of Jesus performed in the afternoon. At St Albans in the 1530s the entire secular choir of Cantor, men and boys was in attendance at the singing of the antiphon, and the Cantor and boys at the mass. At Chester, from at least 1518, John Byrchley and the boys were to perform 'with prycksong and organs' both the Mass of Jesus at six o'clock in the morning, and, following vespers, the Jesus antiphon. At this

---

107 Indentures: 1533 Hodges, 1518 Byrchley, 1529 Elyott, 1538 Foxe.

108 Bowers, 'Liturgy of the Cathedral and its Music', p. 422; *Rites of Durham*, ed. Fowler, pp. 43–4. Indentures: 1486 Hampton, 1522 Boyce. Bowers, 'Musicians of the Lady Chapel', pp. 218–19, 234. PRO, C1/603, no. 1. Indentures: 1515 Tucke, 1538 Edmunds.

109 Indentures: 1515 Speke, 1538 Burre (described as 'Capelle beate marie cantor'), 1518 Byrchley. Quite independently of the evening extra-liturgical antiphon, the standard monastic liturgies stipulated that daily at the end of vespers or compline in quire one of the four standard Marian antiphons be sung. This occasion was commonly known as the 'Salve', 'Salve regina' being the antiphon most commonly performed: Harrison, *Music in Medieval Britain*, pp. 81–2. In a few instances the Cantor was required to attend and participate in this devotion. At Durham Cathedral, he was to be present at this 'Salve' just on Saturdays throughout the year, and on principal feasts and their eves. At Worcester Cathedral from 1486 the Cantor was to be present at the 'Salve' in the monks' quire daily during Lent. Apparently the Cantor's presence there was simply to lend body and distinction to the monks' singing of the plainsong; it was never stipulated that his trained singers also be present, or that polyphony be sung.

latter they were joined by the monks taught and coached by Byrchley in musical skills, so completing the polyphonic ensemble.[110] At Durham, attendance at the Jesus Mass was added to the Cantor's duties in 1513, and at the Jesus antiphon by 1537.[111] The nostalgic author of that memoir of lost monastic practice, the Rites of Durham, allowed himself a sentimental recollection of the attendance of Cantor and boys at both these devotions.[112] The attendance of Cantor and singers at the Jesus Mass and antiphon is also attested for the cathedrals of Winchester, Worcester and Coventry, Gloucester Abbey (Cantor and boys, and probably singing-men, at mass and antiphon), Brecon Priory (Cantor and boys at mass) and numerous others.[113]

The secular singers were not limited to performance in the Lady Chapel and Jesus Chapel. Intermittently, on the Church's greater feast days, they took a role also in the elaborate liturgy executed by the monks themselves in the principal monastic quire. They participated in the grandest of the daytime services, namely first vespers kept on the eve, and High Mass and second vespers on the feast day itself; sometimes they were required at matins as well. 'Feast days', a term rarely precisely defined and evidently expected to be interpreted according to local custom,[114] clearly included all principal feasts and all major doubles, and perhaps also the minor doubles, both in copes and in albs; this could be up to 85 to 100 occasions per year.[115]

Though irregular in its incidence, the duty to be present at the principal services of the monks' liturgy was the most conspicuous instance of the participation of the secular singers. It was always specified in the contracts of Cantors and singing-men; it might also appear among the occasions for which the Cantor was to train his boys. The settings sung at High Mass, matins and vespers on such occasions would include numerous items from the conventional repertories of polyphony, including the Te Deum and (especially) the Magnificat, being the canticles at matins and vespers respectively, and the four movements of the ordinary of the festal High Mass. It appears unlikely that at such service in quire formal places were allotted to the Cantor and secular singers among the monks in their choir stalls. More probably they stood in a group around a

---

[110] Indentures: 1533 Monyngham, 1538 Burre; 1518 Byrchley.

[111] The original contract of Thomas Ashwell, dated 4 December 1513, had followed all previous contracts in containing no such clause; the decision of the Chapter so to augment the Cantor's duties was incorporated into Ashwell's revised indenture, dated 24 December 1513. Indentures: 1513 Ashwell, 1513 Ashwell; also 1537 Brymley.

[112] Rites of Durham, ed. Fowler, pp. 32, 34. Writing fifty years after the event, the author's recollection was a little hazy, and his description is actually of these observances as slightly modified after 1539 for conduct by the staff of the successor secular cathedral, 1539–47.

[113] Indentures: 1482 Pynbrygge, 1510 Goodman, 1538 Fuller; 1486 Hampton, 1522 Boyce; 1515 Speke; 1515 Tucke; 1524 Ferrour.

[114] If a more selective pattern of attendance on feast days was intended, the list was spelled out precisely, as on Indenture: 1534 Smythe (Sempringham).

[115] It might also include some of the remaining feasts less major but still distinguished by the reading of twelve lessons at matins (a further 30 per year). See e.g. Kalendars of Westminster Abbey, c.1384, and St Mary's Abbey, York, c.1400: Missale ad Usum Ecclesie Westmonasteriensis, ed. J.W. Legg, 3 vols., HBS, 1, 5, 12 (1891–97), vol. 1, cols. v–xvi; The Ordinal and Customary of the Abbey of St Mary, York, ed. The Lady Abbess of Stanbrook and J. B. L. Tolhurst, 3 vols., HBS, 73, 75, 84 (1934–51), vol. 1, pp. 9–12.

lectern located on or near the choir step,[116] where they could be joined when appropriate by competent monks deputed to augment them.

It was among those houses where the engagement of a full group of professional singing-men demonstrated a special commitment to the cultivation of polyphony that these services were most particularly distinguished by the appointment of a significant role for the full ensemble of secular men and boys. At Winchester the duties in the monks' quire laid on successive Cantors extended to not only irregular festal but also regular weekly attendance, namely at vespers on Saturday and at High Mass and vespers on Sunday, and also, when required by the precentor, every double feast at first vespers on the eve and at High Mass and second vespers on the day. Cantors Edmund Pynbrygge, Thomas Goodman and Matthew Fuller were required to be present, both singing and playing the organ, weekly at Vespers on Saturday and at High Mass and Vespers on Sunday, and also, when required by the precentor, on every double feast at first Vespers on the eve and at High Mass and second Vespers on the day. The contract of Henry Stempe, singing-man, shows that it was on precisely these occasions that the four singing-men likewise were to attend and participate.[117] Such contribution to service in the monks' quire also appeared among the duties for which the Cantors were to train the singing-boys in plainsong and polyphony, so resulting in the attendance on these occasions of the complete ensemble of singers, men and boys.[118]

At St Albans similar circumstances applied. Here the Cantor Thomas Monyngham was required to participate in service in the monks' quire at High Mass and second vespers on every feast day plus first vespers on its eve, and also at such other services in terms of mass and vespers as were deemed by the precentor appropriate for his presence. The attendance required of the singing-man Walter Burre duplicated these stipulations all but perfectly, and in every likelihood the same obligation was laid on each of the singing-men. To each of these services Monyngham was also to bring his trained group of boys 'knowledgeable in singing polyphony' (scientibus canticum organicum cantare).[119]

Such attendance of a full polyphonic ensemble to sing at festal services in the monks' quire is also found at churches where no professional singing-men were engaged, or less than a full team. Here the men's voices were supplied by the monks or canons of the house trained by the Cantor. At Worcester the men's voices consisted of the Cantor and one singing-man, amplified by certain of the monks who were competent. In 1522 Daniel Boyce was engaged as Cantor, and was required to be present to sing the plainsong and polyphony and to play the organ in the monks' quire at all the 'accustomed' services on principal and double

116 Bowers, 'Musicians and Liturgy of the Lady Chapels', p. 47.
117 Indentures: 1482 Pynbrygge, 1510 Goodman, 1538 Fuller, 1537 Stempe. Likewise, at Coventry Cathedral Priory the singing-man Guy Speke undertook to be present at all the services of High Mass, matins and vespers customary for the singing-men to attend in the monks' quire. Indenture: 1515 Speke.
118 Indentures; 1482 Pynbrygge, 1510 Goodman, 1537 Stempe, 1538 Fuller. This conclusion amends a misapprehension to be found in Bowers, 'Musicians of the Lady Chapel', pp. 224–5, nn. 44, 46.
119 Indentures: 1533 Monyngham, 1538 Burre.

feasts. Such services on these days certainly included High Mass and vespers; specifically to participate in these he was also to train his eight singing-boys, so that the complete ensemble of men and boys was present to sing there.[120]

Meanwhile, at a monastery such as Chester, where no singing-men were employed, it is evident that the Cantor was expected on such occasions to be directing the group of the monks whom he had been teaching in accordance with his contractual obligation. Here John Byrchley undertook to be present in the monks' quire on all festival days at matins and High Mass, and also at any other mass sung at the high altar on such days; he was to be present to contribute both performance on the organ and the singing of 'prycke songe'. To these services he was also to bring his group of singing-boys, so yielding with Cantor and monks a complete ensemble of men and boys on these occasions.[121]

However, not every great monastery wished the services held in the monks' quire to be distinguished with the sound of boys' voices. Historically the voices of young boys had not been heard in the monastic quire since the extinction of the oblate system in the twelfth century, and it appears that among certain of these houses there arose objections of scruple against their engagement now. Consequently, the participation of the singing-boys at festal service in the monks' quire was eschewed, so that the performance of polyphonic music was undertaken by men's voices alone. At Westminster the singing-men had long attended and contributed to the monastic service on the ten greatest feast days of the year,[122] and this practice continued until the dissolution; however, there has yet been found no evidence to suggest that the team of six singing-boys introduced in 1480 ever became involved on these occasions. At Gloucester, where in 1515 John Tucke was required to be present on festivals, playing the organ and participating in the singing of polyphony at first Vespers on the eve and at High Mass and second vespers on the day itself, it may be understood that the monastery's team of three singing-men was present with him;[123] the text of his contract, however, suggests that no attendance here was routinely expected of his singing-boys.

Circumstances at Durham appear to have been similar. Successive Cantors from 1487 onward undertook to be present in the monastic quire at High Mass and vespers on all festal occasions defined as those on which it was customary for the service to be distinguished with organ-playing and with composed and improvised polyphony. It is evident that for this purpose the Cantor was expected to be directing a group consisting of the monks he had been teaching in accordance with his contractual obligation; no provision specifically stipulated that

---

120 Indenture: 1522 Boyce.
121 Indenture: 1518 Byrchley.
122 Bowers, 'Musicians and Liturgy of the Lady Chapels', p. 40.
123 Wherever a monastery undertook the expense of maintaining a group of singing-men as well as a Cantor, it would be natural to expect provision to be made to procure their attendance with the Cantor at festal services in the monks' quire, so ensuring maximum musical impact for the outlay made. This is known to have occurred at St Albans and Winchester, for both of which there survives an example of the contract of a singing-man as well as of a Cantor, suggesting that it may indeed be taken as a general rule.

his boys be present as well.[124] At Cirencester Abbey in 1538 Henry Edmunds undertook to 'kepe' the quire 'with singing of prickid song and playing at the organs' at High Mass, Vespers and Compline on all principal and double feasts and Sundays 'as his predecessors had been accustomed to do'. No stipulation was made that his singing-boys be in attendance, and it appears that Edmunds participated just with his putative team of trained canons.[125]

Thus on many of the greatest occasions of each liturgical year at monasteries such as these, the monks consciously sought to amplify the already elaborate splendour of divine service as executed in a great late-medieval abbey with an extra layer of very distinctive beauty and grandeur. The service resounded with a skilled ensemble's rendering of not less than all four movements of the ordinary at High Mass, and of the Magnificat at first and perhaps second vespers, all executed in the full resplendent magnificence of early Tudor vocal polyphony, extended, resonant, and virtuosic.

Nonetheless, the groups of singers directed by the monastery Cantors did not constitute full-time choirs. Only in that minority of services which was distinguished with polyphony did the secular singers ever participate; the remainder were performed by the monks alone. In consequence, the boys had time to be conventional schoolboys as well,[126] and in general (Glastonbury alone excepted),[127] the singing-men were not engaged on more than a part-time basis.[128] These features had appropriate consequences.

The remuneration in cash and kind offered to the Cantors was on the whole fairly modest; only at Durham and Glastonbury was the reward at all handsome. Consequently, the office of Cantor of a monastery church appears to have tended to attract not the more seasoned musicians, but relatively young men at the start of their careers. For instance, John Hodges must still have been very young when in 1533 he was appointed as Cantor at Llanthony II; following its dissolution in 1538 he was appointed Organist and Master of the Choristers at Hereford Cathedral, and was still in office there in December 1582, all but fifty years later.[129] Edmund Pynbrygge, appointed Cantor at Winchester in 1482,

---

124   Indentures: 1487 Bell, 1496 Foderley, 1502 Tildesley, 1512 Porret, 1513 Ashwell, 1513 Ashwell, 1537 Brymley; *Rites of Durham*, ed. Fowler, pp. 62–3.

125   Indenture: 1538 Edmunds. See also above, p. 34, and n. 68.

126   Bowers, 'Almonry Schools', pp. 208–10.

127   At Glastonbury the abundance of Lady Chapel staff, in terms both of secular priests and lay musicians, was sufficiently great to enable service to be conducted there in the manner of a subordinate collegiate church. Consequently the Cantor had much more of a full-time job, involving – as well as participation in the monks' quire on festivals – attendance at the Lady Chapel's conduct of 'deyly matens masses yevensongs Complens Anteymes and all othe devyne services as hath ben accostomably usid to be songyn yn the seid Chappell of our blessid lody of Glastyngbry': Indenture, 1534 Renynger.

128   Bowers, 'Musicians of the Lady Chapel', pp. 230–1.

129   Indenture: 1533 Hodges. H. Watkins Shaw, *The Succession of Organists of the Chapel Royal and the Cathedrals of England and Wales from c.1538* (Oxford, 1991), p. 132. Somewhat contrary to the spirit of the arrangements established to compensate those indentured employees for whom the dissolution meant a loss of livelihood, Hodges contrived to draw his pension for many years despite having obtained gainful employment elsewhere: PRO, LR6/29/2, m. 10v (1566/7). For further examples of such practice, see Bowers, 'Musicians of the Lady Chapel', p. 234, n. 80.

was still alive sixty years later in 1542 to make a claim for receipt of a post-dissolution pension.[130] Of the twelve men known to have served as Cantor of Westminster between 1480 and 1540, none is known previously to have held a similar post elsewhere, although several subsequently served in distinguished choirs.[131] Christopher Haslam was appointed in 1490 to Beauchief Abbey; a man of this name occurs as one of the priests serving in the church of nearby Dronfield so late as 1533.[132] It is clear that the composer Robert Fayrfax (born 1464) enjoyed some close association with St Albans Abbey, and may perhaps have been Cantor there as a young man before becoming a Gentleman of the Chapel Royal some time before 1497. Henry Edmunds, appointed Cantor of Cirencester Abbey in 1538, was described as forty years old in 1548, when he was organ-player of the parish church.[133] In 1487 Alexander Bell was pleased to leave the rather poorly paid posts of Master of the Choristers in the Oxford choirs of New College (1485) and Magdalen College (1486–87) for the office of Cantor at Durham;[134] however, there he remained for only eight years before moving on again, to become Master of the Choristers at Salisbury Cathedral in 1495.[135] Indeed, it was probably no disadvantage to any monastery that its Cantor was likely to be a relatively young man using the post as a means of gaining experience before moving on to the rewards of a full-time job with a full-size choir. Youthful drive and ambition were, perhaps, what the monasteries appreciated and needed most.

   All the available evidence suggests that in no sense did their part-time status and relatively small membership in any way inhibit the monastery ensembles of Cantor and singers from endeavouring to replicate the standards set by their counterparts at the greater secular churches. Even the grandest of the full-time secular choirs distinguished with composed polyphonic music only a select handful of the services which they sang, and it was precisely the corresponding services in the monastic churches that their ensembles attended also. Moreover,

---

130   Bowers, 'Musicians of the Lady Chapel', pp. 228, 234 n. 80.
131   Bowers, 'Musicians and Liturgy of the Lady Chapels', pp. 51–3.
132   Indenture: 1490 Haslam; BL, Harley MS 594, fol. 125r.
133   N. Sandon, 'Fayrfax, Robert', ODNB, vol. 19, pp. 202–4. Indenture: 1538 Edmunds; J. Maclean, 'Chantry Certificates: Gloucester', TBGAS, 8 (1885), p. 286.
134   Oxford, New College, Account of Bursars 1484/5: MS ONC 7443 (120), Custus Capelle. Oxford, Magdalen College, Liber Computi 1481–88, fol. 115r, Stipendia conductorum, clericorum et serviencium capelle. Durham: Indenture, 1487 Bell. Paying a stipend of £10 per year, Durham could attract and sometimes even retain the services of an experienced man to serve as Cantor. The composer Thomas Ashwell was recruited to Durham in 1513 from the post of Master of the Choristers at Lincoln Cathedral, where he had served for eight years (R. Bowers, 'Music and Worship to 1640', in A History of Lincoln Minster, ed. D. Owen (Cambridge, 1994), 47–76, at pp. 60, 61, 76), and remained at least until 1525 (DCA, Account of Almoner 1524/5(B), Pensiones et Stipendia); this appointment, indeed, proved to be his last known job.
135   SCA, Account of Collector of Choristers' Rents 1495/6, Feoda et vadia; Reg. Harward's Memorials, fol. 1r. In 1512 Robert Perrot (lay clerk, King's College, Cambridge, 1506–09; Master of the Choristers at Magdalen 1510–31, organist 1529–50) secured the same move from Magdalen College to Durham, but instead of implementing it chose to exploit the offer so as to wring from Magdalen College much improved terms to persuade him to stay: R. Bowers, 'Perrot, Robert', ODNB, vol. 43, pp. 817–18.

polyphonic music could be sung just as well with only one voice per lower part as with many; consequently, the nature and extent of the polyphonic repertories undertaken by the monastery ensembles was affected by considerations neither of numerical strength nor of overall extent of work; and in content, and in degree of challenge and grandeur, they appear to have been indistinguishable from those of their secular counterparts.

The nature of the music rendered at service on these occasions is indicated most readily by the surviving records of its having been copied into the singers' choirbooks and sets of part-books, and also by such items of repertory as have actually chanced to survive. Particularly revealing of the vitality and enterprise of the most vigorous of these choirs is the content of the substantial collections of manuscript music which were assembled for them to perform, indicated most clearly by two inventories dating from the 1530s, originating from the cathedral priories of Worcester and Canterbury.

The appointment of a new Cantor could prove to be a potent stimulus for initiating a lively campaign of acquisition of music, and at Worcester, where Daniel Boyce was appointed at Michaelmas 1521, the Warden of the Lady Chapel soon found himself meeting the bills for the copying of much new repertory. Boyce's principal concern was music for the mass. The sum of 11s 8d spent for this purpose on paper and scribe's wages in his first few months would have put some three or four new masses into the repertory. At a cost of 13s 4d in the following year there were added a mass in 'squarenote' and a mass for five voices, and for festal vespers in the monks' quire two new settings of Magnificat. In the following year a small book of 'pricksonge' was created at a cost of 6s 8d, while two Marian antiphons were obtained for 3s 4d;[136] next year again, unspecified 'new songs' were acquired for 7s 6d. The acquisition of books for music sung by just the boys of the Lady Chapel cost 8s 5d in 1531–32,[137] while, as noted above, in 1532 the monk William Wolverley copied out no fewer than eight five-part settings of the Magnificat for use at festal vespers.[138]

An inventory of the overall collection of music used by the Cantor and his singers was taken in 1535.[139] This recorded that the stock of manuscripts of polyphony was kept in the office of the monk designated for the time being as Warden of the Lady Chapel, along with the surplices of the 'maister of the chylderne' and of six of his boys. The provision of music for use at mass predominated; it had to suffice to accommodate daily Lady Mass in the Lady Chapel, weekly Jesus Mass in the Jesus Chapel, and High Mass on festivals in the quire, and was correspondingly substantial. One old-fashioned choirbook contained a collection of masses, some for four voices and some for five; a further choirbook apparently contained a second, similar aggregation. More four-part masses were contained in two individual sets of part-books; two five-part masses were sung

---

136 Accounts of Warden of Lady Chapel, 1521/2, 1522/3, 1523/4: WCL, MS A XVII, pp. 126, 202, 267, *Stipendia*.

137 Accounts of Warden of Lady Chapel, 1524/5, 1531/2: WCL, MSS C414, 414c, [*Stipendia*].

138 At the expense, on this occasion, of the prior: WCL, MS A.xi, fols. 134v, 135v, printed as *Journal of Prior William More*, ed. Fagan, pp. 347, 350.

139 BL, Harley MS 604, fols. 121r, 118r.

from parchment scrolls, while yet more masses for five voices were preserved in a set of part-books of their own. For use specifically in the Lady Chapel there appeared a choirbook containing Marian antiphons, described as 'antems and Salves'; a further collection of antiphons was to be found in yet another choir-book of parchment, plus three or four additional pieces still preserved just on individual scrolls.

Other volumes were for use when the singers took part in the monks' observance of the office on feasts. For use at matins and lauds there was a paper book containing 'yn pryckinge' settings of their canticles (respectively, Te Deum and Benedictus), and of the invitatories at matins (that is, the antiphons to Psalm xciv). A set of five part-books, augmented with sets of scrolls, contained settings of 'Salve festa dies'; this was the *prosa* sung on seven or eight of the greatest feasts in the course of the procession preceding High Mass. Two paper books (apparently choirbooks) containing five-part settings of 'other songs' seem likely to have included, among other material, Wolverley's copyings of Magnificat settings for use at festal vespers, mentioned above. The collection was completed by a 'squarenote book' and 'a paper book of four parts', the contents of which were not recorded.[140]

As well as appropriately comprehensive, in respect of its extension to music both for mass and also for the singers' participation in the monastic office on festivals, this collection was large. Extending to some seven or eight choirbooks big and small, four sets of part-books and an assemblage of odd items still on scrolls, there was sufficient here to provide challenge to the singers, variety and enterprise in what was sung, and constant realisation of artistic distinction in the performance of the liturgical service.

The second inventory, surviving from Canterbury Cathedral Priory, dates from the time of Thomas Wood as Cantor, c.1530–April 1540.[141] It lists the equipment, in terms of books, vestments, and altar adornments, assigned to the Lady Chapel itself. It records the principal missal supplied for the celebrant at the altar (with two small missals in reserve, and an 'olde servyce boke'), and seven graduals provided for the use of the monks and singers deputed to attend and execute the plainsong of Lady Mass. In respect of its volumes of polyphonic music, the collection was of a quantity comparable with that of Worcester, though rather less was recorded concerning its detailed content.

There is no indication that at Christ Church, Canterbury, any need was ever felt for the engagement of professional singing-men; evidently at a monastery so large there were always among those professed a satisfactory number of monks fully capable of singing polyphonic music and of mastering its notation, so that with the Cantor and his eight boys a choir able to sing in no fewer than six parts could routinely be mustered. The repertory was impressive. The books included one 'great black boke', apparently a large choirbook; a further choir-book contained music in four parts, to which belonged further individual quires

---

[140] What may be a last surviving fragment of this collection is the merest sliver of a page from a bass part-book, paper, early sixteenth century, found (and last seen) lying loose between pp. 260 and 261 of WCL, MS A XVII.

[141] CCAL, MS Inventory 29.

of paper conveying the supplementary mean (alto) and bass voices of items in five and six parts. Another choirbook was known as 'mr hawts boke'; 'Mr Hawt' was evidently a member of the local gentry family of that name, cultured, closely associated with the cathedral, and very musical.[142] A further choirbook included music in five parts, and was distinguished by the 'masse off ij tenors' which it contained. The two 'vytatory bokes' listed among the volumes of polyphony, comparable to those at Worcester which contained settings of the antiphons to the invitatory at matins, were clearly for use when the singers were performing not in the Lady Chapel but were contributing to the monks' festal matins in quire. Probably it was for such occasions that three volumes of psalms also were supplied.

Among Canterbury's sets of part-books, music for three voices was included in 'three small qwerys off thomas mann'. Perhaps these were connected to the Thomas Mann who occurs as a London singing-man in 1532, as a lay clerk of St George's Chapel, Windsor, in 1541–47,[143] and as a Gentleman of the Chapel Royal in August 1553.[144] Further sets of part-books extended to four quires containing sequences for the Lady Mass, and also to a set of five books containing unidentified music for five voices; to this latter there was added a sixth book, containing the bass part added when six-part music came to be copied into these books.

Any further items of polyphony there may have been were not considered worth recording. Nevertheless, this acknowledged collection of four to six choirbooks and three sets of part-books, containing music for up to six voices (the maximum number routinely used by composers of this period), is evidence enough of the existence of a substantial and challenging repertory.

These impressions are fully corroborated by the nature of such items of

142 P. W. Fleming, 'The Hautes and their Circle: Culture and the English Gentry', in *England in the Fifteenth Century*, ed. D. Williams, Proceedings of the 1986 Harlaxton Symposium (Woodbridge, 1987), pp. 85–102. This family, of considerable wealth and local influence, was evidently much concerned with music; indeed, Sir William Haute, head of the family in a previous generation (c.1430–1492), had been an accomplished amateur composer, by whom were contributed two pieces to a volume of sacred polyphony compiled for study apparently in Canterbury Cathedral Priory in the mid-1460s: *ibid.*, pp. 94–5; R. Bowers, 'Cambridge, Magdalene College, MS Pepys 1236' in *Cambridge Music Manuscripts 900–1700*, ed. I. A. Fenlon (Cambridge, 1982), pp. 111–14; R. Bowers, 'Wydow, Robert', *ODNB*, lx, p. 631; S. R. Charles, 'Haute, Sir William', *New Grove*, XI, p. 153.

143 H. Baillie, 'Some Biographical Notes on English Church Musicians, chiefly working in London (1485–1569)', *Royal Musical Association Research Chronicle*, 2 (1962), 18–57, at pp. 43–4. Account of Treasurer, 1541/2: Windsor, St George's Chapel, MS xv.59.3, *Stipendia clericorum. Visitation Articles and Injunctions of the period of the Reformation*, ed. W. H. Frere and W. M. Kennedy, 3 vols., Alcuin Club Collections (1910), vol. 2, p. 163, n.

144 *Records of English Court Music 1485–1714*, ed. A. Ashbee, 9 vols. (Snargate and Aldershot, 1986–96), vol. 7, p. 124; vol. 8, p. 11. This Thomas Mann, singing-man, is not known to have had any particular association with Canterbury Cathedral. Alternatively, the books may have been acquired from a Thomas Mann who had been in the priory's service and whose name was entered into the obit book of the Confraternity as a late addition very little prior to 1540: LPL, MS 20, fol. 200v. However, this individual is not known to have had any associations with singing or music.

polyphony for monastic use that survive. The indentures of the later Cantors at Durham required each to compose annually, in honour of St Mary and St Cuthbert, either one new mass for either four or five voices, or – at the discretion of the precentor – other music equivalent to this.[145] There survives a fragmentary Mass 'Sancte Cuthberte' for four voices (including boys) composed by Thomas Ashwell, evidently for performance by his singers at Durham for High Mass in quire on the feast of St Cuthbert.[146] The five-part *Salve regina* composed by John Hampton for the Marian antiphon at Worcester, a five-part Magnificat written by John Nesbett probably for the boys and trained monks of Christ Church, Canterbury,[147] the music of the elder William Cornysh written for the boys and men of Westminster,[148] and the compositions of the monks Robert Holyngborne, William Stratford and John Dygon mentioned above,[149] all testify amply to the sense of seemliness and splendour that was lent to liturgical observance at the monasteries by their ensembles of trained singers. At Westminster there still survive fragments of two early sixteenth-century masses (now anonymous) appropriate for celebration of the Lady Mass,[150] and at Canterbury there remains a fragmentary five-part Magnificat for festal vespers in quire.[151] All this is music of substantial weight and complexity, fully comparable to that sung at any of the grandest of the secular churches.

The extent of collections of music accumulated at other monasteries and perhaps comparable to those of Worcester and Canterbury are dimly suggested by odd surviving references to their augmentation with new material. To Battle Abbey around 1500 there were sent some compositions from William Newark, Master of the Choristers of Henry VII's Chapel Royal;[152] at St Augustine's,

145 Indentures: 1487 Bell, 1496 Foderley, 1502 Tildesley, 1512 Porret, 1513 Ashwell, 1513 Ashwell, 1537 Brymley.

146 BL, Add. MS 30520: a single bifolium from a large choirbook of c.1530. This manuscript may well be of Durham provenance; if so, its other content, part of the Mass 'Leroy' (a Lady Mass) by Nicholas Ludford, may be identified as likewise belonging within the repertory of the Durham singers.

147 *Eton Choirbook*, ed. Harrison, vol. 2, pp. 54–60, vol. 3, pp. 63–8.

148 Bowers, 'Musicians and Liturgy of the Lady Chapels', pp. 54–5; Bowers, 'Cornysh, William (i)', *ODNB*, vol. 13, pp. 494–5; *Eton Choirbook*, ed. Harrison, vol. 1, pp. 116–23; vol. 2, pp. 137–48; vol. 3, pp. 57–8, 59–62.

149 See above, pp. 34–5.

150 WAM, MSS 102A–B, 103; Bowers, 'Musicians and Liturgy of the Lady Chapels', pp. 54–5. Reproduction of MS 103: see J. Wilkinson, *Westminster Abbey: 1000 years of Music and Pageant* (Leighton Buzzard, 2003), p. 35.

151 CCAL, Add. MS 128/7 (a photocopy of the original manuscript, Add. MS 128, no. 46(e), now missing). Sandon, 'Fragments of Medieval Polyphony', pp. 48, 51–3; Bowers, 'Liturgy of the Cathedral and its Music', pp. 421–2. The location of the treble and alto parts, written at the foot of the page where the boys could most easily see them when the manuscript was placed on a lectern, suggests that in this choir both parts were sung by boys. For two pages of keyboard music and a brief three-voice setting of the Jesus antiphon text 'O bone Iesu', entered by John Alcester, sometime monk, into an Evesham Abbey bible at about the end of the 1550s, see T. Dart, 'Notes on a Bible of Evesham Abbey (ii): a Note on the Music', *EHR*, 79 (1964), pp. 777–8.

152 Et in dono domini [abbatis] Magistro Nework clerico capelle domini Regis pro diversis canticis ab eo habendis vjs viijd. Account of Abbot, c.1500: PRO, SC6/Henry VII/861, *Dona et regarda*.

Bristol, in 1506/7 payment was made for the copying of masses into books freshly repaired;[153] at Reading in 1536/7 the Lady Chapel account paid for new books for polyphony, and for repair of the old;[154] at Colchester Abbey in 1526/7 the precentor paid for the composition of a new piece for the start of the procession preceding festal high mass.[155] At Westminster Abbey the existing stock of polyphony was augmented in 1511 by the purchase of 'a pryksong booke of masses antems and other songs'.[156] In 1513/14 at the priory of Holy Trinity, London, masses were copied into the repertory by 'ser Chapman', one of the canons, and by Thomas Rufford, a singing-man.[157] During 1532/3 Thetford priory paid for the carriage of certain 'pricksongbokes' all the way from London,[158] and at Selby the repertory of the secular choir was very substantially augmented during 1536/7, with copies newly made of a Mass 'Assumpta est Maria' for five voices, a Mass 'Iesu Christe', and a votive antiphon (title not given) also for five voices.[159] Collections of polyphony could also be augmented by bequest. To Ulverscroft (Leicestershire) no fewer than six new 'prickseng bokes of masses and antemis' were bequeathed under a will made in about 1535, plus an undefined number to Garendon.[160] The testator was one Richard Sharp,[161] then schoolmaster of

---

153 Et pro notificacione diversarum missarum unacum reparacione diversorum librorum hoc anno ijs viijd. Account of Almoner (by whose office was met much of the expense of maintaining the musical personnel of the Lady Chapel), 1506/7: GRO, MS D674a Z5, *Custus necessarii*.

154 Item pro factione libri epistolarum et aliorum librorum Cantilenarum xjs vjd ... Item Willelmo Gray pro paupiro et reparatione libri cantandi ijs. Account of Warden of Lady Chapel, 1536/7: BL, Add. Ch. 19659, *Expense necessarie*.

155 Et sol' magistro Redham pro factura unius cantus pro asperges. Account of precentor, 1526/7: PRO, SC6/Henry VIII/936, *Allocaciones*. 'Asperges me domine' were the opening words of the antiphon accompanying the aspersion at the beginning of the procession preceding High Mass on Sundays: Harrison, *Music in Medieval Britain*, pp. 58–9.

156 Bowers, 'The Musicians and Liturgy of the Lady Chapels' [Westminster Abbey], p. 55.

157 Accounts of prior 1513/14, PRO, E36/108, fols. 35r, 35v, 35v: Item p^d to ser chapman for paper for to pryk yn as it aperyth by a byll viijd. ... Item to ser chapman for prykyng of a masse xijd. ... Item p^d to Rufford for prykyng of a masse xijd. Thomas Rufford is found later as a singing-man of the parish church of All Hallows the Great, London, and in 1521–22 as Master of the Fraternity of St Nicholas (a fraternity of singing-men and parish clerks of London and its environs): Baillie, 'Some biographical notes on English church musicians', p. 50. *The Bede Roll of the Fraternity of St Nicholas*, ed. N. W. and V. A. James, 2 vols., London Record Society, 39–40 (2004), pp. 203, 274.

158 *Register of Thetford Priory*, ed. Dymond, vol. 2, p. 600.

159 *Monastery and Society*, ed. Tillotson, p. 234. For a Mass 'Iesu Christe' in six parts composed by Thomas Ashwell, Cantor of Durham Cathedral, see *Early Tudor Masses II*, ed. J. Bergsagel, EECM, xvi (1976).

160 Evidently the five 'Chylderen founde of almes' noted at Garendon at the dissolution were the singing-boys of the abbey. At Ulverscroft there were noted 'Chyldren for the Chappell there xiiij'. Fourteen seems too many for a group of Lady Chapel singing-boys; perhaps this was the total number of maintained pupils in the Almonry School, among whom the actual singing-boys formed a smaller group. PRO, E36/154, pp. 106–7, 110–11.

161 A. White, '"Tam in cantu quam in grammatica" – Richard Sharp, an early Tudor song and grammar master', *Durham Research Review*, 5 (1971), 1–7, at p. 3.

Loughborough but possibly identifiable with a former lay clerk (1524–29) of the choir of King's College, Cambridge.[162]

As a factor determining the nature of the repertory sung, the relatively slight numerical strength of the Lady Chapel choirs appears in practice to have been wholly immaterial. The services in the monastery church at which their choirs of men and boys performed polyphonic music were the same as those which the full-time choirs of the greater secular churches enhanced likewise. In respect of depth and richness of tone these small-scale choirs, consisting mostly of some eight to twelve voices, could of course in no sense equal the sheer grandeur of sound yielded by the twenty-five to forty-five voices comprising the greater choirs when all were entabled to sing together;[163] nevertheless, the actual repertories of the two types of choir appear to have been very much the same.

The overall incidence of the employment by monastic bodies of a Cantor and secular singers for the enhancement of the liturgical service with polyphonic music is not easy to attempt to quantify. So far, evidence for their engagement in the period c.1480–1540 has been found for some fifty institutions, great, middling and small. However, the evidence is sparse, and its survival uneven and utterly capricious in its incidence. Perhaps it would not be unrealistic to double that number to around one hundred, to achieve an appreciation of the extent to which, by the mid-1530s, the monastic houses were adopting this conspicuous means of both modernising and enhancing the beauty and the impact of their manner of worship, and were serving society at large as significant academies and employers of musical expertise.

Certainly by 1509–14 such practice was already sufficiently prominent to attract the notice of Desiderius Erasmus during his final sojourn in England; his record of its engagement is illuminating, albeit hardly that of the disinterested observer. Erasmus had no patience with those whom he considered to be mistaking mere ceremonial observance for true piety; he deplored the diversion of the resources of the church to the promotion of what he believed to be superficial irrelevancies, and certainly he entertained no high opinion of the character of the church's professional singing-men. Brought up, moreover, to value the continental music of the generation of Jacob Obrecht, he was unlikely ever to have appreciated the substantially more expansive and virtuosic English style.[164] His experiences in England provoked him to a characteristic response, which appeared in the course of a commentary on I Corinthians xiv.19 (1527). Erasmus readily acknowledged English composition and the singing of the secular men and boys in monastic churches to be 'most melodious' (*modulatissimus*); it was only what he considered to be its usurpation of the place of true piety that

---

162 CKC, Mundum Books vol. 10 part 2 (1524/5), fol. 6r; Libri Communarum, vol. 13 (1528/9), Clerici (weeks 1–39).

163 For comparisons, see e.g. R. Bowers, 'The Cultivation and Promotion of Music in the Household and Orbit of Thomas Wolsey', in *Cardinal Wolsey: Church, State and Art*, ed. S. J. Gunn and P. G. Lindley (Cambridge, 1991), 178–218, at pp. 178–95; *id.*, 'The Music and Musical Establishment of St George's Chapel in the Fifteenth Century', pp. 198–214; *id.*, 'Music and Worship to 1640', pp. 47–62.

164 See e.g. C. A. Miller, 'Erasmus on Music', *The Musical Quarterly*, 52 (1966), 332–49 at 338–9.

he deplored. For improvised faburden, however, which he could have heard only in England, he had nothing but scorn.[165]

> In monasteries, in colleges, in almost every great church, what is to be heard other than the clamour of voices? ... And to this purpose, organ-builders are maintained on great fees, also flocks of boys, whose entire childhood is consumed in learning by heart yelpings of this kind, all the while learning nothing of any good. Also there are maintained the very dregs of men, drunkards foul and fey as very many of them are, because of which pernicious practice the church is burdened with great expense; I ask you to put in mind how many of the poor, imperilled of life itself, could be fed from the stipends of the singing-men.
>
> So gratifying are these endeavours that – especially among the British – the monks do nothing else, and those whose song ought to be of mourning believe that God is pleased with sensuous whinnyings and nimble throat. Among the British, even in houses of Benedictines, youths and boys and vocal virtuosi are maintained in this practice, who each morning sing divine service to the virgin mother with most melodious chattering of their voices and the music of the organ. (The bishops, too, are believed to maintain choirs of this kind in their households.) And occupied with these diversions, they neither arrive at a sound education, nor do they hear anything in which true religion is found.
>
> Moreover, those who are too crass to be able to master the musical art do not think satisfaction done to a feast-day unless they employ a certain perverse kind of music which they call 'faburden'.[166] This neither projects the chant prescribed, nor engages artful harmony. Wherefore, [even] when in this respect restrained music is received into the church, whereby the meanings of the words might quite effectively flow into the minds of the hearers, yet still to some it seems fine for one or another, mingled among the rest, with a great bellowing of the voice to procure that not a single word should be perceived. Herein lies indulgence of the instincts of fools, and deference to those of the base. ... Let us sing with the spirit; but let us sing like Christians, let us sing sparingly, and yet more, let us sing with the mind.

That some such misgivings were not entirely unknown also among Englishmen is suggested by the content of a set of rules for the better governance of the Augustinian canons compiled in 1519 for implementation as legate by Thomas

---

165 Translated from an edited facsimile of the final text of 1535: *Erasmus' Annotations on the New Testament: Acts, Romans, I and II Corinthians*, ed. A. Reeve and M. A. Screech, Studies in the History of Christian Thought, 42 (Leiden, 1990), pp. 507, 508. In this transcription, the text added in 1527 to that of 1519 is enclosed in round brackets. The translation of this passage much quoted in earlier literature from J. A. Froude, *Life and Letters of Erasmus* (London, 1916), pp. 115–16, unfortunately bears little resemblance to the original. The surprise of the much travelled Erasmus at the circumstances he found in England suggests that the employment of Lady Chapel choirs of secular singers in monasteries may have been unknown elsewhere in Europe.

166 It seems that Erasmus did not possess (or, perhaps, pretended not to possess) an ear sufficiently acute to perceive that in fact faburden always incorporated the plainsong, as the middle of its three voices. For a further observation concerning the use by English singers of an apparently improvisatory practice probably to be identified as faburden, see *Desiderii Erasmi Roterodami Opera omnia*, ed. J. Clericus [J. Le Clerc], 10 vols. (Liège, 1703–6), vol. I, col. 930 section A ('De recta Latini Graecique sermonis pronunciatione dialogus'): Nam est huiusmodi musices genus apud Britannos, ut multi inter se concinant, quorum nullus eas sonat voces quos habent codicum notulae ('of whom none sings those pitches which the notes in the books convey').

Wolsey. On the grounds that only holy austerity was seemly for the professed religious, overt condemnation was made of many of these recent innovations, though the author drew a distinction between the genres of music suitable for use in the quire of the canons and those permissible for their secular singers to employ in the outer chapels. At the canons' services conducted in the principal quire only plainsong was to be sung; no harmonised music was to be permitted at all, other than that of the plainest extempore decoration of the simplest chants on Sundays and festivals. The performance of formal polyphonic music, composed and sung from notation, was altogether to be prohibited, and no secular singer, man or boy, was to be permitted to be present at any quire service. However, '[to the canons] we permit that they may cause masses of the Blessed Virgin, of the name of Jesus, and masses of similar nature, which – just as in all monasteries of this kingdom – are accustomed to be sung solemnly outside the canons' quire by lay secular men and boys, to be rendered with polyphonic music and organs, provided only that none of the canons be present except he who celebrates the mass at the altar'.[167]

Even among reformers, that is, there was felt no need for an obligation imposed upon the religious to practise austerity among themselves to hinder in any way the execution of a supplementary ministry of music offered up by seculars in the canons' employment. In any event, there is found no trace of these rules having ever been enforced, and the misgivings to which they gave expression evidently appear never to have been shared by those elsewhere by whom this promotion of polyphonic music was being fostered and encouraged so fully.

Overall, at many religious houses, including some that were minor and many that were middling as well as most that were prominent, the monks undertook during the period 1480–1540 a substantial rejuvenation and invigoration of their manner of conducting divine service. The Cantor and his singers were bringing to their monastery churches a means and a manner of enhancing the efficacy of worship and praise that appear to have been both conspicuous and effective. These houses were displaying in their liturgical observance a degree of energy and initiative sufficient to make clear that they were seeking to establish for themselves a place actively at the forefront of musical vitality and enterprise. The best of the English monasteries were not inanimate but dynamic organisations, and in the sixteenth century – just as in any other – they could have their successes as well as their reversals.

The surviving inventories and accounts appear to provide every reason to believe that in terms of content, breadth, and challenge of repertory the relatively small-scale polyphonic ensembles of the monastic churches yielded little or nothing to their grander counterparts elsewhere. By comparison with the secular institutions, in 1475 monastic worship, at even the best-regulated houses, must have sounded drab, old-fashioned, and dull; by 1535, two generations later, it seems likely that the best bore comparison with almost anyone's. Perhaps it was developments such as these that were being accorded recognition

---

167 MA, vol. 6, part 2, 851–4, at pp. 852–3; Harrison, *Music in Medieval Britain*, pp. 191–2; Knowles, *Religious Orders*, vol. 3, pp. 159–60.

at high governmental level when, in 1536, the authors of the preamble to the Parliamentary statute expropriating the smaller houses went out of their way to commend the larger as 'divers and great solemn monasteries wherein (thanks be to God) religion is right well kept and observed'.[168] Indeed, contemporary appreciation of the contribution made to religion by the monasteries' secular singers may be discerned in the manner in which, eventually, the eighteen successor foundations of Henry VIII actually enhanced their numbers, creating for trained singers posts considerably exceeding those extinguished by the dissolutions.[169]

It is in this context that there is scope to wonder if this substantial revitalisation of the observance of divine service at a fair proportion of the houses of monastics constituted in any way a factor contributory both to the timing of the governmental decision to dissolve them in the second half of the 1530s, and to the resignation and apparent ease with which most monastics appear to have reconciled themselves to their fate. By implementation of the dissolutions, King Henry achieved the utter extinction of a venerable tradition of religious life and devotion, a modest measure of church reform, and a large measure of self-enrichment. This is not the place to enter into any methodical examination of the plausibility of current diagnoses of Henry's motivation and rationale for the dissolutions, but it may now be possible to add, at least for consideration, one or two possible contributory strands not hitherto canvassed.

Firstly, it seems possible that Henry's decisions both to begin and to conclude the dissolutions, once made, may have been hastened upon him at least to some extent by reflection upon this recent evidence of monastic revival. In respect of their observance of the liturgy, institutions which not long before may have been appearing disengaged in conduct and redundant in character had begun to show conspicuous signs of coming back to life. Perhaps, therefore, Henry's exercise essentially in royal cupidity was hastened upon him in the 1530s not solely by a sense of his royal duty to extinguish institutions now allegedly found to be corrupt and decayed, but also by awareness of the emergence of alarming evidence of incipient revival. Conceivably, one strand in the motivation for the dissolution of the monastic houses was the perception, from the royal point of view, of the desirability of acting speedily at the end of the 1530s to lay hands on their assets and endowments before an incipient but real recovery had gained too much momentum readily to be stopped in its tracks.

Secondly, the significant embrace by the monasteries of a manner of worship whose origins lay among the secular church may also have generated internal consequences, all the more damaging for having been unforeseen. The monastic manner of conducting service was gravitating towards, was indeed catching up with, the most spectacular aspects of the secular. Audacious this process may

---

168 J. Youings, *The Dissolution of the Monasteries* (London, 1971), p. 155.
169 The new foundations (including Brecon in Wales and Dublin in Ireland) created eighteen posts for Organist and Master of the Choristers, 136 for choristers, and at least 282 for singing-men (148 for minor canons in priest's orders and 134 for lay clerks; also 36 posts of epistoler and gospeller, commonly occupied by younger singing-men). There were somewhat fewer opportunities for singing-boys and their Masters, but vastly more for professional singing-men, especially for those in priest's orders after the first generation of minor canons (mostly former monks) had passed away.

have been, but it also served to emphasise and corroborate the fundamental underlying commonalities between the secular and the monastic liturgical observance. In a number of respects the monastic way of life had already surrendered its individuality;[170] now the monastic liturgical service was undergoing an enhancement generating similar consequences, which in a context of threatened dissolution might create unprecedented perceptions no less within the monasteries than without.

The more the monastic observance gravitated toward the secular, the more dispensable it might be perceived to be – even by its own practitioners. England in the later 1530s offered a confessional context for the dissolutions very different from that experienced on the continent. In all likelihood, English monks were not unaware of the manner in which in continental Europe dissolutions occurred not in isolation but generally in association with Protestant reform,[171] manifest in the simultaneous abolition of the mass, the entire reform of liturgy, the termination of the traditional Latin service, and the consequent extinction of most if not all of both the historic plainsong and the newer polyphony. In England, by contrast, in 1539–40 none of these potential and painful concomitants of dissolution was even so much as threatened. By the Act of the Six Articles the king had just demonstrated his personal adherence to doctrines central to the traditional faith; moreover, his own Chapel Royal continued to act as a cynosure of all that was finest in the ancient liturgy, and royal policy offered no threat to its indefinite continuance.

It seems, therefore, that as dissolution loomed the monks and regular canons found, albeit unhappily,[172] that acceptance of the implacability of the king's will and acquiescence in their dispersal were by no means impossible – for even if their manner of life and vocation were passing, yet their work was not, but would live on. Within the cathedrals and some 150 collegiate churches, in about one hundred of those greater parish churches which, like the monasteries, had lately established professional choirs of secular singers, in the household chapels of the episcopal and secular aristocracy and, most extravagantly of all, in the Chapel Royal of their king and nemesis, Henry VIII, their central, sacred work of corporate worship, sacrifice and praise, offered through the medium of the Latin liturgy and its elaborate edifices of ceremony, plainsong and polyphony, would yet continue no less proudly than before.

170 B. J. Thompson, 'Monasteries, Society and Reform in Late Medieval England', in *Religious Orders*, ed. Clark, 165–95, at pp. 184–9.
171 E. Cameron, *The European Reformation* (Oxford, 1991), pp. 251–2.
172 P. Cunich, 'The ex-Religious in post-Dissolution society', in *Religious Orders*, ed. Clark, 227–38, at pp. 234–5.

Monastic Murals and *Lectio* in the Later Middle Ages

MIRIAM GILL

Only a small and unrepresentative sample of monastic murals survives from late medieval England. However, this diverse corpus does retain a discernible character. Not only do monastic murals often depict subjects which are distinct from those found in the much larger number of surviving parochial paintings, but they appear to exhibit a certain 'bookishness' in their content and particularly their combination of text and image. Patterns of survival may have served to emphasise this aspect of monastic imagery. However, this tendency is interesting given the prominence of the production and study of books in monastic culture. This paper will seek to illuminate the forms which this bookishness might take. It will illustrate some of these in relation to the surviving murals, and focus, in particular, on the recently discovered fragments of an Apocalypse cycle from the priory at Coventry. The identification of a complex series of scenes from the Book of Revelation in the chapter house of a Benedictine priory reopens previous debates about the significance of the later cycle at Westminster. This paper will suggest that the monastic practice of *lectio divina* particularly associated with the Benedictine Order, together with the experience of monastic life and the liturgical elements outlined in the Rule of St Benedict, may deepen our understanding of the intention behind these two outstanding schemes of later fourteenth-century monastic wall painting.

The Dissolution has had an incalculable impact on our understanding of the visual culture of monasteries in medieval England. Problems of interpretation arise not only from the sheer quantity of material lost through deliberate iconoclasm, greed and neglect, but also from the ways in which the processes of dissolution have distorted what remains. This is evident in both the type of monastic foundations whose fabric has tended to survive intact and the nature and function of the individual buildings of a monastic precinct most likely to be preserved.[1]

The mural paintings which are the focus of this chapter were a ubiquitous form of decoration in medieval England. Parish churches, public buildings and dwellings from royal palaces to humble cottages had painted walls. Hundreds of paintings survive, although often in a damaged and fragmented state, and

---

[1] For the architectural consequences of this see, M. Howard, 'Recycling the Monastic Fabric: Beyond the Act of Dissolution', in *The Archaeology of Reformation, 1480–1580*, ed. D. Gaimster and R. Gilchrist (Leeds, 2003), pp. 221–234.

an additional number of lost paintings are known through antiquarian records. However, most of these are in parish churches. The loss of the murals of so many religious foundations is particularly significant.[2] Firstly, the quality of some of the paintings which survive, together with our knowledge of the patronage of monastic foundations, give us reason to suppose that this body of lost paintings included many of the most artistically accomplished murals painted in medieval England.[3] Secondly, the iconography of the surviving paintings and our knowledge of the intellectual culture of many monasteries suggest that many of these lost paintings may have depicted a different range of subjects from that familiar from the parochial corpus. Thirdly, the range of functions performed by monasteries as institutions, and in particular the specialist buildings which accommodated them, raises the prospect that monastic murals may have included striking instances of the interaction between paintings and their architectural context.

These general issues are brought into relief by consideration of a case study from the decoration of the abbey of St Albans (Benedictine). St Albans is typical of the large Benedictine institutions for male religious whose buildings were preserved after the Dissolution to serve as great churches or cathedrals. Houses belonging to other orders or those in desirable locations for country seats or urban redevelopment often fared less well. For example, in central Coventry the church and most of the domestic buildings of the Benedictine priory were systematically dismantled.[4] The recently uncovered fragments of the Apocalypse cycle discussed later in this essay were probably left on the site only because their complex carvings made them unsuitable for reuse [see plates 1–3].[5]

A wall painting of Doubting Thomas accompanied by a now almost illegible Latin inscription survives on the north wall of the north transept of St Albans Cathedral.[6] It is one of a number of murals still visible within the former abbey.[7] However, it has the unique distinction of being mentioned in an apologia dated

---

2   For a survey of some of the more recent publications on this corpus see M. Gill, 'Monastic Wall Painting in England', MRB, 5 (1999), 32–5.

3   For monastic patronage see, J. Luxford, The Art and Architecture of English Benedictine Monasteries, 1300–1540: A Patronage History, Studies in the History of Medieval Religion (Woodbridge, 2005).

4   I. Soiden, 'The Conversion of Former Monastic Buildings to Secular Use', in Archaeology of the Reformation, ed. Gaimster and Gilchrist, pp. 282–2.

5   The Archaeology of the Medieval Cathedral and Priory of St Mary, ed. M. Rylatt and P. Mason (Coventry, 2003), p. 35. Other worked stones appeared to have been discarded on site for this reason, R. K. Morris, 'Monastic Architecture: Destruction and Reconstruction' in Archaeology of the Reformation, ed. Gaimster and Gilchrist, pp. 242–3.

6   M. Gill, 'The Role of Images in Monastic Education: the Evidence from Wall Painting in Late Medieval England', in Medieval Monastic Education, C. Muessig and G. Ferzoco (London, 2000), pp. 129–131. The inscriptions in this scheme are also discussed in, M. Gill, 'Preaching and Image: Sermons and Wall Paintings in Later Medieval England', in Preacher, Sermon and Audience in the Middle Ages, ed. C. Muessig (Leiden, 2002), p. 168.

7   E. Roberts, The Wall Paintings of Saint Albans Abbey, (St Albans, 1993), pp. 39–41; P. Binski, 'The Murals in the Nave of St Albans Abbey', in Church and City 1000–1500. Essays in Honour of Christopher Brooke, ed. D. Abulafia, M. Franklin and M. Rubin (Cambridge, 1992), pp. 249–278.

to c.1428.[8] This document comprises a defence of church art and an account of the meaning of the images in the north transept. The painting is now abraded but it represents an ambitious example of the International Style; the complex setting of illusionistic architecture is particularly striking. It seems likely that it is close to the apologia in date. The modelling of the figures and the architectural setting resembles that found in the 'Hours of Elizabeth the Queen' which was made in the period c.1420–30.[9]

The apologia reveals that the painting of Doubting Thomas, with its Latin inscription, was once part of a complex constellation of words and images. Moreover, other documentary sources show that this sort of monumental art, combining visual images and extensive texts, was originally to be found in many locations throughout the monastic complex in buildings which are now lost.[10] It is also clear that while the monastic community valued the murals in the north transept they saw them as appealing to and serving a wider range of viewers. In the apologia the scheme is specifically described as 'near the public path, where many persons pass by and go out'.[11] Although this essay will focus on the significance of this sort of combination of words and images for a monastic community, in the context of the later Middle Ages such self-consciously learned schemes might appeal to and be emulated by the laity.[12] By the end of the Middle Ages the interiors of many monastic institutions included 'tables' or notice boards displaying a range of informative and devotional material to visitors and pilgrims.[13]

The scheme in the north transept and the apologia give a tantalising glimpse of a sophisticated interaction between words and images. The scheme itself combined Biblical narrative with emotive 'appeal poetry'. The apologia applies additional layers of meaning and interpretation to the fabric of the chapel. For example, it describes two pillars, probably two piers from the eastern arcade, which were painted respectively red and earth colour and interprets these as symbolising the love of God and the love of neighbour.[14] There is no evidence that these piers were 'labelled' in this way, rather the apologia, possibly in conjunction with preaching and oral instruction, passed on these additional levels of meaning.

---

8   BL, Harley MS 3775, part 11, fols. 122–3r; *Annales Amundesham*, vol. 1, pp. 418–21; *An Account of the Altars, Monuments and Tombs existing AD 1428 in St Alban's Abbey, translated from the original Latin with notes*, ed. R. Lloyd (1873).

9   J. Backhouse, '93: Hours of Elizabeth the Queen', in *Gothic. Art for England, 1400–1547*, ed. R. Marks and P. Williamson, assisted by E. Townsend (London, 2003), p. 229.

10 These are discussed in J. G. Clark, 'Intellectual life at the Abbey of St Albans and the Nature of Monastic Learning in England, c.1350–1440', D. Phil. Dissertation (University of Oxford, 1997), p. 121.

11 Lloyd, *Account of the Altars*, 21.

12 Gill, 'Role of Images', pp. 131–2.

13 See for example, the lists in V. Gillespie, 'Medieval Hypertext: Image and Text from York Minster', in *Of the Making of Books. Medieval Manuscripts, their Scribes and Readers. Essays presented to M. B. Parkes*, ed. P. R. Robinson and R. Zim (London, 1997), pp. 216–17; C. Richmond, 'Hand and Mouth: Information Gathering and Use in England in the Later Middle Ages', *JHS*, 1:3 (1988), 246–7.

14 *Annales Amundesham*, vol. 1, p. 420.

It seems likely that the apologia was one of a series of brief historical works composed to instruct monks about the history and contents of the abbey.[15] This suggests that written texts might have played a role in equipping monks to apply symbolic and multi-layered interpretations to the visual culture of the abbey. Comparable examples of instruction in complex strategies of interpretation can be found in both monastic and secular preaching.[16]

The composition of the apologia and the records of other combinations of words and images at St Albans, suggest that monastic communities may have been places where the design and interpretation of monumental art was regarded as complimenting, and even forming an extension of, the culture of reading and writing. This is a different context from that found in parish churches, even in the later Middle Ages when literacy was more widespread. It is closer to the sorts of relationships between text and image specifically found in the art of the book. At times, this bookishness is so pronounced that it may be possible to claim it as a distinguishing characteristic of monastic art, and possibly one which was self-consciously chosen.[17] In order to see how such an approach might illuminate our understanding of monastic paintings, we need to understand the cultural importance of reading in monastic life.

The horarium of St Benedict provided a minimum of three hours a day during the summer for the practice of *lectio divina*.[18] This 'holy reading' which St Benedict intended to be such an important aspect of monastic routine did not refer to the study of Scripture or works of theology, but indicated a particular pattern of slow and thoughtful reading. This was conceived as the first of the prayerful stages which led to contemplation. St Anselm, in his *Meditations on Human Redemption*, characterised this ruminative process as a form of spiritual ingestion.[19] The anticipated speed of this kind of reading may be indicated by Lanfranc's requirement that each monk at Canterbury read one book a year.[20] Thus, *lectio divina* appears distinct from the process of monastic scholarship which might lead to the composition of works of theology or history. It is closer to the process of memorisation and internalisation required for the learning of the divine office and, in particular, the psalms.

The importance of monasteries and monastic patronage in the production and decoration of medieval manuscripts is well known. However, it is important to separate writing and decoration. The ubiquity of the former is clear from Kauffmann's statement that 'in the early and high Middle Ages the copying of

---

15 I am indebted to Dr James Clark for alerting me to this context.

16 Gill, 'Preaching and Image', 176–7.

17 This possibility of paintings displaying bookish characteristics is raised in relation to the collegiate paintings formerly in St Stephens, Westminster: P. Binski, *Westminster Abbey and the Plantagenets*, (New Haven and London, 1995), p. 184.

18 Quoted in J. Greatrex, 'The Scope of Learning within the Cloisters of the English Cathedral Priories in the Later Middle Ages', in *Medieval Monastic Education*, ed. Muessig and Ferzoco, p. 47.

19 M. T. Clancy, *From Memory to Written Record. England 1066–1307* (London, 1993), pp. 268–9.

20 Clancy, *Memory to Written Record*, p. 160. Lanfranc's injunction was a reiteration of the requirement of the *regula sancti Benedicti*, c. xlviii.

manuscripts formed the principal work of Benedictine monks'.[21] However, it is likely that even in the twelfth century most manuscript illumination was the work of lay artists, such as Master Hugo who was responsible for the magnificent Bury Bible (c.1135).[22] In the later Middle Ages monastic communities remained among the most significant patrons of lavishly illuminated books, particularly those for liturgical use, such as the Litlington Missal (1383–84) made for the Benedictines at Westminster Abbey.[23] Perhaps the collaboration between learned monks and skilled lay artists evident in manuscript production can provide a model for understanding a similar collaboration which must have been present in the production of monumental art.

The surviving corpus of English monastic wall paintings is small but varied. Some paintings were purely decorative. In the early years of the Cistercian order these may have been the only type of paintings commonly executed in their religious houses.[24] Other paintings performed specifically liturgical functions, adorning or accompanying altars or providing the setting for religious ceremonies. The most impressive surviving instance of mural paintings used in this way can be found in the twelfth- and thirteenth-century schemes of Passion subjects in the Holy Sepulchre Chapel at Winchester Cathedral where the Easter ceremonies probably took place.[25] Other paintings interpreted the spaces and functions of the monastery. For example, refectory images of the Crucifixion, such as that found in the Charterhouse of St Anne in Coventry (c.1411–17), invested communal meals with a Eucharistic significance.[26] Some paintings can be seen as intrinsically didactic, such as the lost paintings of the Seven Deadly Sins recorded in the south transept of the Benedictine abbey of Milton, Dorset (painted between 1481–1525).[27]

Since the types of murals to survive are very diverse, this examination of the relationship between monastic murals and bookish culture will focus on selected paintings where such a connection appears most clear and probable. This is not to imply that the centrality of literacy and the experience of *lectio divina* would have had no impact on the way in which other images were considered. Nor is it to suggest that drawing a connection between seeing and reading is the only way of understanding the role of art within monastic culture. However, this is an approach to the question of what characterises monastic art which is supported, not only by the nature of some of the surviving images, but by contemporary definitions of what might constitute the legitimate use of art by monks.

The nature and purpose of monastic art was addressed directly in the monastic

---

21 C. M. Kauffmann, *Romanesque Manuscripts, 1066–1190* (London, 1975), p. 15.

22 *Ibid.*, p. 15.

23 Binski, *Westminster Abbey*, 193–4.

24 D. Park, 'Cistercian Wall Painting and Panel Painting', in *Cistercian Art and Architecture in the British Isles*, ed. C. Norton and D. Park (Cambridge, 1986), pp. 181–210.

25 D. Park and P. Welford, 'The Medieval Polychromy of Winchester Cathedral', *Winchester Cathedral. Nine Hundred Years, 1093–1993*, ed. J. Crook (Chichester, 1993), pp. 123–138; D. Park, 'English Medieval Wall Painting in an International Context', in *Conserving the Painted Past. Developing Approaches to Wall Painting Conservation. Post-Prints of a Conference Organised by English Heritage* (London, 1999), p. 2.

26 Gill, 'Role of Images', 127–9.

27 *Ibid.*, 124–5.

reforms of the twelfth century and the writings of St Bernard of Clairvaux (d. 1153) in particular. While St Bernard is perhaps most famous for his c.1125 polemical denunciation of the grotesques found in Romanesque decoration, his more substantive attack on monastic art was derived from the ideas presented in traditional defences of church imagery.[28] In Bernard's hands, St Gregory's famous justification of art as a didactic aid for the illiterate became a tool to expose the redundancy of monastic art whose viewers were literate.[29]

The writings and the artistic schemes of Abbot Suger (d. 1151) of St Denis have been interpreted by Conrad Rudolph as a deliberate rebuttal of St Bernard's rejection of the idea of religious art for the literate.[30] Suger believed in the inherent value of visual representations, arguing that material images could lead the monk to the contemplation of the spiritual.[31] More significantly, his writings and the typological stained glass at St Denis present a coherent vision of a monastic art accessible only to the Latin literate and theologically erudite.[32] This art was characterised by a reliance on exegetical methods, in particular the typological interpretation of scripture, and the inclusion of extensive inscriptions.[33] For Suger the prominence of text in schemes of images was more than the practical consequence of a learned environment. He believed that theologically sophisticated art with integral text could be understood as an extension of monastic *lectio*.[34]

A specifically English contribution to this debate about monastic art was the manual *Pictor in Carmine* which appears to have been written in a Cistercian house in c.1200, possibly by Adam of Dore.[35] This work has two distinct sections. The introduction combines Bernardine polemic against unsuitable subjects with a self-promoting endorsement of the value of Scriptural images. The body of the book consists of a series of typological subjects accompanied by rhyming Latin couplets. The topicality of *Pictor* may be suggested by the inter-

---

[28] C. Rudolph, *The 'Things of Greater Importance': Bernard of Clairvaux's 'Apologia' and the Medieval Attitude toward Art* (Philadelphia, 1990), pp. 10–12, 39, 51.

[29] For St Gregory's defence of art see L. G. Duggan, 'Was Art Really the Book of the Illiterate?' *Word and Image*, 5:3 (1989), 227. The problems of this definition for our understanding of the role of parochial murals are discussed in M. Gill, 'Reading Images: Church Murals and Collaboration between Media in Medieval England', in *Collaboration: Studies in European Cultural Transition*, ed. S. Wood and S. Bigliazzi (Aldershot: forthcoming).

[30] Rudolph, 'The "Things of Greater Importance"', p. 108; C. Rudolph, *Artistic Change at St Denis. Abbot Suger's Program and the Early Twelfth-Century Controversy over Art* (Princeton, 1990), p. 73.

[31] Rudolph, *Artistic Change at St Denis*, p. 70.

[32] *Abbot Suger on the Abbey of St Denis and its Art Treasures*, ed. E. Panofsky (Princeton, 1979).

[33] In the context of English typological cycles, Heslop observes that verse inscriptions appear to have been fashionable in late Anglo-Saxon England: T. A. Heslop, 'Worcester Cathedral Chapterhouse and the harmony of the testaments', in *New Offerings, Ancient Treasures: Studies in Medieval Art for George Henderson*, ed. P. Binski and W. Noels (Stroud, 2001), p. 297.

[34] Rudolph, *Artistic Change*, p. 71.

[35] M. R. James, 'Pictor in Carmine', *Archaeolgia*, 94 (1951), 141–66; Park, 'Cistercian Wall Painting', pp. 199–200. Worcester Cathedral Priory had an abbreviated version of Pictor (13th c.), now CCCC MS 217.

esting parallels between the author's list of unsuitable subjects and the content of the roof of the nave of Peterborough Cathedral (early thirteenth century), which includes Boethius's Ass and other grotesque creatures.[36] The typological cycle in *Pictor* appears to have been more influential in Central Europe than in England, although parts of it are recorded in an account of a 'table' which may have stood on the altar of the Lady Chapel in York Minster.[37]

Pictor demonstrates both an awareness of the Bernardine controversy and an interest in the development of the sort of 'monastic' art identified in the work of Abbot Suger. Evidence for the execution of complex typological schemes accompanied by Latin inscriptions can be found in English monastic foundations of the twelfth century. The earliest of these schemes identified was associated with the chapter house of the Benedictine community at Worcester, and elements from it are reproduced in a number of later works, including ciboria and illuminated manuscripts.[38] Another important typological cycle was that painted on the backs of the choir stalls at Peterborough (c.1233–45) recorded in the seventeenth century by the local antiquarian, Symon Gunton, before it was defaced by Parliamentary forces. [39] As at Worcester, the original cycle is known only from records of its inscriptions, but the iconography of its images appears to have been carefully reproduced in the prefatory pages of the early fourteenth-century Peterborough Psalter (Brussels, Bib. Roy. MS 9961–2).[40]

Where both original images and accompanying text survive, as in the stained glass programme at Canterbury Cathedral, begun in 1174, it is clear that the images were not simply an accompanying illustration but rather they conveyed and enhanced theological meanings.[41] The typological redemption window in the east end of the Corona (c.1200) includes a scene of two of the spies carrying the grapes of Eschol (Numbers 13: 21–9). While the form of the large bunch of grapes hanging from the pole prefigures the image of Christ on the cross shown above and adds a Eucharistic association, the inscription derives a further moral from the appearance of the two spies. It compares the foremost to the Jewish people who are described as having turned their back on Christ and the second spy is identified as an emblem of the Gentiles who look to Christ.[42] While this layer of interpretation is not inherent in the visual representation, the inscrip-

---

36 For the list of 'undesirable subjects', see James, 'Pictor', 142. C. J. P. Cave, 'The Painted Ceiling in the Nave of Peterborough Cathedral', *Archaeologia*, 87 (1938), 299–304.

37 Gillespie, 'Medieval Hypertext', p. 212.

38 For the longevity of the Worcester scheme, see A. Henry, *The Eton Roundels: Eton College MS 177 (Figurae Bibliorum: A Colour Facsimile with Transcription, Translation and Commentary)* (Aldershot, 1990). Heslop suggests the cycle may be from before 1125, considerably earlier than previously believed. Heslop, 'Worcester Cathedral', 297.

39 Henry, *Eton Roundels*; L. F. Sandler, *The Peterborough Psalter in Brussels and Other Fenland Manuscripts* (London, 1974), pp. 110–15. See also S. Gunton, *The History of the Church of Peterburgh by Symon Gunton*, ed. S. Patrick, a facsimile edition with introduction by J. Higham and index by A. Wilkins (Peterborough, 1990), pp. 95–6.

40 Sandler, *Peterborough Psalter*, pp. 108–15.

41 Heslop's analysis of Worcester explores the difficulties of reconstructing such a scheme from text alone: Heslop, 'Worcester Cathedral', 292.

42 M. H. Caviness, *The Windows of Christ Church Cathedral Canterbury*, Corpus Vitrearum Medii Aevi, 2 (London, 1981), p. 166.

tion is clearly a commentary on the form of this image rather than an allegory of an element in the narrative. The creation of such images implies that visual representations were expected to function as an element within literate culture. They were neither a substitute for it (as parochial art was claimed to be) nor simply an illustration. Rather the specific combination of word and image enabled the development of layers of exegetical meaning.

The bookish nature of these typological schemes has also contributed considerably to our knowledge of them. As the example of *Pictor* suggests, the content of such schemes and the exegetical poems which elucidated them were primarily devised by scholars, rather than painters, although it does appear that John of Worcester (died after 1140), whom Heslop posits as the creator of the Worcester cycle, may also have drawn the illustrations in his historical works.[43] The role of clerics in the development of complex iconographic programmes of monumental art can be found until the end of the Middle Ages, as in the case of the 'magister pictorum', the probable deviser of the elaborate scheme of Marian miracles at Eton College (completed c.1487).[44] Some of the minor works of the poet monk John Lydgate (d. c.1451) include verses intended to accompany images, both devotional representations at Bury St Edmunds, such as the *Image of Pity*, and domestic tapestries with secular themes.[45]

The number of medieval records of inscriptions displayed in monumental schemes suggests their importance in monastic culture. In the realm of wall painting these lists form a rather tantalising supplement to the corpus of art works which now survive. Notable among these are the late twelfth- and early thirteenth-century typological glazing schemes at Canterbury, which are recorded in at least three medieval manuscripts, and the extensive range of images with inscriptions, including exegetical subjects, recorded from Bury St Edmunds.[46] While some records of inscriptions from monastic churches, such as the historical material copied from *tabula* by a member of the female religious community at Kirkstall, represent collations gathered during travels, other such documents, for example the record of the Worcester verses, appear to have been written and used locally.[47] Monastic houses were not the only context in which monumental art was accompanied by inscriptions, examples of the use of inscriptions can be found in later medieval parochial art, but such monastic collations are surely testament both to a commitment to the specific meaning of such art and its status as a theological and intellectual creation.

The exploration of the bookish character of monastic art cannot be confined simply to the presence of inscriptions. Some subjects found in monastic contexts clearly derive from specific literary origins, even when the painting does not

43 Heslop, 'Worcester Cathedral', 298.
44 M. Gill, 'The Wall Paintings in Eton College Chapel: the Making of a Late Medieval Marian cycle', in *Making Medieval Art*, ed. P. Lindley (Donington, 2003), p. 177.
45 *The Minor Poems of John Lydgate*, ed. H. N. MacCracken, EETS, ES, 107 (1911); *The Minor Poems of John Lydgate*, ed. id., EETS, ES 192, (1934).
46 Caviness, *The Windows of Christ Church*, 2; M. R. James, *On the Abbey of S. Edmund at Bury*, 2 vols., CAS (Cambridge, 1895).
47 J. E. Krochalis, 'History and legend at Kirkstall in the Fifteenth Century', in *Of the Making of Books*, ed. Robinson and Zim, pp. 206–29; Heslop, 'Worcester Cathedral', 280.

contain and may never have contained any inscription. The most striking instance of this is the scene of the Man on the Bridge at the Cistercian Cleeve Abbey in Somerset.[48] This painting from the end of the fifteenth century is a unique representation of a sermon exemplum included in the German manuscript tradition of the collection *Gesta Romanorum*.[49] It can be understood as an allegorical representation of the monastic vocation. A man stands on a bridge confronted by the sea, a lion and a dragon, which symbolise the World, the Flesh and the Devil, while above angels display the reward of virtue in the form of the crown of life, and the sword of divine punishment. In the parish church at Halesowen, which was held by the local Premonstratensian Abbey, a unique representation of the miracle of St Nicholas and the hanged man (now lost, but known from nineteenth-century drawings), may demonstrate knowledge of the literary account of this story in the writings of Caesarius of Heisterbach.[50] Intriguing survivals suggest that the transmission of imagery from an erudite monastic context to the monumental art of parish churches was not confined to the direct patronage probably at work at Halesowen. The unusual scene of the Triumph of Mary/Ecclesia found in images related to the lost Worcester cycle is shown on a mid-twelfth-century tympanum at Quenington in Gloucestershire,[51] while the extensive fourteenth-century Passion cycle on the north nave wall of Peakirk church (Cambridgeshire) relies heavily on the prefatory material of the Barlow Psalter (1321–38), which in turn reproduces the Passion sequence of the lost typological cycle at Peterborough.[52]

This brief survey has indicated that some of the painted decoration of English monastic houses can be understood in the context of the ideal of a specifically monastic form of art like that proposed by Abbot Suger and pioneered by him at St Denis. Complex painted schemes were devised by scholars, presumably members of the monastic communities, their inscriptions were recorded and disseminated in written form within and between such communities and their content used as models for manuscript illumination and liturgical objects. Even where paintings contain no inscriptions, their content might be bookish in the sense that it was derived from specific, specialised literary sources.

The remainder of this paper will examine two particularly striking schemes of monastic wall painting which depict the Apocalypse, one at Westminster and the other recently excavated from the site of the Cathedral Priory at Coventry. This analysis will explore how the recent discovery of the Coventry paintings changes our understanding of the Westminster cycle and how the purpose of both cycles can be illuminated by reference to the bookish aspects of monumental art in religious houses.

---

48 C. Babington, T. Manning, and S. Stewart, *Our Painted Past. Wall Paintings of English Heritage*, (London, 1999), pp. 46–7; Gill, 'Role of Images', 120–2.

49 *Gesta Romanorum*, ed. H. Oesterley (Berlin, 1872), pp. 28, 40, 49, 51, 56, 86, 101, 120, 135, 141, 597.

50 M. Gill, 'The Lost Wall Paintings of Halesowen', *WAS*, 3rd series, 16, (1998), 133–41.

51 Heslop, 'Worcester Cathedral', 289, 291.

52 The relationship of Peakirk to the Barlow Psalter is discussed in, E. C. Rouse, 'Wall paintings in the Church of St Pega, Peakirk, Northamptonshire', *ArchJ*, 110 (1953), 135–49. For the Gough Psalter and the Peterborough cycle see, Sandler, *Peterborough Psalter*, 95.

The chapter house of the Benedictine Abbey at Westminster is painted with a ninety-six scene cycle of the Apocalypse dated to the years around 1400.[53] The style of these Apocalypse scenes relates closely to the art of contemporary Flemish and German painters and has often been associated with the work of the famous Hamburg exponent of the International Style, Master Bertram.[54] Four scenes were painted in each bay and thus behind the seat of each cleric. This scheme is combined with a larger image of Christ in Judgement flanked by cherubim executed in a distinctively Italianate style behind the seats occupied by the Abbot and senior members of the community.[55] Some of the scenes have suffered badly from misuse and misguided 'restoration', but those at the start of the cycle are well preserved.[56]

The Westminster cycle was believed to be unique until three significant painted fragments were found at Coventry in the course of excavations under-taken by the Phoenix Initiative on the site of the Benedictine priory and Cathedral Church of St Mary. The first two pieces of painted masonry were found in 2000, the third in 2002 [see plates 1–3].[57] The stones retained areas of high quality, figurative painting. The location in which they were found suggested that they had come from the chapter house and had been discarded when that building was dismantled after the Dissolution.[58] Architectural analysis suggests that the chapter house itself dates from 1300 to 1330.[59] The paintings appear to be slightly later and can be dated to the period c.1360–70 on the basis of stylistic comparison.[60]

The identification of the Coventry fragments with the early chapters of the Apocalypse and the position in which they were found, to the north of the north wall of the chapter house, suggest that the Coventry cycle read from left to right, like that at Westminster, starting from the north-west.[61] The West-minster cycle comprises ninety-six scenes.[62] The number of scenes contained

---

53 Babington, Manning and Stewart, *Our Painted Past*, pp. 10–11, 30–2. This dating, a little later than that in Babington, Manning and Stewart, is proposed in H. Howard, 'Recent scientific examination of the medieval wall paintings of the Chapter House of Westmin-ster Abbey', in *Conserving the Painted Past*, p. 17; S. Hauschild, 'Meister Bertram von Minden', in *Die Kunst des Mittelalters in Hamburg*, ed. U. M. Schneede (Hamburg, 1999), pp. 99–100; Howard, 'Recent Scientific', 24.
54 Park, 'English Medieval Wall Painting', 6.
55 Howard, 'Recent Scientific', 18, 22–3.
56 *Ibid.*, 17.
57 M. Gill, 'The Chapter House Apocalypse Panels', in *The Archaeology of the Medieval Cathe-dral and Priory of St Mary*, ed. M. Rylatt and P. Mason (Coventry, 2003), pp. 82–3. The two stones found in 2000 are discussed in detail in, M. Gill and R. Morris, 'A Wall Painting of the Apocalypse in Coventry Rediscovered', *BM*, 143 (2001), 467–73.
58 Personal communication by Margaret Rylatt, quoted in Gill and Morris, 470. For further discussion see Morris, 'Destruction and Reconstruction', 244–6.
59 Gill and Morris 'A Wall Painting of the Apocalypse', 470.
60 Gill and Morris, 'A Wall Painting of the Apocalypse', 472–3; Gill, 'The Chapter House', 87.
61 Gill and Morris, 'A Wall Painting of the Apocalypse', 471.
62 For discussion of the Westminster cycle see J. G. Noppen, 'The Westminster Apocalypse and its Source', *BM*, 61 (1932), 146–59; B. Turner, 'The Patronage of John of North-ampton: Further Studies of the Wall-Paintings in Westminster Chapter House', *JBAA*,

in the Coventry cycle is not known. Of the three fragments discovered, the first and second may be part of the same scene.[63] The first, a small fragment, shows the head of a venerable figure. The second contains part of a scene of the 'door opened in Heaven' and the 'elders in adoration' (Revelation 6:7–8). The third, part of a central springer with remains of the flanking wall plates, contains the right portion of a scene tentatively identified as the Fourth Horseman of the Apocalypse (Revelation 6:7) and the left portion of a scene which probably shows the Lamb adored by a great multitude, as described in Revelation 7:9–17. However, the presence of the door opened in Heaven and the elders in adoration, a subject not shown in the murals at Westminster, suggests that the Coventry cycle may have included more scenes than the ninety-six depicted there. The exact number of scenes depicted at Coventry on a possible total of fifty-one arcade units is hard to ascertain; it is possible that some of the scenes were of different sizes.[64] It is also possible that, as at Westminster, the cycle of narrative scenes may have been interrupted by larger Judgement images at the east end, behind the Prior's seat.[65]

The Apocalypse paintings at Westminster show how impressive such a monumental cycle could be. However, the fragments found at Coventry reveal a scheme of even greater art historical significance. Firstly, the artistic quality and level of detail is evidently superior to that at Westminster. Secondly, stylistic analysis suggests that the Coventry paintings pre-date those at Westminster. Indeed, artistically they relate most closely to the Italianate style and superb quality of the murals painted in St Stephen's Chapel, Westminster between 1350 and 1363.[66]

The identification of such a remarkable cycle of an earlier date also prompts reconsideration of the Westminster chapter house where the choice of the Apocalypse had previously seemed rather idiosyncratic to Binski.[67] It is certainly significant that several extensive monumental cycles of the Apocalypse survive from the later fourteenth century: the Angers Tapestries made for the wedding of Louis I of Anjou (c.1377); the murals in the Chapel of St Mary in the Karlštejn Castle in Bohemia (c.1357); and the images by Guisto de Menbuoi and workshop in the baptistry at Padua which were completed in 1378.[68] Within the context of religious orders we might point to the great panel painting made for the friary at Hamburg now in the Victoria and Albert Museum and, closer to home, the cycle of bosses in the cloister of the Benedictine Cathedral Priory at

138 (1985), 89–100; Binski, *Westminster Abbey*, 185–95; Babington *et al.*, *Our Painted Past*, pp. 30–2; Howard, 'Recent Scientific', 17–26.

[63] All three fragments are discussed in detail in Gill, 'The Chapter House', 84–6.
[64] Gill and Morris, 'A Wall Painting of the Apocalypse', 471; Gill, 'The Chapter House', 86–7.
[65] Gill and Morris, 'A Wall Painting of the Apocalypse', 471.
[66] For these see E. Howe, 'Divine Kingship and Dynastic Display: the Altar Wall Murals of St Stephen's Chapel, Westminster', *AJ*, 81 (2001), 259–303.
[67] Binski, *Westminster Abbey*, 192.
[68] Gill and Morris, 'A Wall Painting of the Apocalypse', 473.

Norwich.[69] Such comparisons set the ambition and extent of the chapter house schemes in a contemporary European context.

Attention has also been drawn to the role of John of Northampton, the apparent patron of the Westminster cycle.[70] He was a monk at Westminster and his contributions towards the painting scheme are recorded in a fifteenth-century compilation known as the 'Liber Niger'; Turner noted that the sums recorded are insufficient to finance the entire project, but technical analysis confirms that the paintings are essentially one scheme.[71] By contrast, little documentation survives from Coventry Priory. The painting was probably executed while William of Greneburgh was Prior, since he held office from 1361 to 1390.[72] Later fourteenth-century glazed floor tiles found during the excavation of the refectory suggest connections with and possibly patronage from the powerful local Beauchamp family and other possible secular patrons could include Queen Isabella, the Black Prince and Henry, Duke of Lancaster.[73]

However, neither fashion nor patronage sufficiently explain the choice of such a complex and demanding subject for the monumental decoration of two Benedictine chapter houses within one generation. The earlier date and exquisite quality of the Coventry paintings raise the possibility that in this instance the provinces may have inspired emulation at Westminster. But it is to the nature of the subject matter, the Book of Revelation, that we should look in order to understand some of the specifically monastic reasons for this choice.

The Apocalypse is a sophisticated book, full of complex number symbolism; and it presents a disturbing narrative of natural disaster, political dissolution and fiery judgement. Some individual scenes from the Apocalypse are found in English parochial art, for example, St Michael's Coventry (the post-medieval Cathedral) had a late fifteenth-century misericord of the binding of Satan.[74] However, there are no schemes which attempt to present the narrative sweep of the book. Instead, the Doom painting combined a range of Scriptural elements into a single dramatic representation of the final judgement. The Doom appears to have been a very common theme in later medieval parochial art and wall painting in particular. A very fine Doom painting of c.1435 at Holy Trinity, Coventry has been revealed by a recent campaign of restoration.[75]

Several reasons for the absence of Apocalypse cycles from a parochial context present themselves. This extensive and complex narrative requires both an substantial area for comprehensive depiction and the presence of informed viewers. Its length and confusing narrative tend to blunt its didactic edge in

[69] C. M. Kauffmann, *An Altar-piece of the Apocalypse from Master Bertram's Workshop in Hamburg*, (London, 1968); M. Rose, 'The Vault Bosses', in *Norwich Cathedral Church, City and Diocese, 1096–1996*, ed. I. Atherton (London, 1996), p. 366.

[70] Binski, *Westminster Abbey*, 187–8.

[71] Turner, 'Patronage of John of Northampton', 91–2; Howard, 'Recent Scientific', 18, 25.

[72] Gill and Morris, 'A Wall Painting of the Apocalypse', 473.

[73] *Ibid.*, 473.

[74] M. D. Harris, 'Misericords in Coventry', *BAST*, 52 (1927), 246–66. The medieval church of St Michael became the cathedral of the recreated diocese of Coventry in 1918.

[75] M. Gill, 'The Significance of the Site and Historical Setting for the "Doom" Painting', in *Conservation of the 'Doom' Wall Painting, Holy Trinity Coventry, Abstract of Papers Presented at the Symposium in memory of Anna C. Hulbert* (2005), 11–13.

contrast to the uncompromising image of the Last Judgement. However, the Apocalypse did achieve popularity in the Middle Ages, among both clerical and lay people, in the form of an illustrated book. The earliest such books date from the middle of the thirteenth century and the genre appears to have been English in origin.[76] These books presented the narrative of the Apocalypse through a cycle of detailed illustrations. Some contained the full text of the Vulgate accompanied by a popular commentary, such as that of Berengaudus, but others used an abbreviated text in the vernacular; the choice probably depended on the intended reader of the manuscript. Surviving Apocalypse books can be grouped into 'families' which have the same numbers of illustrations and iconographic details and most of these families are named after the earliest surviving exemplar of that tradition.

Nearly all of the major monumental schemes illustrating the Apocalypse are direct transcriptions of one of these Apocalypse books. The Angers Tapestries are based on a source related to the Burckhardt-Wildt Apocalypse.[77] The Hamburg panel follows a visual cycle developed from a Commentary on the Apocalypse composed in c.1248–50 by Friar Alexander, a Franciscan from northern Germany.[78] The communar rolls of the Benedictine community at Norwich record the purchase in 1346–47 of an Apocalypse Book to serve as a model for a cycle of roof bosses.[79] Whether created for a monastic or a secular context, the use of pre-existing illustrated manuscripts makes these cycles of the Apocalypse among the most bookish of images depicted in medieval monumental art.

The cycle at Westminster is no different. The scheme is taken from a version of the Apocalypse Book tradition known as the 'expanded Metz'.[80] It is probable that a fourteenth-century manuscript now in Trinity College, Cambridge provided the model for the cycle (or else was very close to the manuscript which provided the model).[81] Despite its fourteenth-century date, this manuscript and the chapter house paintings faithfully reproduce many compositional details of the earlier model. This is particularly clear in the representation of the twenty-four Elders casting down their instruments. They are shown divided into four groups of six and enclosed within a series of compartments in an ordered arrangement around the central image of Christ in Majesty. However, recent technical analysis has revealed that the Westminster painters did feel able to diverge from their model where necessary. For example, in the same scene it is clear that the artist initially intended to follow the manuscript model which showed seven lamps in a line on either side of Christ's head, but later modified this to show the lamps surrounding him.[82]

---

[76] N. Morgan, *The Lambeth Apocalypse Manuscript 209 in Lambeth Palace Library*, (London, 1990), 42. See also S. Lewis, *Reading Images. Narrative Discourse and Reception in the Thirteenth-Century Illuminated Apocalypse*, (Cambridge, 1995).

[77] G. Henderson, 'The Manuscript Model of the Angers "Apocalypse" Tapestries', BM, 127 (1985), 209–18.

[78] Kaufmann, *Altar-Piece*, 14.

[79] Rose, 'The Vault Bosses', 366.

[80] Noppen, 'The Westminster Apocalypse', 154; Binski, *Westminster Abbey*, 192.

[81] CTC, MS B. 10. 2; Binski, *Westminster Abbey*, 192.

[82] Howard, 'Recent Scientific', 24.

The source or exemplar of the earlier Coventry cycle has proved harder to identify. It is evident from the inclusion of the scene of the Adoration by the Elders that it did not use the model used at Westminster. While the community at Westminster may have wanted to emulate the type of scheme found at Coventry, they clearly used a local manuscript as their model rather than depicting the same scenes or using the same compositions and iconography. More significantly, the type of composition used for the Adoration by the Elders is distinct from that found in the thirteenth-century Apocalypse Book tradition. Rather than placing the Elders in compartments, they are depicted with ambitious naturalism in rows. There is an attempt to suggest complex spatial relationships between them and other elements of the composition such as the door into Heaven.

Two explanations present themselves. The first is that the Coventry cycle is a close transcription of a more artistically developed visual source which has not yet been identified. In this respect, it is worth noting that the rows of elders can be paralleled by the depictions of this scene in the Bible Moralisée, although the differences in shape between its roundels and the unusual forms of Coventry panels make it hard to determine the extent of the resemblance.[83] The second possibility is that the artist at Coventry was using a model which originated in the thirteenth-century Apocalypse Book tradition, but that he was modifying the composition and, in particular, the artistic idiom of the scenes, so as to modernise their appearance. Such a process has been proposed in the case of the work of another Apocalypse cycle with Coventry connections: the great east window at York Minster. This window was created by the Coventry glass painter, John Thornton, between 1405 and 1408. Thornton was given a manuscript from the Minster's library to serve as a model for the eighty Apocalypse scenes included in the window, but he evidently modified his source to meet the expectations of the more naturalistic International Style.[84]

The identification of the exact source of the Coventry painting would undoubtedly enhance our understanding of the culture of the Priory and indeed of the artistic accomplishments of the city in the later part of the fourteenth century. However, whether or not its origins can be traced, it is clear, particularly after the discovery of the third fragment, that this scheme, like that at Westminster, reproduced the content of an illustrated cycle of Apocalypse scenes in monumental form. At Westminster each scene was accompanied by extracts from the Apocalypse and the commentary of Berengaudus written on parchment and pasted onto the wall.[85] Although the fragments to survive from Coventry do not contain evidence of such extensive texts, the scene of the Adoration by the Elders includes an as yet undeciphered speech scroll proceeding from the mouth of St John.[86] It is clear that these schemes not only used books as visual models,

[83] Gill and Morris, 'A Wall Painting of the Apocalypse', 471.
[84] T. French, 'York Minster: the Great East Window', Corpus Vitrearum Medii Aevi, Summary Catalogue, 2 (1995), p. 10.
[85] Binski, Westminster Abbey, 192.
[86] Gill and Morris, 'A Wall Painting of the Apocalypse', 467.

but were characterised by the combination of images and inscriptions identified above as an enduring characteristic of monastic art.

The impression that these two schemes may have functioned as public books for their monastic community is strengthened by their physical context and appearance. In both cases the paintings occupied the lower part of the walls of the chapter house. The scale of the individual images is intimate. At Westminster there are four images in each bay, while at Coventry it is not clear whether each bay contained two or four images.[87] The possible relation of fragments one and two may suggest that the image of the Adoration by the Elders occupied the width of bay, but the tentative identification of the scenes on fragment three tends to suggest that the width of one (or a single) bay contained more than two scenes, since several incidents divide the Fourth Horseman and the Adoration of the Lamb. It is possible that, as on the Hamburg altarpiece, the scene of the Adoration by the Elders was depicted in a larger scale than the majority of scenes.[88] Whatever the number of scenes per bay, the exquisite delicacy and detail of the Coventry paintings suggest that they were intended for close inspection. Both schemes could be studied carefully by those sitting or standing in the chapter house.

However, as Plock has observed, the paintings at Westminster can also be understood as a deliberate declaration of the place which reading and interpretation of scripture held in the community.[89] Like Abbot Suger's typological windows, this 'open book' painted on the walls of the chapter house indicates the monastic community as a place of study and devout reading. The discovery of the earlier Coventry cycle perhaps colours Plock's suggestions that the cycle at Westminster was, in part, a response to Lollard debate about access to and the interpretation of scripture. However, this does not detract from the proposition that the bookishness of the cycles has an ideological purpose as well as a practical function. The earlier lavish scheme at St Stephen's Chapel, Westminster deployed a self-consciously 'learned' combination of images and Latin inscriptions, presumably to complement the collegiate status of the chapel, but positioned the paintings so high up the walls that they were probably illegible to those in the chapel.[90]

It is to a possible practical function that we now come. The placement and execution of both cycles and the addition of the pasted extracts at Westminster point to an expectation that these paintings would be actively used. However, during the formal meetings of the chapter, access to the cycle would have been frustratingly limited, as each bay was potentially obscured by a seated monk. In this context, it is perhaps the message of the Apocalypse as a narrative of judgement and salvation, rather than the specific incidents, which would have

---

[87] This issue is discussed in Gill, 'The Chapter House', 86.

[88] Kauffmann, *Altarpiece*, plate 4.

[89] P. Plock, 'An Image of Reading: exploring tensions of the text in late fourteenth-century England through the Westminster Apocalypse cycle', paper presented at IMC Leeds, July 2000; P. Plock, 'Reading Revelation: the Social Significance of the Apocalypse Mural in Westminster Abbey Chapterhouse', unpublished BA Dissertation (University of York, 1998).

[90] Binski, *Westminster Abbey*, 184–5.

provided food for thought. Such an interpretation accords with Binski's observations about the appropriateness of the central image of judgement to the function
of the chapter house.[91] At Westminster the Abbot sat in front of the image of
Christ the Judge with images of cherubim on either side. The one on Christ's left
hand is based on the moralised diagram which accompanies the treatise by Alain
of Lille (died 1203), *De sex aliis cherubim*.[92] This diagram traces a progression
from confession to the love of God. Binski points to the conjunction between
the images of judgement, allusions to confession and absolution, and the activities of the chapter.[93] Such a conjunction is also present in the description of
the chapter house in Ware's Customary as a 'house of confession, the house of
obedience, mercy and forgiveness'.[94] Binski also points out that documentary
evidence suggests that the chapter house at St Albans also included an image
of the Last Judgement which was the work of Abbot Thomas (1349–96).[95] The
Apocalypse paintings with their more convoluted narrative of divine judgement
could be seen as an extension of this thematic connection to the function of the
chapter house.

However, alongside its thematic appropriateness, it is worth considering the
role which the Apocalypse played in the life and experience of a Benedictine
monk. As has been stated, these cycles present an unusually full and detailed
account of Biblical narrative. The experience of reviewing these small scenes
one by one and reading the inscriptions within or below them would offer a close
parallel to the meditative task of *lectio divina* [for a representation of *lectio divina*
see plate 4]. Indeed, these linear transcriptions of a single narrative are perhaps
closer to that experience than the exegetical form of typological cycles.

A liturgical detail from the Rule of St Benedict adds a further dimension.
The twelfth chapter of the Rule requires that the Sunday celebration of the
office of lauds should include the recitation by heart of one chapter of the Book
of Revelation. This requirement accords the Apocalypse a status like that of
the Psalms within monastic life, as a Biblical text which monks were intended
to memorise in full. This lends a further dimension to our understanding of the
communal function of the murals. It becomes clear that they were probably
intended to recall and refresh aspects of a familiar text. As a means of engaging
in a fresh and meditative way with familiar portions of scripture, we can see
their viewing as a process akin to *lectio divina*. While no direct evidence of such
response has been identified, other features of monastic expression imply the
extent to which familiarity with Scripture enhanced by *lectio divina* coloured
the thoughts of monks. Clark suggests that the extent of monastic exposure to
the words of Scripture can be ascertained from the way in which their personal
expression in Latin often evoked a Biblical idiom.[96]

The chapter house paintings from Coventry Priory represent an important
addition to the small and fragmented corpus of mural painting to survive from

91 *Ibid.*, 191.
92 Alain of Lille, *De sex aliis cherubim*, PL, 1885, 267–80.
93 Binski, *Westminster Abbey*, 188.
94 *Ibid.*, 191.
95 *Ibid.*, 188.
96 Clark, 'Intellectual Life', 121.

English monastic houses. Their chance survival, on carved masonry discarded in the salvage of the chapter house, recalls the factors which further distort this small sample. Their beauty poignantly suggests the high quality of much of the visual culture of monasteries which is now lost to us. Their unusual subject matter reinforces the sense of iconographic diversity gained from medieval and antiquarian accounts of monastic decoration. They also draw attention to the importance of the relationship between books and images in monumental monastic art. Like the typological schemes devised by Abbot Suger they represent a self-consciously erudite form of art, related to the study of scripture and distinct from the types of imagery deployed in parish churches. The Coventry paintings are probably dependent on the form of illustrated manuscripts of the Apocalypse, although their precise model has not been identified. They represent an ideological display of the importance of reading and study and relate specifically to the function of the building in which they were painted. These images were not a substitute for the written words of Scripture, but that does not mean that they were considered as secondary. Rather these images suggest a use of Scriptural art akin to the quintessential monastic practice of *lectio divina* in which a familiar theme was refreshed and renewed by repeated exposure to words and images.

LEARNED CULTURE

The Meaning of Monastic Culture: Anselm and his Contemporaries

G. R. EVANS

Is there a 'monastic culture'? It is important to keep in mind the difficulties of bridging the enormous divide between the understanding the mediaeval monk had of what he was doing and the relatively modern ideas the word 'culture' is likely to bring to mind. *Cultus* to a medieval monk meant simply 'worship'. It was a long and largely post-medieval journey from there to a sense of the English term 'culture' which would fit my title. We are not concerned with cultivation or tillage but with the metaphorical developments of *cultura* which led in one direction to the notion of worship, and in the other to 'culture' in its modern senses of a set of assumptions hanging together in the make-up of a person or system or style, and determining their ways of approaching and doing things. For that we are probably indebted to the influence of the Romantic Movement and nineteenth-century Germany.

We need to begin by drawing a key preliminary distinction, between Eastern and Western monasticism. Western thought set off down a somewhat different track when the late Roman world divided into its Latin and Greek speaking halves; the Western monastic library had few volumes from the Greek Fathers on its shelves in the Middle Ages, and it largely got its Platonism second-hand. This denied Western monasticism direct access to the currents of thought that still eddy on Mount Athos, and which lent a Neoplatonist spiritual colouring to the monastic culture of the Greek East. The Western monk of the earlier Middle Ages cultivated a thoughtful spirituality, affective in its urgings, but essentially rational, and in many respects distinctive to the monastic culture of the West. Medieval English monasticism is of its age and of the West, and whatever the special features of its local exemplifications, its culture is shared with others in that world. I propose to take a few examples of figures responsible for writings which have something to tell us about the way those engaged in living within this culture understood what they were doing; it would be absurd to suggest that Anselm of Canterbury or Aelred of Rievaulx was simply 'English'. That said, it is important not to expect too much by way of intellectual life in medieval English monasticism, at least not as the general rule. Not all medieval English religious by any means attained a high level of education; the monastic school was not a university and already in the twelfth century it is apparent that a Bernard of Clairvaux was at an intellectual if not a political disadvantage when he was confronted with a Peter Abelard or a Gilbert of Poitiers, who had been teaching in the schools which were now well on their way to becoming true universities. But every monk had a spiritual life. That was his work. And this life of the spirit was informed by a theory and a theology. It is there that we should start to look for the core values of English medieval 'monastic culture'.

In his own approximation to a monastic life, begun at Cassiciacum after his conversion and before his baptism, and continued in the community at Hippo,[1] Augustine of Hippo sought to import into Christian culture something approximating to the philosophical *otium* of the late antique world. His model was probably Cicero in his own philosophical retirement, with the corners of secular concern rounded and new priorities special to the followers of Christ. He and his companions spent their time in philosophical conversation, discussing the blessed life and the nature of order, with books as a permanent end result. Benedict of Nursia, setting out a programme for living a dedicated religious life in a community, and at an altogether more pedestrian level, still expected his monks to read and think. The *Regula magistri* allows the monks to ask questions about the reading as well as permitting the Abbot to say a few words of comment or clarification. The Rule of Benedict is more severe, and allows this privilege to the Abbot alone.[2] Chapter 42 of the Rule repeats the instruction that whenever the brothers eat, they should sit down together and one of them should read improving matter such as the Lives of the Fathers, but nothing too testing for there is a more appropriate time for the serious study of Scripture.[3] In a rule for monks attributed to the Complutensian abbot and later Archbishop of Braga and also associated with Isidore of Seville, is a chapter (VIII) on the way the monks are to conduct themselves when they are not engaged in any specific activity or duty. They are not to tell stories or wander about at leisure in an unsettled way. They should be sitting down and concentrating on some manual labour or reading; or they should be at prayer. Those are their proper occupations.[4] So monks are to be occupied in a spiritually profitable way at all times.

In late eleventh-century England, Archbishop Lanfranc sets out in his *Monastic Constitutions* what he considers to be the essentials of the Benedictine life, things which cannot be omitted when a given house chooses to make changes in the detail of its rules for living, as it is to some degree entitled to do. The question is, says Lanfranc, what is necessary to salvation. He lists faith (fides), 'contemptum mundi, caritatem, castitatem, humilitatem, patientiam, obedientiam', with confession, frequent prayer, silence, and things of that kind.[5] By comparison, it is of no importance whether the monks all wash their feet together in the same trough or have individual bowls. Lanfranc's *Constitutions* identify occasions when the monks are to read in the text on the instruction

---

1   G. Lawless, *Augustine of Hippo and his Monastic Rule* (Oxford, 1987).
2   *RB*, 38 (On the weekly reader), ed. A. de Vogüé and J. Neufville (Paris, 1972), p. 574.
3   Sedeant omnes in unum et legat unus Collationes vel Vitas Patrum aut certe aliquid quod aedificet audientes, non autem Eptaticum aut Regum, quia infirmis intellectibus non erit utile illa hora hanc scripturam audire, aliis vero horis legantur.
4   *PL*, 87.1099–1113, and see C. M. Aherne, *Valerio of Bierzo, an Ascetic of the Late Visigothic Period* (Washington, 1949).
5   *The Monastic Constitutions of Lanfranc*, ed. D. Knowles and C. N. L. Brooke (Oxford, 2002), p. 2.

of novices. After dinner (prandium) the monks collect their books from the dormitory and go and study (studendum) in their places in the cloister until the bell rings for vespers. After Vespers they go again to the dormitory to fetch their books and return to the cloister for more study.[6]

But where is the cultivation of any form of 'culture' to fit into the life of a monk if he is to have no leisure in the modern sense of having time for recreation but must be always earnestly at improving work? Where does the *otium* so much desired by Augustine and others in late antiquity belong in the monastic agenda? The two pleasures of leisure, as Pliny identifies them, are reading and relaxation: 'ipse ad villam partim studiis partim desidia fruor, quorum utrumque ex otio nascitur'.[7] It is mostly a question of having enough room to turn round in one's thoughts. Pliny says that a bookish landowner needs only enough land to refresh himself by strolling along perhaps one pathway. On a modest estate he can know every vine and every bush.[8] In a profound sense, the monk can still enjoy *otium*, in the sense of retirement from the world to contemplate what is really important.

The anonymous twelfth-century 'little book on the different orders' says that 'the life of a hermit can be compared to the sheep when it is grazing'. This is a life 'ubi et quies potest esse summa et utilitas fructuum est maxima'. There is nothing wasted in the life of a sheep. It produces wool, leather, meat and milk.[9] There is a similar conception in the literature of a tightness of economy in the life of a truly 'cultured' monk whose intellectual energies are properly harnessed to the production of spiritual fruits.

Among the writings relating to medieval English monasticism, or having an origin there, are a number which tell us a great deal about the assumptions which define this monastic spirituality, with a few sharply English glimpses. Bede's *Life of St Cuthbert* describes how Cuthbert, who was an active small boy who loved competitive games, was prompted to give up idle games by an encounter with a boy younger than himself. From that time on 'the Holy Spirit taught him inwardly'.[10] The monk is to acquire his culture – and it will have different characteristics from the modern ones – by a process of 'formation' in which his mind and heart are taught a pattern and a way of thinking, where the teacher is the Holy Spirit. The monk is to aspire to become a microcosm of heaven in this life precisely because he is enjoying a foretaste of the intellectual and spiritual communication-become-communion, which was Augustine's picture of heaven.

St Hugh of Lincoln (b. c.1140), Carthusian and bishop, became a child oblate when he was eight. He enjoyed his early lessons and submitted readily to the discipline of the religious life. He would say that in truth he had never sampled

6   Ibid., p. 218.
7   Pliny, *Letters*, II.ii.2, ed. R. A. B. Mynors (Oxford, 1963), p. 38.
8   Scholasticis porro dominis, ut hic est, sufficit abunde tantum soli, ut revelare caput, reficere oculos, reptare per limitem unamque semitam terere omnesque viteculas suas nosse et numerare arbusculas possint. Pliny, *Letters*, I.xxiv.4.
9   *Libellis de diversis ordinibus*, ed. G. Constable and B. Smith, OMT (Oxford, 1972), p. 9.
10 *Two Lives of St Cuthbert, Bede's Life*, Chapter 1, ed. B. Colgrave (Cambridge, 1940), p. 159.

the joys (gaudia) of this world. 'Iocos numquam didici, numquam scivi'. Denying himself amusement he applied himself earnestly to the sweetness of heavenly doctrine and he meditated on it day and night. As he became a youth he showed himself full of wisdom and understanding (discretionis et scientie).[11]

In Aelred of Rievaulx we have an important English monastic figure by adoption. He, like Anselm, left a literature which conveys the flavour of the culture he encouraged, this time in a Cistercian environment. In his twelfth-century *De spiritali amicitia*,[12] Aelred envisages monkish friends as present to one another in the same house, and holding their conversations as though there were three not two present: the friends and Christ with them. Monastic friendship is a spiritual exercise.

Aelred of Rievaulx, writing *De spiritali amicitia*, begins with a Prologue in which he describes how when he 'was still a boy at school' he took immense pleasure in being with his friends, 'and nothing seemed sweeter, nothing more delightful, nothing more profitable, than to love and be loved'. His readers would – were meant to – catch the echoes of Augustine's *Confessions*,[13] and Ailred leads them lightly on down a path strewn with patristic allusions, to the story of his first encounters with the serious reading of Scripture and his realisation that there was more to life than 'larking about with one's mates'. And so Book I begins with the memorable opening to the dialogue between Aelred and Ivo, 'Here am I and here are you and I hope that Christ will make a third'.[14] Their talk is in the presence of a divine and human companion. As he lay dying, Aelred had all the monks of Rievaulx called to him and he asked their permission to leave their company as he had done whenever he had had to go on a journey away from the abbey in his lifetime. 'We have a good Lord and now it pleases my soul to see his face'. Reviewing his life, the thing that strikes him most forcibly is that he has 'always loved peace and the salvation of the brethren and inward quiet'.[15]

Aelred's reflections take us to *amicitia* and the 'culture of community'. The Western monk is typically not a solitary, though England had its hermits. For most, the essence of the monastic life, and one of the reasons why Isidore of Seville drew 'monk' (monachus) from monas, in his *Etymologiae*,[16] was that it was lived in unity in community. Moreover, although it was in the physical sense usually quite a small community, composed of the monks who lived together in a particular house, it consciously united itself and its members with the greater eternal community of the City of God.[17] As Thomas of Chobham puts it in his probably late twelfth-century *Summa de arte praedicandi*, there will be a *iocunda societas* when angels and humankind share one heart and one mind. He cites Psalm 132:1, which proclaims how good and how joyous it is for brothers to

[11] *Magna Vita Sancti Hugonis*, ed. D. L. Douie and D. H. Farmer (Oxford, 1985), pp. 6, 8, 9.
[12] CCCM, 1.
[13] Augustine, *Confessions*, I.xi.17.7 and II.ii.2.1
[14] Ailred of Rievaulx, *De spiritali amicitia*, CCCM, 1, pp. 287–9.
[15] Walter Daniel, *The Life of Ailred*, ed. M. Powicke (Oxford, 1950, repr. 1978), pp. 57–8.
[16] Isidore, *Etymologiae*, VII.xiii.1, ed. W. M. Lindsay (Oxford, 1911).
[17] Thomas of Chobham, *Summa de Arte Praedicandi*, IV, ed. F. Morenzoni, CCCM, 82 (Turnhout, 1988), p. 121, line 1039.

dwell together in unity. This is a text much beloved of Aelred of Rievaulx in his *Speculum caritatis* and in his *De spiritali amicitia*.

Saints set examples. That is one of the things they are for, traditionally speaking. They could be brought into the 'community' by report, for would-be fellow-saints to imitate. Monks could expect to hear approved saints' lives read liturgically; a few examples survive of English legendaries put together for that purpose.[18] Hints of saintly conduct in English monastic life are not hard to find in the literature. Hugh of Lincoln never got behind with things. He was never guilty of causing those interruptions or delays in the steady round of the life of the house that his biographer calls *morantia*.[19] He was always present, ready, correct, gathered and focussed. There are also examples to be found in less relentlessly practical people. The eleventh-century *Life* of St Birinus of Dorchester on Thames, 'apostle of Wessex', has some literary pretensions. Among them is a conceit that Birinus himself is the 'school of every virtue':

> Erat omnibus virtutis scola, boni operis forma, magisterium vite, ordo iustitie, firmissima fidei disciplina, severitatis exemplar, speculum honestatis, religionis liber, pagina sanctitatis.[20]

To use a fellow monk or an abbot as an example is to use him as a model, but at a psychological distance. The practice of monastic friendship of a more interactive kind was a great enricher of the 'culture' of medieval monastic life, though it required careful definition and control if it was to serve that purpose, and not lead to dangerous 'special friendships'. The 'culture' of the foretaste of heaven in the community of monastic 'friends' with Christ in their midst was, or was expected to be, a somewhat stately gavotte of souls. The reader of Anselm of Bec cannot help but be struck by the way he ends his apparently affectionately personal and individual letters to Henry and Maurice (at Canterbury with Lanfranc, who was now Archbishop), by telling them to exchange the letters and read one another's, since everything which Anselm has said applies to both alike. Such letters are, to the modern eye, more form than substance, from the point of view of the expression of special affection. Their purpose was quite different. It was to evince the spirit of a common culture of *amicitia*. To Henry the monk he writes 'whatever I have written to Dom Gundulph, I have said to you'. And to Gundulph he writes: 'I have written another letter to Dom Henry; but exchange yours for his throughout; and what is yours is his and what is his is yours' (et tua sit sua et sua sit tua).[21]

The evidence of letters gives us access to a monastic culture which, like the drawing of comparisons with saintly lives lived elsewhere and in other times, extends beyond the particular community, and which the paradox of this 'detached intimacy' is inhabited by 'absent friends'. For the author of classical

---

18   *Three Eleventh-Century Anglo-Latin Saints' Lives*, ed. R. C. Love, OMT (Oxford, 1996), pp. xxix–xxxiii.
19   *Magna Vita Sancti Hugonis*, ed. Douie and Farmer, p.11.
20   *Three Eleventh-Century Anglo-Latin Saints' Lives*, ed. Love, p. 4.
21   Letters 4, 5, *Anselmi Opera Omnia*, ed. F. S. Schmitt (Stuttgart, 1968), vol. 3, pp. 105 and 107.

antiquity, letters are a natural human way of talking to an absent friend. 'I have nothing to write about that I did not say yesterday,' Cicero admits to Atticus, but my illness keeps me awake and it does not allow me to be awake without being miserable (sine summo dolore) so I write as though I were talking to you'.[22] This was a theme equally congenial to Christian letter-writers. Jerome's letter VII was written jointly to three friends, Chromatius, Iovinus, Eusebius. That did not prevent it from being an intimate letter, especially to one who was at the time living in the desert of Chalcis. 'I talk to your letter,' he says, 'and it speaks to me; it is the only thing in these parts which speaks Latin' (nunc cum vestris litteris fabular ... illae mecum loquuntur, illae hic tantum Latine sciunt). When he reads the letter it is as though his friends were in front of his eyes.[23]

Some of the best evidence for Anselm of Canterbury relates to Anselm's time at Bec, but as Eadmer makes plain in his *Vita*, he did not change his approach to the life of a community when he came to England; indeed it was his passionate desire to recreate at Canterbury the life in which he had been happy and fulfilled at Bec.[24] The early letters of Anselm of Canterbury include examples in which he writes to young monks who had left with Lanfranc or joined him at Canterbury, notably the Henry and Maurice mentioned above. He also wrote, with flowery affection but rather infrequently, to the same Gundulph who, while he was at Bec, used to weep when he talked, watering with his tears the seeds Anselm was sowing.[25] In due course Gundulph became Bishop of Rochester and Anselm abruptly stopped calling him *te* and began to call him *vos*, as propriety required. The reader is brought up with a jolt, for this is surely evidence of a theory of friendship rather than of its realities as a vehicle for the stimulation of mutual interest and mutual effort.

Anselm's teaching of the monks at Bec must have had the character of this somewhat abstract and impersonal 'community spiritual exercise', and here we have evidence which takes us inside the life and culture of a community in a way letters cannot directly do. The opening passages of the *Monologion* and other indications throughout his writings – not least the vignette of the weeping Gundulph – show us a group of devoted pupils learning to use their powers of reasoning to think about God, but at the same time engaged in a devotional exercise. The two blended in the *Monologion* and they are there side by side in the *Proslogion*, where chapters of devotional writing alternate with the chapters of argument, the style quite distinct in the two sorts of passage. Anselm their teacher is also Anselm their spiritual mentor and the admiration the monks evidently felt for him is to be applied firmly to the purpose of the cultivation of the rational souls, *animus* and *anima* together.

It has already been suggested that English monastic culture is not normally the culture of the hermit life, although there are notable exceptions in the later medieval period. The strong thrust of Benedictine monastic theory is the fundamental community character of monastic culture, in which the spiritual life is

[22] Cicero, *Letters to Atticus*, 177 (IX.10), ed. D. R. Shackleton-Bailey (London, 1999).
[23] Jerome, *Epistolae*, VII.2, ed. I. Hilberg, CSEL (Vienna, 1910–18), 3 vols., 54, p. 27.
[24] Eadmer, *Life of St Anselm*, II.viii, ed. R.W.Southern (Oxford, 1962), pp. 69ff.
[25] *Vita Gundulfi*, PL 159.817.

a shared life. There is also a contention that the private individual is less likely to get to heaven if he tries to live a holy life on his own in the world. Anselm of Canterbury is far from being the only author urging young men and women not to leave the safe road to heaven, for a crusading adventure (boys) or a marriage (girls) is no substitute.

In a sequence of passages in Walter Daniel's *Life*, we read how a novice 'valde instabilis animo' came to Aelred as novice-master and expressed a wish to leave, of Aelred's distress at seeing him go out into a world where his salvation was at risk, of the way he wandered aimlessly in the woods until he came accidentally back into the grounds of the monastery where Aelred fell on his neck with the words from Luke 2:48 which greet the return of the prodigal son. This was the period, so his biographer says, when Aelred began to write letters 'sensu serenissimas et litera luculentas' and to compose the *Speculum caritatis*, which is an image (imago) 'Dei amoris et proximum'.[26]

In Walter Daniel's *Life* of Aelred there is, however, a passage which suggests that monastic culture in its essence could be attained by an individual living in the most unpromising circumstances, although the story is told with an ending, and the ending is Aelred's decision to become a Cistercian and to live the monastic culture in reality. While Aelred was still living in the world, at the court of the King of Scotland, he dressed simply, in a prophetic foretaste of his future vestment as a monk: 'prognosia quadam veraci future vite sue prophetans laudabilem paupertatem'. He always behaved with 'affabilitas and an immense copia benevolencie'.[27] One of the *militares* of the court became jealous and tried to stir up resentment against Aelred, eventually giving way to an outburst at a full assembly of the court, in the King's presence, reviling and abusing him. Here was the antithesis of the loving community of monastic life. Aelred's response was masterly: 'You say well, excellent knight,' he replied. 'Everything you say is true. For I am sure you hate lying and love me.' 'Monks should read and reread this passage,' exclaims Walter Daniel (legant hunc locum monachi et sepius relegant).[28] Here was the young 'Joseph', not yet a monk, bringing into a most worldly and unpromising environment the essence of the life of the monastic community, where monks love one another in a community of mutual truth-telling for one another's good. It is not possible to discover from the text whether Aelred intended any irony. Probably not.

Medieval kings, barons and bishops did not retire. It is their deaths not their leaving parties which mark the end-dates by which we refer to them. Nor was 'going on holiday' in its more modern sense a feature of such lives, except perhaps for pilgrimage; and if Chaucer is anything to go by, a late medieval pilgrimage was also a holiday. Yet even for those outside the ambit of the professional religious life, there was a culture of anticipating heaven in journeyings that were also consciously spiritual travels. For many centuries, Benedictine monastic life in the West offered an opportunity for retirement from the world from birth. The idea of entering a monastery and entering this culture became an adult choice

---

[26] Daniel, *Life of Ailred*, ed. Powicke, pp. 24–6 at 25.
[27] Ibid., p. 5.
[28] Ibid., p. 7.

towards the end of the eleventh century, in circumstances sketched by Guibert of Nogent in the opening passages of his *De vita sua*.[29] Suddenly old soldiers and their wives were deciding to enter monasteries and live out their lives (separately) as religious. These were, it is true, medieval 'fashions' in retirement that do not seem to have carried the same assumptions that this might be a time for greater intellectual productivity, so we do not always know directly what those who retired did with their time. But that does not mean they were not mentally and spiritually busy; indeed the official presumption was that they were. In the twelfth century we find academics doing it. Peter Abelard, after much moving in and out of monastic life, retired to Cluny. Alain of Lille, following a different fashion, retired to Cîteaux rather later in the century. These retired to give their full attention to the cultivation of their souls and to prayer, the development of the inner man (interior homo)[30] in a solitary conversation with God. They could thus hope to 'catch up' with their more fortunate monastic brothers who had had a lifetime at this task.

But Aelred gives us the solitary journey of the soul of the religious too, portraying this as equally a facet of the spiritual culture of the monk. Aelred encouraged the idea of making little visits to the inner and eternal realm, so that the mind may with practice become accustomed[31] to heavenly experiences and by 'visits' the soul has a foretaste of its future reward, 'ubi quasdam futurae suae remunerationis primitias incipiat praegustare'.[32] The absence of distractions is not merely a necessary precondition for the experience that is being striven for, but in some sense it becomes that experience. As Aelred of Rievaulx puts it, once the withdrawal is complete and the distractions shut out, the sheer absence of unquietness, disorder, gnawing painful feelings, their replacement with delight, tranquillity, harmony, there is a transformation and a secure happiness.[33] Indeed, once all these conditions are fulfilled, the enquiring soul may find it is being helped to go further than it possibly could alone. God takes control and the soul is enabled to go beyond what it could do by itself. 'I entered into my innermost self as well as I could, at your instigation, for you made yourself my helper', says Augustine to God.[34]

But paradoxically, despite Aelred's talk of *securitas*, this concentrated silence and heightened inward spiritual experience is not a state in which human beings

---

[29] Guibert of Nogent, *De Vita Sua*, ed. G. Bourgin (Paris, 1906).

[30] A phrase used by Augustine, for example, Letter 147, 17, CSEL, 44, p. 318, but also quite common in the patristic period.

[31] In hoc statu innumerabilibus caelestium affectuum incentives assuefacta mens.

[32] Aelred of Rievaulx, *De speculo caritatis* II.11, ed. A. Hoste, CCCM, 1 (1971), p. 78, line 471.

[33] Cum enim homo ab hoc exteriori tumultu intra secretarium suae mentis sese receperit, et contra circumstrepentium turbas vanitatum, clauso ostio, interiores gazas perlustraverit, nihilque occurrerit inquietum, nihil inordinatum, nihil quod remordeat, nihil quod oblatret, sed omnia iucunda, omnia concordantia, omnia pacifica, omnia tranquilla, ... oritur hinc subito mira securitas, ex securitate mira iucunditas, Ailred, *De Speculo Caritatis* III. iii.6, ed. A. Hoste, CCCM, 1, p. 108.

[34] Intravi in intima mea duce te et potui, quoniam factus es adiutor meus. Intravi et vidi qualicumque oculo animae meae supra eundem oculum animae meae, supra mentem meam lucem incommutabilem: *Confessions* (VII.x.16)

can long remain in this life. It takes too much effort. The body interrupts. It is hungry. One's shoulder itches. A pretty girl walks past. In Anselm's *Proslogion* the words *paululum, aliquantulum* emphasise that this will be only for a little while.[35] Nor can everyone taking such a holiday hope to experience its high point. 'When the mind is purged,' says Aelred of Rievaulx, 'how much more devoutly, how much more safely' does one enter the divine embrace, and the 'sanctuary' where the soul is face to face with Christ and bathed in an indescribable light and a sweetness beyond common experience.[36] This, for those to whom it is vouchsafed, is a moment of safety that is also a moment of rapture.[37]

It is time to return by way of conclusion to the question of education, and the place of an intellectual or rational strand in this culture of monastic spirituality. Mediaeval English monks from the twelfth century are (by choice or by chance) not in the world of the burgeoning schools and the later universities. Anselm's *Proslogion* begins with poetry and alternates it with prose for the sections of theological argument that require a different kind of precision. His serious theology was not a style of thing so monastic that Anselm's interest in it did not survive his translation to the archbishopric. The only notable difference between the kind of thing he wrote before and after this major change in his life, is the growing sophistication of his awareness that not all his readers were going to be like his monks at Bec, hanging lovingly on his every word; some of them were going to be argumentative, even showing the viciousness characteristic of even the earliest academe. He learned that from his encounter with the ambitious Roscelin of Compiègne, which obliged him to write more than one version of the *De incarnatione verbi* in an effort to clear his name of the imputation of heresy. But it was concerned with the topics which would be taken over by academic theology as the twelfth century proceeded: the existence and nature of God, the Trinity, the incarnation, the sacraments, and the *famosissima quaestio* of the relationship of human free will, with divine foreknowledge, predestination and grace.

Walter Daniel's account of the qualities of Aelred's mind, adjusted for hagiographical conventions, is a useful vignette of one way the distinction could be drawn between the academic and the monastic at the period of their historical bifurcation. Aelred, says Walter Daniel, had by 'infusion of the Holy Spirit' (infusione Spiritus Sancti) a far better grasp of the liberal arts than those who

---

35 Proslogion, 1, Anselm, *Opera Omnia*, vol. 1, p. 97.

36 Factoque silentio ab omnibus corporalibus, ab omnibus sensibilibus, ab omnibus mutabilibus, in id quod est, et sic semper est, et idipsum est, in illud unum perspicacem figat intuitum, vacans et videns quoniam Dominus ipse est Deus [Ps. 45:11] ... sabbatizans sine dubio Sabbatum sabbatorum. Ailred of Rievaulx, *De Speculo Caritatis* III,vi.17, CCCM, vol. 1, p. 113.

37 Cum enim homo ab hoc exteriori tumultu intra secretarium suae mentis sese receperit, et contra circumstrepentium turbas vanitatum, clauso ostio, interiores gazas perlustraverit, nihilque occurrerit inquietum, nihil inordinatum, nihil quod remordeat, nihil quod oblatret, sed omnia iucunda, omnia concordantia, omnia pacifica, omnia tranquilla, ... oritur hinc subito NB the transforming moment theme not confined to conversion mira securitas, ex securitate mira iucunditas, Ailred, *De Speculo Caritatis* III.iii.6, CCCM, 1, p. 108.

learn in the conventional way from a master. These get a sketchy knowledge. They learn 'Aristotelicas figuras et Pitagorice computacionis infinitos calculos'. Aelred understood in the Scriptures and taught others (intellexit in scripturas et docuit), about the God who dwells in light inaccessible and is no *figura* but the truth. This God is himself the object of all knowledge we have in this world (universe doctrine naturalis). But he is a truth who speaks for himself and does not need to be dressed up in fine words in order to be understood (se sola veritas contenta est nec verbis indiget ad deprecandum composites vel intelligendum).[38] This was not an anti-rational stance. Walter Daniel is clear that words derive their full meaning (sufficiencia) from *racio*. Nor is this, in the fullest sense, an anti-intellectual stance. But it is opposed to reliance on technical knowledge. When Aelred, as Daniel puts it, absolutely refused to put the rules of grammar before the truth (refutabat omnino regulas grammaticas veritati anteferre),[39] he had the authority of Gregory the Great's *dictum* that the Holy Spirit is not constrained by the rules of Donatus.

'Consider the meaning of the word monk (vocabulum monachi)', says Jerome (Letter XIV.6). 'What are you, a solitary, doing in a crowd?' (quid facis in turba, qui solus es). I have been suggesting that the mediaeval monk, on the contrary, had come to see the monastic life as a joint enterprise, a partnership with his brother-monks in the company of Christ. Jerome's strictures in this same letter about the need to avoid the Scylla of lust on the one side and the Charybdis of self-indulgence on the other work just as well in community, especially a community where friends tell one another the uncomfortable truth. Jerome was urging his correspondent, Heliodorus, to withdraw himself from the world. He presses Eustochium to do the same thing, at the beginning of the famous Letter XXII.

The author of the *Libellis de diversis ordinibus*[40] does not disapprove of those who have known the contemplative life but have returned for a time to the world to help their fellow-men, even if that has made them get involved in litigation, land-holding and the calling in of revenues. This is what Jacob did after he has embraced Rachel whom he loved (post amplexus desideratae Rachelis) but returned to fertile Leah. The *Libellis de diversis ordinibus* considers the merits of the Cistercian way of life and that of other communities that set themselves apart, searching assiduously for Old Testament precedent.[41] This is a monastic way whose merit lies in unity of life: 'quam concors spiritus simul coadunaverit, ut unum spiritum habentes simul viverent, unum sentirent, in nullo discrepare in alterutrum'.[42]

A community of mediaeval monks or nuns (and I am conscious that I have left out the nuns and any different priorities of theirs in this short paper), has gone apart from the world, but they have done it together. They have formed a

---

38 Daniel, *Life of Ailred*, ed. Powicke, p. 26.
39 Ibid., p. 27.
40 *Libellis de diversis ordinibus*, ed. Constable and Smith, p. 42.
41 Ibid., p. 44.
42 Ibid., p. 48.

community. It is a small and inward-looking community. But it is also a micro-cosm of the world of eternity and therefore in the largest sense outward-looking. It has a capacity to embrace the intellectual activities of the age, but it sees a need to do so selectively and in a manner that conjoins spirituality with the secular intellectual endeavour. It is a living theatre. Liturgical drama takes place there, not only in the sense of such experiences as the *Quem quaeritis*. It is a great play of life that goes on in the successful monastery.

The Monks of Durham and the Study of Scripture

A. J. PIPER

The evidence for the resources available to the Durham monks for the study of Scripture is fuller than for any other medieval monastery in Britain. More books belonging to the community survive than for any other house and there are important inventories of its holdings from the twelfth and the late fourteenth centuries, together with records of substantial gifts, notably those by Bishop William of St Calais (d. 1096) and Bishop Hugh of Le Puiset (d. 1195). The picture that emerges over the span of more than four and half centuries during which the monks formed the cathedral chapter in Durham (1083–1539) is not perhaps startling, and one of its chief values is probably that it is so very full. Nonetheless it is impressive for the way in which the community found the resources to keep abreast of developments in scriptural studies over a very long period, enabling its members to acquire an understanding of the Bible that would have entitled them to hold their heads high among their contemporaries in every generation. It is also very clear that a particularly high priority was attached to obtaining aids to the study of the Psalms, no doubt because they occupied a central place in the liturgy to which the monks devoted so much of their time; as the biblical texts that were the most familiar to junior monks they were an obvious starting point for engaging in scriptural studies, but it may also be that a deeper understanding of these texts was seen as spiritually desirable. The way in which the last generations of monks acquired early printed books for their own needs, and their habit of annotating them, sheds important light on the place that they accorded to Scripture in their studies, a place that the propaganda purveyed by the reformers of the sixteenth century might all too easily obscure.

The Durham monks, like the great majority of medieval English Benedictine communities, were not noted for making major original contributions to the study of Scripture; unlike the mendicants and university men their literary energies were largely directed to the fields of historiography and hagiography, fields in which they could give full play to expressing their corporate *esprit de corps*. The one significant exception is found, not surprisingly, in the early period. The longest, and most popular, work by Lawrence of Durham, prior c.1149–1154, was the *Hypognosticon*, a title which he used to mean an abbreviation.[1] The bulk of its 4684 lines of verse summarise Old and New Testament passages relating to the redemption of man, but, unable to resist the lure of hagiography, the

---

[1] Sharpe, *Latin Writers*, p. 360 lists twenty medieval copies.

ninth and final book brings Lawrence's theme down to his own day, including material about Cuthbert and other English saints.[2] He describes the composition as an activity of his leisure time. A couple of generations earlier, Symeon, the greatest of Durham's historians, could demonstrate his command of Scripture when need arose: in assembling quotations from patristic authorities bearing on views expressed by Origen, he was unable at one point to find an appropriate exposition of Ezekiel 16:55, and so himself quoted relevant verses from Isaiah.[3]

Yet if few monks felt called to write about Scripture it nonetheless suffused almost all that they wrote. Some passages in Symeon's account of the see of Durham from its beginnings down to 1096 are well buttressed by Biblical allusions, a high proportion, not unnaturally for a monk, to the Psalms.[4] When the continuator of the house history, commonly taken to be Robert Greystanes (d. 1333 or 1334), came to describe the peculiar circumstances in which Durham's study-house in Oxford was established in the late thirteenth century he likened this happy development to the redemption occasioned through the sin of Judas.[5] When a fourteenth-century prior wrote to the monks at the cell of Holy Island and ordered them to desist from ridiculing the prior there, he noted 'in antiqua lege Moysi precipiebatur ut presbiteros eligeret scilicet seniores quorum gloria est canicies que sapientiam denotat et designat'.[6] As well as controversial writings, Uthred of Boldon (d. 1397), greatest of all Durham's theologians, produced treatises on the monastic life which take the gospels as their touchstone.[7] When monks came to preach, as many did in the later Middle Ages, they naturally needed a sound knowledge of the Bible and its interpretation.[8]

When Bishop William of St Calais founded Durham's Benedictine community in 1083, by bringing together the twenty-three monks who had re-established monastic life at Jarrow and Wearmouth some years earlier, they inherited from the previous community of St Cuthbert a stock of books. To judge by those that survive, gospel-books held in high honour figured prominently, most notably of course the Lindisfarne Gospels. But there was also an impressive abbreviated

---

2   A. G. Rigg, *A History of Anglo-Latin Literature 1066–1422*, (Cambridge, 1992), pp. 54–56, with a substantial summary of the contents.

3   R. Sharpe, 'Symeon, Hildebert and the Errors of Origen', in *Symeon of Durham Historian of Durham and the North*, ed. D. Rollason (Stamford, 1998), pp. 282–300, esp. 293–94.

4   Symeon of Durham, *Libellus de Exordio atque Procursu istius hoc est Dunhelmensis Ecclesie*, ed. D. Rollason, (Oxford, 2000), p. 337.

5   M. R. Foster, 'Durham Monks at Oxford *c.*1286–1381: a House of Studies and its Inmates', *Oxoniensia*, 55 (1990), 101 n. 12, correcting the text as printed *Historiae Dunelmensis scriptores tres* ... [ed. J. Raine], SS, 9 (1839), p. 73 line 2 'peccatum. Inde' to 'peccatum Iude'.

6   BL, Cotton MS Faustina A. VI, fol. 9r.

7   W. A. Pantin, 'Two Treatises of Uthred of Boldon on the Monastic Life' in *Studies in Medieval History presented to Frederick Maurice Powicke*, ed. R. W. Hunt, W. A. Pantin and R. W. Southern (Oxford, 1948), pp. 363–85.

8   One of the earliest indulgences, dated 1277, for those hearing the monks preaching refers to them doing so in the cathedral or the city of Durham, DCM (Durham University Library, Archives & Special Collections, Durham Cathedral Muniments), 1.13.Pont.11. *Rites of Durham ... written 1593* [ed. J. T. Fowler], SS, 107 (1903), pp. 46 in the cathedral galilee 'every holy day and Sunday ... at one of the clock after noone', and 88 where the connection between the study of Scripture and preaching is made.

copy of Cassiodorus' commentary on the Psalms (B.II.30)[9] to which two replacement leaves were added during the earlier twelfth century, presumably because
the originals were damaged, while a somewhat scruffy copy of Bede on the Apocalypse, 'with a full use of the later insular system of abbreviations', (A.IV.28) was
replaced under Symeon's direction at the same period (B.IV.16).[10]

Bishop William was not slow to supplement the stock, along lines he presumably deemed desirable. Not only is his munificence attested by the fact that he
gave forty-nine books, judging by the list entered in the Bible that he gave,[11] but
by the very high quality of those that survive. As is well known, the selection
reflects the much wider movement at this period in England to build up holdings
of the Fathers.[12] What deserves greater emphasis than it has generally received
is that the focus was rather more sharply defined than that, being primarily
on patristic writings on Scripture, together with Bede's, and in consequence
Ambrose, whose concerns were more theological or moral than scriptural, was
represented by only one book.

Between Bishop William's death in 1096 and c.1160, when a catalogue was
compiled,[13] the monastic book-collection underwent remarkable expansion,
and not only in terms of sheer numbers. It became very much more diverse,
with holdings across a wide range, including for instance an impressive group of
classical texts, probably used for teaching and subsequently to disappear almost
without trace. The foundations laid in the late eleventh century had been built
upon, with more of Bede's commentaries, Ambrose's one major work of exegesis,
his commentary on Luke, and Origen's homilies on Luke, and Chrysostom's on
Hebrews. Jerome's commentaries on the Major Prophets had been acquired, but
not apparently those on Matthew or Mark, works which are not recorded at any
time in Durham. Augustine on Genesis *ad litteram* and his *De consensu evange-
listarum* were now present, and also the collection of sermons on the Epistles
and Gospels, *De uerbis Domini et apostoli*. To the Hrabanus on Matthew given by
Bishop William had been added the *florilegium* of Adalbert of Metz from Gregory
on Job, Haimo of Auxerre on Isaiah, the Pauline epistles and perhaps on the
Apocalypse in an abbreviated form, Robert of Tumbalena on the Song of Songs,
and Berengaudus on the Apocalypse. Although this was by no means a full set of
the Biblical commentaries available in England by c.1130, no popular work was
conspicuous by its absence.[14]

---

9   Manuscripts with press-marks of this kind are in Durham Cathedral Library (DCL).
10 R. A. B. Mynors, *Durham Cathedral Manuscripts to the End of the Twelfth Century*, (Oxford,
    1939), nos. 26 and 70, also pl. 38b (B.IV.16 fol. 2v).
11 *Catalogi veteres librorum ecclesiae cathedral Dunelm*, SS, 7 (1838), pp. 117–18, soon, like
    all the other catalogues referred to below, to be superseded in the Durham volume in the
    Corpus of British Medieval Library Catalogues.
12 R. Gameson, *The Manuscripts of Early Norman England (c. 1066–1130)*, (Oxford 1999),
    pp. 20–7.
13 *Catalogi veteres*, pp. 1–9.
14 This sentence is based on Gameson, *Manuscripts of Early Norman England*, pp. 159–83
    (index of authors and texts), as are the numbers of manuscripts known to him given
    hereafter. The Durham monks later acquired Alcuin on John 0, and on Genesis 0, and
    Hilary on Psalms 0. There is no record of them ever having owned manuscripts containing
    Alcuin on Song of Songs 1, or Ecclesiastes 1, Ambrosiaster on the Pauline epistles 1,

By the latter part of the twelfth century the acquisition strategy of the monks would not of course have been primarily directed at the works of the Biblical commentators but at that relatively newfangled tool, the gloss, which was in process of sweeping all before it. By c.1160 they had made a modest start, with the original entries in the catalogue recording copies of Genesis, two of Isaiah, Matthew, Mark and the Apocalypse, also copies of Anselm of Laon, Ivo of Chartres and Gilbert de la Porrée on the Psalms and eight others, and five on the Pauline epistles; given the date of the catalogue it is perhaps doubtful whether any of the copies of the Psalms or the Pauline epistles can have contained the great gloss by Peter Lombard.[15] The eleven Psalms exactly matched the number of all the others put together, while the interest in the Pauline epistles was part of a wider pattern.[16]

Four of these glossed books came from Prior Lawrence (d. 1154): Anselm and Ivo on the Psalms, Isaiah and one of the Pauline epistles. Although all of these were in some sense duplicates they do raise the more general question of how far the monks themselves were responsible for the development of their book-collection, how far books given to them fell in with their plans; in theory an unsolicited gift might not be particularly welcome, but in fact the records of the collections do not mention any significant number of works that stand out as thoroughly eccentric, so it seems safe to conclude that donors, not unnaturally, set out to please the monks with the books that they gave. This certainly appears to be the case with the most munificent of all benefactors of their collections, Bishop Hugh of Le Puiset (1153–95) who gave a total of seventy-five books.[17] As well as two complete Bibles, the larger of them of surpassing magnificence, replete with illuminated historiated initials and fashionable blind-stamped bindings on each of the four volumes, he gave some twenty Biblical glosses, some of them the best that money could buy, as befitted a man with a highly developed taste for lavish display. A precise chronology of his gifts, based on a close scrutiny of the surviving books, remains to be established, but if they are assumed to have been given immediately after the completion of the c.1160 catalogue, then Hugh added to the monks' coverage of glosses the Pentateuch, the Minor Prophets, Luke and John, together with Peter Lombard on both the Psalms and the Pauline epistles. He also provided them with the immensely popular contemporary reworking of Biblical history by Peter Comestor, the *Historia scholastica*, and another copy of Gregory on Job.

For all his impressive aristocratic connections Bishop Hugh liked to surround

Caesarius of Arles on the Apocalypse 1, Haymo of Auxerre on the Song of Songs 1 + ?1, or Minor Prophets 0, Hilary on Matthew 1, Hrabanus on Pentateuch 0, Samuel and Kings ? 1, Judith 0, Ecclesiasticus 0, Jeremiah 0, Maccabees 0, or the Pauline epistles 0, Origen on Matthew 1, Paschasius on Lamentations 1 or Matthew 1, or Pelagius on the Pauline epistles 1.

[15] C. F. R. de Hamel, *Glossed Books of the Bible and the Origins of the Paris Booktrade* (Woodbridge, 1984), pp. 7–8, on the chronology of Lombard's publication; in giving the number of glossed books in the Durham catalogue as thirty-one he includes those recorded in added entries.

[16] De Hamel, *Glossed Books*, p. 4.

[17] *Catalogi veteres*, pp. 118–19.

himself with the new breed of university clerics, men who could sport the style 'Master'. Among them was Robert de Addington, who was in Paris for a time, probably from the late 1170s to the early 1190s, and came back as a 'Master'.[18] Among the thirty-eight books that he deposited at St Victor's, six or seven survive as his gifts to the monks; with the exception of Peter of Poitiers's Distinctions on the Psalms, all of them were Biblical glosses and contributed very substantially towards completing the monks' coverage. Robert in fact possessed what appears to have been a full set, so if all of these passed to the monks they will have achieved complete coverage by c.1200, a major landmark in their acquisition of the necessary tools for the study of Scripture, and one that was to stand them in good stead some two centuries later. It is possible that Robert was partly financed in his book-collecting activities by the monks; if so, they were willing to lay out funds on acquiring gloss-books of high quality, some clad in fashionable Parisian blind-stamped bindings.

The evidence for the growth of the monastic library over most of the thirteenth century is almost entirely confined to inscriptions in the surviving books. Among these are numbers of gloss-books and one, containing Isaiah, Jeremiah and Lamentations, was a duplicate that was quite clearly deliberately acquired, for it has an inscription explicitly stating that it was bought from the executors of Mr William, who was presumably William of Durham (d. 1249), of University College, Oxford fame, donor of copies of Kings, the Sapiential books and Maccabees with gloss.[19] Further copies came in of the Historia scholastica (B.I.33), and of Gregory on Job (B.II.32), the latter originally belonging to Durham's cell at Coldingham. Two Englishmen among the modern commentators in the Paris schools were represented: the Franciscan Alexander of Hales on the Gospels, a gift of Mr Gilbert Aristotle,[20] and works of the most renowned commentator to be produced by later medieval England, Stephen Langton, in two books, one containing Ecclesiasticus (A.III.28) and the other the Heptateuch, Kings, three of the Sapiential books, and the Major and Minor Prophets (A.I.7). The latter was given by Ralph, prior of Durham's cell at Finchale; he presumably knew exactly what would be a welcome addition to the collection, even in a manuscript that might aptly be described as utilitarian. Parts of four Langton commentaries are also found in a notoriously complex manuscript (A.III.12), which includes dicta on the Psalms by Robert Grosseteste (d. 1253). Later in the thirteenth century the vicar of one of the monks' churches in Scotland gave them a substantial manuscript, of no great age, and this would have been particularly welcome since one of its four texts was Alcuin on St John's gospel, a rarity, for which there is no earlier evidence of a copy in the monastery.[21]

The crowning glory among the thirteenth-century acquisitions was the responsibility of Prior Bertram of Middleton (1244–58): he procured for the

---

18 Mynors, Durham Cathedral Manuscripts, pp. 78–82.
19 The inscription recording the purchase, A.III.18 fol. 1, is in the same hand as that recording William's gift, A.II.7 fol. 1. Other acquisitions are A.IV.14 Luke, A.II.15 Gospels, A.III.15 various books, A.III.22 Ezekiel and Daniel, A.III.14 Sapiential books, A.II.8 various books.
20 B. Smalley, The Gospels in the Schools c.1100–c.1280 (London, 1985), pp. 146–7.
21 B.III.17; the other texts are Jerome on Isaiah and Ezekiel, and Anselm of Laon on John.

house a nearly complete set of the postils that run under the name of the Dominican Hugh of St Cher, probably composed c.1232–36, very much in the tradition
of Langton's version of the 'biblical moral' school, and destined to become the
great warhorse among later medieval Biblical commentaries.[22] This put Durham
up in the vanguard so far as aids to the study of Scripture was concerned, but,
while the volumes were large, with generous margins, the script was the tight
university type and in one volume (A.III.21) the spaces left for the initials
were never filled; this has *pecia* numbers in the margins, one of the very earliest
examples in England of this evidence for commercial production in a university
context [see plate 5].[23] Interestingly Prior Bertram also saw fit to obtain a further
copy of Bernard's sermons on the Song of Songs (B.IV.23), the highly spiritual
treatment of Scripture matching the more technical.

It was probably late in the thirteenth century that a Durham monk called
Thomas of Westoe built up a collection of over twenty books while studying
in Oxford. He made a list of them, perhaps when returning to Durham in or
before 1309.[24] His chief purpose seems to have been to equip himself to grasp
the theological controversies engaging the attention of university men during
the 1290s. His one notable deviation from this course was the acquisition of
the postils on the Psalms and Luke by Nicholas de Gorron (d. c.1295), also
those on the Pauline epistles which were perhaps the work of Peter of Taren-
taise sometimes attributed to Nicholas (A.III.13, 31). In seeking to supersede
the Biblical commentary of Hugh of St Cher, Nicholas failed and the Durham
monks did not show great enthusiasm for his work.[25] When Thomas acquired
these texts it was probably not clear that the judgement of history would go this
way and in any case his acquisition may have been to a degree opportunistic:
there is evidence that the two surviving manuscripts may have been a booksell-
er's unwanted stock.[26]

Thomas was a pioneer among Durham monks studying in Oxford and was
probably there when the decision was made to establish a study-house. Thanks
to a very generous gift by Bishop Hatfield of Durham this small establishment
was transformed in the 1380s into a college where eight young monks and

---

[22] Smalley, *Gospels in the Schools* pp. 118–19, 143. When the chronicler's incomplete
statement is put with the surviving manuscripts, only Isaiah, Jeremiah and Ezekiel are
wanting.

[23] DCL, A.I.12–13, 15–16, A.III.21. Graham Pollard, 'The *pecia* system in the medieval
universities', in *Medieval Scribes, Manuscripts and Libraries. Essays presented to N. R. Ker*,
ed. M. B. Parkes and A. G. Watson (London, 1978), p. 146 and pl. 41.

[24] M. R. James, *A Descriptive Catalogue of the Manuscripts in the Library of Jesus College,
Cambridge*, (London, 1895), pp. 91–2. DCM, Loc.VIII:39, Loc.VII:23.

[25] A copy of the postils on the Pauline epistles in three volumes is recorded in the cloister
collection (*Catalogi veteres*, p. 68), and Prior Ebchester (1446–56) acquired, in circumstances that are not clear, a fine copy of the Pentateuch (A.I.6) that had belonged to
Bishop Langley (d. 1437).

[26] A.III.13 and 31. M. B. Parkes, 'The Provision of Books', *The History of the University of
Oxford II: Late Medieval Oxford*, ed. J. I. Catto and T. A. R. Evans (Oxford, 1992), p.
469.

eight seculars could attend the university, presided over by a warden.[27] This put Durham on a par with Christ Church Canterbury in having its own college and meant that a considerably higher proportion of Durham monks had university experience than in the great majority of Benedictine houses. How far this made their approach to Scripture untypical is, however, difficult to assess.

It was probably in 1315 that a list was drawn up of the books at the study-house.[28] This reveals a collection of some forty-six volumes, of a fairly diverse nature, which perhaps reflects the fact that it had been recently assembled, presumably by moving books that could be spared elsewhere, given that Durham was in no position to lay out large sums on new books at the time. Aids to the study of Scripture numbered nine, with both Augustine and Bede on Genesis and one volume of Gregory on Job, a glossed copy of the Pauline epistles, postils on Job, the Sapiential books, Isaiah, Jeremiah, Daniel, the Minor Prophets and the Catholic epistles, the *Historia scholastica* and William Brito's guide to difficult words in the Bible. It is interesting to note that Bede on Genesis and one volume of postils were not at the study-house but had been pawned at Merton College; they were evidently not regarded as indispensable. This, and the modesty of the collection, probably reflects the fact that the Durham monks in Oxford at this period had completed their education in the cloister, thereby acquiring a thorough grounding in Scripture, and possibly that they were not heavily engaged in preaching. A century later the situation was significantly different.

One of the more distinguished Durham monks in Oxford in the early fourteenth century was Robert Greystanes; the remarkable infrequency with which he is mentioned in the records as being at Durham between 1305 and 1330 suggests that he spent much of this time in Oxford.[29] To judge by the style of the script and the decoration, it was while he was there that he arranged the making of six books. One of them was a copy of Hugh of St Cher's Biblical concordance (A.I.2), a fine book, with an ornamental initial on a gold ground to each letter of the alphabet.[30] Four of the books are primarily assemblages of works by Augustine, in line with the interest then current in Oxford.[31] Apart from the sermons 'De verbis Domini' the works are theological, rather than scriptural, but a seventh book (B.II.15) is extremely close in appearance to two of the Greystanes books (B.II.19 and 20) and was made from a copy long in Durham's possession (B.II.14) of the third and final part of Augustine on the Psalms.

The only other surviving Oxford book-list dates from about 1395.[32] It is much longer than the earlier one, recording some 115 books, and it is much more

27 R. B. Dobson, 'The Black Monks of Durham and Canterbury Colleges: Comparisons and Contrasts' in *Benedictines in Oxford*, ed. H. Wansborough and A. Marett-Crosby (London 1997), pp. 61–94.

28 Printed H. E. D. Blakiston, in *Collectanea. Third Series*, ed. M. Burrows, OHS, 32 (1896), pp. 36-7.

29 Emden, *BRUO*, vol. 2, p. 814.

30 Two of Greystanes' fellows in the community gave concordances: Gilbert of Elwick and Thomas of Lound, see below at n. 42: *Catalogi veteres*, p. 53.

31 W. J. Courtenay, *Schools and Scholars in Fourteenth-Century England*, (Princeton, 1987), pp. 317–24.

32 Ed. Pantin, in *Formularies which bear on the History of Oxford*, I, ed. H. E. Salter, W. A. Pantin and H. G. Richardson, OHS, New Series, 4 (1942), pp. 241-4.

systematically ordered, having sections for various types of book. All save one of the Biblical works are in the first section, for theology books, and they number fifteen. All nine books recorded eighty years earlier are there, and the others are much the same in character, apart from what appears to be an incomplete copy of Josephus' *Jewish Antiquities*, which reworked Biblical narratives and other sources to trace the history of the Jews down to A.D. 70, with brief references to Christ.

Early in the fifteenth century the collection at Oxford was supplemented by two consignments of books from Durham, one in about 1408 and the other in 1409.[33] The first comprised twenty-one books and twelve of these were Biblical gloss-books, an almost complete set, together with some sort of index to the glosses on the Old Testament; it was now clearly seen as desirable that the young monks studying there should have ready access to it as part of their education. The consignment also included Langton on Ecclesiasticus. The second had far fewer Biblical books: one gloss-book and the thirteenth-century copy of Hugh of St Cher on the first half of the Old Testament, which was said in a letter to Archbishop Kemp by Prior Wessington in 1436 to be better written than the duplicate kept in Durham.[34] Old books were evidently thought to serve young monks well.

Just as the fourteenth century saw the production of the most important lists of the collection at Oxford, so too at Durham itself, culminating in the final decade of the century, with fragmentary drafts of catalogues surviving from the middle of the century onwards. Surviving books shed some light on the process of acquisition, but it is frustrating that the thirteenth-century monks do not appear to have attached much importance to inscribing their books with owner-ship notes. Consequently it is not until the mid fourteenth century that it is certain that they possessed a fine late twelfth-century two-volume copy of the *catena* of extracts on the Pauline epistles from Augustine compiled by Florus of Lyon (B.II.34, Cambridge Sidney Sussex Coll. 32), and, much more tantalis-ingly, a thirteenth-century three-volume copy of the commentary in French on the Psalms that has been attributed to Simon of Tournai (A.II.11–13). How this came into the collection and whether it was much used is totally uncertain; in the mid fourteenth century the second volume was in the keeping of one Robert de Hilton, who was not a member of the community, and by that time all three volumes were normally kept in the book-store in the Spendement, along with another apparently in French which subsequently disappears from sight.[35] During the fifteenth century, however, they were brought out and placed in the fixed reference collection in the *Libraria*. During the first half of the fourteenth century a gift from the vicar of one of the monastery's parishes contained Aqui-nas's *Catena aurea* on Matthew and Mark (A.I.11); this was sufficiently valued to be placed in the main cloister collection, but not apparently to the point where any attempt was made to acquire Luke or John. At the same period, one

[33] *Catalogi veteres*, pp. 39–41.

[34] *Ibid.*, pp. 124–5.

[35] DCM, Misc. Ch. 2475 nos. 13–18. For a book of gospels and homilies in French in the novices' cupboard in 1395, see n. 45 below.

of the most academically distinguished monks, Thomas of Lound, procured an alphabetical *tabula* to Gregory on Job (B.III.27); this was very much a foretaste of things to come during the second half of the fourteenth century, when the compiling and copying of such reference tools became something of a mania among certain Durham monks.

The first extant fourteenth-century catalogue dates from *c.*1345 and records some 140 books, but is evidently incomplete.[36] It clearly covers books kept inside the Spendement, the strongroom opening off the western walk of the cloister at the northern end, and shows that the monks had divided their principal book-collection into two parts, by putting books that were less called for into a secondary sequence in the Spendement. Some were works that had fallen out of fashion, but others were duplicates that would otherwise have cluttered up the cupboards of the cloister collection, duplicates that could therefore be loaned out or moved elsewhere without inconveniencing users of the cloister collection; most of the books sent down to Oxford in the first decade of the fifteenth century were taken from the Spendement.

In its present state the catalogue begins with the section for the Psalms, previous sections being lost. Thirty-eight volumes are recorded, among which there were twenty glossed copies; four of these are described as 'antiqua glossa', which, to judge by surviving books (A.III.9, A.IV.3), meant marginal and interlinear glossing, as against the continuous text of Peter Lombard's great gloss. Whether all the sixteen other books contained Peter's text is very doubtful; one did (A.II.10), the first of nine entries that specifies 'fully glossed'.[37] Difficulty in determining precisely what texts the entries cover is frustrating, but perhaps of secondary importance to the fact that only five of the thirty-eight entries refer to simple psalters, without gloss or commentary. The holding of aids to the study of the Psalms was clearly considerable, especially when there were doubtless others in the cloister cupboards, but it is not without parallel: at other large Benedictine houses for which there is comparable documentation, notably St Augustine's Canterbury and St Mary's York,[38] a similar phenomenon may be observed.

The fragmentary catalogue continues with the Prophets, almost all fifteen being gloss-books, but including Bede on 1 Kings. Although there were a clutch of copies in northern England,[39] this was not a common text in English Benedictine libraries, reflecting a lack of popularity which may account for the fact that it was kept in the Spendement. Subsequently the Durham monks seem to have re-evaluated its worth, moving it first into the cloister collection late in the fourteenth century and then into the reference collection in the *Libraria*.[40] The section for the Gospels records plain texts or gloss-books, and the sections for the rest of the New Testament are missing.

At about the same time as the books in the Spendement were catalogued,

[36] DCM, Misc. Ch. 2475, see Mynors, *Durham Cathedral Manuscripts*, p. 11.

[37] Misc. Ch. 2475 no. 1.

[38] James, *Ancient Libraries*, pp. 200–1; *EBL*, pp. 732–3.

[39] R. H. and M. A. Rouse, *Registrum Anglie de libris doctorum et auctorum veterum*, CBMLC, 2 (1991), no. 7.11.

[40] *Catalogi veteres*, p. 64 A ('super Samuelem').

some listing of those in the cloister appears to have taken place and a fragment of the result survives.[41] Although this is not entirely easy to interpret it
does include three volumes of an incomplete concordance, placed beside that
procured by Robert Greystanes, and the value put on such tools during the earlier
fourteenth century can be seen in two further concordances given by Robert's
contemporaries, Gilbert of Elwick and Thomas of Lound.[42] The chief interest of
the fragment lies in a group of fifteen entries which probably lists books used for
reading aloud in the refectory. This can be set beside the later twelfth-century
list of books read at the evening collation, which were mainly concerned with
the monastic life, and the late fourteenth-century list of books for reading in the
refectory, which were very largely hagiographical.[43] By contrast the fragment's
most marked feature is the high proportion of Scriptural material, including the
second volume of Bishop St Calais' Bible, Augustine on the Psalms, Jerome on
Isaiah, Gregory on Ezekiel, Florus' *catena* on the Pauline epistles, Bede on the
Catholic epistles, and probably Anselm of Laon on Matthew and Berengaudus
on the Apocalypse. It was chiefly the novices who would have been fed this
good solid diet of patristic and other authorities, since the more senior monks
were commonly allowed to eat elsewhere and partake of meat.[44] If the selection of books was indeed made with the novices in mind, to form part of their
introduction to some of the core works on Scripture, it seems unlikely that this
practice of making good use of mealtimes would have been abandoned, all the
more so since there is no sign that such works were to be found in the novices'
cupboard in 1395, where Scripture was served by a Brito and a book of gospels
and homilies in French.[45] What seems more probable is that the passionals and
such like, which formed a major part of the refectory collection later, were used
more or less all the time for some of the reading, while other texts, brought in
when required, provided rather meatier matter. A portion read aloud during a
meal was perhaps expounded later in the cloister by the monk in charge of the
novices.

It may well have been at the annual chapter meeting in May 1384 that the
Durham monks decided to make one of their major investments in Biblical
commentary, by commissioning a copy of Nicholas de Lyra (d. 1340). There
can be little doubt that this was a direct consequence of the condemnation of
the opinions of Wyclif that began in 1377. Before that Durham's most distinguished theologian of the period, Uthred of Boldon, had already locked horns
with Wyclif over civil dominion, and it was Benedictines who played a leading
part in initiating proceedings against Wyclif at the papal curia in 1377. De Lyra's
reputation stood high, for he offered a major advance on what was already available by his ability to compare the Hebrew of the Old Testament with the Latin
Vulgate; Wycliffe admired him and the prologue to the Wycliffite Bible recom-

---

41 DCM, Misc. Ch. 7144; Mynors, *Durham Cathedral Manuscripts*, p. 11.
42 *Catalogi veteres*, p. 53.
43 *Ibid.*, pp. 9 and 80–1.
44 Dobson, *Durham Priory*, pp. 64 and 208–9.
45 *Catalogi veteres*, pp. 81–2.

mended that particular use should be made of him.[46] Clearly those who sought to rebut Wyclif could not afford to be outflanked by an opponent with a superior command of Biblical scholarship. Nor did the Durham monks stint when it came to having their copy made: it was on a very grand scale, and written in *textura*, for the most part by an exceptionally proficient Breton scribe, William le Stiphel, a scribe who had already worked for Uthred.[47] He completed the first half of the Old Testament, up to Judith, in 1386, as he recorded in a colophon that refers to the direction of the subprior, who normally played an important part in library matters at Durham, but he had not got far into the Psalms when he was succeeded by two other scribes who lacked his skill; they finished the Psalms and one of them wrote Acts, the Catholic Epistles and the Apocalypse (A.I.3–4) [for the first of these volumes see plate 6]. So far as can be seen the project was never completed.

The two Lyra volumes soon found their place in the cupboards in the north walk of the cloister which housed the monastery's principal collection. The catalogue drawn up in 1395 reveals an entirely conventional arrangement, with books grouped according to their subject matter in separate sections, with entries lettered alphabetically.[48] The fact that law and grammar rather unexpectedly precede Scripture is probably explained by the way in which the north end of the west cloister walk was used: the chancellor operating out of the Spendement and the monk instructing the novices there would have found it particularly convenient for such books to be near at hand.

The first of the seven sections devoted to Scripture records seven complete Bibles and the second part of another; the first is described as glossed, but a set of the whole Bible fully glossed between two covers would have been inconceivably large. The next section, headed 'various books of the Bible glossed', is the largest and does indeed include a considerable number of gloss-books, but it was not apparently deemed necessary to have all the historical books, for Joshua, Judges and 1–2 Chronicles are absent. On the other hand there were four copies of the Psalms glossed, a term evidently used loosely given that a surviving manuscript shows that one of these was the only known copy of William of Bramfield's commentary;[49] there was also a copy of Cassiodorus' commentary, and an unidentified commentary was added between 1412 and 1425. Only one other book of the Old Testament is represented by a separate commentary, the rare work by William of Newburgh (d. *c*.1200) on the Song of Songs, which was added to this section for want of anywhere else. All the other commentaries are parts of large-scale undertakings in separate sections: Langton, St Cher, and Lyra. This is the result of the Durham monks following the normal pattern of medieval English library management in having separate sections for major authors, such

[46] A. Hudson, *The Premature Reformation. Wycliffite Texts and Lollard History* (Oxford 1988), pp. 243–4.
[47] To judge by four surviving leaves, DCL C.I.6, fols. 306-309v, of which one was clearly a discard, being left unfinished, the original plan was more modest: while these leaves are similar in size to those of the surviving volumes the script is not *textura* but a much more economical cursive, albeit very professionally executed.
[48] *Catologi veteres*, pp. 46–79.
[49] Oxford, Bodl., Laud MS lat. 36.

as Augustine and Bede, where their writings on Scripture were placed; Gorran was treated in this manner. The effect was the dispersal of Biblical resources, and this suggests that browsing was not an important way for monks to advance their studies. Presumably a monk could be expected to be sufficiently well trained to know his way around the collection, or at least to consult a fellow-monk who did, but, in the wake of the major reorganization of the book-collections during the earlier fifteenth century, the need for some sort of union catalogue was recognised. It could be seen, however, as a modest concession that a newly acquired copy of the relatively rare compendium on the literal sense of the whole Bible, designed as a preaching aid, by the Franciscan Peter Aureoli (d. 1322), was placed at the head of the section, rather than being tagged on at the end. On the other hand, a volume of the twelfth-century Benedictine Osbern Pinnock 'on the Bible' was added to the grammar books.

The New Testament was divided into three sections. A high proportion of the books are described as glosses, but again the term was certainly used rather loosely: a surviving book (A.I.9) reveals that it covers, among other items, Peter Comestor's lectures on Matthew and Luke, and Langton on the Catholic Epistles and the Song of Songs. The named authors are Alexander of Hales, on the Gospels, and Haimo of Auxerre, on the Pauline epistles. One addition, the popular sermons by Philip Repingdon (d. 1424) on the Sunday gospels, strikes an unexpected note, for it seems clear that the shelves containing the section devoted to sermons were not so full that this book could not have been placed there; it was perhaps this former Wycliffite's reputation as an upholder of orthodoxy that made him a suitable companion for scriptural commentators.

The sixth section is headed 'Books of concordances' and that is true of most of the ten books entered, but the last four are tools of a somewhat different kind. Two are *Distinctiones* of the kind that reached the height of their popularity in the late twelfth and early thirteenth centuries, both by Englishmen, one the fairly rare compilation by William de Montibus (d. 1213),[50] and the other the more popular work by Maurice. The third was the well-known *De proprietatibus rerum* by Bartholomew the Englishman (d. 1250). All three would have been particularly useful to preachers wanting to flesh out a string of Biblical texts in a way that a conventional concordance did not, and it seems clear that this was the need to which the choice of these books was directed from the fact that the fourth was one of the most widely used preaching aids, the *Manipulus florum* by Thomas of Ireland (d. c.1335); those seeking inspiration from existing sermons had a selection available in the cloister cupboards, and an ample supply in the Spendement.[51] When, however, a comparable tool, the *Tabula septem custodiarum*, was added early in the fifteenth century it was placed in the final section; it had been copied by one of the Durham monks who spent time at Durham College, Oxford and also included the *Concordantiae morales* attributed to Antony of Padua.[52]

[50] J. Goering, *William de Montibus (c. 1140–1213). The Schools and the Literature of Pastoral Care*, (Toronto 1992), pp. 261–303, listing headwords.

[51] *Catalogi veteres*, pp. 75–6 and 103–6.

[52] *Registrum Anglie*, pp. xcviii–cxxvi.

The final section of Scripture comprises four copies of the ever-popular *Historia scholastica*. Peter Lombard's *Sentences*, hagiography and history follow and then begins the long sequence of sections for individual writers, beginning with Ambrose. Here were to be found virtually all the patristic manuscripts given to the monks by Bishop William three centuries earlier, together with those acquired fairly soon afterwards; so far as the study of Scripture was concerned, the foundations had been well laid. The demand for certain works was sufficient for duplicates to be provided: there were two copies of the third and final part of Augustine on the Psalms, two on John, two of Gregory on Job, two on Ezekiel, and three of Bernard on the Song of Songs. On the other hand, the duplicates of Jerome on Isaiah and Ezekiel were incidental, in that they came with Anselm of Laon on Matthew and Alcuin on John, and similarly a copy of the lost commentary on the Apocalypse by the unknown Richard Castleton apparently found its place in the cloister cupboards for the sake of its companion, Nicholas Trivet on Augustine's *De civitate Dei*. With two copies the Durham monks exhibited the enthusiasm found in Oxford for the imperfect commentary on Matthew by an Arian whose mildly heretical work gained currency through being misattributed to John Chrysostom. A monk wishing to consult Aquinas on Matthew and Mark would have been obliged to look for it on shelves otherwise full of his theological writings.

During the second decade of the fifteenth century the monks undertook a major reorganization of their book-collections in the wake of the construction between the south transept and the chapter house of a purpose-built bookroom, which they called the 'Libraria'; this probably functioned as a reference collection, perhaps with the books chained to the ten presses.[53] To judge by notes added to the Spendement and cloister catalogues they initially moved about 150 volumes into it, but the later fifteenth-century pressmarks in surviving books suggest that the number rose to over 320, as the scope of the collection was expanded. As originally conceived, its focus was on Scripture, theology and law, and the great majority of the books were from the cloister cupboards, representing a distillation of the main working collection. The only Scriptural works not found in the cloister that were moved directly from the Spendement to the *Libraria* were an anonymous commentary on Isaiah and a versified Bible which was probably Peter of Riga's *Aurora*, a work that was gaining in esteem at the time, witness the transfer of another copy into the cloister; Bede on 1 Kings and Acts went first to the cloister, while the transfer of a copy of the *Historia scholastica* from the Spendement meant that those in the cloister were undisturbed.

These moves offered the opportunity to adopt a somewhat different approach to the arrangement of the books in the *Libraria*, and the monks departed from the practice of putting all the works of a single author together. Instead, subject matter became the principle of arrangement and so, for instance, Origen's Old Testament homilies (B.III.1) stood next to Jerome on Isaiah (B.II.8) in the first of the five presses mainly given over to works bearing on Scripture; Aquinas on Matthew and Mark (A.I.11) was placed in the second press, not the sixth, which

---

53 Described Dobson, *Durham Priory*, pp. 365–9.

was full of his scholastic works. What users of the books had previously had to hold in their minds' eye they could now see in front of them on the shelves.

The gaps left on the cloister shelves by moving books to the *Libraria* were exploited to achieve a change of emphasis in the collection. Thirty volumes were brought out of the Spendement; a third of these contained sermons and almost doubled the number of such volumes available in the cloister, none of which had been transferred to the *Libraria*, perhaps because they were commonly perused at leisure rather than being consulted for reference. Here the monks could seek inspiration in putting their Scriptural knowledge to good use.

University men of fourteenth- and fifteenth-century England were enthusiastic compilers and collectors of *tabulae* or indexes, the Durham monks among them.[54] Indeed, once they realised how valuable such tools were as a means of access to important texts, they galloped ahead of most of the field. Numbers of the manuscripts that they had owned for centuries were enhanced by the addition of *tabulae*, while new manuscripts were acquired that consisted entirely of *tabulae*. The case of pseudo-Chrysostom on Matthew provides a good illustration.[55] There is evidence that the Durham monks owned five copies of the text; only one of these, recorded as having a *tabula*, does not survive, and two that do survive (B.II.3, B.IV.3) contain the same *tabula*, which is the one most frequently found. A slightly extended version of this is in one of the books (B.IV.43) that consist entirely of *tabulae*, but three volumes of a similar nature have different *tabulae*; two (B.III.31, Edinburgh Univ. Lib. 106), based on the commonest *tabula* but with no other surviving copies, are the same, while the third (B.III.29) is again different, and is found in three older copies, all connected with Oxford. Thus the monks possessed seven *tabulae* to pseudo-Chrysostom, in various forms, one of which seems to have been made locally. They were evidently intent on having the appropriate tools to make best use of this popular if dubious work, and a similar story could be told of most of the basic patristic texts.

The acquisition of *tabulae* may be seen as the final phase in the advance of Scriptural studies in England prior to the advent of the New Learning, which Durham monks probably first encountered in the shape of Colet's lectures in Oxford in the late 1490s; and they could justly regard their resources as completely adequate during almost all the fifteenth century, apart from the absence of the popular commentary on Wisdom by Holcot (d. 1349), which they quickly remedied (A.III.27). In fact, however, numbers of manuscripts were added to their stock during this period, almost all of which contain texts that were very rare in England, and taken as a group suggest a very considerable appetite for the unusual. True, in theory some texts might not have been deliberately acquired, simply coming as part of a book wanted for the sake of its other contents, but there are no clear instances of this; even where they form part of composite manuscripts, the rare texts constitute the principal contents of physically separable sections.

[54] *Opus imperfectum in Matthaeum*, Corpus Christianorum, ed. J. van Banning, 87B (1988), pp. ccxlvi seq.
[55] *Ibid.*, ed. Van Banning, pp. ccxlvi–cclvi; MSS B.IV.32, fols. 168 seq. and B.IV.43, fols. 33 seq. were not known to him.

The general works were the *Distinctiones* of Nicholas Gorran (d. *c*.1295, Cambridge, St John's Coll. 112); the Scriptural *exempla* of Nicholas de Hanapis (d. 1291), alphabetically arranged with the preacher in mind (B.IV.30), followed by the Biblical *Summa* in verse, perhaps by the Dominican Theobald of Crete; and two copies of the *Compendium* composed in 1319 by Peter Aureoli, one in the cloister, which is now missing, and the other (B.IV.20) placed in the *Libraria* by Prior William Ebchester (1446–56). Bishop Langley (d. 1437) gave a copy of William of Nottingham's commentary on Clement of Lanthony's gospel harmony so massive that it must have required a separate lectern to make it useable (A.I.1). Among discrete portions of Scripture the Psalms remained as popular as ever, with Prevostin of Cremona (d. 1210) on the first eighty, and two copies of the *Collectarius* by Peter of Harenthals (d. 1391), probably deriving from a copy in Oxford (A.IV.5, Oxford, St John's College, MS 14). Other Old Testament books were Nequam on the Song of Songs (Lambeth Palace 23), pseudo-Gorran on Proverbs (A.III.26), and Moses Maimonides on the Prophets (B.II.3); for the last, a copy now in Munich is the only one recorded by the greatest compiler of modern reference tools for the history of the study of Scripture in the Middle Ages, Friedrich Stegmüller. New Testament rarities included Peter Comestor (d. 1187) on John, and two incomplete commentaries on the Apocalypse, one by Victorinus (d. 304), the other by Joachim of Fiore (d. 1202), in a manuscript that William Ebchester had made and assigned to the *Libraria* in 1458.

Less obvious, but in fact much more spectacular, is the mid fourteenth-century manuscript containing John Chrysostom on Paul's letters to Timothy, Titus and Philemon, and on Hebrews, translated into Latin by Burgundio of Pisa (B.II.5); while the fact that Burgundio made such a translation is recorded, it is generally believed that it has not survived.[56] The manuscript appears to have been made in England, and it was certainly in Oxford in the autumn of 1414, when it was pawned in a loan-chest; it appears to have been acquired for Durham by William Seton, probably before he became a Doctor of Theology *c*.1460.[57] That the work of this renowned twelfth-century translator should survive in this way is not in fact quite so astonishing as it seems: its history could well run parallel to that of the English family of pseudo-Chrysostom on Matthew proposed by Father van Banning, whereby at some time between 1151 and 1230 an Englishman obtained a copy of it from Italy in a state originating from the hand of Burgundio, a state for which no witness now survives in Italy.[58] Given that he received help from Beryl Smalley and Richard Hunt, it is perhaps surprising that Father van Banning did not go on to mention an obvious Englishman with a highly developed enthusiasm for Chrysostom, namely Robert Grosseteste, although he did

---

[56] The translator is clearly identified by Thomas Rud, *Codicum manuscriptorum ecclesiae cathedralis Dunelmensis catalogus classicus* (Durham and London, 1825), pp. 101–2.

[57] Professor Sandler has suggested to me that the fine opening initial is akin to the decoration found in the Bohun manuscripts, see also L. F. Sandler, *Gothic Manuscripts 1285–1385*, I (London, 1986), pp. 34–6. Erased inscriptions on the front flyleaves record that the book was pawned in Oxford, and that it belonged to William Seton, without styling him *Magister*; Seton entered the Durham community in 1428, see also Emden, *BRUO*, vol. 3, pp. 1671–2.

[58] *Opus imperfectum*, ed. Van Banning, pp. cxlviii, clxxviii–clxxxiv.

know that Grosseteste's name was attached by Bale, for reasons unknown, to a popular *tabula* to pseudo-Chrysostom; perhaps he was deterred by his awareness that this work is not among the patristic writers recorded as read by Grosseteste prior to *c*.1235–40.[59]

In the second half of the fifteenth century all students of Scripture found the ground begin to shift beneath their feet as printed books became increasingly available. Initially there was no enormous change in the range of works available: printers with slender resources generally chose to invest in the publication of works with an established reputation, for which they were sure that there was a ready market. Thanks to their personal allowances, Durham monks were part of that market. The first known was Mr William Law: soon after incepting as a Doctor of Theology between 1477 and 1480 he wrote his name in four volumes of Lyra on most of the Old Testament, lightly annotating the first two of them (DCL Inc. 1a-d). One of his contemporaries owned Lyra on the second half of the Old Testament (Inc. 1f), while a generation and more later the hand of Dr Peter Lee is found in a full five-volume set (Ushaw Coll. XVII.E.4.6–10); in 1536 another scholarly monk, William Wylom, acquired a repertory to this commentary (DCL Inc. 15a), and the immensely learned Dr Thomas Swalwell (d. 1539), most prolific among the monks as a purchaser of books, owned a full seven-volume set of Hugh of St Cher (Ushaw Coll. XVIII.B.3.5–11). Printers were clearly right to sink their funds in such venerable warhorses of the later medieval scene.

Gaining in confidence, printers became more adventurous and the monks repaid them, albeit somewhat slowly. At Durham College there was a copy of the commentary on the Decalogue by Johann Nider O.P. (d. 1438. Ushaw Coll. XVIII.A.4.1). In 1510, a year in which he laid out 10s. on a large volume of Jerome's Biblical writings (Downside 970), Swalwell also manifested his interest in the new Biblical learning by paying 5s. for Jacques Lefevre d'Etaples's fivefold edition of the Psalms published in the previous year (York Minster XI.G.4); his approval of his contemporary (d. 1536) was marked by the acquisition of his commentary on Matthew and Mark (Ushaw Coll. XVII.E.5.5), but the pattern of his annotations indicates that he was only interested in Matthew, although when it came to the *enarrationes* on the gospels by the Carthusian Denys Ryckel (d. 1471) his notes are scattered throughout (Ushaw Coll. XVIII. B.6.10). The Psalms continued to command attention: in 1534 William Wylom acquired Augustine's work, but Swalwell was more venturesome and owned a copy printed in 1530 of the *catena* by the Carthusian general, François du Puy (d. 1521), which he passed on to the young Stephen Marley, one of the monks whom he repeatedly favoured in this way (Ushaw Coll. XVII.G.4.5). Not that Swalwell undervalued Augustine: when he was much younger he had paid 5s. for Augustine on John, apparently before he attained the rank of Doctor of Theology in 1503 or a little later (DCL Inc. 45). The commitment of the last Durham monks to the study of Scripture is amply demonstrated, particularly

---

[59] *Ibid.*, pp. vii-viii, cclv–clvi. S. H. Thomson, *The Writings of Robert Grosseteste Bishop of Lincoln 1235–1253* (Cambridge, 1940), pp. 263 and 122–4.

during the 1530s, lending support to those who argue that the moderates among the reformers, left to themselves, might have achieved most of what was needed. Certainly, in their own day these monks stood high enough in the eyes of those who knew them for Robert Ridley, chaplain to Bishop Tunstall, to present them with at least some volumes of the Complutensian Bible, the great polyglot with texts in Hebrew, Greek and Latin that stands as one of the finest achievements of the new Biblical learning (Hereford Cath. A.ix.2–3; Lincoln Cath. F.1.14).

Modern scholars are well aware that possessing books is not necessarily the same as reading them, but it would be anachronistic to suggest that this applied to a medieval monastic community; books were far too costly to be acquired for purely ornamental purposes, although in the case of law books there was very probably an element of providing resources to attract able lawyers into the monastery's service. In general, the value placed on books inhibited monks from annotating those belonging to the community, although in the earlier fourteenth century this did not apply to the first generations of monks who went to Oxford. Matters were markedly different with the printed books that they acquired for themselves. Many are full of marginalia that shed invaluable light on the minds of these men, a source that remains very largely unexploited.

Margins spattered with quantities of notes were not, however, a feature of many of the printed books relating to Scripture; this cannot mean that these books were not much used, as no monk would have expended the very considerable sum involved in acquiring a multi-volume commentary simply to fill his shelves or impress his fellows. What it must mean is that such were books were used differently from those which were heavily annotated, and here it is the latter which offer an important clue. A number of them have the great bulk of the annotation concentrated in the first part of the book, suggesting that the monk making the notes began at the beginning and read through to a point at which he gave up. Most of the Scriptural texts were probably not read in this way, but used instead for reference, being dipped into when help was wanted with a particular text of the Bible; this may confirm that it was relatively rare for a monk to settle down and make a consecutive study of one of the books of the Bible, although an exception is perhaps to be seen in a two-volume set of Origen's commentaries where there is very little annotation except to the opening chapters of Job.[60] The pattern of recurrent sporadic usage is well illustrated by Swalwell, thanks to the fact that his handwriting became markedly shaky during the last decade of his life (1530–39); in the margins of his Hugh of St Cher, notes from this period mingle with others made when his hand was much firmer.[61]

Two of Swalwell's books present a very different picture. The margins of his copy of Peter Comestor's *Historia scholastica*, effectively the standard textbook for the literal sense of Scripture, are replete with long discursive notes that appear to date from the earlier part of his long career as a monk (c.1483–1539).[62] While it is possible that these were made purely for his own personal use, a strong case

---

[60] Ushaw Coll. XVII.G.4.1–2.
[61] *Ibid.*, XVIII.B.3.7 sigs o5v, L6v.
[62] *Ibid.*, XVIII.C.2.9.

could be made for seeing them as his notes used when giving instruction to the junior monks, men whom he had earlier sought to teach Latin and would subsequently induct into the mysteries of the Lombard's *Sentences*.[63]

It may have been the same audience that accounts for the way in which one volume of his seven-volume St Cher stands apart from the rest: whereas his notes are generally sparse, he annotated the majority of the pages in the volume containing most of the psalms. These notes are clearly intended as an aid to exposition, and confirm how the Durham monks used the lynchpin of their liturgical round for wider purposes. To the general spiritual significance of the psalms, Swalwell brought a number of contemporary concerns touched on elsewhere in his annotations, such as the Eucharist,[64] confession,[65] almsgiving[66] and the importance of works,[67] also predestination and the impossibility of salvation outside the Church.[68] Two topics feature particularly prominently: the importance of preaching and the conduct of the clergy. On the former he was evidently ready to castigate preachers who lacked *subtilitas*.[69] What drew most of his fire, however, was clearly unsatisfactory clergy, men strong in understanding who nonetheless lived badly, destroying the walls of Jerusalem and polluting the tabernacle of God.[70] Above all, prelates were repeatedly denounced, and the particular references to those who did not live in their benefices and to legates suggest that Swalwell may well have had in mind Cardinal Wolsey, who was bishop of Durham for six years (1523–29) but never set foot in the diocese, and had not endeared himself to the religious by his suppression of a number of small houses.[71] While it is no surprise that Swalwell should have held such trenchant views, it is perhaps unexpected that he gave repeated vent to them while expounding the Psalms to his fellow-monks, metaphorically beating the great Cardinal about the head with a psalter.

---

[63] A. J. Piper, 'Dr Thomas Swalwell: monk of Durham, archivist and bibliophile (d. 1539)', in *Books and Collectors 1200–1700: Essays presented to Andrew Watson*, ed. J. P. Carley and C. G. C. Tite, (London, 1997), pp. 84–6.

[64] Ushaw Coll. XVIII.B.3.6, fols. 51, 174, 299v.

[65] *Ibid.*, fol. 142. See also Ushaw Coll. XVIII.C.3.5 (Augustine on John) fol. 83v.

[66] Ushaw Coll. XVIII.B.3.6, fol. 74v. See also *ibid.*, XVIII.B.3.7 sig. L6v 'de dantibus elemosinam spe laudis vel lucri terreni'.

[67] *Ibid.*, fol. 78v 'qualiter omnia opera in fide facienda sunt'; See also Ushaw Coll. XVIII.C.5.2, fol. 178v 'contra docentes verbo et non opere'.

[68] Ushaw Coll. XVIIIB.3.6, fols. 65, 175. See also *ibid.* XVIII.C.5.2, fol. 191 'nullus de se sine doctore aptus est scire sacram scripturam'.

[69] Ushaw Coll. XVIII.B.3.6, fol. 72.

[70] *Ibid.*, fols. 73, 133 and 187v.

[71] *Ibid.*, fols. 175, 170; Knowles, *Religious Orders*, vol. 3, pp. 161–4.

Worcester Monks and Education, c.1300

R. M. THOMSON

One of the outstanding features of Worcester Cathedral library is the number of surviving books, dateable from the late thirteenth century onwards, associated with the monks' studies at Oxford.[1] The impetus behind these studies is well known: a growing awareness by the Benedictine Monks generally that they needed to participate in the intellectual life of universities in the same way as the Friars. From 1277 on, the General Chapters of the English Black Monks issued decrees aimed at the formation of a house of studies at Oxford, and in 1291 the newly formed Gloucester College was made the common property of the southern province.[2] By this time Worcester was already sending monks to Oxford,[3] and by the early 1300s university-based intellectual life at the Cathedral Priory was not only active, but probably more active than it would ever be again. The community was keen to engage in this enterprise; it anticipated by decades Pope Benedict XII's injunction to Benedictine monasteries in 1336 to support at least one monk out of twenty annually at university.[4] The evidence shows that Worcester supported two monks annually at Oxford virtually continuously from the 1290s until the Dissolution.[5] Of the total known monastic population across that period, about one in nine was a university graduate at any one time.[6] This paper focuses on the earliest group of these participants, with the aim of demonstrating that they are worth more attention than they have been accorded.

At least thirty-two books now at the Cathedral can be associated with Oxford

---

[1] For much of what follows I am indebted to J. Greatrex, 'Benedictine Monk Scholars as Teachers and Preachers in the Later Middle Ages: Evidence from Worcester Cathedral Priory', *Monastic Studies* 2 (1991), 213–25, and M. B. Parkes, 'The Provision of Books', in *The History of the University of Oxford, vol. II: Late Medieval Oxford*, ed. J. I. Catto and T. A. R. Evans (Oxford, 1992), pp. 407–83. The manuscripts are described in R. M. Thomson, *A Descriptive Catalogue of the Medieval Manuscripts in Worcester Cathedral Library* (Woodbridge, 2001).

[2] M. W. Sullivan, 'The Religious Orders 1220–1370', in *The History of the University of Oxford I: The Early Oxford Schools*, ed. J. I. Catto (Oxford, 1984), p. 215.

[3] John de Arundel and William Grimley, 1291/2: Greatrex, *BRECP*, pp. 771, 814.

[4] *Concilia*, ed. Wilkins, vol. 2, pp. 585–651, at p. 595; Greatrex, *BRECP*, p. 214. This was reiterated by the General Chapter *c*.1363: *Chapters*, ed. Pantin, vol. 2, p. 75.

[5] Out of a total monastic population at any one time of forty to fifty: Greatrex, *BRECP*, pp. 754, 758–9.

[6] Greatrex, 'Benedictine Monk Scholars', p. 216.

University:[7] that is, they were made, obtained, or used there. The focus of the earliest peak of this enthusiasm seems to have been one John of St Germans,[8] the only Worcester monk to have achieved real intellectual distinction, not only within England but on the Continent as well. Of Cornish origin, he was a student at Oxford by 1295, a monk of Worcester by 1298. In 1302 he was nominated, in controversial circumstances, to the bishopric of Worcester, but resigned before the pope in the same year. He was invited to lecture in theology at St Augustine's Abbey, Canterbury, in 1308. He left his mark, literally, in some of the books there: a late eleventh-century copy of Eutropius has a brief annotation by him, so has a twelfth-century copy of Augustine, *Contra Faustum*, and he may have written a longer note on Boethius glosses in Oxford, Bodl. Digby MS 174, containing Boethius, *De Consolatione*, and scientific works.[9] From there he was sent to the University of Paris in 1310, along with two other local monks. There he took his Doctorate in Theology c.1312, and was Regent in the Theology Faculty until 1315. In 1317 or 1320 he was requested to return to St Augustine's, and that is the last we hear of him. Whether he ever came back to Worcester, or how much longer he lived, is not known. However, the fact that so many of his books remain there suggests that he did. A commentary on Aristotle's *Posterior Analytics* I–II is attributed to him in the fifteenth-century manuscript Oxford, Magdalen College, MS lat. 162, fols. 183–246v.[10] It was long ago printed among the works of Duns Scotus, but the attribution is not accepted by modern scholarship.[11] As it survives in continental manuscripts, it may have been a work of St Germans' Parisian period.

The activity of John of St Germans is registered in more Worcester books than any other single monk.[12] He was the owner of F. 4, F. 8, F. 149, and Q. 20. He wrote some of F. 56 and Q. 59, and most of F. 69, Q. 64 and Q. 99 [the latter

---

7   F. 3, 4–6, 10, 18, 35, 37, 44, 55–6, 63, 65, 69, 73, 86, 96–7, 101–2, 118, 130, 139, 165, Q. 20, 27, 33–4, 45–6, 54, 99.

8   For John of St Germans 'de Cornubia', see Emden, *BRUO*, vol. 3, p. 1626; *BRECP*, pp. 869–70, T. Sullivan, *Benedictine Monks at the University of Paris A.D. 1229–1500; A Biographical Register* (Leiden &c., 1995), no. 602 (pp. 311–12).

9   CCCC, MS 276, fol. 23v; Oxford, Bodl. Bodley MS 826, fol. i; Digby MS 174, fol. v[v].

10 'Scire autem opinamur unumquodque cum causam recognoscamus et quoniam ... nisi tantum in uniuersali c. An aliquod accidens persone predicetur etc. Expliciunt questiones et tituli tam primi libri quam secundi posteriorum analeticorum dat' a domino IOHANNE DE SANCTO GERMANO DE CORNUBIA Amen.'

11 'Scire autem opinamur unumquodque cum causam rei cognoscimus et quoniam illius est causa et quoniam impossibile est alia se habere hanc propositionem descripsit Aristoteles': pr. *Iohannis Duns Scoti ... Opera Omnia*, ed. L. Wadding (13 vols., Leiden, 1639), vol. 1, pp. 342–430, using 'codices MSS. tres Bibliothecae Vaticanae, quartum Monasterii S. Mariae de Populo, quintum Collegii Gregoriani Benedictinorum'. Not mentioned in the entry for St Germans in *BRUO*; Sharpe, *Latin Writers*, p. 307, noting another copy seen by Leland at St Mary's Abbey York (ascr. Grosseteste). C. Lohr, 'Medieval Aristotle Commentaries, Johannes de Kanthi – M', *Traditio*, 27 (1971), 251–351 at 278, besides the Magdalen College MS, cites only Toledo, Biblioteca del Cabildo 19. 25 (s. XIV), foliation unknown. But the number of early editions of the work, and Wadding's remarks, suggest that there must have been many more copies in the late Middle Ages; some of these may still be extant.

12 Specimens of his handwriting are reproduced in Thomson, *Descriptive Catalogue*, pl. 35a–c.

illustrated in plate 7]. He was possibly the annotator of F. 16, F. 107 and Q. 57, certainly of F. 157, F. 169, Q. 12, Q. 23, and Q. 53. These books came to him from various sources. F. 4, probably made at Oxford, was used there by St Germans, who pledged it in 1295. As he does not call himself a monk of Worcester he may not yet have professed. F. 4 also has notes by St Germans recording loans to and from other Oxford students, not all of whom were monks. F. 8 was made in England but pledged by St Germans in a Paris chest. F. 56 was probably written at Oxford by a consortium of Worcester monks, including St Germans. It belonged to the Cathedral Priory by the mid fourteenth century, when another monk was using it, probably again at the university. Q. 59 and 64 were definitely made by Worcester monks including St Germans, but perhaps at the Cathedral Priory. F. 69, partly written at Oxford by St Germans, seems to have continued to circulate among students there before coming to the Cathedral late in the fifteenth century. F. 107 and Q. 53 were professionally made, probably at Oxford, perhaps purchased by St Germans who annotated them. F. 149 was written in France and bought there by him. Q. 12 and 23 are also French, presumably more of his Parisian purchases. F. 169 was written in England, probably at Oxford, doubtless the place where it was glossed by John and two other Worcester monks. Q. 20 is particularly interesting because of the autograph letter on f. 34v, addressed to a group of Canterbury monks. It describes John's attempts to obtain for himself and for them copies of a recent commentary on the Sentences which he attributed to James of Viterbo.[13] Even at a centre such as Oxford this was fraught with difficulty. The main text in the manuscript, the work of an indifferent scribe, is the imperfect result of his endeavours. Q. 99 was written entirely by St Germans, over a period of time but always in a university context, at both Oxford and Paris [see plate 7].

John of St Germans was only one, though perhaps the central figure, of a little circle of scholar-monks at Worcester. Other members of the circle also left their marks in books. Among them can be identified, with the greatest frequency, the names and hands of John Preston, Henry Fowke and Richard Bromwych. Preston[14] first occurs as a Worcester monk in 1335; he was studying at Oxford 1336/7, and lived until at least 1349. Fowke professed in 1303, was sub-sacrist c.1317, subprior c.1324, cellarer c.1326/7, penitentiary 1338, and was still alive in 1340/1.[15] He is not known to have studied at Oxford, but his work on the manuscripts shows a level of education which makes it hard to imagine that he did not. Bromwych was a monk of Worcester by 1301, precentor in 1318, prior of Abergavenny 1320–?25, when his return was requested by the prior and convent of Worcester; he was still alive in 1337.[16] He certainly studied at Oxford. Preston gave F. 11 and CCCC 24, both in 1348, and he may have annotated F. 134, 149, 169 and Q. 99; his comparatively nondescript hand is not always easy to identify.[17] Henry Fowke, on the other hand, wrote both formal

13 Transcribed in Thomson, *Descriptive Catalogue*, p. 132, and see pl. 35a.
14 Emden, *BRUO*, vol. 3, p. 1518; Greatrex, *BRECP*, p. 865.
15 Greatrex, *BRECP*, pp. 807–8.
16 Emden, *BRUO*, vol. 1, pp. 277–8; Greatrex, *BRECP*, pp. 782–3.
17 Thomson, *Descriptive Catalogue*, pl. 32a–b.

and cursive book hands, the formal version usually easily recognisable.[18] He was particularly concerned to make the books usable by himself and others by means of finding-aids. He owned F. 77, 124, and 139, Q. 85, which he paginated, and Oxford, Bodl., Rawl. C. 428. He wrote some of Q. 18, concordances in Q. 24, indexed F. 141 and Q. 64, indexed and foliated Q. 65, and wrote a table of contents in F. 2. He probably foliated Q. 46, which a note in his hand identifies as having been written by the monk John Dumbleton. He probably annotated F. 170. He seems to have commissioned the manufacture of F. 131, in which he wrote notes and an index. On endleaves of F. 62, F. 131 and 142 he copied drafts of his own letters. Richard Bromwych, like Preston, was primarily an annotator. He owned F. 62, 79, 101, 139 (autograph), 156, and Oxford, Bodl., Bodl. 442. His extensive annotation is easy to identify because of his frequent employment of humorous profile monks' heads with staring eyes: his notes are found in F. 32 (with a concordance apparently also in his hand), perhaps F. 37, F. 46, F. 54, F. 57 (with concordances), F. 63, F. 105, F. 108, F. 132 and Q. 25 [F. 105 is illustrated in plate 8].[19]

These men collaborated in various ways. Thus Q. 12, obtained by St Germans in Paris, was foliated and annotated by Fowke, who also foliated, indexed and annotated Q. 53, an Oxford book with text and notes by St Germans. Both of them may have annotated Q. 57, as they certainly did F. 157, a collection of sermons given to the Cathedral Library by Clement de Hertford, rector of Chaddesley Corbett in Worcestershire, in 1305. Q. 64, largely in St Germans' hand, contains text by Fowke, who foliated and indexed it. Preston and Fowke may have annotated F. 8 and F. 16, books associated with St Germans. Bromwych and perhaps Preston annotated F. 101, a book probably made at Oxford, used there at first by Westminster monks, then pledged by Bromwych who presumably gave it to Worcester. F. 62 was bought by Fowke from Bromwych after c.1325. F. 139 is the autograph copy of Richard Bromwych's commentary on the Sentences, which he passed on to Fowke, who gave it to the Cathedral Priory, recording both transactions in an inscription on f. 1v. The two men annotated F. 142.

Other monks went to university at about this time, but were not so obviously part of this circle. Ranulph de Calthrop, who was studying at Oxford in 1312/13 together with John of St Germans, incepted as D. Th. in 1312, and was briefly lecturer in theology at Ramsey Abbey, whence he was recalled at the end of 1318. He owned F. 124, which he gave to Fowke, and in the front of F. 139 is a draft of the commendatory speech for his inception, by and in the hand of Richard Bromwych.[20] A presumably older monk, John Aston, was studying at Gloucester College in 1294–95. He was cellarer in 1295, penitentiary in 1308 and 1319.[21] Q. 13 and Q. 33 are his university notebooks.[22] The first of these is important because it contains unique sophisms, attributed to contemporary logicians: William Scarborough, John Berwick and Peter of Cornwall, as well

18 *Ibid.*, pl. 37a–c.
19 Thomson, *Descriptive Catalogue*, pls. 33–4.
20 Greatrex, *BRECP*, p. 784.
21 Greatrex, *BRECP*, p. 772.
22 Thomson, *Descriptive Catalogue*, pl. 29.

as works of Roger Bacon and William Shirwood, Iohannes Dacus and Dominic Gundisalvi. Q. 33, still in its original limp parchment wrapper, contains Aston's theological notes, including comment on Lombard's Sentences, and sermon outlines. Finally, there is William Grimley, who occurs as a monk of Worcester in 1283 and 1308, and was at Oxford in 1292.[23] His name is in F. 98, F. 146 and the tenth-century MS Q. 5.

The degree of interaction between the bishops and monks is always hard to assess (Bishop Nicholas of Ely, who died in 1268, left a Bible to the convent).[24] But one should not forget Bishop Thomas Cobham, 1317–27, founder of what he intended to be the first University Library at Oxford, to which he bequeathed his personal books. I have argued elsewhere that one of these may now be Hereford Cathedral O. IV. 14.[25] One can only speculate as to what impetus he might have given to studies at Worcester and to the connection with Oxford; his own example must have counted for something.

What was in these books and how did the monastic scholars obtain them? They fall into several classes. First of all (proceeding in descending order of frequency), there are standard curriculum texts, such as Peter Lombard's Sentences, or works of Aristotle, often annotated by the students. Among the surviving books are eleven copies of the Sentences with glosses, and twenty of commentary.[26] Secondly, there are copies of works by contemporary Oxford and Parisian theologians and logicians, of which the most important survivor is F. 69 (and the early fifteenth-century F. 118). Thirdly, there are collections of or including academic sermons, such as Q. 46 and 99, and, finally, sets of lecture notes such as John Aston's in Q. 33.

As to how the students obtained them: the university statutes required graduate students to have their own copies of the necessary textbooks, and the Constitutions of Benedict XII required Benedictine houses to provide their scholars with them.[27] In the case of Worcester they could be taken to Gloucester College by monk-students for the duration of their studies. It seems likely that the College built up a collection which outlasted the stay there of individual monks.[28] Thirdly, new books could be ordered to be made commercially in Oxford, and for this purpose the Cathedral Priory sometimes provided the monk-student with a grant. In 1294/5, for example, the cellarer gave to John Aston, then at Oxford, the substantial sum of 20s. 'ad libros'.[29]

There is evidence of commercial manufacture, doubtless at Oxford, for a number of books, most of which were in early use there.[30] The copies of Aquinas

23 Greatrex, *BRECP*, p. 814; Thomson, *Descriptive Catalogue*, pl. 36.
24 *Annales Wigorniae*, in *Annales Monastici*, ed. H. R. Luard, 5 vols., RS (1864–69), vol. 4, p. 480.
25 R. A. B. Mynors and R. M. Thomson, *Catalogue of the Manuscripts of Hereford Cathedral Library* (Woodbridge, 1993), pp. xxii, 30–1.
26 Glossed copies of the Sentences: F. 8, 46, 53, 64, 88, 98, 134, 176, Q. 32, 47, 88. Commentaries: F. 2, 39, 43, 50, 54, 56, 60, 67, 69, 107–9, 139, 164, 167, Q. 20, 31, 35, 69, 71.
27 *Concilia*, ed. Wilkins, vol. 2, p. 597.
28 F. 101 may be an example, and so may some of those books listed in note 35 below.
29 *Early Compotus Rolls of the Priory of Worcester*, ed. J. M. Wilson and C. Gordon, WHS, (1908), p. 30 (roll C. 52).
30 See G. Pollard, 'The University and the Book Trade in Mediaeval Oxford', in *Beiträge zum*

on the Sentences books 1 and 3, F. 107 and 108, are in the same hand. Very similar to these and to each other in script and/or decoration are F. 11, 15, 16, 18, 20, 22, 41, 51, 60, the volumes of Aquinas F. 101–5 and 109, Q. 27, 72 and 97. F. 131, 141 and 168 are handsome law-books decorated with vinet initials in the same hand, the first two at least purchased by the monk Henry Fowke. Finally, flourished initials in the same style, and sometimes by the same scribes, are found in thirteen books.[31] Then as now, too, second-hand books could be got from other students by purchase or exchange.[32] Finally, the students could make their own books, as did John Aston and John Dumbleton.[33] One book from Oxford does not come into any of these categories, but must be singled out for its extraordinary interest: F. 103, a well-used set of stationers' *peciae* c.1300, containing Aquinas' *Secunda Secundae*. It was probably bought by a Worcester monk, after it had become too worn for further commercial use, in the course of the fourteenth century.

The 1336 Constitutions of Benedict XII forbade monks studying at university to pledge or otherwise alienate their communities' books.[34] At Worcester this nonetheless happened extensively: a dozen surviving books from the fourteenth and fifteenth centuries carry pledge-notes (*cautiones*) by local monks.[35] The university was clearly a place where books could be lost to a monastic community, but they could also be obtained for it by the same means. Other pledge-notes in surviving Worcester books are of previous owners, either monks of other houses or secular clerks.[36] A note on the rear pastedown of F. 101 shows how freely the books of a particular community could circulate between Oxford scholars: 'Memorandum quod Magister Galfridus de Kelminton habet in custodia sua istum librum et librum magistri H. de Gandauo in quo continentur vii. quodlibeta eiusdem [= F. 79] quos accepit de manibus fratris Ricardi de Bromwych monachi Wygornie et tradantur domino Alexandro monacho Norwychio uel alicui socio Norwychio Oxonie commoranti'. We have already met Bromwych; Geoffrey Kylminton, a secular, was Fellow of Merton College in 1296–97; Alexander (de Sprowston), monk of Norwich, is known to have been at Oxford 1304/5–1313/14. Another example also concerns Bromwych: Oxford, Bodl., Bodley MS 442, a fine twelfth-century copy of Hilary of Poitiers, written in the Worcester scriptorium. An inscription on fol. i includes a partially erased Worcester *ex libris*, followed by 'quem exposuit frater Ricardus de Bromwico [monachus] eiusdem loci Philippo de Lustushulle pro uno paruo libello distinctionum super Psalterium et tabula super originalibus sancti Augustini'.

Berufsbewusstsein des mittelalterlichen Menschen, ed. P. Wilpert, Miscellanea Mediaevalia: Veröffentlichungen des Thomas-Instituts an der Universität Köln, Bd. 3 (Berlin, 1964), pp. 336–44; Parkes, 'The Provision of Books', pp. 413–24.

[31] F. 8, 20, 22, 31, 37, 77, 79, 96, 100, Q. 17, 42, 53, and 87.

[32] A particularly complex set of arrangements for books moving between students is exemplified by F. 4: see the description in Thomson, *Descriptive Catalogue*, under 'History' (p. 5). And see F. 69, 73, 96, 118, 130, Q. 34, 54.

[33] Q. 13 and 33, 46. This seems to have been also true of F. 56.

[34] *Concilia*, ed. Wilkins, vol. 2, p. 597.

[35] F. 4, F. 8, F. 37, F. 86, F. 101–2, F. 118, F. 130; Cambridge, Peterhouse, MS 71, BL Harley MS 3066, Oxford, Bodl., Auct. MS D. inf. 2. 4; Bodley MS 442.

[36] F. 6, F. 18, F. 55, ?F. 59, ?F. 63, F. 97, F. 101, F. 130, F. 135, Q. 34.

Lusteshall was a monk of Winchester, who died in 1316/17;[37] the manuscript was pledged again at Oxford in 1491, by which time it was in the hands of a secular Master.

The Black Death is probably sufficient explanation for a falling away from these standards at Worcester, both quantitatively and qualitatively, for another fifty to seventy years. In this article I have merely broken the ground with respect to the books and studies of the Worcester monks c.1300: the community was clearly intellectually alive, and in particular the commentaries of John of St Germans and Richard Bromwych deserve attention.

[37] Greatrex, *BRECP*, p. 711.

The Culture of Women

What Nuns Read: The State of the Question

DAVID N. BELL

In 1995 I had occasion to publish a study of books and libraries in the nunneries of medieval England. It was entitled *What Nuns Read: Books and Libraries in Medieval English Nunneries* [hereafter *WNR*][1] and was divided into two parts. The second part comprised a list of all those books, manuscript and printed, surviving and not surviving, which (at the time) had been traced to English nunneries. The first part contained a summary of the second part, and also (especially in Chapter 3) a discussion of what could be learned from these materials with regard to the learning and literacy of English nuns in the Middle Ages, especially the later Middle Ages. The Anglo-Saxon nuns – different women in a different world – were not my concern. My conclusion, which now needs some slight amendment, was that

> The old and well-worn adages – 'Nuns' libraries were always small', 'Only Anglo-Saxon nuns had any pretensions to learning', 'Nuns in the later Middle Ages could not read Latin', and so on – require some revision; and although it would obviously be just as silly to state the direct opposite – 'Nuns' libraries were always large', and so forth – it is possible (I would say probable) that what has long been accepted as unquestioned and canonical may not be quite true. I am not, therefore, calling for radical revision with regard to the scholarly attainments of women religious in the later Middle Ages, but only arguing for a modicum of honest reassessment.[2]

WNR was not, of course, the first book to deal at length with female religious in England. Eileen Power's *Medieval English Nunneries* had been published in 1922 and still remains an invaluable repository of information. Nowadays, naturally, we must read it with caution, for Miss Power was too deeply influenced by the work of George G. Coulton, whose views were far from unbiased, and her main sources – primarily the series of episcopal Visitations edited by A. Hamilton Thompson – were somewhat too limited, but the book remains of interest and use. The author could also write English, which, these days, is not a common accomplishment.

Following Power's publication, the study of English nuns and nunneries

---

[1] Published by Cistercian Publications (Kalamazoo and Spencer). The books and articles listed here are restricted to those which deal exclusively with the learning and literacy of English nuns after the Norman Conquest or which have useful things to say on the subject. It is not intended to be a comprehensive bibliography of medieval English nuns and nunneries.

[2] *WNR*, p. 79.

lapsed into desuetude for about half a century.[3] It is only in 1980 that we see the first real trickle of what, in due course, would become a flood of material dealing with medieval women religious.[4] That the renewed interest in women religious coincided with the rapid development of feminism and the women's movement is not, of course, a matter of chance. Many of the works produced between 1980 and 1995 have no relevance, or only marginal relevance, to the situation in England;[5] but a few important studies appeared – some of them very important – and present-day researchers must remain indebted to (among others) Anne Clark Bartlett, Susan Groag Bell, Claire Cross, Ian Doyle, Vincent Gillespie, and Barbara Harris.[6]

[3]   A few useful works appeared, notably the work of M. D. Legge, including *Anglo-Norman in the Cloisters: The Influence of the Orders upon Anglo-Norman Literature* (Edinburgh, 1950), 'The French Language and the English Cloister' in *Medieval Studies Presented to Rose Graham*, ed. V. Ruffer and A. J. Taylor (Oxford, 1950), pp. 146–62, and *Anglo-Norman Literature and its Background* (Oxford, 1963). Also valuable were *In A Great Tradition: Tribute to Dame Laurentia McLachlan, Abbess of Stanbrook*, by the Benedictines of Stanbrook (London, 1956); A. I. Doyle, 'Books Connected with the Vere Family and Barking Abbey', *TEAS*, New Series, 25 (1958), 222–43; *The Life of Christina of Markyate: A Twelfth Century Recluse*, ed. C. H. Talbot (1st edn., Oxford, 1959); C. R. Dodwell, F. Wormald, and O. Pächt, *The St Alban's Psalter* (London, 1960) (= *WNR*, Markyate 1); *The Bridgettine Breviary of Syon Abbey*, ed. A. J. Collins, HBS, 96 (1969 [for 1963]) (= *WNR*, Syon 8); S. Jónsdóttir, 'Enskt saltarabrot á Íslandi', (Andvari, 1967), pp. 159–70, and 'Heilagur Nikulás í Árnasafni', in *Afmaelisrit Jóns Helgasonar, 30. júní 1969* (Reykjavík, 1969) (= *WNR*, Carrow 3). See also *idem*, tr. P. Foote, *Illumination in a Manuscript of Stjórn* (Reykjavík, 1971). The seventies were sparse, excepting the work of Hogg and Parkes: *The Rewyll of Seynt Sauioure and Other Middle English Brigittine Legislative Texts, Vol. 2: The MSS CUL Ff. 6. 33 and CSJC 11*, ed. J. Hogg (Salzburger Studien zur Anglistik und Amerikanistik, Bd. 6/2; Salzburg, 1978), and *The Rewyll of Seynt Sauioure, Vol. 4: The Syon Additions for the Sisters from the British Library* Ms. Arundel 146, ed. J. Hogg (Salzburger Studien zur Anglistik and Amerikanistik, Bd. 6/4; Salzburg, 1980). M. B. Parkes, 'The Literacy of the Laity', in *Literature and Western Civilization: II. The Medieval World*, ed. D. Daiches and A. K. Thorlby (London, 1973), pp. 555–77, reprinted in *id.*, *Scribes, Scripts and Readers: Studies in the Communication, Presentation and Dissemination of Medieval Texts* (London and Rio Grande, Ohio, 1991), pp. 275–97.

[4]   For example, *Beyond Their Sex: Learned Women of the European Past*, ed. P. Labalme (1980); S. H. Cavanaugh, 'A Study of Books Privately Owned in England: 1300–1450', unpublished Ph.D. dissertation (University of Pennsylvania, 1980).

[5]   For example, P. Dronke, *Women Writers of the Middle Ages: A Critical Study of Texts from Perpetua (d. 203) to Marguerite Porete (d. 1310)* (Cambridge, 1984); M. L. King, *Women of the Renaissance* (Chicago and London, 1991).

[6]   See A. C. Bartlett, *Male Authors, Female Readers: Representation and Subjectivity in Middle English Devotional Literature* (Ithaca, 1995). On pages 149–71 of this work, the author prints 'A Descriptive List of Extant Books Owned by Medieval English Nuns and Convents', but this has been superseded by the material in *WNR* and the later work of Mary Erler; S. G. Bell, 'Medieval Women Book Owners: Arbiters of Lay Piety and Ambassadors of Culture', in *Women and Power in the Middle Ages*, ed. M. C. Erler and M. Kowaleski (Athens, GA, 1988), pp. 149–87. As the title implies, the article is primarily concerned with the laity, but the article is too important to omit; C. Cross, 'The Religious Life of Women in Sixteenth-Century Yorkshire', in *Women in the Church. Papers read at the 1989 Summer Meeting and the 1990 Winter Meeting of the Ecclesiastical History Society*, ed. W. J. Sheils and D. Wood, SCH, 27 (Oxford, 1990), pp. 307–24; A. I. Doyle, 'Publication by Members of the Religious Orders', in *Book Production and Publishing in Britain 1375–1475*, ed. J. Griffiths and D. Pearsall (Cambridge, 1989), pp. 109–23; 'Book Produc-

My own study, WNR, was gratefully indebted to much of this earlier work and, at the time of its publication in 1995, provided what I hoped was a comprehensive listing of all manuscripts and printed books which had been traced to English nunneries. There were about 144 such houses in England in the later Middle Ages; books are listed from forty-six (just less than a third, and recent research has not increased this number[7]); and there are miscellaneous records from a dozen more. In sum, we have books or records of books from fifty-eight nunneries, representing about 40% of the total number.

WNR lists and describes 141 manuscripts, together with 17 printed books, 10 of which are from Syon. The number is not large, but we must beware of

tion by the Monastic Orders in England (c. 1375–1530)', in *Medieval Book Production: Assessing the Evidence*, ed. L. L. Brownrigg (Los Altos Hills, 1990), pp. 1–19; V. Gillespie, 'Vernacular Books of Religion', in *Book Production and Publishing in Britain*, ed. Griffiths and Pearsall, pp. 317–44; B. J. Harris, 'A New Look at the Reformation: Aristocratic Women and Nunneries, 1450–1540', *JBS*, 32 (1993), 89–113 (an important article).

From this period see also J. Burton, *The Yorkshire Nunneries in the Twelfth and Thirteenth Centuries* (Borthwick Papers, 56; York, 1979). This is a useful but brief account (54 pages) based on one chapter of the author's doctoral dissertation; D. K. Coldicott, *Hampshire Nunneries* (Chichester, 1989); R. Gilchrist and M. Oliva, *Religious Women in Medieval East Anglia: History and Archaeology, c. 1100–1540* (Studies in East Anglian History, 1; Norwich, 1993); R. Gilchrist, *Gender and Material Culture: the Archaeology of Religious Women* (London, 1994); and id., *Contemplation and Action: The Other Monasticism* (London and New York, 1995). Dr Gilchrist's interests are primarily archaeological; C. F. R. de Hamel, *Syon Abbey. The Library of the Bridgettine Nuns and Their Peregrinations after the Reformation* (Roxburghe Club, 1991). Despite the publication in 2001 of Vincent Gillespie's edition of the Syon catalogue (see n. 61 below), this remains an indispensable study; B. Hill, 'Some Problems in Washington, Library of Congress MS Faye-Bond 4', in *In Other Words: Transcultural Studies in Philology, Translation, and Lexicology Presented to Hans Heinrich Meier on the Occasion of his Sixty-Fifth Birthday*, ed. J. Lachlan Mackenzie and R. Todd (Dordrecht and Providence, 1989), pp. 35–44; P. Hodgson, 'The Orcherd of Syon and the English Mystical Tradition', in *Middle English Literature: British Academy Gollancz Lectures*, ed. J. A. Burrow (Oxford, 1989), pp. 71–91; A. M. Hutchison, 'Devotional Reading in the Monastery and in the Late Medieval Household', in *De Cella in Seculum: Religious and Secular Life and Devotion in Late Medieval England*, ed. M. G. Sargent (Cambridge, 1989), pp. 215–27. Her 'What the Nuns Read: Literary Evidence from the English Bridgettine House, Syon Abbey', *Mediaeval Studies*, 57 (1995), pp. 205–22, is heavily dependent on the researches of Christopher de Hamel and my own work in WNR; C. Paxton, 'The Nunneries of London and Its Environs in the Later Middle Ages', unpublished D. Phil. Dissertation (University of Oxford, 1993); S. Thompson, *Women Religious: The Founding of English Nunneries after the Norman Conquest* (Oxford, 1991); J. H. Tillotson, *Marrick Priory: A Nunnery in Late Medieval Yorkshire* (Borthwick Papers, 75; York, 1989).

Several important papers also appeared in collections other than those noted above: *Sisters and Workers in the Middle Ages*, ed. J. M. Bennett et al. (Chicago, 1989); *Women and Literature in Britain, 1150–1500*, ed. C. M. Meale (Cambridge, 1991, 1996 [2nd ed.]); *The Uses of Manuscripts in Literary Studies: Essays in Memory of Judson Boyce Allen*, ed. C. Morse, P. Doob, and M. Woods (Kalamazoo, 1992) (especially the contribution by Josephine Koster Tarvers).

[7]   Recent research has suggested a number of possible identifications, but they do not fall within the strict criteria used in WNR. Jeanne Krochalis, for example, has suggested that Library of Congress, MS 4 – an English translation of a French version of the Benedictine Rule – comes from the nunnery of Lyminster in Sussex, but her arguments, though cogent, remain circumstantial. See J. Krochalis, 'The Benedictine Rule for Nuns: Library of Congress, MS 4', *Manuscripta*, 30 (1986), 21–34.

comparing it with the impressive collections which have survived from some men's houses. The greatest accumulations of surviving manuscripts come not from small and isolated monasteries, but from major Benedictine houses which were also cathedrals, or which were converted into cathedrals in 1540 and 1541, and the circumstances here are obviously quite different. But if we compare the numbers of surviving manuscripts which have been traced to English nunneries with those which have survived from the houses of the English Cluniacs, Premonstratensians, Gilbertines, Trinitarian Friars, and Austin Friars, the comparison is much more favourable.

When we examine the dates of these various books, one thing stands out: no less than about sixty-five percent of all surviving volumes (including, as we shall see, recent discoveries) date from after 1400. This is precisely the period which was marked by a general increase in vernacular literacy and a corresponding decrease in the cost of books,[8] and it is not mere coincidence that the majority of surviving volumes from English nunneries date from this time.

With regard to the content of these volumes, over half are primarily liturgical, and because of this it is sometimes suggested that the book collections in English nunneries must have comprised primarily liturgical works. Such a conclusion would be too hasty. Many liturgical books were objects of conspicuous consumption, and some of those that have survived are quite magnificent. And if there were adherents of the Old Religion who, after the Dissolution, wanted to continue to practise their faith – and such there were[9] – a Psalter or Breviary might have been more use to them than a copy of the letters of Cyprian of Carthage.[10] In short, there are sound reasons for the survival of substantial numbers of liturgical volumes, and we cannot assume that the proportion they occupy among surviving books is an accurate reflection of the wider situation.

Let us now turn to the contents of the non-liturgical volumes.[11] These are to be found in three languages: Latin, French, and English. In 1995 I listed about sixteen volumes (23%) in Latin, seven (10%) in French, and no fewer than forty-eight (67%) in English. As we shall see below, the number of volumes in English has increased by about a dozen, and the percentages now need to be adjusted accordingly: about 20% of the non-liturgical books are in Latin, 10% in French, and 70% in English.

The material in Latin is, for the most part, unexceptional: biblical books, *vitæ sanctorum*, and common standard texts such as works of Ambrose, the *De*

---

8   See *WNR*, pp. 13–17.
9   See, for example, C. Cross, 'Community Solidarity among Yorkshire Religious after the Dissolution', in *Monastic Studies: The Continuity of Tradition*, ed. J. Loades (Bangor, 1990), pp. 245–54; *id.*, 'The Reconstitution of Northern Monastic Communities in the Reign of Mary Tudor', *Northern History*, 29 (1993), 200–4; and *id.*, 'Yorkshire Nunneries in the Early Tudor Period', in *Religious Orders*, ed. Clark, pp. 152–3. Other relevant articles by Claire Cross may be found listed in C. M. Newman, 'Bibliography of the Writings of Claire Cross', in *Life and Thought in the Northern Church c.1100–c.1700: Essays in Honour of Claire Cross*, ed. D. Wood, SCH, Subsidia, 12 (Woodbridge, 1999), pp. 563–74.
10 Of which there was a copy at Nunnaminster: see n. 23. below.
11 The following discussion is, for the most part, no more than a summary of the material presented in chapter 3 of *WNR*; but it is important to know where we stand before we can discuss where we should go.

consolatione philosophiæ of Boethius, the Rule of St Benedict, Peter Comestor's *Historia scholastica*, and so on.

Volumes in French were to be found at nine houses. They include a bible, metrical versions of biblical books, lives of the fathers, lives of saints, the *Château d'amour* of Robert Grosseteste, the Bestiary of Guillaume le Clerc, and Peter of Peckham's *Lumière as lais*.

As for works in English, they are so many that a summary is hardly possible. They include works by writers like John Capgrave, Geoffrey Chaucer, Walter Hilton, Thomas Hoccleve, Peter Idley, Nicholas Love, John Lydgate, William of Nassington, Richard Rolle, and Richard Whitford, and a whole bunch of well-known anonymous works and translations such as the *Ancrene Rule*, *The Book of the Craft of Dying*, *The Chastising of God's Children*, *The Cleansing of Man's Soul*, *Cursor Mundi*, *The Tree and Twelve Fruits of the Holy Ghost*, *The Doctrine of the Heart*, *The Dream of the Pilgrimage of the Soul*, and the *Golden Legend*.

Now what do these statistics tell us? First of all, it is essential to note that the actual number of surviving books which, in England, can be traced with certainty or high probability to any particular house tells us virtually nothing about the size of its library. They are, if I may quote Francis Bacon, 'some remnants of history which have casually escaped the shipwreck of time'.[12] The Cistercian abbey of Meaux, for example, had a collection of almost four hundred books: about half a dozen have survived. And if it had not been for the fortunate survival of the library catalogue,[13] we could never have guessed the size and variety of the collection. No formal catalogue has survived from any English nunnery, and comparison with those in Europe is perilous. I would say useless. There is, however, a record of 'certayne bookes yn the Abbey of Barkynge', and a list of thirty-nine volumes once to be found in the library of Winchester St Mary's (Nunnaminster) in the first decades of the fourteenth century. Let us say a word about each of these.

The Barking list appears in two manuscripts at present preserved in the Essex Record Office at Chelmsford: MSS D/DP F234 and D/DP F235. Both are copies of the will and probate inventory of William Pownsett of Eastcheap, who was steward of the estates of Barking in the years immediately preceding its dissolution in 1539. Pownsett himself died in March 1554, and we may presume that the inventory of his goods was made very shortly after his death. Included in the 'Inventory at East Chepe' is a list of twenty-nine books, with valuations, headed – as we have seen – 'Certayne bookes yn the Abbey of Barkynge', and it is possible, though by no means certain, that some or all of these books once formed part of the nuns' library. A list of the books, with identifications, may be found in WNR[14] and in *English Benedictine Libraries: The Shorter Catalogues* edited by Dr Richard Sharpe and his colleagues.[15] Almost all of them appear to

---

12 Francis Bacon, *Advancement of Learning* (1605), Bk. II.ii.1.
13 See *The Libraries of the Cistercians, Gilbertines and Premonstratensians*, ed. D. N. Bell, CBMLC, 3 (1992), pp. 34–82 (Z14). The manuscript is BL, Cotton MS Vitellius C VI, fols. 242v–246, and the catalogue was compiled in the early fifteenth century by the former abbot of Meaux, Thomas de Burton.
14 *WNR*, pp. 116–20.
15 *EBL*, pp. 13–16 (B7).

have been printed books, and almost all are in Latin. There is nothing in French, and the only volume certainly (or almost certainly) in English is 'Isopps fabel', which cannot be other than Caxton's translation of the fables first published in 1484.[16] Whether Erasmus's *Enchiridion militis Christi* is in English or Latin (the title was the same for both versions) is impossible to determine (in *WNR* I opted for Latin), and the language of the 'ij bookes, one of the decres of the lawe, the other of the distinctions of the lawe', valued at 3s. 4d.,[17] is unclear. My own conclusion in *WNR* was that

> we cannot be certain whether the books listed in the Pownsett inventory belonged to the deceased steward or the suppressed nunnery; and if, as I suspect, they represent a mixture of the two, we cannot be certain of what belonged to whom.[18]

Dr Sharpe's conclusion is that the books probably came from the abbey, but

> that is not to say that these were books necessarily from the library of the nuns: they may, for example, have been left behind by a chaplain near the time of the abbey's suppression. The list must be read with some scepticism.[19]

This is true. And given such uncertainty, there is little further to be said about William Pownsett's list, and which, if any, of the books belonged to the nuns is impossible to determine. What, then, of Nunnaminster?

Our record here comes from the *Registrum librorum Anglie*,[20] that union catalogue of theological works compiled by English Franciscans in the first decades of the fourteenth century (it must have been completed by 1331[21]). By an inexplicable oversight, I forgot to include this list in *WNR* and am happy now to give it the attention it deserves. Nunnaminster – Sancte Marie Winton' – is number thirty-two in the list of libraries in the *Registrum* and thirty-nine titles are recorded.[22] As we would expect from the *Registrum*, all are in Latin and they include fourteen works by Augustine and ps.-Augustine, the *Registrum* of Gregory the Great, four works by Ambrose, Hilary's *De Trinitate*, three commentaries by Jerome and ps.-Jerome (on the Psalter, Isaiah, and Matthew), Bede on Luke and the Apocalypse, Isidore's *De fide catholica contra Iudaeos*, the *De cruce* of Hrabanus Maurus, the *Contra Arianos, Sabellianos, Photinianos dialogus* attributed to Athanasius, but actually by Vigilius of Thapsus, Cyprian's letters, the *De corpore et sanguine Domini* of Paschasius Radbertus, Eusebius's *Historia ecclesiastica* translated by Rufinus, a collection of homilies by (probably) Haimo of Auxerre, four works by Anselm and ps.-Anselm of Canterbury, the letters of Ivo of Chartres, Alcuin's *De fide sanctæ Trinitatis*, and a treatise *De officiis divinis*

---

[16] B7.7.
[17] B7.10.
[18] *WNR*, p. 117.
[19] *EBL*, p. 14. Professor Ian Doyle's opinion (expressed to me in a personal communication) is that the books undoubtedly belonged to the chaplain.
[20] *Registrum Anglie de Libris Doctorum et Auctorum Veterum*, ed. R. H. and M. A. Rouse, CBMLC, 2 (1991).
[21] See *ibid.*, p. cxxxiv.
[22] *Ibid.*, p. 264.

attributed incorrectly to Peter Damian, which might be the work of this title usually attributed (equally incorrectly) to Alcuin.[23]

This is a fairly impressive list, but since none of the volumes has survived, it is impossible to tell their date and whether and how much they were used. What we cannot and must not do is repeat the old absurd adage that since all later medieval nuns were essentially illiterate, the bulk of the manuscripts must have been pre-Conquest, and that after midnight on 31 December 1066, they did nothing more than lie dormant in the unused armarium of the abbey. Since the books were still there in the early fourteenth century – the date of the *Registrum* – they were probably still there at the Dissolution; and if, in about 1517, bishop Richard Fox (a devout prelate with a strong dose of common sense) saw fit to present the Winchester nuns with an *ordo professorum*, accompanied by his own English commentary,[24] he presumably thought that they were not cerebrally dead or even intellectually moribund.

On the other hand, neither of these two lists tells us anything about the size of the libraries at Barking and Nunnaminster. The Barking list is too uncertain to use, and the Nunnaminster entry in the *Registrum* merely tells us that in the early fourteenth century the house possessed at least thirty-nine volumes in Latin. More revealing are the pressmarks which appear on certain surviving volumes, for since the essential principles of library cataloguing differed little from house to house, the *distinctio* and *gradus* assigned to a particular book can often provide a useful indication of the overall size of the collection.

Only three of the manuscripts listed in Part II of *WNR* contain pressmarks. Recent research by Dr Mary Erler may have added one more to this number, though that cannot be regarded as certain. But although the examples are few, they are certainly of interest. One of the three (or four) is from Barking; the others are from Campsey.[25] The Barking volume is marked B.3, two psalters from Campsey bear the pressmarks O.E.94 and D.D.141, and Dr Erler has discovered an early sixteenth-century 'C 32' on the second folio of a third manuscript from Campsey.[26] What, then, does this imply? It implies that Campsey, which was moderately wealthy and probably housed about twenty nuns, might have had a huge library. Just how huge we do not know, but if there were at least 94 books in one *distinctio*, 141 in another, and 32 in a third, and if there was a plurality of *distinctiones* (as would seem to be the case), we could have a collection which would rival that of any of the great libraries of medieval England.[27] In some nunneries, therefore, the book collections might have been very much larger than has hitherto been supposed, and such bald and uncompromising statements as 'convents seem to have owned hardly any books' are better avoided.

Let us now turn from the question of libraries to the question of literacy.

---

23 For all these identifications, see *ibid.*, *in loc.*
24 CUL, MS Mm.3.13 (*WNR*, p. 214 [Winchester, 1]).
25 See *WNR*, pp. 42–4.
26 M. C. Erler, *Women, Reading, and Piety in Late Medieval England* (Cambridge, 2002), pp. 34–5. The manuscript is CCCC., MS 268 = *WNR*, p. 123 (Campsey 2).
27 Even if the books were acquired second-hand, there is no reason to believe that the pressmarks – those on the psalters are both fifteenth century – were added before they came to Campsey.

Once again we are dealing with three languages: Latin, French, and English. In the thirteenth century (generally speaking) learned clerks thought and spoke in Latin; ordinary persons of the upper classes thought and spoke in French;[28] the lower classes thought and spoke in various dialects of English. Then in the course of the fourteenth century, English began to take over as the *lingua materna*. Of the three languages, however, Latin remained, as it were, the constant – it was the language of learning and the liturgy – and unlike French and English, it always had to be learned. One did not just pick it up from parents or peers.[29]

When speaking of Latin literacy, however, it is, I think, useful to divide it into four levels. This is something I first suggested in *WNR*, and, with some refinement of the fourth and highest level,[30] the scheme still works. The first and simplest level is the ability to read a text without understanding it, and that this was done is not in doubt (even at Syon). The second level is to read and understand a common liturgical text, and what evidence there is clearly shows that the majority of monks and nuns were well aware of the meaning of what they were singing. The third level involves reading and understanding non-liturgical texts or less common texts from the liturgy; and the fourth level is the ability to compose and write a text of one's own.

The third and fourth levels are the most interesting, and we shall begin with a brief discussion of the third: the ability to read and understand a non-liturgical text. Were there nuns who could do this? The answer, certainly, is yes, but their numbers are unknown. There is no reason to suppose that the Latin volumes listed in *WNR* or the thirty-nine volumes at Nunnaminster were never read. In some cases, we should not be surprised to find surviving volumes in Latin. Syon, Barking, and Dartford were all known as centres of learning, and Latin books are recorded from all three. But Elstow, Heynings, Horton, Lacock, Nuneaton, Polsloe, Romsey, Swine, Wherwell, Winchester, and Wintney also possessed at least one Latin volume,[31] and some of these houses (so far as we know) were far from being intellectual centres. Furthermore, we must also bear in mind that the

---

[28] In addition to the works cited in *WNR*, pp. 57–8, see also W. Rothwell, 'The Role of French in Thirteenth-Century England', *BJRL*, 58 (1976), 445–66, and D. A. Kibbee, *For to Speke Frenche Trewley. The French Language in England, 1000–1600: its Status, Description and Instruction* (Amsterdam, 1991).

[29] How the language was learned is not my concern in this survey. To examine the matter would lead us into the whole question of women's education in the Middle Ages, and that is a wide-ranging study in its own right.

[30] In her introduction to *Voices in Dialogue. Reading Women in the Middle Ages*, ed. L. Olson and K. Kerby-Fulton (Notre Dame, 2005), p. 1, Dr Olson is kind enough to say that she finds this four-fold scheme 'very useful'. But she adds, quite rightly, that at the fourth level – the ability to compose and write a text of one's own – 'a number of complications enter the picture at once. Two separate types of writing are referred to here – intellectual writing or the composition of texts, and physical writing or the copying of texts – and sometimes it is very difficult to know ... where to draw the line between these two activities' (p. 2). A. I. Beach, in her *Women as Scribes: Book Production and Monastic Reform in Twelfth-Century Bavaria*, Cambridge Studies in Palaeography and Codicology, 9 (Cambridge, 2003), p. 65, accepts the principle of this division, and adds a useful footnote 'on the difficulties of defining literacy' (pp. 65–6, n. 1).

[31] All are listed in *WNR*. At Swine, however, it is uncertain whether the twelve Latin texts donated to the convent by the vicar of Swine in about 1400 (see *WNR*, pp. 168–70, and

number of surviving manuscripts tells us nothing about the size of the library. It is therefore my contention that more nuns than we suppose might have been able to construe a Latin text, and more nunneries than we suspect might have taught the language.

In the twelfth century this was certainly the case, and Latin literacy among women, even among women of 'humble' (*infimus*) stock might have been fairly widespread. The case of Baldwin of Forde's mother is particularly interesting.[32] But there is also clear evidence that in some nunneries the study and use of Latin was continued well into the fourteenth and fifteenth centuries. In 1316 the abbess of Romsey had no difficulty in reading muniment rolls in Latin.[33] Three years later, at Polsloe and Canonsleigh, the bishop required any nun who wished to speak during periods of obligatory silence to use Latin (though they were not required to use it grammatically).[34] In 1395, the chambress at Lacock wrote a note, in Latin and in the first person, setting out the expenses for the veiling of one of the Lacock nuns.[35] At Dartford, instruction in Latin continued until at least 1481;[36] and the novices at Syon may have been having Latin lessons as late as the sixteenth century.[37] Nor must we forget the evidence of the manuscripts: the Romsey collection of *vitæ sanctorum*[38] was written in the early fourteenth century. The date of the Lacock copy of the *Dictionarius* of William Brito is fourteenth–fifteenth century.[39] Swine received a donation of twelve Latin treatises in about 1400[40] and Thomas Reymound gave a copy of the *Liber gestorum Karoli* – a text from the Charlemagne Cycle – to Polsloe in 1418.[41] In short, although it is almost certainly true that from the early fourteenth century onwards, only a minority of nuns (and perhaps of monks too, a fact which should not be forgotten), could read and understand a non-liturgical text in Latin, I would contend that that minority was greater than has hitherto been supposed.

When we come to examine the fourth and highest level of literacy, however, the evidence is scarce indeed. Excluding the Anglo-Saxon period, which is not here my concern, female scribes and female authors in England appear to have been extremely rare. There is no parallel with the situation in Europe, especially in the Germanic area, which (as Jeffrey Hamburger[42] and Alison Beach[43] have

---

Bell, *Libraries of the Cistercians*, pp. 144–6 [Z25]) were intended for the nuns or for their chaplain.

32 See *ibid.*, pp. 84–5, n. 41.

33 *Ibid.*, p. 65.

34 *Ibid.* The injunction might also have been aimed at reducing idle chatter.

35 *Ibid.*; W. G. Clark-Maxwell, 'The Outfit for the Profession of an Austin Canoness at Lacock, Wilts. in the Year 1395, and other Memoranda', *ArchJ*, 69 (1912), 117–24.

36 *WNR*, pp. 63, 65, and see now Lee, *Nunneries*, pp. 157–8.

37 *WNR*, pp. 61, 65.

38 *Ibid.*, p. 161 (Romsey 1).

39 *Ibid.*, p. 146 (Lacock 1).

40 See n. 31 above.

41 *Ibid.*, p. 160.

42 J. F. Hamburger, *Nuns as Artists: the Visual Culture of a Medieval Convent* (Berkeley, 1997), which deals primarily with the Benediktinerinnen-Abtei St Walburg in Eichstätt; *id.*, *The Visual and the Visionary: Art and Female Spirituality in Late Medieval Germany* (New York, 1998).

43 Beach, *Women as Scribes* (see n. 30 above); *id.*, 'Claustration and Collaboration between

demonstrated) was dramatically different. There is an early twelfth-century Latin manuscript from Nunnaminster which was written by an anonymous scriptrix,[44] but the evidence for scribal activities on the part of nuns in the centuries following is very scarce. In *WNR* I drew attention to some half-a-dozen liturgical texts possibly or probably written by nuns for their own use (though some of the cases are far from certain),[45] and although the careful researches of Veronica M. O'Mara have suggested one or two further examples,[46] the end result is disappointing.

As for English nuns composing treatises in Latin, the evidence is rarer still. At the very end of the eleventh century or the beginning of the twelfth, Muriel, described as a *versifatrix*, was a nun at Wilton, and her poetry was much esteemed, though none of it has survived.[47] But after Muriel there is no one, unless we accept Alexandra Barratt's suggestion that the eleven elegiac couplets on the death of Matilda, abbess of Wherwell, were composed by her successor Euphemia.[48] But when we list the names of the women who, from the twelfth to the mid-sixteenth century, composed in Latin – and there are more than two dozen of them – they are all European: French, Germanic, Hungarian, Italian, or Spanish.[49] This is not to say that there were no English nuns writing in Latin

---

the Sexes in the Twelfth-Century Scriptorium', in *Monks and Nuns, Saints and Outcasts: Religion in Medieval Society. Essays in Honor of Lester K. Little*, ed. S. Farmer and B. H. Rosenwein (Ithaca, 2000), pp. 57–75; and *id.*, 'Listening for the Voices of Admont's Twelfth-Century Nuns', in *Voices in Dialogue*, pp. 187–98 (with John van Engen's important response on pp. 199–212). See also G. J. Lewis, *By Women, For Women, About Women: the Sister-Books of Fourteenth-Century Germany* (Toronto, 1996). For female scribal activity in other parts of Europe, see V. M. O'Mara, 'Female Scribal Ability and Scribal Activity in Late Medieval England: the Evidence?', *Leeds Studies in English*, New Series, 27 (1996), 87–130.

44 *WNR*, p. 216 (Winchester 4), and see now P. R. Robinson, 'A Twelfth-Century Scriptrix from Nunnaminster', in *Of the Making of Books. Medieval Manuscripts, Their Scribes and Readers. Essays Presented to M. B. Parkes*, ed. P. R. Robinson and R. Zim (Aldershot, 1997), pp. 73–93.

45 See *WNR*, pp. 66–7.

46 See O'Mara, 'Female Scribal Ability and Scribal Activity', pp. 99–104, and the comments in Robinson, 'Twelfth-Century Scriptrix', pp. 89–93. Depictions of English women writing are even rarer, if they exist at all. In her 'Scriba, Femina: Medieval Depictions of Women Writing', in *Women and the Book: Assessing the Visual Evidence*, ed. L. Smith and J. H. M. Taylor (London and Toronto, 1997), pp. 20–44, Lesley Smith finds only one depiction in a manuscript in England (CTC., B.II.22, fol. 100r: see *Women and the Book*, ed. Smith, p. 32), and that manuscript is probably Flemish. Depictions of women reading are, of course, legion. That some English women could write is not in doubt, but, as O'Mara has said (p. 96), there is only 'the slightest evidence' of their abilities. We might also add that, from a palaeographical point of view, it is quite impossible to distinguish a male from a female hand – unless, that is, one has preconceived notions as to what a 'female' hand should be.

47 J. S. P. Tatlock, 'Muriel: The Earliest English Poetess', *PMLAA*, 48 (1933), 317–21.

48 A. Barratt, 'Small Latin? The Post-Conquest Learning of English Religious Women', in *Anglo-Latin and its Heritage. Essays in Honour of A. G. Rigg on his 64th Birthday*, ed. S. Echard and G. R. Wieland, Publications of the Journal of Medieval Latin, 4 (Turnhout, 2001), pp. 62–4. The manuscript, now in St Petersburg, is Wherwell 3 in *WNR*, pp. 212–13.

49 For a list, see *WNR*, p. 67.

– the problem of anonymity remains a problem – but we do not know their names.

The case with French is different. We have, in fact, examples of Anglo-Norman literature written both for nuns and by nuns, though there is much more of the former than the latter. We know of three nuns who were actually authors of works in Anglo-Norman, and their works are all preserved in the same manuscript, a collection of saints' lives from Campsey.[50] Sometime in the second half of the twelfth century, Clemence of Barking wrote a life of St Catherine of Alexandria. Between 1163 and 1169 another nun of Barking – she does not give her name – translated Aelred of Rievaulx's life of Edward the Confessor. And at the very beginning of the thirteenth century, a nun called Marie took Thomas of Ely's Latin life of St Etheldreda of Ely and translated it into pedestrian French verse as the life of St Audrey. Where Marie came from is unknown, but her piety was greater than her poetry.[51]

It is, however, eminently probable that more was written by women than we know, and the desire for (or imposition of) anonymity, so touchingly exemplified in the statement of the anonymous translator of the life of Edward the Confessor,[52] has resulted in the names of many female authors being irretrievably lost. The anonymous translator from Barking may have been but one of many whose fear of 'presumption' prevented them from leaving a record of their identity.

When we turn to works in English, we find that they are recorded from twenty-eight – almost half – of the houses from which we have records of books, and they account for more than two-thirds of the non-liturgical works listed. There can be no doubt that this percentage reflects a strong preference on the part of women religious for texts in the vernacular – and not only any texts in the vernacular, but (as we shall see) the most up-to-date texts available. As a consequence of this, the spiritual and devotional life of the English nuns might well have been richer and fuller than that of their brethren, who, for the most part, were still mired in the consequences of a conservative and traditional education. There are many who would rather read Walter Hilton's *Ladder of Perfection* than the *Contra Arianos* of Vigilius of Thapsus.[53]

In these matters of learning and literacy, it is easy to imply that the situation in men's houses during this period was radically different: that nuns were ignorant while monks were learned; that nuns wrote nothing while monks wrote much. Before making such facile contrasts one should remember that, after the twelfth century, ignorance of Latin was common in monasteries as well as in nunneries,[54] and before one succumbs to the easy temptation of contrasting the

---

50 Now BL, MS Add. 70513 = *WNR*, pp. 124–5 (Campsey 5).
51 On these texts, see *ibid.*, pp. 69–71, to which may now be added J. Wogan-Browne, 'Rerouting the Dower: The Anglo-Norman Life of St Audrey by Marie (of Chatteris)', in *Power of the Weak: Studies on Medieval Women*, ed. J. Carpenter and S-B. MacLean (Urbana, 1995), pp. 27–56.
52 See *WNR*, p. 70, for a translation.
53 There were copies of *The Ladder of Perfection* at Campsey, London Franciscans, Shaftesbury, and Syon. For the *Contra Arianos* at Nunnaminster, see n. 23 above.
54 See *WNR*, p. 64.

large number of male monastic authors with the dearth of females, one must
bear in mind certain pertinent points. There were five times as many male
houses as there were female, and many of the former housed far larger numbers
of religious. Most of the monasteries, however, produced no writers at all, and
those that did generally did so in the twelfth and thirteenth centuries. Out of
more than eighty Cistercian houses, for example, only two or three could be
called centres of learning,[55] and although we know that Meaux had a large and
splendid library, there is hardly any evidence for its being used as a basis for
scholarship.[56] As for the rest of them, the appearance of an occasional isolated
writer serves only to draw attention to what, for the most part, was a literary
desert. To draw a comparison between a large monastery in the twelfth century
and a small nunnery in the fifteenth gets us nowhere; but if we were to compare,
say, the Cistercian nunnery of Catesby and the Cistercian monastery of Bruern
in about 1400, I doubt we would find much difference.

In the years following the publication of *WNR*, much further work has
appeared. As Dr Joan Greatrex has said,

> Research and writings on late medieval women religious have experienced a quick-
> ening in pace and an expansion in scope in the last decade. Studies of individual
> houses and groups of houses have resulted in monographs, articles and unpub-
> lished theses exploring an impressive variety of themes: these include economic
> organization and estate management; family connections; patrons and benefac-
> tors; monastic art and architecture; intellectual pursuits, attainment and writings;
> prosopographical analyses; and the contrasts in conditions pertaining within male
> and female houses.[57]

In the area of 'intellectual pursuits, attainment and writings' there are now
a number of significant studies, notably by Alexandra Barrett, Barry Collett,
Claire Cross, Mary Erler, John Friedman, Rebecca Krug, Paul Lee, Marilyn Oliva

[55] Forde and Rievaulx certainly stand out, and in the later Middle Ages, Buckfast seems to
have had a university tradition (see David N. Bell, 'Monastic Libraries: 1400–1557' in *The
Cambridge History of the Book in Britain*, Vol. III, ed. L. Hellinga and J. B. Trapp [Cambridge,
1999], pp. 232–3). Elizabeth Freeman's recent study, *Narratives of a New Order: Cistercian
Historical Writing in England, 1150–1220*, Medieval Church Studies, 2 (Turnhout, 2002),
concentrates on Rievaulx, though the author also deals with historical writing from Kirkstall, Fountains, and Coggeshall.

[56] For the Meaux library, see n. 13 above. Apart from Thomas de Burton himself, I know of
only two authors from the abbey: Alan of Meaux, who wrote a series of verses on Susanna
(Sharpe, *Latin Writers*, p. 33, no. 76), and John of Meaux, who wrote two sets of *forma
literarum* (see D. N. Bell, *An Index of Cistercian Authors and Works in Cistercian Libraries
in Great Britain*, Cistercian Studies Series, 130 (Kalamazoo, 1992), p. 94 [not in Sharpe]).
It may, of course, be argued that scholarship was not the main business of a Cistercian
monk, but this is a more complex matter than many suppose: see, for example, D. N. Bell,
'The Libraries of the Religious Houses in the Late Middle Ages' in *A History of Libraries in
Britain and Ireland*, Vol. 1, ed. T. Webber and E. Leedham-Green (Cambridge, 2007).

[57] J. Greatrex, 'After Knowles: Recent Perspectives in Monastic History', in *Religious Orders*,
ed. Clark p. 46.

and Nancy Bradley Warren.[58] There are also important essays to be found in

[58] A. Barratt, 'Books for Nuns: Cambridge University Library MS Additional 3042', *Notes and Queries* 242 [N.S. 44].3 (1997), 310–19; and 'Small Latin?', cited in n. 48 above (pp. 51–65). I would also add the same author's 'A Reconstruction of an Old French Anthology of Religious Prose', *Romania*, 410–11 (1982), 371–3 (relating to *WNR*, pp. 112–15 [Barking 13]), which I overlooked in *WNR*; B. Collett, 'Female Monastic Life in Early Tudor England. With an Edition of Richard Fox's Translation of the Benedictine Rule for Women, 1517', *The Early Modern Englishwoman 1500–1750: Contemporary Editions* (Aldershot, 2002) (this is a very sound edition with a good introduction); id., 'Organizing Time for Secular and Religious Purposes: the Contemplation of Sinners (1499) and the Translation of the Benedictine Rule for Women (1517) of Richard Fox, Bishop of Winchester', in *The Use and Abuse of Time in Christian History*. Papers read at the 1999 Summer Meeting and the 2000 Winter Meeting of the Ecclesiastical History Society, ed. R. N. Swanson, SCH, 37 (Woodbridge, 2002), pp. 145–60. On this topic see also J. Greatrex, 'On Ministering to "Certayne devoute and religouse women": Bishop Fox and the Benedictine Nuns of Winchester Diocese on the Eve of the Dissolution', in *Women in the Church*, pp. 223–35. For Cross see the articles cited in n. 9 above, to which may be added C. Cross and N. Vickers, *Monks, Friars and Nuns in Sixteenth-Century Yorkshire*, YAS, 150 (Leeds, 1995). The Yorkshire nuns are also the subject of the unpublished doctoral dissertation of A. C. Macdonald, 'Women and the Monastic Life in Late Medieval Yorkshire', unpublished D.Phil. thesis, (University of Oxford, 1997). For Erler see *Women, Reading, and Piety*, cited in n. 26 above. Her earlier articles are listed on p. 201 of her study; J. B. Friedman, *Northern English Books, Owners, and Makers in the Late Middle Ages* (Syracuse, 1995). This supersedes the author's earlier 'Books, Owners and Makers in Fifteenth-Century Yorkshire: The Evidence from Some Wills and Extant Manuscripts', in *Latin and Vernacular: Studies in Late-Medieval Texts and Manuscripts*, ed. A. J. Minnis (Cambridge, 1989), pp. 111–27. He is primarily concerned with lay ownership, but his study contains much valuable information. R. Krug, *Reading Families: Women's Literate Practice in Late Medieval England* (Ithaca, 2002). Krug's study is primarily, but not exclusively, concerned with laywomen. For Lee see note 36 above. M. Oliva, *The Convent and the Community in Late Medieval England: Female Monasteries in the Diocese of Norwich, 1350–1540*, Studies in the History of Medieval Religion, 12 (Woodbridge, 1998) (an admirable study), and 'Unsafe Passage: the State of the Nuns at the Dissolution and their Conversion to Secular Life', in *Vocation of Service*, pp. 87–104; Nancy B. Warren, *Spiritual Economies: Female Monasticism in Later Medieval England* (Philadelphia, 2001).
    For other studies that touch on this theme see J. Burton, 'The 'Chariot of Aminadab' and the Yorkshire Priory of Swine', in *Pragmatic Utopias: Ideals and Communities, 1200–1630*, ed. R. Horrox and S. Rees Jones (Cambridge, 2001), pp. 26–42; K. Cooke, 'The English Nuns and the Dissolution', in *The Cloister and the World: Essays in Medieval History in Honor of Barbara Harvey*, ed. J. Blair and B. Golding (Oxford, 1996), pp. 287–301; M. Cre, 'Women in the Charterhouse? Julian of Norwich's Revelations of Divine Love and Marguerite Porete's Mirror of Simple Souls in British Library, MS Additional 37790', in *Writing Medieval Women: Female Spiritual and Textual Practice in Late Medieval England*, ed. D. Renevey and C. Whitehead (Toronto, 2000), pp. 43–62. For this manuscript, see *WNR*, p. 173 (Syon). A. M. Dutton, 'Passing the Book: Testamentary Transmission of Religious Literature to and by Women in England 1350–1500', in *Women, the Book and the Godly: Selected Proceedings of the St Hilda's Conference 1993*, vol. 1, ed. L. Smith and J. H. M. Taylor (Cambridge, 1995), pp. 41–54; M. Goodrich, 'Westwood, a Rural English Nunnery with its Local and French Connections', in *The Vocation of Service to God and Neighbour: Essays on the Interests, Involvements and Problems of Religious Communities and their Members in Medieval Society*, ed. J. Greatrex, International Medieval Research, 5 (Turnhout, 1998), pp. 43–57; M. J. Harrison, *The Nunnery of Nun Appleton*, Borthwick Papers, 98 (York, 2001); T. Hunt, 'An Anglo-Norman Treatise on Female Religious', *Medium Ævum*, 64 (1995), 205–31. This is an edition, with introduction and commentary, of a thirteenth-century poem on a nun's vocation. B. M. Kerr, *Religious Life for Women c.1100–c.1350:*

collections published since 1995.[59]

As a consequence of this wide-ranging research we can increase the number of surviving manuscripts and books which have been traced to medieval English nunneries, and we have a convenient list of seventeen such volumes published by Mary Erler in 2002.[60] In the first part of the first Appendix to her *Women, Reading, and Piety in Late Medieval England*, Dr Erler lists books which certainly or almost certainly came from Amesbury, Canonsleigh, Dartford, Derby, Elstow or Wotton, the London Minoresses, Nunnaminster, Syon, and Wherwell. The second part lists other volumes which may possibly have come from Amesbury, Barking, Bruisyard, Denny, Malling, and Syon. Of these identifications, some are more probable than others. In part one, for example, two of the volumes from Syon might have belonged to either the brothers or the sisters,[61] one – if it was indeed from Syon – was almost certainly part of the brothers' library,[62] and one, though certainly written for a nun by a nun, has only tenuous connections to Syon.[63] And in the second part of the list, I remain uncertain about the volume possibly attributed to Bruisyard (lay ownership is perhaps more probable),[64] and unconvinced about the Gallican Psalter possibly attributed to Syon.[65] There is

---

Fontevraud in England (Oxford, 1999); W. F. Pollard, 'Bodleian MS Holkham Misc. 41: A Fifteenth-Century Bridgettine Manuscript and Prayer Cycle', *Birgittiana* 3 (1997), 43–53; L. Smith, 'Benedictine Women at Oxford: the Nuns of Godstow', in *Benedictines in Oxford*, ed. H. Wansbrough and A. Marett-Crosby (London, 1997), pp. 95–107 (text), 293–6 (notes). This is a rather disappointing study of an interesting topic, but Dr Emilie Amt of Hood College, Frederick, Maryland, has in hand a comprehensive history of Godstow and an edition of its cartulary: see 'The History and Cartulary of Godstow Abbey', in *MRB*, 10 (2004), 34–5; B. L. Venarde, *Women's Monasticism and Medieval Society: Nunneries in France and England, 890–1215* (Ithaca, 1997). The author's main interest lies in the foundation of nunneries in the earlier period.

59 *Women, the Book and the Godly: Selected Proceedings of the St Hilda's Conference 1993*, ed. L. Smith and J. H. M. Taylor (Cambridge, 1995); *Women and the Book: Assessing the Visual Evidence*, ed. L. Smith and J. H. M. Taylor (London, 1997); *Medieval Women in their Communities*, ed. D. Watt (Toronto, 1997); *The Cultural Patronage of Medieval Women*, ed. J. H. McCash (Athens, GA, 1996); *The English Medieval Book: Studies in Memory of Jeremy Griffiths*, ed. A. S. G. Edwards, *et al.* (London, 2000); *Medieval Monastic Education*, ed. G. Ferzoco and C. Muessig (London, 2000); *Medieval Women: Texts and Contexts in Late Medieval Britain. Essays for Felicity Riddy*, ed. J. Wogan-Browne, *et al.* (Turnhout, 2000); *Writing Women Religious*, ed. D. Renevey (2000); *Writing Medieval Women: Female Spiritual and Textual Practice in Late Medieval England*, ed. D. Renevey and C. Whitehead (Toronto, 2000); *Voices in Dialogue. Reading Women in the Middle Ages*, ed. L. Olson and K. Kerby-Fulton (Notre Dame, 2005).

60 Erler, *Women, Reading, and Piety*, pp. 139–46 (Appendix I). I exclude the six books from unidentified houses listed on pages 143–4.

61 LPL, MS 72 (cf. *Syon Abbey with the Libraries of the Carthusians*, ed. V. Gillespie and A. I. Doyle, CBMLC, 9 (2001), p. 226 [SS1.755a]) and Longleat House, Marquess of Bath MS 14 (Erler, *Women, Reading and Piety*, pp. 142–3).

62 LPL, MS 432 (Erler, *Women, Reading and Piety*, p. 142–3). On this manuscript, see further Domenico Pezzini, '"The Meditacion of Oure Lordis Passyon" and Other Bridgettine Texts in MS Lambeth 432', *Analecta Cartusiana. Studies in St Birgitta and the Bridgettine Order*, 1 (1993), pp. 276–95.

63 Oxford, Bodl., Holkham MS Misc. 41 (Erler, p. 143).

64 CGCC, MS 124/61 (Erler, *Women, Reading and Piety*, p. 145).

65 Oxford, Bodl., Auct. MS D.4.3 (Erler, *Women, Reading and Piety*, p. 146).

no evidence that the owner, Rose Tressham or Tresham, was actually a nun at the house, and although her family certainly had Syon connections (Clemence Tressham was unquestionably a Syon sister[66]), there is no sound evidence that the Psalter formed part of the sisters' collection.

Syon, however, accounts for almost half of the seventeen books recorded in part one of Dr Erler's list (including four of the six printed volumes), and that is not surprising. The number of books traced to the house is far greater than to any other nunnery, but Syon was always an anomaly.[67] Of the non-liturgical volumes listed by Dr Erler, all but one are in English. The exception is a few additional folios from an Anglo-Norman miscellany from Derby already recorded in WNR.[68] Not one of the books is in Latin, despite the Latin title of Wynkyn de Worde's 1495 edition of the Vitas patrum from Dartford and Syon.[69] Most of the books, both manuscript and printed, date from the fifteenth and early sixteenth centuries, and one – London, BL, MS Sloane 779 from the London Minoresses – is a manuscript copy, dated 1484, of the printed texts of Caxton's Game and playe of the chesse (1474) and Cordyal (1479).[70]

If we include these newly discovered volumes in the lists in WNR, what is the result? The result is that their effect on the various percentages – books from Syon, books in English, French, and Latin, books produced later than 1400, and so on – is small,[71] and the effect on my general conclusions is simply to reinforce them. Indeed, when I suggested ten years ago that the scholarly attainments of women religious in the later Middle Ages needed only 'a modicum of honest reassessment', I now think I was being too cautious. This is not to say that every nun at, say, the chronically poor Cistercian priory of Whistones in Worcestershire could read Ciceronian Latin – they were too busy begging in the streets to learn it[72] – and it is not to say that the majority of nuns were eagerly awaiting the next work from the pen of Erasmus. Nor is it to say that every anonymous text in whatever language produced in England before the Dissolution was written

---

66 See WNR, pp. 184–5 (Syon 16 and 17); Erler, Women, Reading, and Piety, p. 142.

67 On the importance of (vernacular) reading for the sisters of Syon, see E. Schirmer, 'Reading Lessons at Syon Abbey. The Myroure of Oure Ladye and the Mandates of Vernacular Theology', in Voices in Dialogue, pp. 345–76. The recent (and superb) edition of the Syon catalogue edited by Gillespie (n. 61 above) is exclusively concerned with the brothers' library.

68 WNR, pp. 135–6 (Derby 1); Erler, Women, Reading, and Piety, p. 140 (Manchester, John Rylands University Library, French MS 6).

69 CUL, Inc.3.J.I.2 [3538], and Manchester, John Rylands University Library, MS 15441 (Erler, Women, Reading and Piety, pp. 140, 141).

70 Erler, Women, Reading and Piety, pp. 140–1.

71 I am counting the collection of fifteen English incunable tracts in the volume once belonging to Dame Margaret Nicolson, a nun of either Elstow or Wotton, as one volume. That was how they were bound when they were in Dame Margaret's possession, and that was how the book arrived in the British Museum in 1757. See T. A. Birrell, 'The Printed Books of Dame Margaret Nicollson: A Pre-Reformation Collection', in Essays on English and American Literature and a Sheaf of Poems Offered to David Wilkinson on the Occasion of his Retirement from the Chair of English Literature at the University of Groningen, ed. J. Bakker et al. Costerus, New Series, 63 (Amsterdam, 1987), pp. 27–33 (Erler, Women, Reading and Piety, p. 140).

72 See WNR, pp. 10 and 25, n. 37.

by a nun. Of course not. But the evidence is slowly mounting that the modicum of reassessment that I called for in 1995 is a larger modicum than I supposed at the time.

It must be added here that although, for obvious reasons, I have emphasised the importance of Dr Erler's Appendix I, the material that it contains does not represent the main thrust of her study. Its importance lies in the detailed examination of what nowadays we would call 'networking': the tracing of networks of female book ownership and the ways in which women were responsible for the circulation of devotional and religious literature. Dr Erler concentrates on the interaction between lay women and women religious in late medieval England, and although she was not the first to do this,[73] her careful survey provides us with a great deal of interesting detail.[74] We should add, however, that this was not a phenomenon restricted to women. By a close examination of inscriptions in manuscripts, James Clark has demonstrated much the same thing for laymen and monks,[75] and my own researches on the inscriptions in printed books have led me to believe that such networking was even more common than Dr Clark has suggested.

The mention of printed books leads me to another matter which has seen significant advances since 1995. In *WNR* I pointed out that when we consider the variety of books in English which can be traced to medieval nunneries, one of the things which stands out is the up-to-date nature of the material. Good examples come from Barking, Dartford, the London Minoresses, Shaftesbury, Syon, and the much poorer and less consequential nunnery of Thetford.[76] But the best example is surely Elizabeth Throckmorton, last abbess of Denny, who is briefly discussed in *WNR*, but who happily appears in much more detail in Mary Erler's *Women, Reading, and Piety*.[77] She certainly owned a copy of Tyndale's

---

[73] See, for example, B. A. Hanawalt, 'Lady Honor Lisle's Networks of Influence', in *Women and Power in the Middle Ages* (n. 6 above), pp. 188–212, and 'Female Networks for Fostering Lady Lisle's Daughters', in *Medieval Mothering*, ed. J. C. Parsons and B. Wheeler (New York, 1996), pp. 239–58. Hanawalt, however, is concerned primarily with laywomen, as is C. M. Meale in her '"… alle the bokes that I haue of latyn, englisch, and frensch": Laywomen and Their Books in Late Medieval England', in *Women and Literature in Britain, 1150–1500*, ed. C. M. Meale (Cambridge, 1991, 1996 [2nd ed.]), pp. 128–58. On the interaction between laywomen and nuns, see C. Cross, 'Les couvents de femmes et la société laïque dans le nord de l'Angleterre à la veille de la Réforme', in *Université Paris-Val-de-Marne. Groupe de recherches sur l'histoire et la pensée religieuses anglaises, Vie ecclésiale: communauté et communautés* (Paris, 1989), pp. 177–91; and Marjorie C. Woods, 'Shared Books: Primers, Psalters, and Adult Acquisition of Literacy among Devout Lay Women and Women in Orders in Late Medieval England', in *New Trends in Feminine Spirituality: The Holy Women of Liège and their Impact*, ed. J. Dor et al., Medieval Women, 2 (Turnhout, 1999), pp. 177–93. Neither of these interesting papers appears in Erler's bibliography. Marilyn Oliva, in *Convent and the Community*, pp. 64–72, deals with such networks among Norfolk nuns and laity, and there is a useful and important discussion in Paul Lee's *Nunneries*, pp. 142–9.

[74] See Erler's index, p. 223 s.v. networks.

[75] In his 'Monks, Books, and the Laity in Late Medieval England', a paper delivered at the 38th International Congress on Medieval Studies at Kalamazoo, Michigan, in May 2003.

[76] See *WNR*, pp. 72–3.

[77] *Ibid.*, pp. 73–4; Erler, *Women, Reading, and Piety*, pp. 106–15, and see Erler's index p. 225 s.v. Throckmorton.

controversial translation of Erasmus's *Enchiridion militis christiani* and was one of the first readers of the English version of the work.[78] But at a similar period – the 1520s – other nuns were reading similar texts. John Ryckes's *Image of Love*, another dangerous book which also echoed certain views of the continental reformers, was probably written for the nuns of Syon, and in 1525 sixty copies of the work were sent by the printer to Syon itself.[79]

The point of this is to disprove, clearly and unequivocally, that the old idea that in the years preceding the Dissolution – actually the period from about 1400 to the 1530s – all English religious houses, both male and female, were in a state of laxity, decadence, degeneration, and general corruption. 'It is still widely understood', writes James Clark,

> that England's monasteries and mendicant convents descended into a headlong decline more than a century before Henry VIII set about to destroy them. In their last years the lives of the religious were little more than a travesty of their early ideals and they drifted towards their end 'not in an heroic struggle ... but with a fox hunt and a jolly dinner party under the greenwood tree'.[80]

Dr Clark's mention of monasteries presumably includes nunneries,[81] but his discussion of the level of learning of fifteenth- and sixteenth-century nuns is regrettably brief.[82] It is quite clear that they too, just like their confrères in men's houses, experienced a revitalisation of monastic life from about 1450, and although it is not difficult to find examples of real decadence, the overall picture shows less decadence than mediocrity. John Thomson speaks of 'a tendency to slovenliness and a lack of positive spirituality',[83] and much clearly depends upon time, place, and circumstances. The great houses of Syon and Dartford cannot be regarded as typical of women's houses, but neither can Cookhill in Worcestershire, where the poverty of the house was 'almost the chief feature of its known history',[84] or Rothwell in Northamptonshire, where the local bishop was forced to allow the nuns to break their enclosure to beg for alms.[85] We might be able to demonstrate a deep interest in contemporary theology at Denny, but, as Claire Cross has pointed out, the situation further to the north in Yorkshire might have been very different.[86] But enough evidence survives to demonstrate clearly

[78] See *ibid.*, pp. 106–9.
[79] *Ibid.*, p. 107.
[80] J. G. Clark, 'The Religious Orders in Pre-Reformation England', in *Religious Orders*, ed. Clark, p. 3.
[81] When it came to describing decadence, Eileen Power's classic study, *Medieval English Nunneries*, provided all too much unsifted information.
[82] Clark, 'Religious Orders in Pre-Reformation England', pp. 21–2.
[83] J. A. F. Thomson, *The Early Tudor Church and Society, 1485–1529* (London, 1993), p. 199. According to Charles Talbot (who is generally pessimistic), the general level of observance 'seems to have been pedestrian rather than bad or relaxed' (*Letters from the English Abbots to the Chapter at Cîteaux 1442–1521*, ed. C. H. Talbot [London, 1967], p. 15).
[84] See *WNR*, p. 25, n. 37.
[85] *Ibid.*
[86] See Cross, 'Yorkshire Nunneries in the Early Tudor Period', p. 151. The problem with Cross's argument, however, is that it is heavily based on the paltry number of books

that for many houses, both male and female, the old paradigm of a Golden Age followed by irredeemable decadence and final dissolution is no longer viable.[87]

Where, then, do we go from here? It seems to me that the suggestions I put forward in 1995 have been confirmed and/or reinforced by more recent work, but some of that more recent work clearly indicates the limitations of my own and other studies. One of the most important areas which demands further research is the question of the *mise en page*. Consider, for example, the Shaftesbury Psalter [see plate 9].[88] Not only is this a collection of texts, of psalms and prayers, it is also magnificently illuminated. There are six full-page miniatures before the text of the Psalms and two after it, and such illumination plays a major role in a number of other Psalters (the Winchester Psalter, which soon passed into the possession of Shaftesbury, opens with no fewer than thirty-eight full-page miniatures[89]) and, of course, in innumerable Books of Hours. But the unknown abbess who commissioned the Shaftesbury Psalter [see plate 9][90] would not have seen these images merely as pretty pictures: she would have seen them as an integral part of the text. Indeed, she would have seen the images as text, for ruminative meditation on the illuminations could have been just as rewarding as meditation on the psalms and prayers themselves.[91]

We are not, however, dealing only with illuminations. A medieval manuscript is more like a modern newspaper than a modern book:[92] apart from the pictures which supplement the text, it has various devices to catch the eye and lead the reader from one section to another. The most obvious of such devices

surviving from the Yorkshire nunneries. But as we have seen, the number of survivors may be quite unrelated to the actual size of a monastic library.

[87] For further discussion of the revitalisation of monastic life in England in the century before the Dissolution, see D. N. Bell, 'Printed Books in English Cistercian Monasteries', *Cîteaux: Commentarii cistercienses*, 53 (2002), 127–62 (especially pp. 132–43).

[88] Now BL, Lansdowne MS 383 (= *WNR*, p. 166 [Shaftesbury 5]).

[89] Now BL, Cotton MS Nero C IV (= *WNR*, pp. 165–6 [Shaftesbury 4]). See Francis Wormald, *The Winchester Psalter* (London/New York, 1973).

[90] C. M. Kauffmann, *Romanesque Manuscripts 1066–1190* (London and Boston, 1975), p. 83 suggests Emma, but that is not certain.

[91] See, for example, the collected papers in *Medieval Texts and Images. Studies of Manuscripts from the Middle Ages*, ed. M. M. Manion and B. J. Muir (Reading and Paris, 1991), M. M. Manion and B. J. Muir, *The Art of the Book: Its Place in Medieval Worship* (Exeter, 1998), and (especially) *The Illuminated Psalter: Studies in the Content, Purpose and Placement of Its Images*, ed. F. O. Buttner (Turnhout, 2005). For a brief discussion, see D. N. Bell, 'A Token of Friendship? Anselmian Prayers and a Nunnery's Psalter. Response to Mary Jane Morrow: Where Do We Go from Here?', in *Voices in Dialogue*, pp. 119–21. Vincent Gillespie speaks of 'Medieval Hypertext' ('Medieval Hypertext: Image and Text from York Minster', in *Of the Making of Books*, pp. 206–29). Further insightful comments may also be found in J. F. Hamburger, 'The Visual and the Visionary: the Image in Late Medieval Monastic Devotions', *Viator*, 20 (1989), 161–82, and M. Gill, 'The Role of Images in Monastic Education: the Evidence from Wall Painting in Late Medieval England', in *Medieval Monastic Education*, ed. G. Ferzoco and C. Muessig (London, 2000), pp. 117–35. One could now present an extensive bibliography on this important subject. See also Dr Gill's essay in the present volume, pp. 55–71.

[92] It is illuminating to read Maurice Mouillaud and Jean-François Tétu's *Le Journal quotidien: événement, mise en page, illustration, titres, citations, faire savoir, faire croire* (Lyon, c.1989) with manuscripts in mind.

are the actual layout of the page, and the size and colour of the letters, especially the initials. Scholars began to devote attention to this important question in the 1970s, but a major step forward was taken in 1990 with the publication by Les Éditions du Cercle de la Librairie of the excellent series of studies in *Mise en page et mise en texte du livre manuscrit* edited by Henri-Jean Martin and Jean Vézin. So far as I am aware, the most recent volume to consider the matter is Lesley M. Smith's *Masters of the Sacred Page: Manuscripts of Theology in the Latin West to 1274* published by the University of Notre Dame Press in 2001.

A good example of the importance of the *mise en page* can be seen in a paper by Neil R. Ker published in 1979.[93] In this study, Ker compares two manuscripts of Jerome's commentary on Habakkuk. A fragment from Christ Church, Canterbury is almost certainly a direct copy of another manuscript from Canterbury, but the scribe of the former adopted a layout quite different from that of his exemplar, and the impact, accordingly, is also quite different.

In other words, if I were now to prepare a totally revised edition of *WNR*, I should include a great deal more information on the physical form of their books and the layout of the pages (especially in the liturgical volumes), but I would also have to change the title from *WNR* to something like 'How Nuns Experienced Books'. It would be an interesting study, if only I had the courage to attempt it.

Another limitation of my 1995 study was that in listing the books which could be traced to nuns' houses, I did not (save in rare instances) include the books relating to the administration and business dealings of the various houses. It is true that I included as an Appendix a list of cartularies and related documents pertaining to thirty-five houses (more have been discovered and some have been edited since then[94]), but I did not deal with them in any detail. I suspect that much remains to be discovered in this area, though one example must suffice in this brief survey. In *WNR* I drew attention to the *Rentale* of Dartford for 1507–08 (now BL, MS Arundel 61) drawn up by its remarkable prioress, Elizabeth Cressener, an intelligent, efficient, and far-sighted administrator with

---

[93] N. R. Ker, 'Copying an Exemplar: Two Manuscripts of Jerome on Habakkuk', in *Miscellanea codicologica F. Masai dicata MCMLXXIX*, ed. P. Cockshaw *et al.* (Ghent, 1979), vol. 1, pp. 203–10.

[94] See *MRB* 2 (1996), 2–11 s.v. Canonsleigh (Augustinian canons/canonesses), Flamstead (Benedictine nuns: see n. 98 below), Lacock (Augustinian canonesses: see n. 99 below), Nuneaton (Benedictine nuns of the Order of Fontevrault), and Studley (Benedictine nuns); *ibid.* 3 (1997), pp. 9–32 s.v. Aconbury (Augustinian canonesses), Broomhall (Benedictine nuns), Flamstead (Benedictine nuns), Harrold (Augustinian canonesses), Lillechurch/ Higham (Benedictine nuns), Marham (Cistercian nuns), Markyate (Benedictine nuns), Norwich/Carrow (Benedictine nuns), Nun Coton (Cistercian nuns), Nuneaton (Benedictine nuns of the Order of Fontevrault), Romsey (Benedictine nuns), Wintney (Cistercian nuns), and Wix (Benedictine nuns); and *ibid.*, 5 (1999), pp. 4–21 and 26–27 s.v. Barking (Benedictine nuns), Castle Hedingham (Benedictine nuns), Dartford (Dominican nuns), Syon (Bridgettine nuns), Wilton (Benedictine nuns), and London/Haliwell (Augustinian canonesses). I have not included the Gilbertines. On Marrick priory (Benedictine nuns), see *ibid.*, 5 (1999), pp. 48–53, and n. 6 above. For the cartulary of Chatteris (Benedictine nuns), see now *The Cartulary of Chatteris Abbey*, ed. C. Breay (Woodbridge, 1999). For the cartulary of Nunkeeling (Benedictine nuns), see D. M. Smith, 'The Cartulary of Nunkeeling Priory: A Guide to its Contents' in *MRB*, 7 (2001), 14–38.

important connections with certain devout laymen in the local community.[95] Since that time Paul Lee has discovered another Dartford rental for 1521–22 – London, Society of Antiquaries, MS 564 – which is every bit as detailed as that in the Arundel manuscript. Elizabeth Cressener is again named in the heading, and this second volume is a further testament to her administrative genius.[96]

It is, I think, probable that the number of what we might call non-business books – liturgical texts, devotional texts, and so on – which can be traced reliably to specific English nunneries and added to the present lists of surviving volumes is limited, and their discovery is often a matter of serendipity. There are plenty of surviving manuscripts which were certainly or very probably written for religious women, but identifying the women and/or the houses is another question. This is not a suitable area for guesswork. But business books are another matter, and – I speak from experience – there is much to be discovered among the documents at present preserved in the PRO and in local record offices. The discoveries may not, for many, be as exciting as finding a hitherto unknown copy of *The Cleansing of Man's Soul* from some small nunnery in Xshire or Yshire, but in the Middle Ages – just as now – many an abbess found her work cut out with economics, business, litigation, and the general care of her house, her properties, her staff, and her nuns.

There is also, I suspect, much still to be discovered from the contents of medieval wills, and as more of these are examined, more bequests will be found. In 1995 I included all that I could find in this area, but there was never any question of that listing being comprehensive. Since that time Marilyn Oliva has reported bequests of books to nuns at Campsey, Flixton, and the Gilbertine house of Shouldham,[97] and Dr Oliva was working in the limited area of the diocese of Norwich.

In short, there still remains much work to be done in the study of the learning and literacy of medieval religious women, and work is what it will take. It is far easier to write yet another hundred pages on the ideas of Julian of Norwich or the problems of Margery Kempe than it is to discover, say, a new rental in some local repository (open for two hours a day on alternate Wednesdays in Leap Years) or edit the cartulary of the Benedictine nuns of Flamstead Priory[98] or the charters of the Augustinian canonesses of Lacock Abbey.[99] I would suggest that a sound start would be the preparation of a prosopographical index of medieval English nuns. Dr Joan Greatrex has suggested that the time is ripe for such a study of the sisters of Syon,[100] but there is no reason to stop there. I have not the least

---

95   *WNR*, p. 13. See now Lee, *Nunneries*, index p. 239 s.v. Cressener, Elizabeth (senior). Dr Lee shares my admiration for this extraordinary woman.

96   Lee, *Nunneries*, pp. 48–55.

97   See Oliva, *Convent and the Community*, p. 69 (see also Erler, *Women, Reading, and Piety*, p. 163, n. 70). Further examples of the rich mine of information to be found in testamentary dispositions may be found in Oliva's 'Patterns of Patronage to Female Monasteries in the Late Middle Ages' in *Religious Orders*, ed. Clark, pp. 155–62.

98   C. A. Butterill, 'The Cartulary of Flamstead Priory (St Giles-in-the-Wood), Hertfordshire', unpublished MA thesis (University of Manitoba, 1988).

99   K. H. Rogers, *Lacock Abbey Charters*, WRS, 34 (Devizes, 1979).

100   Greatrex, 'After Knowles', p. 43.

doubt that many of us have the beginnings of such an index in our computers, and it is quite possible that some centralised list is already being prepared. But if it is not, it should be, and it would be of immense benefit in identifying women whose names appear in medieval books and whose status – lay or religious – is at present unknown. An excellent example of this sort of index is the invaluable information on abbesses and prioresses to be found in the revised edition of *The Heads of Religious Houses: England and Wales, I. 940–1216* (Cambridge, 2001), and its continuation in *The Heads of Religious Houses: England and Wales, II. 1216–1377* (Cambridge, 2001).[101] But a glance at the sources on any single page of these superb reference tools will indicate the formidable labour involved in the compilation.

In conclusion, the studies which have been produced since 1995 have reinforced my own suggestion that the intellectual attainments of later medieval women religious have been gravely underestimated. I still think that *WNR* was, for its time, a useful contribution to the debate, but I must be the first to recognise that in listing the surviving books it is now (inevitably) somewhat incomplete (and, I hope, will become more incomplete as time goes by), and in other areas (especially the questions of the physical structure of the books and the *mise en page*) it is seriously deficient. But that is as it should be. Unlike, for example, a study of the financial situation of Dartford in 1521, we are not here dealing with a circumscribed and limited topic. The area of research is ever expanding, more is being discovered each year, but, as Thomas Babington Macaulay reminds us, 'Knowledge advances by steps and not by leaps'.[102] There are few areas in which this is more true than in the continuing study of the learning and literacy of medieval English nuns.

---

[101] Both published by Cambridge University Press in 2001. For additions and corrections to the nunneries, see *MRB*, 6 (2000), 22–35, and *ibid.*, 7 (2001), 11 (Polsloe).

[102] T. B. Macaulay, *Essays and Biographies. History*, Edinburgh Review, May 1828.

Private Reading in the Fifteenth- and Sixteenth-Century English Nunnery

MARY C. ERLER

When we think of monastic reading we imagine it performed in common: in the refectory during meals, or at collation in the evening, or in the daily chapter. Although private prayer was from earliest times part of the monastic day[1] and private reading is mentioned in Benedict's Rule, opportunities for such reading expanded at the end of the Middle Ages. Such private practice represented a shift away from the more common, older form of reading – that is, by listening – to the newer form of reading by looking.[2] In particular, moments for individual reading in the monastery may be linked with a development which episcopal visitors struggled to suppress: the growth of privacy within a communal setting.

The opportunity for such solitude presented itself through two gradual and much-opposed evolutions in the traditional monastic rule: the decay of shared dining and the division of the common dorter into separate cells.[3] Each of these changes was strongly criticised by contemporaries, who feared their effect on monastic life. Their effect on communal reading, however, was perhaps as powerful as their influence on communal spirituality. These practices moved religious life away from the older form of reading and toward the new. The visitation injunctions, for instance, which commanded religious superiors to restore refectory dining abandoned in favour of small-group meals[4] are so frequent as to make us wonder how widespread the presence of a lector in the refectory still was. It may be that this eating practice had unlooked-for effects. When meals were no longer taken with the community and when, as a result, refectory reading no longer reached the ears of an entire house, the corollary may have been not only an increase in private dining but also in solitary reading.

---

1   Benedicta Ward briefly surveys the development of books of private prayer from the third to the eleventh century in the introduction to *The Prayers and Meditations of St Anselm with the Proslogion*, ed. B. Ward (London, 1973), pp. 36–7.
2   Classic examinations of this shift include P. Saenger, 'Silent Reading: Its Impact on Late Medieval Script and Society', *Viator*, 13 (1982), 367–414 and J. Coleman, *Public Reading and the Reading Public* (Cambridge, 1997).
3   Power, *Nunneries*, pp. 316–23. David Knowles suggests that the trend toward monastic privacy began early, soon after the Conquest: *Religious Orders*, vol. 2, p. 244.
4   Power cites fourteen female houses to which strictures against private rooms were addressed, often giving several occasions upon which the house was reproved, from 1279 to 1492: *Nunneries*, p. 320 & n. 1. Research comparing male and female houses in this regard has not yet appeared.

Similarly, when cloth or wainscot partitions effectively carved small cells out of a shared dorter, the incidence of private reading seems liable to increase. Describing male Benedictine houses Barbara Harvey says, 'From the late thirteenth century onwards, the General Chapter of the English Black Monks found it necessary to condemn the introduction of any kind of partition into dormitories – a sure sign that the innovation was already becoming popular.'[5] Roger Chartier has argued that it had become common in the sixteenth century to read before going to sleep[6] and monastic rules for women, together with some later devotional texts, suggest that even nuns may have read in this way. As intriguing as the issue of when private reading took place is the question of where it was possible. The development of private space has been traced in secular households, space which was used either for reading and devotion or for business.[7] It seems likely that a parallel development was occurring in religious households. Although these changes were part of male monastic life as well as female, this essay will look at the ways in which such currents were visible in nuns' houses.

What texts were read in these solitary moments? Copies of the most popular devotional reading survive which bear nuns' names: Hilton's *Scale of Perfection* or the *Prick of Conscience* for instance.[8] Some smaller and more idiosyncratic nuns' books, however (described below), may illustrate more sharply the element of individual choice in reading. Though all religious rules forbade such privately owned books, by the late fifteenth century they were common. These personal possessions make visible the meditative private reading which alternated with public communal reading over the course of a monastic lifetime.

Finally, texts addressed to religious women have a good deal to say about interior posture, the productive disposition to be cultivated while reading. In the late fifteenth and early sixteenth centuries these final fruits of a centuries-old understanding of monastic reading, taken together with changes in the monastery's physical space, may underlie and support the growth of new forms of reading. Examined attentively, all these elements – the when, where, what, and how of late medieval religious womens' private reading – can illustrate ways

5   B. F. Harvey, *Living and Dying in England 1100–1500: The Monastic Experience* (Oxford, 1993), p. 130.

6   R. Chartier, 'General Introduction: Print Culture', in *The Culture of Print: Power and the Uses of Print in Early Modern Europe*, ed. *id*. (Princeton, 1989), pp. 1–10.

7   M. Girouard, *Life in the English Country House: A Social and Architectural History* (New Haven and London, 1978); C. Carpenter, 'The Religion of the Gentry of Fifteenth-Century England' in *England in the Fifteenth Century*, ed. D. Williams (Woodbridge, 1987), pp. 53–74; G. Ziegler, 'My Lady's Chamber': Female Space, Female Chastity in Shakespeare', *Textual Practice*, 4 (1990), 73–90; S. Roberts, 'Shakespeare's "Creepes into the Womens' Closets about Bedtime": Women Reading in a Room of Their Own' in *Renaissance Configurations: Voices/Bodies/Spaces, 1580–1690*, ed. G. McMullan (New York, 1998), pp. 30–63.

8   *Scale* Owners: Campsey (Elizabeth Wylby), London Minoresses (Elizabeth Horwode), Shaftesbury, Syon (Catherine Palmer, Rose Pachet, Joan Sewell). *Pricking of Love* owners: Dartford (Beatrice Chaumber, Emma Wynter, Denise Caston, Alice Braintwath, Elizabeth Rede): Bell, *What Nuns Read*, pp. 224–5.

in which the progression away from public reading took place within female religious houses.

To consider first the treatment of reading in monastic rules for women,[9] the frame of the monastic day contained two different kinds of space and time. The desired and chosen obligation of divine office was performed in public space and marked off the day's public times. The more immediate choices involved in personal reading found a home in private space and time, positioned between these larger public markers.

The Augustinian Rule speaks about reading in only two places. The first guides the response to refectory reading: 'From the beginning of the meal to the end listen to the customary reading without noise or protest against the Scriptures, for you have not only to satisfy your physical hunger, but also to hunger for the very word of God'.[10] The second passage reads: 'Books will be available every day at the appointed hour, and not at any other times'.[11] This was historically recognised as a hard saying. In the twelfth century, Robert the scribe, prior of the male house of Bridlington (Yorkshire), wrote an exposition of the rule in which he argued 'against those who suggest that St Augustine intended reading to take place during only one hour a day'. Anne Lawrence notes that 'such assertions [might] reflect an argument amongst the Yorkshire Augustinians at this time on the question of reading and studying'.[12]

Since the Augustinian Rule is so brief on the subject of reading, the following discussion will focus mostly on the Benedictine Rule, which speaks at four points about reading in the daily life of a monastery.[13] First, of course, is reading in the refectory (chapter 38). The lector – only someone capable of reading for the community's profit – shall continue for an entire week; silence is to be strictly observed except when, in Bishop Fox's sixteenth-century translation for nuns,

[9]   For an overview of mss containing female rules C. D'Evelyn, 'Instructions for Religious' in *A Manual of the Writings in Middle English, 1050–1500*, ed. J. B. Severs (Hamden, Ct., 1970), vol. 2, pp. 458–81, provides an overview of manuscripts of women's rules. To this should be added J. Krochalis 'The Benedictine Rule for Nuns: Library of Congress MS 4', *Manuscripta*, 30 (1986), 21–34, and in response B. Hill, 'Some Problems in Washington: Library of Congress MS Faye-Bond 4' in *In Other Words: Transcultural Studies in Philology, Translation and Lexicology Presented to Hans Heinrich Meier* (Dordecht, 1989), pp. 35–44. For a recent analysis of fifteenth-century womens' rules in relation to mens', see N. B. Warren, 'Saving the Market: Textual Strategies and Cultural Transformations in Fifteenth-Century Translations of the Benedictine Rule for Women', *Disputatio*, 3 (1998), 34–50 and *id.*, *Spiritual Economies: Female Monasticism in Later Medieval England* (Philadelphia, 2001), chapter 2.

[10] *The Rule of Saint Augustine, Masculine and Feminine Versions*, tr. R. Canning (London, 1984), 3. 2.

[11] *Ibid.*, 5. 10.

[12] A. Lawrence, 'A Northern English School? Patterns of Production and Collection of Manuscripts in the Augustinian Houses of Yorkshire in the Twelfth and Thirteenth Centuries', in *Yorkshire Monasticism: Archaeology, Art and Architecture from the 7th to the 16th Centuries*, ed. L. R. Hoey, BAACT, 16 (Leeds, 1995), pp. 145–53 at 148.

[13] G. Holzherr, *The Rule of St Benedict: A Guide to Christian Living* (Dublin, 1994).

'perauenture the prioresse wolde breuely declare ought/ for the edyfyenge of hir susters'.[14]

The record of what was read in English women's refectories is not so full as that from Germany where, in the absence of more plentiful English evidence, the several kinds of texts to which those nuns were exposed can suggest the nature of female religious reading. In the refectory of Saint Catherine's convent, Nuremberg, the German nuns heard parts of the New Testament, texts of the Mass and their interpretation (they preferred Willhelm Durandus's *Rationale divinorum officiorum* in German), sermons (especially Johannes Tauler), tracts and saints' lives, all in excerpts which had been selected to fit the time available.[15]

Physical evidence in one surviving nuns' book from Campsey (Suffolk) confirms that hagiography was read in their frater. BL, Additional MS 70513, a fourteenth-century volume which contains the lives in French of St Elizabeth of Hungary, St Paphnutius, St Paul the Hermit, St Thomas of Canterbury and a host of others, also carries the notation 'Ce livre [est] deviseie a la priorie de Kampseie de lire a mengier'.[16] In addition, A. I. Doyle has suggested that the Longleat copy of Nicholas Love's *Mirror of the Life of Jesus Christ* may have been intended for collation reading at Syon, based on its markings. [17]

Second, chapter 42 of the Rule describes the evening reading in the chapter house which preceded compline. It was called collation, from John Cassian's *Collationes* or conversations with the hermits of the eastern deserts, written in the 420s, which Benedict recommended should be read. Episcopal strictures directed toward 'both men and women' frequently forbid socialising after collation and compline instead of retiring. Nuns were so reproved, for instance, at Heynings, Lincolnshire in 1440.[18]

No nun-owned manuscripts of the *Collationes* survive, though the Syon brethren owned three;[19] but it is possible that the popular *Chastising of God's Children*, which was owned by the community or its members at the women's houses of Campsey, Easebourne, Esholt, and Syon[20] and which was influenced by Cassian's work, might have been read at collation. Its twenty-six relatively short chapters led its editors to call it 'a work which could very well provide a daily reading in English ... for about a month'.[21] BL, Cotton MS Vespasian A XXV, a fifteenth-century metrical version of the Benedictine Rule from West Yorkshire,

---

14 STC, 1859, E3[V]. For Fox's translation of the Rule see also Barry Collett's essay below.
15 M-L. Ehrenschwendtner, 'A Library Collected by and for the Use of Nuns: St. Catherine's Convent, Nuremberg', in *Women and the Book: Assessing the Visual Evidence*, ed. J. H. M. Taylor and L. Smith (London, 1996), pp. 123–32 at 124.
16 Bell, *What Nuns Read*, p. 108.
17 A. I. Doyle, 'The Study of Nicholas Love's Mirror, Retrospect and Prospect' in *Nicholas Love at Waseda: Proceedings of the International Conference, 20–22 July 1995*, ed. S. Ogura et al. (Woodbridge, 1997), pp. 163–74 at 169–70.
18 *Visitations*, ed. Thompson, vol. 2, p. 135.
19 *Syon Abbey*, ed. V. Gillespie and A. I. Doyle, CBMLC, 9 (2001), p. 739 (SS 1. 766b, 774a, 839).
20 Bell, *What Nuns Read*, p. 228.
21 *The Chastising of God's Children and the Treatise of Perfection of the Sons of God*, ed. J. Bazire and E. Colledge (Oxford, 1957), p. 44.

says the nuns shall sit together at this time after supper, 'and rede lessons of hali writ/ Or els of liues of hali men/ þat' gastly comfort may þam ken'.[22] Bishop Fox's suggestion is 'a boke called collacions or els Vitas patrum', the amount to be read is four or five leaves 'or elles as moche as oon houre wyll permit'.[23] Barking owned a French miscellany in which *Vitas Patrum* was the first text, and perhaps the signature of Martha Fabyan in a printed edition of 1495 may belong to a Barking nun of that name, while either a Latin or a French version was one of the Duchess of Gloucester's books willed to her minoress daughter Isabel in 1396.[24] The *Myroure of Oure Ladye* recommends at collation

> some spyrytuall matter of gostly edyfycacion. to helpe to gather to gyther the scaterynges of the mynde. from all oute warde thynges. And therfore all maner of bokes oughte not to be redde at that tyme but onely the bokes that ar inwardely spyrytuall. and easy to vnderstande that all sowlles may be fedde therwyth and holpen thereby. to kepe themselfe in inwarde peace and stablenesse of mynde all the nyghte folowynge.[25]

The fifteenth-century Franciscan Rule for women implies that reading at collation in their houses was usually scripture, since it gives directions for what to do 'after þe firste or secunde verse of þe lessoun'.[26] Earlier, however, in the fourteenth century, collation in male monasteries could sometimes take the form of a sermon made by a monk on a scriptural text.[27] A copy of the Northern Homily Cycle survives which belonged to Denny Abbey (Cambs.); it contains sixty-one sermons, in English verse, which might have been read during collation at this female Franciscan house.[28]

Versions of the Rule made for women do not differ from male ones in what they have to say about reading except in Benedict's final chapter (the fourth place where reading is mentioned in his Rule), which lists a few valuable books. J. Frank Henderson points out that here the northern verse version of the Rule for nuns adds 'haly virgins', to Benedict's recommended readings, 'thus including women's lives as models for themselves'.[29]

So far the Benedictine Rule has spoken of public reading. Chapter 48 gives the varying times of day throughout the year that private reading was to be done. Here the well-known Lenten book distribution is specified, the one described in

---

22 *Three Middle English Versions of the Rule of St Benet*, ed. E. A. Kock, EETS, OS, 120 (1902), p. 106; *A Linguistic Atlas of Late Mediaeval English*, ed. A. McIntosh et al., 4 vols. (Aberdeen, 1986), vol. 1, p. 108.

23 STC, 1859, EIᵛ. These two texts, plus the suggested length of four or five pages (though not the time of one hour) are found in Benedict's Rule, 42. 3 and 6.

24 Bell, *What Nuns Read*, pp. 110, 115, 151.

25 *The Myroure of oure Ladye*, ed. J. H. Blunt, EETS, ES, 19 (1873), p. 165. *Myroure* is here glossing Benedict's advice in *RSB*, 42.4 that the Heptateuch or Kings, with their stimulating sexual content, should not be read at this time.

26 *A Fifteenth-Century Courtesy Book and Two Fifteenth-Century Franciscan Rules*, ed. W. W. Seton, EETS, OS, 148 (1914), pp. 102–3.

27 *Visitations*, ed. Thompson, vol. 1, p. 227; vol. 3, p. 234.

28 Bell, *What Nuns Read*, p. 134.

29 J. F. Henderson, 'Feminizing the Rule of Benedict in Medieval England', *Magistra*, 1 (1995), 9–38 at 33.

so much detail in the Barking ordinal but present more briefly in all versions of the Rule. BL, MS Lansdowne 378, for instance, the northern prose version for nuns, simply says, 'At te bigining of lentyn sal be broght intil þe chapitur alle þe bokis, and ilkain take þaris & rede it ouir'.[30] The abbreviated version of the Rule which Caxton devised for both men and women religious in the *Book of Divers Ghostly Matters* is the only one to specify what the Lenten reading should be: 'In the tyme of lent echon by theyr-selfe haue the bible/ the whiche they owe to rede complete and hole besyde theyr seruyse/ and the seyde bible is to be delyuerd vnto them atte begynnynge of lent'.[31]

Besides Saturdays, when Benedict specifies all were to read, two times were available for private reading: just before the day's work began and just after the main (noon) meal, a time of rest which could also be used for reading. Lansdowne 378 says that from Easter to Michaelmas after the midday meal all shall rest in bed, with silence. 'Yef any wille þat tyme loke lescun, loke þat sho rede sua, þat sho ne noy noht þe oþir'.[32] That private reading might still be oral, even in the sixteenth century, is shown by Bishop Fox's translation of the same passage: 'They shall reste a wyle in their beddes/ with all silence/ or els if she woll gyue hir selfe to reding let hir so rede softli bi hir selfe/ that she trouble none other'.[33] Similarly, the prioress of St Catherine's, Nuremberg, wrote to a Swiss nunnery at St Gall advising its nuns to spend leisure time after the noon meal with spiritual reading. Some of the German nuns took this opportunity to write their own books for private prayer and contemplation, choosing their copy texts from the convent's library.[34]

After the last hour, compline, one devotional text suggests that private reading time may have intervened before sleep. In fact the text is suggestive regarding both the times and places of private reading. The *Tree and xij Frutes*, which was owned in a printed copy by a Syon nun, recommends perusing the *Stimulus Amoris*: 'I wold þou were occupied namly [especially] on holy dayes with redyng of deuoute bokes as is *Stimulus amoris* or such oþer In þe wich specialy I recomende to þi meditacioun þe holy passioun of oure lord ihesu and namly after complyn and after matynes', that is, the last thing at night and early in the morning.[35]

The Syon rule specifies that after compline nuns should go to the dorter, where each woman had a separate cell. Apparently, private night prayers were then said sitting up in bed.[36] 'In ther bedes, they schal sytte, and ʒeue thankynges

30 *Three Middle English Versions*, ed. Kock, p. 33; McIntosh, *Literary Atlas*, p. 114.
31 *Three Middle English Versions*, ed. Kock, p. 132.
32 *Ibid.*, pp. 32–3.
33 STC, 1859, F1ᵛ.
34 Ehrenschwendtner, 'A Library', p. 124.
35 *A Devout Treatyse Called the Tree and xii. Frutes of the Holy Goost*, ed. J. J. Vaissier (Gronigen, 1960), p. 32.
36 The *Consuetudines Corbeienses* mentions 'those who sit and read in bed': *Consuetudines Corbeienses*, ed. J. Semmler, CCM, 1 (1963), 417, cited in N. Bauer, 'Monasticism After Dark: From Dormitory to Cell', *American Benedictine Review*, 38 (1987), 95–114, n. 30. The position for prayer seems to have been more conventional at Wherwell; here an accident occurred at matins when 'the nuns were in the dorter, some in bed and some in prayer before their beds': Power, *Nunneries*, p. 169.

to god, with some special, but no longe prayers or they slepe'.[37] That there may have been some time for private reading in one's bed is suggested by the Rule's reference to the searchers 'depute by the abbes, [who] schal euery nyghte serche and se, sone after complen ... yf the sustres be in ther celles, and wheyther they be alone, and how they be occupied ... and whether þer lyghtes be quenched'.[38] Thus Chartier's suggestion that bedtime reading came into use in the sixteenth century may be relevant in a monastic setting as well as a secular one. If indeed private reading was the last action of the day it thus added an individual closure to a communal one, the collective recitation of compline.

Movement away from common meals toward more intimate dining has been noticed as a phenomenon of religious life, both male and female, from the late thirteenth century on. Power's examples of episcopal attempts to restore community dining in the nuns' frater have been much quoted.[39] Small rooms where individual obedientiaries ate with two to five other nuns were inveighed against, and Knowles gives parallel examples for male monasteries.[40]

A similar phenomenon was occurring in lay life. Margaret Wood has described the evolution of the storage space under the medieval house's solar (bed-sitting room) into a room where the lord and his family 'could retire from the adjoining high table. In this smaller, less draughty room ... the family more and more tended to dine apart from the servants and retainers, leaving the great hall to the latter ...'.[41] She quotes from *Piers Plowman* (1362):

> Elyng [wretched] is the halle   vche daye in the wyke
> There the lorde ne the lady   liketh nou3te to sytte
> Now hath vche riche a reule   to eten bi hym-selue
> In a pryue parloure ...[42]

Roberta Gilchrist has seen female religious life, and particularly its architecture, as imitative of its secular peers;[43] but in the case of lay and religious withdrawal from communal eating spaces, it is not easy to say in which direction the influence moved, or if both simply shared a common current. Felicity Heal notes that at the beginning of the fourteenth century, Edward II was using his chamber for eating, and she suggests that in aristocratic circles the shift from hall to parlour may have been complete by the end of that century, though gentry houses perhaps continued communal meals until the early sixteenth century. Here too, as in the religious sphere, there was opposition to the privatisation of eating. The

---

37 *The Rewyll of Seynt Sauioure*, 4. The Syon Additions for the Sisters from the British Library MS Arundel 146, ed. J. Hogg, Institut für Anglistik und Amerikanistik, Universität Salzburg (Salzburg, 1980), p. 177.

38 *Ibid.*, 184.

39 Power, *Nunneries*, pp. 316–17.

40 Knowles, *Religious Orders*, vol. 2, pp. 244–45.

41 M. Wood, *The Medieval English House* (London, 1965), p. 91.

42 *The Vision of William Concerning Piers the Plowman*, ed. W. W. Skeat (London, 1886), B Text, X. 94–97.

43 R. Gilchrist, *Gender and Material Culture: The Architecture of Religious Women* (London and New York, 1994), pp. 122–3; *id.*, 'Medieval Bodies in the Material World: Gender, Stigma, and the Body', in *Framing Medieval Bodies*, ed. S. Kay and M. Rubin (Manchester, 1994), p. 58.

visitation injunctions which inveighed against the decline of community life in religion are paralleled by the manuals of secular household service where 'the habit of eating in separate chambers is vigorously opposed and it is always argued that the lord, his guests, and his whole household must sit down together'.[44]

This subdivision of function into smaller and more specialised rooms,[45] seen here in spaces used for eating, found a parallel in the development of private sleeping spaces out of a shared larger room. As in the matter of private dining, both male and female monastics were warned, from the thirteenth century on, against partitioning the dorter with panels or curtains,[46] though in some cases the latter seem to have been allowed.[47] At the Dissolution however, sales of wainscot dorter partitions from both male houses (Lilleshall; Dale; Barnwell) and female ones (Gracedieu; Catesby) show that such individual rooms were much in use.[48]

Though for the most part the growth of private space has been traced in secular buildings, particularly in the late fourteenth and fifteenth centuries with the emergence of closets used both for religious and business purposes,[49] nonetheless the spaces in religious houses may likewise have offered a venue for the development of private life, and especially for the act of solitary reading. Like the secular closet, the small bedrooms made by dividing the monastic dorter may have facilitated the growth in reading which is so notable a feature of the fifteenth century. At the very end of the medieval period, a Dissolution inventory from Minster in Sheppey (Kent) allows us to see with considerable vividness what such private female space looked like.

The Minster cells' tinyness is evident, since none of them included a chair or a table.[50] For comparison, the Oxfordshire womens' priory of Littlemore had

---

44 F. Heal, *Hospitality in Early Modern England* (Oxford, 1990), pp. 40–2.
45 Speaking of the two centuries from 1480 to 1680 Nicholas Cooper says 'the fundamental change is ... from spaces that were shared to spaces that are private, and from rooms with more general functions to more specialised ones': *Houses of the Gentry 1480–1680* (New Haven and London, 1999), p. 273.
46 E. C. Butler, 'Dom Besse's "Moine Benedictin"', *DR*, 18 (1899), 117–27; Harvey, *Living and Dying*, pp. 130–1; V. Jansen, 'Architecture and Community in Medieval Monastic Dormitories', in *Studies in Cistercian Art and Architecture* 5, ed. M. P. Lillich, *Cistercian Studies*, 66 (1998), pp. 59–64.
47 Power, *Nunneries*, pp. 319–20 n. 3.
48 Mackenzie E. C. Walcott, 'Inventories and Valuations of Religious Houses at the Time of the Dissolution, from the Public Record Office', *Archaeologia*, 43 (1871), pp. 201–49 at 208, 222, 226, 241.
49 C. M. Woolgar, *The Great Household in Late Medieval England* (New Haven and London, 1999), pp. 65, 177.
50 Mackenzie E. C. Walcott, 'Inventories of ... the Benedictine Priory of SS. Mary and Sexburga in the Island of Sheppey for Nuns', *Archaeologia Cantiana*, 7 (1868), 272–306. Better equipped was Durham in whose dorter 'where all ye Mounkes & ye Novices did lye, euery Mouncke [had] a little chamber of wainscott verie close seuerall by them selues & ther wyndowes towardes ye cloyster, euery wyndowe servinge for one Chamber by reasoune ye partition betwixt euery chamber was close wainscotted one from an other, and in euerye of there wyndowes a deske to supporte there bookes for there studdie ...': *Rites of Durham*, ed. J. T. Fowler, SS, 107 (1902), p. 65. The dorter at four Yorkshire womens' houses (Thicket, Handale, Nunkeeling, Arthington) ranged from 15–16 feet wide by 48–60 feet long. With a community of 16 (Thicket had 16 stalls in the church), individual

twelve cells, six on each side of a central corridor, each about 2.4 × 3 metres or 7 × 9 feet.[51] In her small space each Minster nun 'had made provisions for storage'. The most extensive belonged to Dame Agnes Browne who had 'a square cofer carvyd ... and in the wyndow a lytell cobard of wayncott carvyd and ij lytell chestes'. The scantiest was Dame Dorothe Toplyve's, who had only 'a casket coveryd with lether'. Thirty years earlier, in 1505, Alice Chester, a vowess living at the London minoresses', left to one of its nuns what she calls a 'closet' – presumably a chest.[52] Whether many or few, such chests, cupboards, and coffers would have been where personal possessions such as books were kept.

The chambers had certain common elements. Besides boxes and chests for storage, each nun had some bedding (all but two had feather beds) and some dishes. But a personal note was sometimes sounded: the painted papers which were part of Margaret [...ocks]'s cell constitute one of the earliest mentions of wallpaper,[53] while Anne Clifford owned two devotional *objets d'art*: a table with a crucifix of wood painted and an image of Our Lady painted. Two of the nine nuns had curtains; two had cushions: Elizabeth Stradlynge's of silk, Margaret Ryvers' of carpet work. In the absence of chairs, private reading, like private praying, may have been done in bed. The development of such private space within a communal, larger, space would of course make easier the acquiring of possessions like books, and might assist their solitary perusal, as well. That books were kept in the cells seems certain. A monk of Christ Church, Canterbury, who died in 1509, had at least twenty-five manuscripts in his cell at his death, while a second member of this house who died in 1517 had seventeen.[54] In these small identical spaces, shadowed by the Rule and its refusal of possessions, we can see nonetheless the evidence of private life, of individuation, as potent here as in the secular closet.

But even in more public spaces, personal reading may have been carried on. The rumination of scripture was a common reading practice. A modern commentator on the Benedictine Rule speaks of 'a lengthy oral repetition of individual words or sentences of Scripture which, humming them to oneself, one thus relishes to the full and makes part of oneself'.[55] We may catch a glimpse of such meditative reading in the Syon Rule, which enjoins silence in the library

---

cells would measure 60 square feet, about the same size as Littlemore's 7 × 9 feet: W. Brown, 'Description of the Buildings of Twelve Small Yorkshire Priories at the Reformation,' *YAJ*, 9 (1800), 197–215. For discussion of the size of nuns' cells at Amesbury, see B. M. Kerr, *Religious Life for Women c. 1100–1350: Fontevraud in England* (Oxford, 1999), p. 109.

[51] Gilchrist, *Gender and Material Culture*, pp. 122–3.

[52] PCC, 35 Holgrave; Prob. 11/14, fol. 175.

[53] Other early wallpaper fragments likewise come from a nuns' cell at Wienhausen in Lower Saxony, about 1564. Wallpaper seems not to have been particularly expensive in these years. At Antwerp sixteenth-century printed and coloured ceiling papers were found in 'five relatively modest houses'. G. Wisse, 'Manifold Beginnings: Single-Sheet Papers' in *The Papered Wall: History. Pattern. Technique*, edited by L. Hoskins (London, 1999), pp. 8–21.

[54] C. F. R. de Hamel, 'The Dispersal of the Library of Christ Church, Canterbury, from the Fourteenth to the Sixteenth Century' in *Books and Collections 1200–1700: Essays Presented to Andrew Watson*, ed. J. P. Carley and C. G. C. Tite (London, 1997), pp. 263–79 at 270.

[55] G. Holzherr, *The Rule of St. Benedict: A Guide to Christian Living* (Dublin, 1994), p. 233.

'whyls any suster is there alone in recordynge of her redynge'.[56] The modern meaning of 'record', to write down, was operative at this time, but so too was the older sense of 'recorden', to make the text part of oneself by committing it to memory. Thus in Syon's library a woman may have written excerpts from her reading in a personal manuscript, a *florilegium*, or she may have committed her reading to memory using the soft but audible murmur of rumination.

This interior retracing of the text has an exterior counterpart, again from Syon. The editor of *The Tree and xij Frutes* observed that in one of its manuscripts the letters had been carefully darkened by retracing, and he attributed this work to Syon nun Dorothy Codryngton.[57] It may be that, like oral repetition, this activity was intended as an exercise in mental retention as well as physical preservation, one in which reforming the manuscript's letters produced a deep familiarity with its text.

A few English nuns' manuscripts seem intended especially for personal perusal. For instance: a small, grubby, fifteenth-century book, Oxford, Bodl. MS Add. A.42, contains reflections on the religious life sent by a male spiritual director to 'My deare susterys Mary and Anne wyth all the other devo3th dyscyples of the schole of Cryste in youre monastery of Amysbury' (Wiltshire). The occasion was the two womens' religious profession, sometime between 1507 and 1530, and the book had come in response to their initiative. Their advisor says he has been

> Remembryng and consyderung your good and re[l]ygyouse desyres to have hadde sum goostly comforte and sum maner off instructyon of me, nowe att þe tyme of your professyoun, and specyally apon the wordes of the same and the substancyallis, whereby, as ye thow3th, yow my3th wyth Goddys helpe be the more apte and abylle to the performans of the same professyoun.[58]

Its worn and darkened pages may represent the form in which the writer originally sent his counsel or it may have been re-copied for a particular owner.

Amesbury's 1539 pension list contains three Annes (although no Marys), who might have been professed between 1507 and 1530, respectively numbers four, five, and twelve in the seniority list, after the prioress and subprioress: Anne Newman, Anne Predeaux, and Anne Bulkeley. Each received a pension of 100s.; Newman and Bulkeley were still alive in 1555–56.[59] It is tempting to identify the devout and ardent women addressed in Additional A.42 with the Anne Bulkeley whose name is found in another tiny humble manuscript, BL Harley MS 494. It contains the inscription 'dne Anne Bulkeley attinet liber iste' on the first leaf's verso; the same name is written in a display script on the second leaf (fo.1) as well: 'domina Anna Bulklie'.

Though Harley 494 has not been identified as a nuns' manuscript, the use of

---

[56] *Rewyll of Seynt Sauioure*, ed. Hogg, p. 72

[57] *Devout Treatyse Called the Tree*, ed. Vaissier, pp. xxxvii–xxxviii.

[58] Y. Parrey, '"Devoted Disciples of Christ": Early Sixteenth-Century Religious Life in the Nunnery at Amesbury' *BIHR*, 67 (1994), 240–8 at 245.

[59] MA, vol. 2, pp. 340, 334n.

'domina' may suggest its owner was the Amesbury nun. Its collection of texts written in several hands recalls another nun's manuscript, Sister EW (Elizabeth Woodford) of Syon's miscellany in LPL MS 546,[60] though Harley 494 is less competently produced and some of its texts more popular. Since the Harley manuscript includes two devotions which had been printed in the 1520s and 1530s, it seems likely, though not certain, that parts of the manuscript were copied from these prints; if this were so the manuscript could be dated between 1532 and 1539, the year of Amesbury's dissolution. The first devotion, A Dyurnall for deuoute soules, printed three times by Robert Wyer between [?1532] and [?1542],[61] recommends as reading for each day of the week a particular chapter from the Speculum Vite Christi. The second devotion, Syon author William Bonde's chapter on the ceremonies of the Mass, was probably taken from his Pylgrimage of Perfection printed in 1526 and 1531.[62] MS Harley 494's small size, disorderly layout, and various hands characterise it as a personal product, perhaps put together by its owner and a group of friends.

These two individual collections, Elizabeth Woodford's and Anne Bulkeley's, look back to the fifteenth-century household miscellanies of interest to secular women and perhaps written by them, like the Findern anthology, and look forward to female commonplace books of the seventeenth century.[63] They are early examples of collections for which women chose, and in which they wrote, texts particularly meaningful to them, texts which they then read over at times which they likewise chose. Within female religious life too, the Woodford and Bulkeley manuscripts have precedents. BL, Cotton MS Galba A XIV and BL, Cotton MS Nero A II are parts of an eleventh-century miscellany, perhaps from Nunnaminster, which contains a collection of devotions written by many hands and representing a personal selection.[64]

The opportunity for individual choice is reflected in Additional A. 42 as well, which represents an initiative taken by the nuns Mary and Anne to obtain spiritual reading. In lives whose spiritual direction and whose reading was regulated with a high degree of control, these female-owned manuscripts register the presence of the personal in intellectual and spiritual matters. As individual monastic space was more frequently found, so we might posit a similar growth of individual effort in obtaining or in producing one's own reading, the books that would be perused in that private space.

Reading required a certain disposition, an attentive poise. The Dietary of Ghostly Health, printed four times between 1520 and 1527, is marked as a Syon text by its woodcut of St Bridget writing. Its anonymous author sent the book to 'my good systers' as a New Year's gift since 'dyuerse of you haue giuen tokens vnto me wherefore hauynge nothyng redy to gyue vnto you agayne I purpose in

[60] V. O'Mara, 'A Middle English Text Written by a Female Scribe', Notes & Queries, 235 (1990), 396–8.

[61] STC, 6928, 6928. 5, 6928a.

[62] J. R. Rhodes, 'Private Devotion in England on the Eve of the Reformation', unpublished Ph. D. dissertation, 2 vols., (University of Durham, 1974), vol. 2, pp. 12, 49, n. 340.

[63] S. McNamer, 'Female Authors, Provincial Setting: The Re-Versing of Courtly Love in the Findern Manuscript', Viator, 22 (1991), 278–310.

[64] A Pre-Conquest English Prayer Book, ed. B. Muir, HBS, 103 (1988), p. xxxiv.

my mynde to prepare one token for you all'.[65] The general advice is thoughtful: 'In your study & redynge of bokes/ se yt they be conuenyent [suitable] for you. And marke wel all suche thynges as make to the ensample of good lyfe/ both for to fele at yourselfe/ & to she [sic, for 'shew'?] it vnto others for ye same entente'. Even private reading should be prefaced by a gathering of attention; one should begin: 'Ye grace of the holy ghost lyght on vs both soule and body'. The reading concluded, some gesture toward retention should follow: 'And after your redynge/ remember breuely what ye haue redde & than say thus (Confirma hoc deus quod operatus es in nobis), with a pater noster'.[66] The *Dietary* makes several points: even solitary reading was to be shared with others. It involved intellectual effort; the practice of recall and retention was an integral part of reading. Set off from daily life by beginning and ending in prayer, reading retained its identity as a spiritual practice.

This same intimate joining of reading and mental prayer is visible in the introduction to the *Faits and the Passion of Our Lord Jesu Christ*, a fifteenth-century set of prayers written by one religious woman for another, both probably from Syon.[67] The author says, 'I wolde ye couden the sentence [understood the meaning] withoutyn the book, for an ye so coude, ye schulden fele mochil more comforth and unyon in God to seye it so inforth than forto seie it be scripture' [to say it mentally rather than to read it]. This passage draws on the traditional understanding of meditative reading, the rumination and assimilation of spiritual truth through reading. Its goal was the internalisation of the text, a process which then issued in prayer, or perhaps, particularly in the gift of tears. Reading was thus a way into prayer. As Paul Gehl says, 'long and arduous study led to a momentary release of prayerful insight, a glimpse through a doorway at the top of a steep stair'.[68]

Such internalisation of one's reading was at least as old as St Anselm. Somewhat more recent was the kind of Franciscan-associated response to reading which Mary Carruthers found in a Latin rule for women from the second half of the fourteenth century,[69] wrongly attributed to St Jerome and perhaps written for a convent of Tuscan nuns.[70] It describes 'how each sister should follow the reading'. With absorbed, intent mind, she should actively, emotionally, enter into the reading. She sighs anxiously when, in prophecy or historical narrative, the word of God shows enmity to the wicked: 'she is filled with great joy when the favour of the Lord is shown to the good'. Given Syon's affection for St Jerome, and the dissemination of this rule as Jerome's, it may be that a similar

65 STC, 6834, A2.

66 *Ibid.*, A6.

67 *Women's Writing in Middle English*, ed. A. Barratt (London and New York, 1992), pp. 217–18; W. F. Pollard, 'Bodleian MS Holkham 41: A Fifteenth-Century Bridgettine Manuscript and Prayer Cycle', *Birgittiana*, 3 (1997), 43–53.

68 P. Gehl, '"Competens Silencium": Varieties of Monastic Silence in the Medieval West', *Viator*, 18 (1987), 125–60 at 143.

69 The pseudo-Hieromian rule is printed in *PL*, 30. 435 C–D. For Carruthers' discussion of meditative reading see M. Carruthers, *The Book of Memory: A Study of Memory in Medieval Culture* (Cambridge, 1990), pp. 164–74.

70 E. F. Rice Jr., *St Jerome in the Renaissance* (Baltimore and London, 1985), pp. 128, 246.

passage in the *Myroure of Oure Ladye* was influenced by such a text. Distinguishing between books made to inform the mind and those made to excite the emotions ('to quyken ... the affeccyons of the soule'), the *Myroure* says 'When ye rede these [latter] bokes ye oughte to laboure in your selfe inwardly. to sturre vp your affeccyons accordingly to the matter that ye rede. As when ye rede maters of drede, ye ought to set you to conceyue a drede in your selfe. And when ye rede maters of hope, ye oughte to sturre vp yourselfe to fele comforte ... and so fourth of other'.[71]

As instructive books moved the reader to reformation of life, other sorts of books induced a reformation of feeling, and some books could do both. Guidance like the *Myroure's* assisted the reader in distinguishing various kinds of texts and constructed a suitable posture for different sorts of reading upon which the reader might model her own. Such counsel produced a range of nuanced readerly responses. Aimed originally at women, but finally reaching a broad undifferentiated audience, this instruction was responsible for shaping in the reader a sophisticated and flexible reading of the text, a reading *habitus* which might be deployed in perusing secular works as well.

We may thus wonder about the effect of monastic formation on reading, a traditional training that included both the older technique of memorisation and the newer training in empathy, particularly when these approaches were combined with the development of physical spaces for private reading. Surely the woman who read alone in such a small space, remembering the text strongly enough to summon it at will and feeling with the words, generating the emotions appropriate, moved substantially in the direction of psychological interiority.

In work on secular architecture, the early modern closet has been associated with 'the construction of a new modern subjectivity'.[72] Religious life too was affected by the same trends in the built environment: the evolution of smaller, more individual rooms and the corresponding focus on activities suited to these spaces.[73] Thus in institutional religious life the long-sustained pressure against the communal ideal and toward a more individual orientation which has generally been viewed as representing a decline from an elevated monastic ideal, might instead be seen as the precondition for a new sort of reading practice. In women's religious houses the availability of places for private reading was linked with reading techniques productive of interiority. These physical spaces and this interior formation together combined to ease the shift away from the medieval notion of public reading and toward the modern conception of reading: singular, solitary, a locus for the interior.

---

[71]   *Myroure of oure Ladye*, ed. Blunt, p. 69.

[72]   A. Friedman, *House and Household in Elizabethan England* (Chicago, 1988), p. 77.

[73]   David N. Bell has provided a magisterial survey of Cistercian regulations regarding privacy, from 1287 to 1666: 'Chambers, Cells, and Cubicles: The Cistercian General Chapter and the Development of the Private Room', in *Perspectives for an Architecture of Solitude: Essays on Cistercians, Art and Architecture in Honour of Peter Fergusson*, ed. Terryl N. Kinder (Toronto, 2004), pp. 187–98.

Holy Expectations:
The Female Monastic Vocation in the Diocese of Winchester on the Eve of the Reformation

BARRY COLLETT

Just months before Martin Luther propounded theological ideas that later contributed to the dissolution of monasteries, the Bishop of Winchester, Richard Fox, translated the Benedictine Rule for nuns, *Here Begynneth the Rule of Seynt Benet*, published by Richard Pynson in January 1517 [see plate 10]. A few months earlier he wrote the 'Fourme and order of the ceremonies perteinyng to the solempne profession of benediction and consecration of holy virgins', using the original Latin ordinal (based upon chapter 58 of the Rule), but adding explanations and instructions in English.[1] Fox's expansions and interpolations in these works reveal much about his thinking, and although historians often must conjecture what might or might not be implied by particular words and phrases, his concept of the female monastic vocation is discernible in these two sources.[2] We do not know how the nuns themselves understood their vocation, but four slender points suggest that they agreed with him: he and the nuns knew each other; the four heads of houses themselves asked him to write for them; they would have recognised that what he wrote accurately followed the Rule, and that his English interpolations flowed naturally from the Latin; finally, a Benedictine prioress and other nuns (not at Winchester but at Stamford) annotated their copy of *Here Begynneth* with approval.[3]

---

[1]   Two copies of *Here Begynneth* survive, one in the BL in mint condition; the other, heavily annotated, belonged to Margareta Stanburne prioress of St Michael's Benedictine Priory, Stamford, and is now in Oxford, Bodl. Two copies of 'Fourme and order' survive. One is in CUL, MS Mm. 3. 13, undated, given to the nuns of Saint Mary's Winchester, and printed in William Maskell, *Monumenta, Ritualia ecclesiae Anglicanae* (London, 1846), vol. 2, pp. 307–31. The second copy is Bodleian, Barlow MS 11; the recipients are unknown, but the profession was for Holy Cross and St Peter, the dedication of Wherwell Abbey. M. C. Erler, 'Bishop Richard Fox's Manuscript gifts to his Winchester Nuns: A second Surviving Example', *JEH*, 52/2 (2001), 334–7. See also plate 10.

[2]   Official sources of the Winchester houses include the episcopal registers of Archbishop Morton, CCCR, CCP, Register R, *Sede vacante*, fols. 108–157 (1500) and the episcopal registers of Fox (1501–28) in HRO. There are also state papers and letters, monastic cartularies (the Wherwell cartulary is BL, Egerton MS 2104a), the records of the Court of Augmentations, account rolls for both Wherwell and Romsey (NA, SC6–983–34).

[3]   J. G. Clark, 'The Religious Orders in Pre-Reformation England', in *Religious Orders*, ed. *id.*, pp. 21–2.

Fox's two works are valuable, first because they reveal individual nuns' and also community expectations of monastic life in 1517, and therefore how these women defined their monastic vocation. Second, modern studies of English nunneries have tended to separate practical from spiritual and intellectual matters, but these two sources are based directly upon the Rule which covers all aspects of the monastic life: consequently, an analysis of the expectations will provide us with a reasonably balanced view of monastic life.[4]

In 1485, Richard Fox was a middle-aged cleric in Paris, a political exile from Richard III. He joined the earl of Richmond's entourage, helped plan the invasion of England, and was present at Bosworth. He became Privy Seal and confidential adviser to Henry, who appointed him successively bishop of Exeter, Bath and Wells, Durham, and finally Winchester, where he remained from 1501 until his death in 1528. In 1516, Fox left government and was replaced by Thomas Wolsey, his own protégé. When he returned to Winchester, Fox wrote to Wolsey, regretting his neglect of the work of God, and stating his intention to act effectively in the time remaining to him: to 'be occupied in my cure wherby I maye doo soom satisfaccion for xxviij yeres negligence ... to serue woldly with damnacion of my saule and many other sawles whereof I haue the cure'.[5] Fox surveyed his diocese, identified problems, and began a programme of reform.

One problem was common to all four female houses of the diocese, the three Benedictine abbeys of Romsey, Wherwell, St Mary's within-the-city of Winchester (Nunnaminster) and the Cistercian Priory of Wintney.[6] Novices were supposed to read, learn and understand the Rule before being professed, and afterwards to continue reading it, and teaching it to younger novices. But the Rule was in Latin, and although heads, obedientiaries and a number of other nuns could read Latin, many could neither read the Rule nor understand the passages read aloud during chapter and refectory. Literate nuns (*dogmatistae*) took it in turns to translate the Rule into English and explain it to others, but some nuns claimed that they still remained uncertain about the vocation to which they had committed themselves. Fox commented that at times a nun would claim 'that she wyste nat what she professed, as we knowe by experience that some of them have sayd in tyme passed'.[7] Clearly, there was an expectation of the female monastic vocation, not always articulated, that women who became nuns would receive sufficient education to understand their vocation, and to some extent become learned women, according to individual ability. We shall return to this point.

If the heads of houses (and the bishop) were to meet this expectation fully they needed a good English translation to ensure better understanding of the

[4] Lee, *Nunneries*, p. 6.
[5] Fox's letter to Wolsey, 23 April 1516, declining to return to London to assist with a problem in foreign affairs. *Letters of Richard Fox*, eds. P. S. Allen and H. M. Allen (Oxford, 1929), pp. 82–3. His reference to twenty-eight years is not clear. Wolsey later adapted this remark to his own deathbed use.
[6] *VCH Hampshire*, vol. 2, p. 107. Nunnaminster was founded at the end of the ninth century by Alfred and his queen, Eahlswith. Unusually, the priory of Hartley Wintney, near Reading, was subject to the bishop.
[7] Here *Begynneth*, A.ii.v.

Rule, perhaps a book which nuns could themselves read and also use as a tool for learning the original Latin. Moreover, a good English translation and its pedagogic value for education would help recruit more nuns. Fox described how the three abbesses and the prioress made an 'instant' (urgent) request to him, and his response:

> specially at thinstant requeste of our ryght dere and welbeloued doughters in oure lorde Ihu[s] Thabbasses of the monasteris of Rumsay, Wharwel, Seynt Maries within the citie of Winchester, and the prioresse of Wintnay: oure right religious diocesans, we haue translated: the sayde rule into oure moders tonge, co[m]mune, playne, rounde englisshe, easy, and redy to be understande by the sayde deuoute religiouse women.[8]

It is not known whether the four heads of houses approached Fox or whether he pressured them to make the request. The former is most probable, partly because Fox was inclined to cooperation rather than compulsion, and partly because nuns were decisive women, capable of taking their own initiatives and not easily pushed around.[9] In particular, heads of houses were responsible for small but busy corporations: they had to oversee the worship, spiritual capabilities, education, daily lives, sickness, death and burial of everyone within their convent; they had to understand complicated internal and external problems, consult with their house's secular officials, make financial and legal decisions, negotiate endowments, administer property, building maintenance and finances, balance a limited budget for housekeeping, and oversee the buying of food and clothing, and the employment of domestic staff such as bakers or butchers – though the abbess delegated many tasks to obedientiaries such as the sacristan or the cellarer. These obedientiaries were similarly capable women, such as Avelene Cowdrey the sub-prioress of Wherwell in 1516. She came from a gentry family, was educated, accustomed to give orders, and as sub-prioress was probably involved in the request for an English translation. Fox approved when the nuns elected her abbess in 1518 because she was 'pleasant to god and true to the king'. Her successor was Anne Colte, a woman of spirit, who had a close relationship with John Stokesley the bishop of London, resisted the crown's attempts to alienate one of Wherwell's farms, and when urged to retire on a pension demanded to speak to the king in person.[10] Other heads of religious houses and their obedientiaries were women of this calibre, each with their own experience, competence and understanding of monastic life. Moreover, being aware of the need for reform – at least in Romsey abbey – the need for greater dedication to the monastic vocation in all nunneries, and a need for more nuns,

---

8   Here *Begynneth*, preface, A.ii–iii.
9   H. G. D. Liveing, *The Records of Romsey Abbey: an account of the Benedictine house of nuns, with notes on the parish church and town (A.D. 907–1558)* (Winchester, 1906), pp. 211–16.
10 *VCH Hampshire*, vol. 2, pp. 49, 135–7.

they themselves were capable of taking the initiative, or at least matching Fox's interest in a translation of the Rule.[11]

Mid 1516 was timely for the nuns to act. Bishop Fox was now in residence, and the troubled Romsey abbey had a new abbess: in 1515, Anne Westbrook had been elected abbess, replacing Joyce Rowse. Dame Anne had previously been the sexton, responsible for the fabric and contents of the church, including furniture, vestments and vessels, preparation of the altar, bell-ringing and the digging of graves. This businesslike abbess, with a sense of order and discipline, set out to reform the abbey, and in 1516 she joined the request for a translation.[12] Senior nuns in each house probably conferred amongst themselves and with other houses, and agreed that a translation of the Rule was necessary. In his words, they urgently requested him to translate it into 'oure moders tonge, co[m]mune, playne, rounde englisshe, easy, and redy to be understande'. This 'instant requeste' to the bishop demonstrates the first expectation of the female monastic vocation, that by virtue of their status, collectively as a community and individually as heads and obedientaries, nuns possess and exercise independent authority both within the cloister and towards the outside world. Fox's own term 'oure right religious diocesans' clearly implies that he considered female heads of houses to possess such authority.

A sense of independent authority took strength from the social background and education of nuns who came from yeoman and gentry families in rural and urban southern England: some had had access to schools, primers and liturgical and devotional books at home and when they entered the monastic life could already read and write English and even Latin.[13] Now whatever sense of authority their upbringing and earlier education had given them was being used to increase learning within the monastic life. Their request demonstrates the second expectation of the female monastic vocation already mentioned: that able nuns should be educated for their vocation. If they were not already literate in English and Latin it was expected that they should become so, and, if already literate, it was expected that they should go on learning. In the early sixteenth century most nuns at the Dominican priory at Dartford could read English and liturgical Latin, and some had more advanced learning, reading books of classical literature, popular histories such as The Brut, and vernacular spiritual writings; and several nuns had a strong intellectual and spiritual rapport with their friar chaplains.[14] If this were the case at Dartford, it is quite possible that the

[11] For a detailed account of the responsibilities and capabilities of heads, seconds-in-command and obedientiaries see Marilyn Oliva, The Convent and the Community in Late Medieval England: Female Monasteries in the Diocese of Norwich, 1350–1540 (Woodbridge, 1998), pp. 75–102. Oliva's conclusion is that the nuns were 'hands on' highly sophisticated managers of accounts and practical running of their houses, took responsibility for servants and guests and handled limited resources reasonably well, even in hard times. Unfortunately, I have not been able to consult the recent work of Valerie Spears on leadership in female houses.

[12] The next abbess, Elizabeth Ryprose (1523–39) also kept the abbey under stricter control, but occasional further episodes of sexual misbehaviour, quarrelling, slander and backbiting meant that Romsey's community life was still troubled at the dissolution.

[13] Power, Nunneries, p. 253.

[14] Lee, Nunneries, pp. 214–21.

heads and senior nuns of the four Hampshire houses had similar rapport with the clergy.

Fox did not commission the translation but decided to do it himself. There were several Latin texts available to him: Wintney abbey's library had a female-gendered Latin text with early Middle English translation, but most probably he used *Regula & vita beatissimi patris Benedicti* also published by de Worde, in 1512.[15] For the translation he may have consulted the Wintney Middle English version, though there is little similarity, or the French translation by Guy de Jouenneaux, *Regula beatissimi benedicti e latino in gallicum sermone[m]*, published by Geoffroy de Marnef in Paris in 1500. On the other hand, Fox was a competent Latinist and wrote a lively and exuberant English, and was well able to translate the Rule without borrowing from other translations: moreover, the English expansions and comments are undoubtedly his own work.

In addition to the two expectations of the female monastic vocation already discussed (the convent's standing and authority in the community, and the education of nuns), the text itself reveals five more expectations. The first is that nuns were not to imitate monks in ways that modified or denied their female identity. Fox did not wish to impose masculine practices on nuns, nor would he delete passages or bowdlerise the text because they were women – another acknowledgment of their independent minds. He told them that he translated Benedict's entire Rule, even the chapters and passages that applied only to men: 'And that no parte of seynt Benetts rule be by vs conceyled or hid for them/ we haue therfore translate the sayde chapiter applyenge it to the monkes oonly/ accordynge to the originall text as followeth/ without any me[n]cion maki[n]ge of mi[n]chi[n]s'. Thus, the nuns would know exactly how they, as female monastics, lived differently from males. His only changes were small adjustments appropriate for England, for example specifying apples as the fruit dish, and daily quantities of beer instead of wine.[16]

There may even have been 'worldly' manifestations of femininity within the nunneries of Winchester. Marilyn Oliva has discovered that East Anglian nuns wore comfortable sometimes secular clothing, even silk waist bands, and a recent study of Italian convents during the later, and much stricter, post-Tridentine period challenges the stereotype of nuns wearing drab, featureless habits: there is evidence that their dress and attire was fashionable, almost 'worldly'.[17] At Wherwell, Avelene Cowdrey's portrait, painted during the early 1520s, showed a woman with intelligent eyes and determined mouth, holding a book,

---

15 The Wintney version is BL Cotton Clauius D. III. Both Latin and English texts are gendered for women. The critical edition is M. M. Arnold Schroër, *Die Winteney-Version der Regula S. Benedicti, Lateinisch und Englisch* (Halle: Max Niemeyer, 1888), with supplement by M. Gretsch, Tübingen: 1973. Also recently printed was *Regula & vita beatissimi patris Benedicti cum miraculis a beato Gregorio. ix papa conscripta* (London: Wynken de Worde, probably 1506) [STC, 12351]. 'Gregorio. ix' is obviously a printer's error. Also, Fox could have used one of the many other Latin texts published on the continent.

16 A 'hemina' was generally reckoned as half a pint, but a modern scholar reckons it at half a bottle; *RB 1980*, pp. 238–9.

17 Oliva, *The Convent and the Community*, pp. 186–90. S. Evangelisti, 'Monastic Poverty and Material Culture in Early Modern Italian convents', *HJ*, 47/1 (2004), 1–20. Nuns dressed stylishly, at times wearing high-heeled shoes, wigs, furs and other elegancies.

elegantly dressed in her well-designed nun's habit, the veil fashionably drawn back to show her handsome face, a full forehead and her hairline.[18] As a well-dressed abbess, without being lax, she was an example of how Fox, who must have known of the portrait, expected nuns to be competent in their vocation but retain their femininity, a point also evident in the copy of 'Fourme and order of the ceremonies' that he gave Wherwell abbey. It contains five delicate illustrations, initial letters illustrated with the faces of nuns, distinctly womanly faces, affectionately drawn, perhaps likenesses of the abbess and obedientiaries, possibly including Avelene Cowdrey when she was sub-prioress in 1516 [see also plate 11].[19] Moreover, if gentry families in Winchester diocese used local nunneries as finishing schools for their young women, as they did in Yorkshire, then the nuns must have provided a level of deportment and education that was satisfactory to the gentry.[20]

Fox also knew that because nuns had come from 'the world', they were familiar with female domestic matters, had not expunged them from their memories, and could learn from allusions to them. He wrote in terms of ordinary lay life, using familiar 'worldly' intimate terms to describe both physical and spiritual temptations. In the Rule's allusion in chapter 7 to the self-centred distress of a newly weaned child (si exaltavi animam meam, sicut ablactatus est super matrem suam) Fox elaborated the imagery of a child denied his mother's breast, 'if I haue not mekely behaued me/ but exalted my mynde by pryde/ vayne glorye/ or presumpcion/ then let my punishement be lyke vnto the punishement of a sokynge childe the whiche is wayned & denied his moders breste/ and then doth p[er]ishe'.[21] In another passage, despite his intention to translate the Rule fully, he seems to have respected female maternal tenderness by softening the Prologue's allusion to killing temptations as one might kill infants by dashing them against a rock, albeit the rock of Christ (et parvulos cogitatos ejus tenuit, et ellisit ad Christum). Instead, he translated the passage simply as 'temptacions/ and entisinges/ ... brokyn & resisted ... at the firste monicion of them'.[22] Also, in the chapter on chastity he appealed to the nuns' female understanding of love and sex, by expanding the Rule's concise 'Non adulterari' beyond the physical act to what he called the 'spiritual fornication' of excessive self-esteem, the sinful elements of pride and greed in sexuality:

ye breke not your chastite/ that is to saye/ that ye doo no maner of aduoutrye/ fornicacion/ inco[n]tinencie nor any other synne or vucle[n]nesse of the flesche/ &

18 VCH Hampshire, vol. 4, p. 170, for details of the Coudray family of Basingstoke and monastic houses. The portrait, held in private hands, is reproduced in D. K. Coldicott, Hampshire Nunneries (Chichester, 1989), p. 87.
19 Oxford, Bodl., MS Barlow 11, pp. 2, 7, 8, 10 (twice). The face on p. 8 is reasonably similar to the portrait of Avelene Cowdrey. On p. 1 there is an illustration resembling breasts. See also plate 11.
20 C. Cross, 'Yorkshire Nunneries in the Early Tudor Period', Religious Orders, ed. Clark, p. 145.
21 Here Begynneth, C.i.v. For a discussion of the uncertain syntax and meaning of the passage, see RB: 1980, pp. 192–3.
22 Here Begynneth, A.iv.r.

in lyke wyse ye shall doo noo spirituall fornicacio[n]/that is to say/ ye shall worchip no falce gods nor loue inordinatly youre selfe nor any other erthely creature.[23]

Clearly, Fox understood chastity as much more than abstinence from sexual acts: chastity, like sexual intercourse itself, included self-giving and tenderness, which self-centred people lack, being guilty of 'spiritual fornication' even when physically chaste. This remarkable passage shows Fox's depth of understanding of human sexuality – and presumably that of the nuns for whom he wrote his comment.

Fox, himself an early riser, was sympathetic to nuns who found it difficult to wake up in the morning and needed to be roused gently. In chapter 22, in a brilliant extension of the Latin 'surgentes vero ad opus Dei invicem se moderate cohortentur' he transformed the two words 'moderate cohortentur' (quietly encourage) into the vivid admonition 'they that be furste vp and redy toward the seruyce of god shall make som softe and sobre styrrynge/with the sou[n]de of their mouthes/or of their fete/or knockynge vppo[n] the beddes sydes/to a wake theym that be sluggardes'.[24] He was also sympathetic to nuns who found learning laborious: he translated concise Latin phrases with expansive, lively, English, frequently alluding to contemporary life, weaving pedagogic devices into the text, especially repetitions, synonyms, and recollections such as 'in the manner aforesaid', and 'O dere susters (sayth seynt Benet)', and expanding the Rule's biblical examples with brief allusions to inspire curiosity, such as extending the Latin to explain how Eli, the priest who fell and broke his neck, was negligent about correcting his children.[25] In short, Fox understood that nuns were still conversant with the outside world and subject to difficulties experienced by laywomen. He was *simpatico*: and made an effort to internalise their memories, experiences and attitudes.

The fourth expectation within Fox's extensions and extrapolations was that nuns would live a close-knit family life, including patriarchal and matriarchal relationships. He used lay domestic imagery of father and daughter to describe the nuns' relationship with God, a kind, loving and forbearing father who 'of his owne kyndnes' listens with sweetness and favour to the petitions of his daughters '... myne [e]yes be open & fixed vppon you/ & myne erys allway redy to your prayers & peticions/ & before ye shall call vppo[n] me I shall p[re]uent you/ & shall say/ lowe here I am/ redy to youre desyres'.[26] Similarly, he emphasised the role of abbess as a mother to the nuns, expanding the Rule's simple statement that 'Abba' means father, to read 'that is to say fader/ of the whiche name all abbottes & abbasses take their names: thabbot to be to his coue[n]t a fader/ & thabbasse a moder'.[27]

The nun entered this family and household through the formal rite of profession as set out in Fox's 'Fourme and order of the ceremonies', probably written in 1516, based mainly on the Sarum Pontifical but with the addition of extensive

---

23 *Here Begynneth*, B.iii.r.
24 Here *Begynneth*, D.iii.v.
25 *Here Begynneth*, B.i.v. the Latin is simply 'memor periculi Heli sacerdotis de Silo'.
26 Here *Begynneth*, Prologue, A.iii.v. Prevent you: to come even before you ask; Lowe: Lo.
27 *Here Begynneth*, A.vi.r.

stage directions in words and stylised illustrations, bringing out both the ceremony's theatrical drama and its communal nature. At the mass that followed,
the newly professed nuns served at the altar: they 'muste at the hygh masse offre
brede and wyne and also be co[m]muned and howseld'. When she offered the
elements, each nun had a 'sudary' or a towel over both her hands; the imagery of
these 'housling towels' is rich: they were napkins to carry prayer books – food of
the Word – and also napkins to hold the food of the Eucharist. In her right hand
the nun held a paten with a host and in the left hand a cruet containing wine.
Then, 'they shall shyft the hoste' from their paten onto the paten held by the
deacon, after which they gave the cruet of wine to the bishop, kissing his hand
as they did so. The bishop then put 'so[m]me deale' into the chalice. After the
bishop's own communion the nuns were 'howselled' (communicated), kneeling
to take the consecrated bread from the bishop and standing to receive the consecrated wine from a priest, that is, not kneeling before the priest, but standing at
the same level as him.

> he shall howsell the virgins ther that day p[ro]fessed kneylyng at the sayde aulter
> grece [step] in order wi[th] *confiteor, misereatur* and *absoluto[n]em,* theyr veyles
> hitherto cov[er]yng theyr faces as a fore, and then they shall receyve wyne of a
> p[re]ystes hande standing at the sayde grece as the man is, and after that yet stan-
> dyng in the same place they shall there syng to gether.[28]

Thus, as newcomers to this family ritual, the nuns served at the family holy
table, communicating in both kinds as they did at high feasts and probably other
convent masses.

The smooth running of a family household requires affection and competence,
not offending or inconveniencing others, or forming rivalries and factions. Fox
took the Rule's preoccupation with conflict management and emphasised it
even further, pointing out that it took an effort to make relationships within the
convent resemble the bonds between parents, children and siblings in a 'worldly'
family. Thus, he expanded the Rule's fifth 'instrument' of doing no theft (Non
facere furtum), to include the irritating habits of borrowing or taking things,
which cause friction in all households:

> The v. [instrument] is that ye doo no thefte/that is to say/ ye shall not take nor vse
> the goods of an other fraudulently/nor without the owners wyll lycence or asse[n]t/
> nor that ye religiose sisters take/ receyue/ or kepe ony thynge/without the certeyne
> knowlege & speciall graunt or licence of the abbasse.[29]

More positively, he knew that affectionate family bonding creates self-restraint,
tolerance and good humour, which in turn create and maintain an orderly,
companionable and happy community. Within this family, Fox wrote, it becomes

---

[28] Oxford, Bodl., Barlow MS 11, pp. 24–9. Deale was Rhenish wine, probably hock. Marilyn
Oliva kindly pointed out the imagery of the 'housling towels', and referred me to M. E. C.
Walcott, 'Inventories of St Mary's Hospital, Dover, St Martin New-Work, Dover, and the
Benedictine Priory of SS Mary and Sexburga in the Isle of Sheppy for Nuns', *Archaeologia
Cantiana,* vii (1868), p. 294, n. 4 'Howseling towels: four towels were required ... and until
a recent period, women carried their prayer books to church in a white handerchief, which
was a relic of the howseling cloth.'

[29] *Here Begynneth,* ch. 4, B.iii.r–v.

easy to obey authority, to be not self-centred, 'plesant vnto other', and have the community function 'effectuosly'.

> It is a narowe and strayte waye that leedith vnto euerlastinge lyfe. that is to say not lyuyng after there owne wyll/ ne beinge obedient to their owne desyres and vnlefull pleasures/ but continuinge their lyfe vnder the Iugement and power of a nother/ lyuinge in monasteries ... this sealfe same obedience shall then be acceptable vnto god and plesant vnto other/whan that thinge which is co[m]maunded is effectuosly brought to ende/ not ferefully/ slowly/ or fayntly/ ne with grutch or denyeng nor arguinge nor resoning it.[30]

The fourth expectation, of living in a family, overlaps the fifth expectation of the female monastic vocation in *Here Begynneth*, that a nun will grow in holiness through self-discipline. The Rule simply states that the monastic's task was to pursue the kingdom of God and his justice, but Fox added 'by ryghtwose service/ workes/ and doing to god'.[31] He recognised human difficulties, often inability, to do good works, 'where through the fragilite of nature/ and the infirmite of our selfe we be insufficient and vnhable so to do'. Fox illustrated his point with a practical example of the self-deceptive procrastination that tackles lesser tasks in order to avoid greater ones.[32] Thus, the abbess 'shall not haue any apparent or probable cause/ to be busy and solicite aboutes wordly goodes/ takynge the lesse heede to the spirituell & goostly sowles'.[33] This not only refers to procrastination in exercising authority, but echoes his own recent regret that prolonged royal service had delayed 'takynge the lesse heede' to his spiritual duties. All abbesses (and by implication all nuns) must get their priorities right and live focussed, disciplined lives. To emphasise the danger, Fox used particularly vivid English to translate the Rule on the disorganised and degenerate lives of Sybarite pseudo-monks:

> whiche lyue not vnder obedience of any sup[er]ior/ ne vnder any Rule that is good & approued/ nor be tried in monasters: as golde is by the furnace/ but be more lyke vnto ledde/ supple & plyable to all vicis/ And fayning the[m]selfe to be religiose/ vnder the simulate habite/ & to[n]sure of religiose men/ be in all their dedes: vayne/ y dell/ and worldly.[34]

Such temptations are overcome only by organised and self-disciplined resolution. Drawing from his experience in high office, Fox emphasised resolution, urging nuns to be determined and intrepid – not suddenly to be afraid and desert the task 'at a chop'.[35] Without hectoring or coercion, he gave straightforward advice about overcoming weaknesses, acknowledging that the nuns had within themselves the power to fulfil their vocation.

Fox described this fifth expectation of the female monastic vocation – growth in holiness through self-discipline – as a skilled occupation, working as part

30 *Here Begynneth*, B.vi.r–v.
31 *Here Begynneth*, ch. 2, B.ii.r.
32 *Here Begynneth*, Prologue, A.iv.v.
33 *Here Begynneth*, Ch. 2, B.ii.r.
34 *Here Begynneth*, Ch.1, A.v.v. Fox did not expand the passage, but used his English to emphasise the point.
35 *Here Begynneth*, A.v.r. A 'chop' is a problem or difficulty.

of a team. He consistently translated the Rule to emphasise competence and efficiency, each nun doing the work for which she has responsibility, being 'composed and ordered' both in herself and within the communal life of the convent. Since the nun is a craftswomen, she requires tools for the job. At the beginning of chapter 4 (The instruments of good works) Fox inserted his own striking prologue on the necessary instruments and skills:

> Like as all worldely artificers have materyall instrumentes apte for the accomplyssheme[n]t of their worldely werkes, in lyke wyse there be instrumentes spirituell, for the crafte of religiose lyuinge, by the whiche religiose persons, bothe in this p[re]sent lyfe, may honestly & after the pleasure of god be derected, composed, & ordred, & also after the same lyfe, they may blessedly reigne with christ i[n] heue[n].[36]

The expectation of growth in holiness through 'the crafte of religiose lyuinge' is set in a much wider context than the individualistc 'spiritual' concept of John Alcock, Bishop of Ely, whose almost contemporary tract on Carthusian nuns concentrated upon the nun's interior marriage to her heavenly bridegroom, entirely apart from the world.[37] In contrast, the spiritual aspirations of Fox's nuns were closer to those of pious laywomen who regularly worshipped God and tried to grow in holiness whilst living 'in the world', married, having a family, with worldly possessions, and living within the kind of obedience necessary to family life and work.

We shall return to this fifth expectation, of growth in holiness. In the meantime, to summarise the argument, Fox and the nuns of Winchester saw the female monastic vocation as several overlapping expectations; first, that senior nuns would possess a degree of independent authority; second, that nuns would receive appropriate education and intellectual training; third, that they would remain conscious of their sex as women; fourth, that they would live within a monastic family; fifth, that each nun would grow in holiness using valuable spiritual tools and craft skills.

The sixth expectation of the monastic vocation in *Here Begynneth* was a development of the fourth and the fifth: that the competence of individual nuns would operate collectively to create corporate efficiency, so that the monastic community would be a smoothly functioning community, effectively fulfilling its purpose. The need for order and cooperation was inherent in the Rule, but Fox's commentary also reflected a type of mirror-for-princes advice, the paradigm of a smoothly functioning community based less upon the authority of one person and more upon the interacting responsibilities and competent discharge of each person's responsibilities.[38] During his political life, Fox had emphasised clear

---

[36] *Here Begynneth*, B.iii.v.

[37] John Alcock, *Desponsacio virginis xpristo. Spousage of a virgyn to chryste. … Here endeth an exhortacyon made to relygyous Systers in the tyme of theyr consecracyon*, Westminster: Wynken de Worde, c. 1497 (reprinted 1499, 1501). Reprinted Amsterdam and Norwood, New Jersey, USA: Walter J. Johnson, *Theatrum Orbis Terrarum* (1974).

[38] For this style of political advice, see B. Collett, 'The Three Mirrors of Christine de Pizan', in *Healing the Body Politic: The Political Thought of Christine de Pizan*, ed. K. Green and C. J. Mews (Disputatio 7) (Brepols, 2004), pp. 1–18; id., *The Art of Good Governance in Italy and England. Tito Livio Frulovisi's De Republica of 1434*.

knowledge and understanding as prerequisites for both individual and corporate efficiency, and he now applied that principle to the monastic life. In the long opening sentence of his preface he made this point much more explicit in English than in the Rule's Latin. Presumably, the heads of houses agreed with him:

> For asmoche as euery p[er]sone ought to knowe the thyng that he is bounde to kepe or acco[m]plisshe/ and ignorance of the thynge that he is bounde to do/ cannot nor may not excuse him/ and for so moche also/ as the reding of the thynge that a persone is bounde to do & execute/ except he vnderstande it/ is to the executinge therof no thyng vailliable/ but only thyng i[n]utile/ trauell in vayne/ and tyme loste.[39]

Corporate efficiency required each nun to do her spiritual, intellectual and domestic work with skill and competence: this was part of her monastic vocation, and the work of the abbess required particularly sound judgments and effective decisions. To remind her how essential it is to take advice from colleagues, Fox expanded the Rule's admonition on the point by explaining that sound advice must be sought from senior nuns 'of long continuance and experience in the monastery according as it is'.[40]

But what kind of smoothly functioning nunnery did Fox envisage? We can construct some sort of answer from the visitations of the nunneries in 1501, Fox's translation of 1516–17, and the reports of Cromwell's commissioners during the 1530s. In 1501, Dr Thomas Hede was appointed by the prior of Christ Church, Canterbury to visit the monastic houses of the diocese of Winchester. As he came through the gatehouse of the convent of St Mary's within-the-city of Winchester, or Nunnaminster, on 2 March 1501, Dr Hede entered an enclosed small village of well-kept buildings, the largest of which was the church and bell tower, with a cloister and chapter house.[41] Close by were the abbess's lodgings and the nuns' dormitory (dorter), with the infirmary (farmery) standing a little apart. There was the refectory (frater), and beside it the buttery (which stored butter, bread and ale), the pantry, kitchen, larder for storing meat, the barn, two bakehouses, a small brewery, two grain storehouses (garners), stables for the convent's horses, three mills for grinding corn, the priests' lodgings, and the plumber's house.[42]

When Fox was making his translation, Nunnaminster's population was probably close to the figures noted by Cromwell's commissioners in May 1536, when there were 102 persons in the convent.[43] At the heart of the community were 26 nuns, of whom 22 were professed, 5 priests and 13 lay sisters: these 44 'religious'

---

39 *Here Begynneth*, A.ii.r.
40 *Here Begynneth*, ch. 3, B.iii.v.
41 The prior of Christ Church, Canterbury held the right to hold metropolitan visitations, though the incumbent bishops generally opposed them. Between the death of Archbishop Morton on 12 October 1500 and the election of Henry Dean on 26 April, Winchester was vacant and Prior Thomas successfully asserted his rights, sending Hede as his Visitor.
42 Oliva, *The Convent and the Community*, pp. 75–6, similarly describes East Anglian convents.
43 The following details for Nunnaminster are from *VCH Hampshire*, vol. 2, pp. 123–6.

persons were a spiritual élite dedicated to worship, prayer and growth in holiness under the authority of the abbess. Their prime task was liturgical worship, and five nuns with good voices, one precentor and four cantors, were appointed for the services. The abbess, prioress, sub-prioress and sacristan had administrative and other duties, and in consideration of their additional responsibilities, each had a personal servant. There were nine female servants altogether, including three washerwomen. Twenty-six children, of 'lords, knights and gentlemen', were accommodated and educated within the convent, and a boy cared for the altar and made it ready for services. Older nuns taught younger nuns and the children. The 58 'non-religious' people also included 20 officials, both women and men, who attended to practical matters: there was a receiver to administer property and a clerk, both of whom had servants, a purveyor (cater), the plumber (who had a house within convent grounds), a butler, a cook, under-cook, and for the nuns a convent cook and under-convent cook. A gardener (curtiler) supervised the convent's gardens, the brewer made ale in the brewery, the miller operated the corn mills, the porter and under-porter fetched and carried, and three servants waited at tables. There were also three male corrodians, pensioners housed and fed for life in return for a benefaction to the convent.

Dr Hede spoke with the abbess of Nunnaminster, Joan Legh (1486–1527), now abbess for 15 years, and with the prioress and other nuns. All gave accounts which satisfied him: the prioress, Margaret Fawcon said that every nun dined in refectory except one who was aged; and the sub-prioress, Agnes Tystede, said that all nuns rose at night for matins except the sick and aged. Elia Pitte, the librarian, said that the library was functioning well. Christiane Bawdwin, the precentor, Agnes Trusset, second cantor, Agnes King, third cantor, Agnes Massaw, fourth cantor, Alice Tystede, scrutator (the scrutineer at abbey elections and probably related to Agnes Tystede), Agnes Byrcher, Margaret Shafte, Agnes Cox (senior *dogmatista*), Margaret Legh, mistress of novices, and the sacristan, all said *omnia bene*. One defect was that the convent could no longer maintain hospitality because during the later fifteenth century it had experienced financial difficulties with high costs of repairing buildings, payments of tenths and other imposts, and had to be given relief through royal renewal of the abbey's income earning rights.[44] Otherwise, Hede's report was favourable. Thirty-five years later, Cromwell's commissioners, who could be expected to be hostile, similarly reported that the nuns were 'clean, honest, and charitable in conversation, order and rule synce the furst profession of thym, which is also reported not only by the Mayors and Comynalyte of the Citye of Winchester but also by the most worshipfull and honest persons of the Contre adjoynynge thereunto' (their praise did not include the word 'holy' – an omission that may reflect the commissioner's view of the monastic vocation).[45] Obviously some defects were hidden and much was glossed, but Nunnaminster's smooth functioning gives

[44] These were a view of frankpledge, assize of bread and ale, and waif and stray at their towns of Urchfont and Allcannings, both in Wiltshire. Clearly, the abbey had difficulty in collecting tithes, traders' dues and claiming stray property, including animals, within its jurisdiction.

[45] *VCH Hampshire*, vol. 2, pp. 49, 124–6, based upon CCCR, CCP, Register R, *Sede vacante*, fols. 108–157. In 1536, Nunnaminster's gross annual value was just over £245.

some idea of what the nuns expected of their vocation and what the bishop and community expected of them.

Dr Hede then visited the nunnery of Wherwell on 31 March 1501. He questioned Abbess Matilda Rowse and the nineteen nuns, six of whom were novices. Their testimony adds to the picture of how a nunnery was expected to run: the monastic cycle of prayer was properly observed day and night, silence was kept at proper times, finances were well managed, the annual balance sheet was properly presented, rents had risen, the house was not in debt, no valuables were pledged, the common seal was locked away and there were sufficient stores of grain and other necessities for a year. Notes taken when Wherwell surrendered to the crown in November 1539 give us a physical description of the nunnery much as it had been in Fox's time. The church choir and steeple were lead roofed, the cloister roof tiled with lead guttering, the chapter house, refectory, dormitory, convent kitchen and lodgings next to the granary were also tiled; there was an infirmary, a mill and mill house next to the slaughterhouse; the brewery and bakehouse both had adjoining granaries, and there were stables and a barn in the outer court, and a good water supply. As the nuns of Wherewell worshipped, prayed and studied, the sounds and smells of matter-of-fact activities went on around them, milking, brewing, baking, slaughtering, horses clattering by, grain and other foodstuffs being stored, buildings being maintained, all part of the day-to-day workings of the small enclosed community within which they fulfilled their religious vocation.[46] The abbess, prioress, sacristan and precentor and eighteen of the nineteen other nuns, asserted that 'all was well' – snug and trim – 'omnia bene', with the spiritual, intellectual and practical elements of their religious vocation.

When Dr Hede visited Wintney priory on 3 April 1501, it was not operating with the same efficiency as Nunnaminster and Wherwell, and his report gives us a glimpse of a small and less perfect community. Thirty-nine persons were living at the priory, of which only ten were nuns; the others comprised two priests, a waiting servant, thirteen farm workers (hinds), nine women servants, and two corrodians, both with a servant. Anna Thomas the prioress and three nuns stated that the house had an annual income of £50 and a debt of 20 marks (£13 6s. 8d.), of which 15 marks had been repaid at some unknown date. Wintney priory was also omnia bene, except that the kitchen and the brewery were in poor condition and there was a low proportion of 'religious' in the priory (26 per cent as opposed to 43 per cent at Nunnaminster). When the commissioners arrived in May 1536, they reported that Wintney's nuns were 'by reporte of good conversation' and wished to remain as religious, but £72 16s. was owing to the house, although this debt may have been a strategy to salt away resources in the face of the forthcoming dissolution.

The least efficient community, both in worldly and spiritual terms, was Romsey abbey, the wealthiest nunnery in the diocese, possessing many endowments and legal powers. The abbey church, a large building of freestone, covered with lead, and 'worth £300 or £400 or more' was surrounded by the dormitory, infirmary, refectory, and other buildings, a wind-driven corn mill, at least four watermills,

---

[46] VCH Hampshire, vol. 2, pp. 135–7.

a fulling mill, fulling stocks and a fishery.[47] But the abbey had internal problems which had begun with Elizabeth Brooke, abbess for thirty years (1472–1502). She was a strong-willed woman who was accused of being arrogant and having numerous sexual liaisons with stewards and others. When Bishop Waynflete tried to remove her, the nuns mustered support from the local gentry and appealed to Rome, and when she was forced to resign in 1478, they re-elected her. She continued to behave as before, and on 29 October 1492 Archbishop Morton's visitation accused her of having a sexual relationship with Terbock, the gold-digging abbey steward; neglecting the abbey's resources; financial mismanagement; allowing the walls of the church, and the roofs of the choir, refectory and dorter to decay, and nuns to frequent the town's taverns. Now Hede was told that the abbess had male and female visitors at all hours. She and other nuns had meetings at the kitchen window, and the convent's male cook's wife carried messages between nuns and lay persons to arrange assignations, and Thomas Hampton the doorkeeper let people into the convent by the cloister door or left it unlocked.[48]

Elizabeth Brooke died on 12 May 1502, but her successor, Joyce Rowse (1502–15), had her own problems with excessive eating and drinking, and she too permitted lax behaviour, so that the abbey continued to have a poor reputation. In January 1507 Fox intervened to remove the sub-prioress for incontinence, administered strong censures for slander to others, and forbade two priests, Master Folton and the unnamed 'Vicar of Romsey', to have any contact with the nuns.[49] These were extreme cases, but the laxity of other nuns mostly consisted of being casual about worship, prayer and study: some slept in, or spent time in town, chatting with people, visiting their families and friends, eating, drinking and sometimes flirting, activities which might, though not inevitably, have hindered their monastic vocation.

Nevertheless, several nuns at Romsey were dissatisfied, and the community split into two factions, for and against the abbess, although some nuns, such as Cecil Reed the sub-prioress, apparently did not take sides. Hede's visitation concentrated on these factions. In answer to his questions, the prioress criticised the abbess for her indifference to delinquencies, and the precentor criticised her for neglect of the abbey's town properties; the almoner and a cantor told Hede that the quantity and quality of food had diminished; Ellen Tawke made a sarcastic allusion to the abbess's thirty years of neglect; Avice Haynow, also sarcastic, said that the roofs of the chancel and dorter were so decayed that when it rained the nuns were unable to remain either in church or in bed. The sub-sacristan Anne Harvey, whom the abbess allowed to wear her hair long, accused Emma Powes of sexual incontinence with the vicar, although since Anne was also friendly with the vicar, who left her a bequest in his will, she may have

47 VCH Hampshire, vol. 2, pp. 129–32; There is a comprehensive list of the manors and realty held by the four nunneries of Winchester diocese in Coldicott, Hampshire Nunneries, pp. 176–87.
48 Liveling, Records of Romsey Abbey, pp. 222–6.
49 BL, Landsdowne MS 963, fol. 55. 'An. 17 H. Temp mun de Romesay dna Gaudete olim Jvyse Rowse. 17 Junii'. Liveling, Records of Romsey Abbey, pp. 211–16. HRO, Episcopal Register, Fox, iv, fol. 80.

been jealous of Emma. Emma counter-attacked, alleging that the abbess, who favoured Anne, had not maintained the church or dorter roofs in good repair.

The condition of Romsey was clearly not how the female monastic vocation was envisaged. For forty-three years, two abbesses had allowed a nunnery to run down in both worldly and spiritual functions. Fox knew from long experience in politics and administration that misused authority damages a community, and that an organisation divided by factions and disputes cannot function as it ought. Fox almost certainly had in mind the dysfunctional history of Romsey abbey, including the sisters who criticised their abbess and each other, when he translated the passages on dissension. In *Here Begynneth*'s chapter 4, Instrument 3, he emphasised the dangers of dissension and factionalism and backbiting by expanding 'Non occidere' to include slander.[50] In Instruments 39 and 40, the Latin 'non murmurosum' and 'non detractorem' he translated as 'ye be not trowblous/ busy quarelynge/ or grutchynge' and 'ye be no detractor/ bakbyter ne slaunderer nor reuylor of any person'. At the end of chapter 40, he expanded the Latin '… ut absque murmurationibus sint', with an additional phrase to show that community life required 'that susters leede their lyue to gydder without grutchynge'. On a second-in-command being appointed by an authority other than the abbess, he emphasised the threat to harmony by translating 'Hinc suscitantur invidiae, rixae, detractiones, aemulationes, dissensiones, exordinationes' into the vigorous English 'Therof be raysed Inuies/ wrothes/ striues/ backbytings/ hatreds/ dissencions/ makynge & marrynge/ discordes & discorders.'[51]

Another cause of discord was class conflict:

> She that cam of higher or noble linage or of a fre kynrede: shall not be p[re]ferrid in order of sto[n]dinge: or vnto office / by fore a nother of lower byrthe or of a bonde stocke … notwithsta[n]dinge there diuersite and condicion of byrth or any suche other thinge. … For be she bonde/ be she fre/ be she of noble/ or ignoble blode/ and lynage/ all be oon in our lorde Ihu chiste [sic]/ and vnder oon lorde dothe bere equall borden of seruyce. For god takith no consyderacion ne regarde to the persone/ but to the vertuose workes and merites.[52]

The passage clearly addressed class distinctions, but we cannot be sure that there were any nuns of bond or ignoble lineage in Winchester, or whether Fox was simply following the Rule. Since presumably there were nuns of low social status, Fox's translation would have served as an instrument of education to help equalise or even eliminate class differences. There is no reason to think that superiors and obedientiaries were chosen on social status rather than administrative ability, or that they differed from East Anglian nuns, shown by Marilyn Oliva's prosopographical analysis to have been mainly of lower gentry origin.[53]

---

50 *Here Begynneth*, B.iii.r. At this point the Anglo-Saxon text adds an item on fornication, '… ne slean man; ne unriht haeme', which may correspond to Fox's inclusion of 'deedly synne'.

51 *Here Begynneth*, B.iv.v; E.iv.v; G.iv.v. 'Marrying' here means connecting from person to person, spreading. A 'discorder' was one who foments discord.

52 *Here Begynneth*, fols. A.vi.v–B.i.r.

53 *RB*, 2, 'The qualities of an abbot', says that he is not to give rank to one born free over one born a slave simply because of their social status. On this point *RB* is a conflation

The seventh expectation of the female monastic vocation was that a nun, living within her well-run coenobitic community, would gain heaven through her love of God. The fourth chapter of the Rule (Instruments of good works) instructs the monastic to love God totally with heart, soul and strength (Dominum Deum diligere ex toto corde, tota anima, tota virtute). But there are two distinct views of a nun's love of God and her pattern of salvation. In *The Spousage of a Virgin*, John Alcock described complete withdrawal from the world, subduing the pleasures of the flesh through total absorption in divine marriage with Jesus Christ. The banns between the two parties (the 'hyghe and moost myghty prynce ... Chryste Jesu of Nazareth' and the nun) were read as if for a parish wedding, lawful impediments were called for, followed by a sermon on marriage. The nun-wife, now called Nazarena, made her vows, then delivered herself from the world into the embracing presence of Christ, her husband and lover to whom she gave herself in the depths of her soul and mind, with the extreme sanctity of the clean blood of the virginity of Mary. In Alcock's eyes the nun's love was an intense spiritual experience, which rejected the outward and physical and redirected her energies of love, including sexual energy, into a controlled, concentrated spiritual experience, an isolating dedication to Christ, turning away from the world.[54] This was a semi-Pelagian pattern of cloistered strenuous effort, meriting salvation through the sublimation of human love, separating nuns from the laity and even from each other: Alcock barely considered skills for living in community.

Fox's description of the nun's love for God significantly differs from that of Alcock in several respects. Both agreed that the love must be unreserved and entire, but Fox expressed it in far more human terms by describing how to love. He extended the Rule's Latin injunction with additional English words 'applying all your thoughts only to him and with all your mind, that is to say applying all your studies, wits and delights only to him and with all your might, that is to say applying all your bodies strength and powers only to his service'. This description of being exuberantly in love with God is more human than Alcock's ascetic injunctions, and has a different theological focus, being much less meritorious and semi-Pelagian. Although Fox told nuns the nuns to attend to the service of Christ with outward fasts and devotions, he added, 'yet more in devocion of mynde and herte', meaning that their service to Christ should not be dominated by individualistic pious observances.[55] Love is centred upon God, but not in isolation from others, for the nun is a responsible and interacting member of her community.

Fox was applying to convents ideas drawn from his experience in politics and administration, and six months later set out similar ideas in the foundation charter of Corpus Christi College. Analogous themes occur in Thomas More's *Utopia* of 1516, a fictional society in which competence and reason create a

of Ephesians 6:8 and Galatians 3:28. Oliva, *The Convent and the Community*, pp. 52–61, 105.
[54] Alcock, *Spousage of a Virgin*, A.iii.r–v, A.vi.r–v, B.i.r, C.ii.r. Alcock has no reservations about marriage and lay piety.
[55] Barlow MS 11, pp. 24–9. I am now preparing an article on semi-Pelagian ideas in pre-Reformation monastic houses.

self-sufficient, smoothly operating community, and in Fox's chaplain Richard Whitford's *Werke for Householders*, possibly written in 1516 but published in 1535, which describes the ordered functioning of a quasi-monastic lay household. These ideas on ordered communal life may reflect the three authors' dissatisfaction with Henry VIII's government in 1516.[56]

Interaction was expected to be directed outward as well as inward, towards 'the world' beyond the cloister, including the local community. Just as Fox expected nuns not to be totally absorbed in rituals and prayers, neither did he seek to diminish their consciousness of 'the world'. Nuns had multiple families: their adopted family within the cloister, their natural family outside – parents, uncles, aunts, cousins and family servants – with whom they retained emotional and practical ties – and a third 'family' of friends and acquaintances, including lay people living in the nunnery. The connections were numerous and nuns maintained a high profile in local life: at Romsey the lay fraternities of St George and St Laurence kept lights and an altar in the conventual church from 1475 or earlier and almost every will of the early sixteenth century made a bequest to one or other confraternity. Links between nuns and parish were further demonstrated when Elizabeth Brooke was re-elected abbess in September 1478, and the prioress and convent gave powers to the diocesan chancellor to proclaim Elizabeth in the abbey church, in the English tongue, before clergy and parish laity.[57] Marilyn Oliva has clearly described the situation in East Anglia, where nuns dispensed alms and hospitality to the poor and indigent, executed and granted probate of wills, prayed for the community and facilitated intercessory prayer, boarded and educated children, accommodated local parishioners in their chapels and buried them in their cemeteries.[58]

All this intimately bound generations of people to their local convents and made convent communities a crucial part of the social and cultural landscape. Continuing connections between the outside world and the nunnery gave nuns an 'embeddedness' in local society, described by Paul Lee as 'combining a life of prayer with interaction with pious laity … a broad and balanced spirituality that did not leave them unaware of the needs of the world'. The same applied to the contemporary Cistercian monks of Sibton abbey in Suffolk, their visitors, servants and employees – including females.[59] Similarly, Sylvia Evangelisti

---

56 This point is briefly argued in B. Collett, *Female Monastic Life in Early Tudor England With an edition of Richard Fox's Translation of The Benedictine Rule For Women, 1517*, 'The Early Modern Englishwoman 1500–1750: Contemporary Editions', ed. B. S. Travitsky and P. Cullen (New York and London, 2002), pp. 10–15. *Werke for Householders* was published in 1535, but probably written in 1516.

57 Liveling, *Records of Romsey Abbey*, pp. 183–4, 213–16.

58 Oliva, *The Convent and the Community*, pp. 138–59. Oliva uses sentiments and bequests in wills and other patronage to conclusively demonstrate lay recognition of nuns, and pp. 174–83 demonstrates that the gentry and yeomen families gave greater patronage to female houses than to male, especially local convents, in 'Patterns of Patronage to Female Monasteries in the Late Middle Ages', in *Religious Orders*, ed. Clark, pp. 155–62, Oliva extends her earlier argument that patronage of nunneries enhanced the social standing parish gentry and yeoman families.

59 Lee, *Nunneries*, pp. 218, 220. *The Sibton Abbey Estates; Select Documents, 1325–1509*, ed. A. H. Denny, SRSP, ii (1960), pp. 33–40.

concludes that even in post-Tridentine Italy nuns met relatives and friends and had dealings with the outside world: they were 'not as separate from the world as one might think, convents were places for female contemplative life which in fact merged into the culture and society that created them'.[60] The nunneries of Winchester seem also to have been 'embedded' in society in ways similar to that found by Lee at Dartford, Oliva in Norwich, and Evangelisti in later Italian nunneries.

On the eve of the Reformation the female monastic vocation comprised seven inter-connected spiritual, intellectual and practical expectations by which the monastic life was to be lived and its successes or failures judged by church authorities, laity and the nuns themselves.[61] An analysis of these expectations leads us to three conclusions. First, at the heart of vocations were spiritual goals of holiness, perfection and salvation, for which purpose nuns separated from the world. Yet, their separated conventual life was also consciously lived within the local community. Their vocation was not 'spiritual' as distinct from 'worldly', but 'spiritual' within 'the world' to which they were still linked, a paradox both strengthening and dangerous. The strength was that the laity appreciated the spiritual and social contribution of nuns, and the danger that social contacts could distract nuns from spiritual goals. Yet, distractions rarely involved spectacular sins, and more often consisted of minor compromises with the world through generally acceptable social activities and relationships that did not necessarily mean laxity, let alone corruption. The distinction between nuns socialising and being 'lax' is uncertain, varied and nuanced, and as long as nuns did not blatantly neglect or scandalously transgress religious obligations, socialising did not necessarily threaten their monastic vocation. Consequently, we must be careful when defining the 'laxity' or strength of nunneries, and remember Joan Greatrex's observation that misbehaviour recorded in visitation records does not necessarily demonstrate the death of monastic ideals.[62]

The second conclusion is that being separated from, but also an active part of the world required learning, piety and an ordered reasonable life in community. In a sense, the nuns were expected to demonstrate how grace perfected nature, and the process of perfection brought good governance in its train. The female monastic vocation involved a family which nurtured both nuns and local community, thereby providing a paradigm for lay family life and other corporate bodies – confraternities, schools, colleges, and the nation.

Finally, when nuns were separated from the world but were also an integral part of it, the female monastic road to salvation was not as clearly defined as that of the stricter orders, whose complete enclosure provided a meritorious route to salvation. On the other hand, if nuns led a less austere life, not entirely isolated but often seeing and speaking to the people for whom they prayed, as they did in the diocese of Winchester, then these nuns were loving God (their seventh

---

60 Evangelisti, 'Monastic Poverty and Material Culture', p. 19. Nuns made and sold objects and commissioned art and other work from outsiders.
61 Most of these expectations were, of course, held in common with male monastics.
62 J. Greatrex, 'After Knowles: Recent Perspectives in Monastic History', in *Religious Orders*, ed. Clark, pp. 46–7. 'It would be closer to the truth to recognize that human nature lies in a state of perpetual tension between the two, the ideal and the reality.'

and greatest expectation), and demonstrating human affection in ways resembling the forthcoming Protestant doctrine of faith. Consequently, except for
their unmarried state and ordered offices, female religious were much like devout
people outside the convent. Fox's translation of the Rule, and the abbesses'
request for it, perhaps marks a shift towards a Pauline, rather than semi-Pelagian, understanding of the monastic vocation, and this may be what they meant
by 'reformacion' of the monastic life. These theological issues, however, are a
separate matter.

THE CULTURE OF THE COMMUNITY

Culture at Canterbury in the Fifteenth Century: Some Indications of the Cultural Environment of a Monk of Christ Church

JOAN GREATREX

Daily life and routine in an English medieval monastic institution can be fairly accurately described. There is an abundance of source material for a prosopographical approach to these close-knit communities that lived under obedience to a rule, were governed by customs and regulations covering almost every waking moment, and carefully preserved a written record of past acts and achievements. Individual biographical details, however, are scarce and depend largely on the survival of a few personal notebooks and letters that contain little information that would be considered essential for successful biography today.

The cultural environment within the medieval monastic context is even more elusive than biographical data since, in essence, it deals with intangible evidence concerning the intellectual and spiritual labours of monks and their thoughts and attitudes. With the aim of elucidating the foundations on which monastic civilisation in medieval Europe first developed and on which it always remained dependent, the Benedictine scholar monk Dom Jean Leclercq, produced in 1960 a masterly study which bears the title, in its English translation (by Catherine Misrahi), *The Love of Learning and the Desire for God*. The accompanying subtitle, 'a study of monastic culture', makes it clear that the author's approach would focus on the two identifying characteristics of monastic culture named in his title: understanding and faith. Leclercq finds the literary sources of monastic culture in Holy Scripture, patristic tradition and classical literature, and in this last category he includes history and letter writing.[1] The monks of western Europe diligently pored over the books of both the Old and New Testaments, committing lengthy passages to memory including the entire Book of Psalms; they zealously studied and preserved the writings of the Church Fathers; and they utilised and adapted the literary heritage of Graeco-Roman antiquity, converting the pagan writings of Latin authors into Christian models

This paper has undergone a lengthy period of gestation during the course of which I have been the grateful recipient of the comments and suggestions of several scholars whom I now acknowledge with thanks: Professor Christopher Brooke, Dr Lynda Dennison, Dr Ian Doyle, Professor Richard Sharpe, Dr Michael Stansfield.

[1] Leclercq, *Love of Learning*, p. 76 and Chapters 5 and 7 *passim*.

of grammar and style.[2] The intellectual stimulus of the twelfth-century renaissance and its thirteenth-century continuation made a significant impact upon Benedictine cloisters thanks largely to the élite group of monks selected for university studies; it was mainly they who were responsible for the acquisition of copies of many of the biblical and theological writings that proliferated in this period. For the majority of medieval monks, who spent most of their days in the cloister, monastic life was, as it always had been, sustained by the two pillars of devotion which are at the heart of monastic culture as defined by Dom Leclercq: the spiritual growth of the individual through his daily *lectio divina* nourished by scripture and accompanying exegetical texts, and the daily liturgical worship of the community in the *opus Dei*.[3]

There can be no doubt that in the fourteenth and fifteenth centuries monks continued to seek out volumes in their libraries for consultation and also for pleasure; and in the greater English monasteries there were impressive book collections, that at Christ Church, Canterbury, amounting to over two thousand volumes.[4] What is uncertain and, indeed, virtually unknown is the frequency and earnestness with which they did so; probably only a small number made a sustained effort to broaden their minds and deepen their understanding. Moreover, time for reading would have been in short supply for the many monks who were obliged to fulfil administrative and other assignments in addition to taking part in the daily round of liturgical offices.

This is the general background into which I now propose to insert an individual monk, namely William Glastynbury, together with his notebook, in order to make use of passages scattered through the latter from which to glean some evidence of the cultural environment within the Christ Church community of his day.[5] The evidence is tantalisingly meagre and at best fragmentary, but sufficient, I venture to say, to make the undertaking worthwhile.

A short biographical introduction is necessary to make it clear that William was an ordinary if not a typical monk of his time, intelligent without being scholarly, and both conscientious and diligent. He entered the cathedral priory in February 1415, joining a group of five other novices who had preceded him by several months. The earliest entry in his notebook, subsequent to his admission, is an inventory entitled *pro exhibicione sua*, which lists some thirty items of clothing, bedding and other personal needs with the cost of each article specified – 'the monk's trousseau' in the apt phrase of W. A. Pantin.[6] For all the items in his keeping William knew that he would be held responsible to his

2 *Ibid.*, p. 56.
3 See my forthcoming *Ideal and Reality: a Comparative Study of the English Cathedral Priories, c. 1270–1420* (Oxford University Press).
4 Before the death of Prior Henry Eastry in 1331, 1831 titles were listed in the catalogue of books compiled under his orders; many of the volumes contained at least several treatises, and more volumes from time to time were continually being added. The catalogue is transcribed in M. R. James, *The Ancient Libraries of Canterbury and Dover* (Cambridge, 1903), pp. 13–142.
5 The known biographical details of Glastynbury are to be found in Greatrex, *BRECP*, p. 169. His notebook is MS 256 in the library of Corpus Christi College, Oxford [hereafter Corpus MS 256].
6 W. A. Pantin, *Canterbury College Oxford*, OHS, new series, 4 vols., 1 and 2 (1947), 3

superiors in accordance with the Benedictine Rule.[7] In the period prior to his priestly ordination he was instructed by one or more novice masters; and he was also assigned to a senior monk for individual supervision in preparation for a final examination (redditus) by a committee of seniors. William received priest's orders at the hands of Archbishop Henry Chichele on 1 April 1419 when he was probably about twenty-four years of age, the minimum set by canon law.

Neither William nor any of the other novices in his group were selected to proceed to higher studies at Canterbury College, Oxford; and none of them appear to have been assigned to hold office in the monastery until the late 1420s. Some of them probably continued their studies within the cloister when not occupied with some form of practical training in one or more of the administrative departments. A few of the notebook entries suggest places where William may have been employed as an assistant, although they may merely reflect his own personal interest in, for example, the financial organisation of Christ Church and the administration of the manorial estates and their revenues.[8] More significant and certain were his concern to have to hand an historical record of the priors from the time of William the Conqueror, and of the gifts and acquisitions of manors and churches from St Augustine's arrival as archbishop in AD 597.[9]

By the mid-1430s, if not before, William began to play a more visible role; between 1435 and 1443 he was appointed to five different offices in succession for short periods of from one to three years, namely those of fourth prior, anniversarian, novice master, magister mense and chaplain to the prior.[10] None of these could be classed as major responsibilities in terms of the administrative or financial competence required, but all of them would have demanded maturity, tact and an understanding of human nature. His last known office, held from 1443 to 1446 and probably his most important, was that of bartoner, the obedientiary in charge of the home farm which lay on the north side of the city of Canterbury. Frequent visits were essential in order to oversee farming operations, supervise the employees and pay their wages, and arrange for deliveries of farm produce to the priory. William faithfully recorded precise details of his receipts and expenses during his tenure of this office to assist him when he drew up the final account at the end of the accounting year.[11]

The notebook was also the repository of items of personal interest to its owner, and it is by examining these that we begin to perceive something of William's cultural framework. We encounter, for example, his choice of some reading material for spiritual edification and reflection, his several attempts to

(1950), 4 (1985), 4, p. 119; the list has been transcribed by Pantin in full from fol. 180r of the Corpus manuscript, p. 118.

7   *RB 1980*, Chap. 33 on private ownership, pp. 230–1 and Chap. 55 on clothing and footwear, pp. 260–5.

8   Corpus MS 256, fol. 91r; and see C. Eveleigh Woodruff, 'The Chronicle of William Glastynbury, Monk of the Priory of Christ Church, Canterbury, 1419–1448', *Archaeologia Cantiana*, 37 (1925), 121–51 at 128.

9   Corpus MS 256, fols. 80v–81r (priors) and fols. 82r–87r (manors and churches).

10   Greatrex, *BRECP*, p. 169. For the years in which he held these offices and the folio references in Corpus MS 256 see *ibid*.

11   Corpus MS 256, fols. 36r–62r.

keep a chronicle of contemporary events within the community and beyond, selections from his correspondence with fellow monks together with a list of twenty-eight epistolary salutations [see plate 12] and his detailed description of the iconography of the late twelfth-century theological windows.

The few brief extracts from William's reading of the Bible which were jotted down in the notebook allow us to visualise him as he strove to penetrate beneath the actual wording of the texts to their deeper meaning. He quotes, for example, St Paul's letter to the Ephesians: 'Avarus quod est idolorum servitus'; and then he goes on to explain how and why avarice is equivalent to idolatry in a paragraph that may represent his own thoughts, or it may have been copied by him from an unidentified commentary.[12] Another topic over which he laboured was that of predestination and its correct interpretation, thus showing himself to have been in company with countless other Christians through the ages who have striven to understand the doctrine implicit in this controversial term. In a paragraph under the heading *Predestinacio* he quotes again from Ephesians while pondering over the relationship between predestination and grace.[13] To assist him he consulted Augustine's treatise *De praedestinatione sanctorum*, of which there were at least two copies in the monastery library, copying the passage where Augustine explains that 'praedestinatio est gratiae praeparatio'.[14] William doubtless read the remainder of the bishop's statement, although without noting it down, namely that gratia 'vero iam ipsa donatio'. If the letter to the Ephesians was lying open in front of him he would have found further clarification in chapter two: 'Gratia enim estis salvati per fidem. … Dei enim donum est.'[15] From the above extracts, the writings of St Paul and St Augustine appear to have played an influential role in William's growth in spiritual understanding. On another folio under the title *Verba peccatoris ad deum* he copied a passage from one of Augustine's sermons on the nativity of Christ of which, he noted for future reference, the incipit was 'Rogo vos'. His choice of quotation was one that makes a plea for the divine mercy, and it contains the memorable line spoken by the sinner 'despperatus ad omnipotentem venio: vulneratus ad medicum curro'.[16]

Stored in William's memory and kept fresh by daily repetition, verses from the Psalms did not need to be written down as aids to recollection. He would have been able to call to mind, for example, without effort, the many verses that extol the fear of the Lord. However, in his reading of the Old Testament book, Ecclesiasticus, he found additional phrases that must have suggested fresh insights attached to the words 'timor dei': 'quoniam nichil melius est quam timor dei nichil dulcius quam respicere in mandatis domini' and again 'timor dei scientiae religiositas'.[17]

The virtue, indeed the love, of silence was instilled into the mind and heart of the Benedictine novice from the moment of his admission to the monastery.

12 Ephes 5:5; Corpus MS 256, fol. 2v.
13 Ephes 2:10; Corpus MS 256, fol. 17r.
14 Augustine, 'De Praedicatione Sanctorum', *PL*, 44, cols 959–92 at 974–5.
15 Ephes. 2:8.
16 Sermo 117, *PL*, 39, cols 1977–82 at 1977; it is one of a group of sermons described by Migne as 'sermones suppositii'.
17 Chap. 23: 37–8 and Chap. 1: 17.

He encountered it in the sixth chapter of the Rule, entitled *De taciturnitate*, when it was first read to him and also in the seventh chapter on the fourth and ninth of the degrees of humility, and these he was required to commit to memory along with the entire Rule.[18] According to an unidentifiable sentence jotted down by William, he was apparently troubled by the means of discerning the circumstance in which speech would be necessary in order to refute error; at such times, so the quotation affirmed, silence would surely be tantamount to encouraging and supporting false doctrine.[19]

Medieval Benedictines may have had their eyes firmly fixed on heaven but their feet remained on the ground, and they were devoted to history. They read, transcribed and composed a variety of historical works because, for them, the passage of events on both the local and the world scene was situated within the background of a universal history, the history of salvation.[20] William's 'chronicle' of contemporary events was in itself unremarkable, and the surviving fragments leave no indication as to the possibility that he attempted anything more ambitious than these sporadic efforts scattered through the notebook. Nevertheless, his seemingly instinctive desire to record both what he witnessed near at hand and also what he was able to learn of the more distant affairs in church and realm secures him a place among the countless and largely unknown members of his order for whom interest in history prompted the desire to record it for posterity. The practical results of William's historical leanings include: a list of his brethren who died or departed between 1415 and 1449 (that is, the entire span of his monastic life); a record of exeats of some monks for their recreation in 1438 and of appointments to and removals from obedientiary office in the years 1438 to 1441 as announced at the daily chapter meeting; an account of the 1438 and 1439 visits of the aging archbishop, Henry Chichele, to the cathedral priory; and a description of the ceremonial welcome given by the prior and community to the queen, Margaret of Anjou, wife of Henry VI, when she paid a visit to the shrine of St Thomas in 1447.[21]

Examples of William's interest in events occurring further afield are reflected in his list of nine cardinals who attended the Council of Constance (1414–18), among whom the first name was the 'Cardinal of St Cross', Henry Beaufort. In fact, William's statement was premature because, although Beaufort was an active participant at the Council and was promoted to the cardinalate by Martin V in 1417, the king refused to allow him to accept it.[22] One item on the

18 *RB 1980*, Chap. 6, pp. 190–1 and Chap. 7, pp. 196–7 v. 35 and pp. 200–1 v. 56.
19 Corpus MS 256, fol. 8r; the Latin reads 'Contentus est tacere cum possis redarguere vel errorem adulando fovere'.
20 See the remarks of Dom Leclercq, which amplify this statement, in *Love of Learning*, pp. 156–60 especially p. 157.
21 Corpus MS 256, fol. 162v/168v (deaths and departures); fol. 177v/182v (exeats); fols. 117r–118r (changes of offices); fols. 118r and 119r and Woodruff, 'Chronicle', 130–2, 134–5 (Chichele's visits); fol. 63r and Woodruff, 'Chronicle', pp. 126–7 (visit of the queen). The young queen's visit was also recorded by another Christ Church monk, John Stone. Although he, like William, was probably present for the occasion, his version of the proceedings differs slightly from William's, *The Chronicle of John Stone, Monk of Christ Church, 1415–1471*, ed. W. Searle, CAS, 34 (1902), p. 42.
22 Corpus MS 256, fol. 120v; see G. L. Harriss, *Cardinal Beaufort, a Study of Lancastrian*

agenda of the long-lasting Council of Basel (1431–49) also finds a place in the notebook, possibly prompted by an interest in ecumenism on William's part. He wrote down, presumably for future reference, the four articles presented by the Hussite leaders to the assembly of ecclesiastical delegates with the urgent petition that their position be recognised and accepted.[23]

It was by word of mouth passed on by brethren who were sent abroad and also by correspondence that William, while remaining in the cloister, was kept informed of conciliar and other events. John Langdon, for example, a fellow monk, was one of the English representatives at Constance along with Beaufort who was a friend of the Christ Church community and a frequent visitor.[24] The subprior, John Salisbury, attended sessions at Basel in 1433, and William reports his departure in December 1432 in a letter to John Wodnesburgh who was then at Canterbury College, Oxford, and was probably the college warden.[25] Other news from Basel would have filtered through to William from the same John Wodnesburgh who, at Oxford, was kept up to date on Council affairs because of the six university delegates in attendance.[26] The friendship between John and William would have begun when they were in the noviciate and a correspondence between them must have ensued after John was sent to Oxford c.1418 as a student in canon law. Unfortunately the only surviving letters are dated c.1432/3, four from John to William and two from William to John. In their form and content we find that the general rules of dictamen have been followed, most noticeably in the opening phrase or salutation which although brief is careful to recognise rank or title.[27] William acknowledges John's slightly senior status by 'vestra paternitas' and John responds politely with 'reverendo ac discreto viro'. Both then demonstrate their mutual affection by 'confrater karissime', dispensing with flowery formulae, and the conclusion is equally brief, with 'per vestrum in omnibus' usually sufficient.[28] The contents are informal, as befits a long-standing friendship; nevertheless, in construction and style the grammar masters would have found little to correct apart from a lack of elegance which would have

Ascendancy and Decline (Oxford, 1988), pp. 94–8. However, Beaufort's promotion was favourably received in 1427 during the regency of Henry VI, *ibid.*, p. 152.

23 Corpus MS 256, fol. 11r and Woodruff, 'Chronicle', p. 125.

24 For John Langdon see Greatrex, *BRECP*, p. 217 (John Langdon I). Beaufort was admitted into the Christ Church confraternity and a house within the precincts was put at his disposal, Emden, *BRUO*, vol. 1, p. 142. In 1445 when William was serving as bartoner he was responsible for a delivery of pigs and piglets to the Cardinal's kitchen, Corpus MS 256, fol. 51r.

25 John Salisbury was to become prior of Christ Church in 1436; see Greatrex, *BRECP*, p. 275 (John Salisbury I). Biographical details for John Wodnesburgh are in *ibid.*, pp. 323–4 (John Wodnesburgh III). William's letter, along with other correspondence in the notebook has been transcribed by Pantin in *Canterbury College*, vol. 3, p. 91, no. 103 (Corpus MS 256, fol. 185v/190v).

26 John Wodnesburgh passed on to William the news about the six Oxford delegates to Basel in a letter dated August [1432] and copied by William into his notebook, Corpus MS 256, fol. 185r/190r; see Pantin, *Canterbury College*, vol. 3, p. 89, no. 100.

27 For a definition and description of the *ars dictaminis* see M. Camargo, *Ars Dictaminis, Ars Dictandi*, Typologie des Sources du Moyen Âge occidental, fasc. 60, (Turnhout, 1991), pp. 17–28.

28 Pantin, *Canterbury College*, vol. 3, pp. 88–93 (nos. 98–105).

been out of place.[29] It is to be noted that in one of the letters John asks William to send him a book which he believed to be at the time in William's possession, namely the *De interpretatione hebraicorum nominum*, probably the work of Jerome, of which at least six copies were listed in Prior Eastry's early fourteenth-century catalogue.[30] To assist him in his correspondence William compiled a list of twenty-eight salutations, some clearly appropriate for prelates and religious superiors and others suitable for more general use; it is quite possible that he composed some of them himself [see plate 12].[31]

The series of twelve aptly named 'theological windows' located in the choir, presbytery aisles and eastern transepts of the cathedral had been in place at least a century and a half before they captured William's attention. With their typological juxtaposition of Old and New Testament subjects they form a liturgical cycle of the Christian year, each window consisting of between twelve and twenty-one panels of varying shapes and sizes with explanatory verse inscriptions.[32] For the largely illiterate laity these acted as visual aids in bringing the biblical stories to life in much the same way that the illuminated medallions in the *Bible moralisée* manuscripts illustrated the texts for the few who could afford to own them.[33] Both types of imagery would have been more easily understood with the assistance of an interpreter capable of explaining the connection between the Old and New Testament scenes portrayed and the sequence of events narrated. Did William assume the role of guide from time to time when he encountered pilgrims gazing at the windows? By doing so he would have fulfilled a pastoral responsibility appropriate to the vocation of a cloistered monk, and the appearance of the descriptive record of the windows in his notebook would be explained.[34] However, he may have turned to the windows simply to infuse light and life into his own meditations and intensify their meaning. It is insignificant that William's description of the images and inscriptions is not a slavish copy of either of the two other surviving Christ Church manuscripts that contain similar texts.[35] He may have made use of them since they are both

---

[29] The rules of the epistolary genre included the importance of ensuring that letters were 'correct and elegant' in composition and style and displayed a working knowledge of the *ars dictaminis*; see Giles Constable, *Letters and Letter Collections*, Typologie des Sources du Moyen Âge occidental, fasc. 17 (Turnhout, 1976), pp. 11–13.

[30] The letter is in Corpus MS 256, fol. 185r/190r and Pantin, *Canterbury College*, vol. 3, p. 88, no. 98. Copies of Jerome's *De interpretatione* are listed in James, *Ancient Libraries*, nos 197 (p. 38), 209 (p. 40), 910 (p. 89), 940 (p. 91), 1090 (p. 101), 1229 (p. 108).

[31] Corpus MS 256, fol. 171v/176v; examples are 'salutem et perpetuam anime et corporis sanitatem', 'salutem et spem discrecionis et consilii', 'salutem et sinceram in domino caritatem', 'salutem et tam debitam quam devotam reverenciam'.

[32] Only a small proportion of the glass of these windows has survived, but with the aid of the medieval descriptive records most of the original scenes are known; the details are competently presented in M. Caviness, *The Windows of Christ Church Cathedral Canterbury*, Corpus Vitrearum Medii Aevi, 2 (Oxford, 1981), pp. 77–156.

[33] See, for example, *Bible Moralisée, Codex Vindobonensis 2554, Vienna, Österreichische Nationalbibliothek*, Manuscripts in Miniature No. 2, ed. G. B. Guest (London, 1995).

[34] Woodruff has transcribed them in his 'Chronicle', pp. 139–50; in Corpus MS 256 they occupy fols. 185r/190r to 188r/193r.

[35] The other surviving descriptions of the windows are in CCCC, MS 400, part iv, p. 121–7 (late thirteenth century) and CCAL, MS C246 Roll (early fourteenth century).

earlier, dating from the late thirteenth and the early fourteenth centuries, but Madeline Caviness judges that the three are 'sufficiently different to be considered independent'.[36] We may deduce from William's detailed treatment of the theological windows that his interests extended beyond an appreciation of the written word to that of visual representation, both being put to practical use as aids to understanding and devotion.

In this single manuscript notebook that has miraculously been preserved, a disparate collection of memoranda, documents, journal entries, historical notes and letters, albeit haphazardly arranged and incomplete, has proved sufficient to delineate an ordinary Benedictine monk in the cultural setting of the fifteenth-century cloister of Canterbury cathedral priory. The quotations extracted by William from his spiritual reading suggest the initial stages of a planned florilegium, or collection of memorable texts from chosen authors to be savoured in future moments of repose; the historical passages reflect a keen interest in past and current events and the desire to preserve them in a written record; the selections from his correspondence and the accompanying forms of address provide evidence for training in the *ars dictaminis*; and his prolonged study of the iconography of the theological windows points to an observant nature and an appreciation of the value of colourful imagery to infuse life into biblical narratives.

---

[36] Caviness, *Windows of Christ Church Cathedral*, p. 79.

1. Fragments of an Apocalypse cycle from the chapter house, Coventry Cathedral Priory.

2. Fragments of an Apocalypse cycle from the chapter house, Coventry Cathedral Priory.

3. Fragments of an Apocalypse cycle from the chapter house, Coventry Cathedral Priory.

4. *Lectio divina*: detail of a decorated capital from an anthology of historical texts compiled for John Moorlinch, a monk of Glastonbury Abbey, in c. 1400.

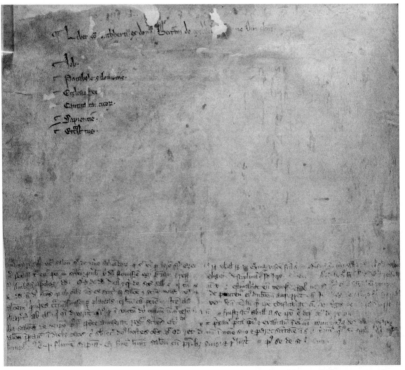

5. The final volume of the six-volume edition of Hugh of Saint-Cher's postils presented to Durham Priory by Prior Bertram of Middleton (1244–58), showing the *exdono* inscription. The other volumes survive as Durham Cathedral Library MS A. I. 12–16.

6. A leaf from Nicholas of Lyre's postils, copied by the Breton scribe, William Le Stiphel for the monks of Durham Priory. Two further volumes survive as Durham Cathedral Library MS A. I. 4–5.

7. The first full leaf of text from a collection of reports of academic disputations made at Oxford (1298–1302) and Paris (*c.* 1310–11) by John of St Germans, monk-scholar of Worcester Priory.

8. Detail showing the distinctive profile head *siglum* used by Richard Bromwych, monk-scholar of Worcester Priory, in this case drawing attention to a passage in an early fourteenth-century copy of Thomas Aquinas's *Quaestiones disputatae X de potentia Dei*.

9. A leaf from the Shaftesbury Psalter, compiled c.1130–1140, showing the Virgin and Child enthroned. The figure kneeling at the foot of the frame is probably the unidentified abbess of Shaftesbury that commissioned the manuscript.

10. [Richard Fox, bishop of Winchester], *Here Begynneth the rule of seynt Benet*, R. Pynson [London, 1516]. Title page.

11. The formula of profession from the text of the *Regula Benedicti* given to the nuns of Wherwell by Bishop Richard Fox of Winchester. The formula confirms the identification, since the dedication of the house is given as of St. Cross and St. Peter. Fox presented copies of the Rule to the four nunneries of his diocese, Nunnaminster (St Mary's Winchester), Romsey, Wherwell and Wintney. The Nunnaminster book also survives, as Cambridge, University Library, MS Mm. 3. 13.

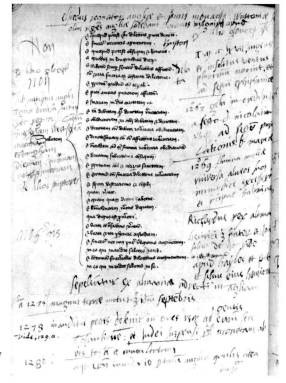

12. The commonplace book of William Glastynbury, monk of Christ Church, Canterbury; here a leaf containing epistolary salutations.

14. The opening lines of Anselm of Canterbury's *Epistolae*, from an English manuscript of the twelfth-century of unknown provenance.

13. The opening lines of Aelred of Rievaulx's *De spiritali amicitia*, from a manuscript of c.1200 which belonged to Revesby Abbey, where Aelred had held the abbacy (1143?–46).

15. Detail of a portrait of the fourteenth-century horologer, Richard of Wallingford, abbot of St Albans, showing the pioneering clock for which he was widely celebrated. Taken from the St Albans, *Liber benefactorum*, a codex first compiled in 1380.

The Monastic Culture of Friendship

JULIAN HASELDINE

The culture of friendship in pre-modern Europe was broadly commensurate with political culture. Friendship could provide a conceptual vocabulary for almost any relationship of importance outside the ambit of close kin. Some notion of friendship seems to have been inextricable from most social or political institutions, such as patronage, lordship and military allegiance – indeed even ideas about kinship itself were interwoven with friendship. But it is hard to recover the precise role of so ubiquitous, even apparently commonplace, a concept. References to friends and friendship scattered throughout the texts of chronicles, charters, histories, letters, sermons and so forth, can easily escape our attention. The writers presumably thought in most cases that they needed no explanation. From the perspective of a modern culture in which friendship is valued as an essentially private experience, they can appear as mere clichés, as hollow as the notion of the friendship of nations.[1] Yet friendship had been at the centre of the tradition of political thought since antiquity, and recent research has demonstrated its centrality to political life and social order in the Middle Ages.[2] Gerd Althoff's work, for example, was among the first to show the importance of friendship to the functioning of order in early medieval society. His approach has been described as part of a 'new constitutional history'.[3] Huguette Legros, more recently, has demonstrated how the *chansons de geste* of the central

---

[1] To say that friendship is valued primarily as a private relationship is not to say that it functions exclusively or even primarily as such, or originates only in contexts described as 'private'. Rather, we routinely describe our social experience in terms of distinctions between private and public (of, for example, private 'life' and professional or public 'life') which are conventions not necessarily reflective of real experience. The work, for example, by Mark Granovetter in the 1980s on the role of personal relations in organisations was among the first to demonstrate the artificial nature of such distinctions: e.g. 'Economic Action and Social Structure: The Problem of Embeddedness', *American Journal of Sociology*, 91 (1985), 481–510.

[2] How far western medieval ideas were influenced by ancient theories of friendship, and how far they arose in the specific cultural contexts of post-Roman societies, later to be recast in classical terms, is a complex question. The general point, however, is that it would be anachronistic to assume, without investigation, that terms like *amicitia* were being used simply as decorative clichés.

[3] See G. Althoff, *Verwandte, Freunde und Getreue: zum politischen Stellenwort der Gruppenbindungen im früheren Mittelalter* (Darmstadt, 1990), and id. *Amicitiae und Pacta: Bündnis, Einung, Politik und Gebetsgedenken im beginnenden 10. Jahrhundert* (Hannover, 1992). Althoff also discusses his approach and historiographical position in id., 'Friendship and Political Order' in *Friendship in Medieval Europe*, ed. J. P. Haseldine (Stroud, 1999), pp.

Middle Ages reflect a comparable culture of friendship: 'Avoir un "ami" c'est d'abord avoir un "allié"'.[4] An increasing amount of research has focused on the impact of the friendship bond on the organisation of medieval society and the functioning of its politics, often recovered from scattered and cryptic references in the sources.[5]

In the monastic world friendship is apparently less elusive. The heightened expressions of friendship found in monastic letter collections for example, or its treatment in sermons or treatises, are an important part of medieval literary culture. Such explicit interest in friendship flourished particularly in what has come to be known as the twelfth-century Renaissance. The fact that monastic writers were generally more concerned than others to elaborate their ideas about friendship has led to a tendency to assume that monastic *amicitia* is essentially distinct from other forms of friendship: that it is, for example, more personal and sincere; that it is concerned with individual emotions where other expressions of friendship are more pragmatic; that it is affective and deep where they are instrumental and shallow; and that it is therefore in some sense more 'real'.[6] Monastic friendship has indeed frequently been interpreted as a language of the emotions, significant of a new interest in the inner man or woman. Of course there is here a critical question of genre and the nature of the surviving evidence: we should not assume that literary forms favoured by monastic writers express ideas that are exclusively monastic, nor that a preponderance of monastic writing in a particular genre necessarily conveys an especially monastic experience. But the study of the monastic culture of friendship does raise important questions that go beyond these considerations, including what we mean by more or less 'real' friendship. Medieval authors, of course, wrote of true and false friendship, but meant by this something very different from our test of emotional warmth and sympathy.[7] Monastic friendship certainly acquired both a powerful voice and a new popularity in the Middle Ages, and especially perhaps in the eleventh and twelfth centuries, but it did so in a culture long imbued with particular ideas and

91–105 at 91–2. The phrase 'new constitutional history' was applied by Timothy Reuter: 'Pre-Gregorian Mentalities', *JEH*, 45 (1994), 465–74 at 466.

4   H. Legros, *L'amitié dans les chansons de geste à l'éopque romane* (Provence, 2001), p. 403.

5   See e.g. the bibliographies in Althoff, *Amicitiae und Pacta*, pp. xviii–xxxii and *Friendship in Medieval Europe*, ed. Haseldine, pp. 275–7.

6   But it must be noted immediately that friendship in courtly literature, especially verse, was neither derivative of nor discrete from monastic friendship, as Ziolkowski has shown: J. M. Ziolkowski, 'Twelfth-Century Understandings and Adaptations of Ancient Friendship', in A. Welkenhuysen, H. Braet and W. Verbeke eds., *Mediaeval Antiquity*, Medievalia Lovaniensia, ser. 1, stud. xxiv (Leuven, 1995), pp. 59–81.

7   True friendship was not defined in terms of feelings or emotional preferences but rather with reference to its origins and ends – virtue operating to the public good in classical terms, divine love working to the good of the community of the faithful, or the ascent to God, in Christian terms. It was precisely emotional attachment or warmth of feeling which true and false friendship could have in common, hence the need to distinguish them by other criteria. For an introduction to medieval friendship and the classical tradition, with extensive bibliography, see J. McEvoy, 'The Theory of Friendship in the Latin Middle Ages: Hermeneutics, Contextualization and the Transmission and Reception of Ancient Texts and Ideas, from *c.* AD 350 to *c.* 1500' in *Friendship in Medieval Europe*, ed. Haseldine, pp. 3–44.

practices of friendship. To look to medieval monastic culture for 'the discovery of the friend' – of the 'true' friend in the modern sense – would be to presume both the existence and the specific content of a distinctively monastic concept of friendship. It is clear that monastic writers made important contributions to thought about friendship, and these may amount to a new direction in the experience of the relationship, or its articulation, in western culture; but it is only by setting them in the context of this existing intellectual and practical tradition that we can determine in what sense it might be valid to talk of a distinctive monastic culture of friendship.

There have been, broadly speaking, two complementary approaches to interpreting medieval friendship. Put simply, the first involves close reading of those texts which deal extensively or directly with friendship, or which provide rich examples of its use, in order to arrive at an understanding of the concept. The second attempts to identify as many instances of the language of friendship as possible, from the prolix to the cryptic, and to correlate them to external circumstances such as political co-operation, dispute resolution, career advancement and so forth, in order to identify patterns in the deployment of the language and to trace the possible influence of networks of friends. Needless to say these are rarely mutually exclusive concerns – indeed cannot strictly speaking ever be so – but rather complementary emphases. Indeed many studies combine both approaches precisely because both have in common the need to take into account the literary and philosophical traditions which shaped the language used at many levels, from the meaningful use of topoi to the most fundamental philosophical assumptions.[8] It is, however, probably fair to say that the former has been prevalent and has put in place a rich and valuable literature, and that the latter is still developing (indeed in important respects on the foundations of the former) both methodologically and in the amount of work done.[9]

Determining whether there was what amounted to a distinctively monastic culture of friendship, then, means understanding the connections, or lack of connection, between these two spheres of friendly interaction – between on the one hand the heightened expressions of friendship which monks (among others) were producing, and, on the other, the long tradition of friendship as an integral part of social and political relations, which certainly continued to play a major part in the institutional politics of monasteries. Do we have two cultures of friendship, one (exclusively perhaps or predominantly monastic) character-

---

8   As Margaret Mullett noted in 1999: '[re] the connection in Byzantine mentality between the intimate affective individual relationship and the widespread uses of *philia* for political purposes. Here I am in no doubt that one major step forward lies in the carrying out of a full network study of the writers of the period, testing what they say about friendship against what they do with it in their lives': 'Friendship in Byzantium: Genre, Topos and Network' in *Friendship in Medieval Europe*, ed. Haseldine, pp. 166–84 at 175.

9   Examples of the latter type of approach include I. S. Robinson, 'The Friendship Network of Gregory VII', *History*, 63 (1978), 1–22; J. McLoughlin, '*Amicitia* in Practice: John of Salisbury (c.1120–1180) and his Circle' in *England in the Twelfth Century, Proceedings of the 1988 Harlaxton Symposium*, ed. D. Williams (Woodbridge, 1990), pp. 165–81; J. P. Haseldine, 'Understanding the Language of *Amicitia*: The friendship circle of Peter of Celle (c.1115–1183)', *JMH*, 20 (1994), 237–60; J. Barrow, 'Friends and Friendship in AngloSaxon Charters' in *Friendship in Medieval Europe*, ed. Haseldine, pp. 106–23.

ised by a new interest in the intimate personal experience, the other continuing to use the same vocabulary in a more traditional, instrumental way? Or do we rather have a continuation of the ancient tradition of disinterested friendship, regarded as part of the socio-political fabric, which monastic writers simply articulated with greater sophistication? Monastic friendship literature also poses a further problem, one which has long been recognised by some historians.[10] Not only is it elaborated with greater literary style, but it is apparently more ardent, even erotic, in its expression. And this ardent language is used in very different contexts, with intimates and strangers often seemingly addressed in the same terms. Therefore we need to understand a language whose terms of reference, especially regarding the appropriateness of apparently strongly emotive expressions, are obviously different to our own, while at the same time considering the relationship of this language to a long-standing tradition of friendship in western culture.[11]

Interest in friendship among monks, as has been frequently observed, was revived, and flourished with particular vigour, in the eleventh and twelfth centuries, and this presents us with yet another problem of interpretation. It is often taken as a truism that the *Rule of St Benedict* opposes friendship – although it is more accurate to say that it says little or nothing about it.[12] No analysis of monastic culture can avoid the overwhelming presence of the *Rule*. It is hard for us to imagine the saturating effect the *Rule* and the liturgy must have had on all aspects of the life experience of monks, pervading language as much as daily routine – and particularly so as our own interactions with rules and services (religious or in the very many wider uses of the terms) have little resonance with that of the pre-modern religious. And at the same time it is hard to avoid the notion that friendship was part of the world that Benedict had sought to escape. Nor does friendship appear to be a phenomenon that commentators saw the need to accommodate to the *Rule*. Certainly the established commentaries, Smaragdus's on the *Rule* and his *Diadema Monachorum*, for example, say little about it.[13] But what makes this a particularly interesting problem is that the

10 Notably R. W. Southern: see pp. 183–4 below.

11 An additional difficulty here may be our natural inclination to take what are modern, individualistic and romantic linguistic conventions simply as unmediated expressions of true feeling and to apply this to medieval texts.

12 As indeed Brian Patrick McGuire noted at the beginning of his influential study of friendship and community: B. P. McGuire, *Friendship and Community: The Monastic Experience, 350–1250*, Cistercian Studies Series 95 (Kalamazoo, 1988), p. xiv. C. 69 is most frequently cited in this connection, but see also *RB*, cc. 2, 54, 63 and 71 – although none of these passages treat friendship directly.

13 *Smaragdi Abbatis Expositio in Regulam S. Benedicti*, ed. A. Spannagel and P. Engelbert, CCM, viii (Siegburg, 1974) (also *PL*, cii. 689ff.): there are some uses of the term but no extended discussion, and one instance (c. liii) where the term is used to refer to outsiders; the *Diadema Monachorum* (*PL*, cii. 593–690) does discuss it briefly (c. xli., col. 637). Nor does friendship figure, beyond a few passing references, in the commentary of Hildemar (sometimes ascribed to Paul the Deacon): *PL*, cvi. 394, also R. Mittermüller ed., *Vita et Regula s. Benedicti una cum expositione Regulae III: Expositio regulae ab Hildemaro tradita* (Regensburg, 1880), and *Bibliotheca Casinensis*, IV.ii. *Florilegium Casinense* (Monte Casino, 1880), 12–173. Note also that M. A. Schroll, *Benedictine Monasticism as Reflected in the Warnefrid-Hildemar Commentaries on the Rule* (New York, 1941) makes no mention of

flourishing of monastic friendship literature in the eleventh and twelfth centuries coincided with a monastic reform and revival based on a self-proclaimed
return to literal interpretations of the *Rule*. Needless to say, claims to literal
interpretation are not the same as the actual recovery of past situations, and the
new monasticism of the late eleventh and early twelfth centuries was no less a
creative reinterpretation, reflective of its own time, than any other revivalist
movement. Nevertheless, we do need to account for such a marked resurgence
of interest in friendship at the time of an ascetic revival driven by a call for
the literal interpretation of a text – the *Rule* – which seems to exclude it from
consideration, and in which it is community, not individual relations, which is
presented as the essential context for salvation.

Monks could not of course have ignored friendship. It had been an integral
part of political culture since Plato and Aristotle, albeit known to them princi-
pally through Cicero and the Church Fathers.[14] They could probably no more
meaningfully have separated friendship from politics than we could rights from
politics. So to take it as significant simply that they were aware of it may be to
over interpret. Yet their enthusiastic adoption of it does require explanation.[15]
At first sight, then, there seems to be an inexplicable tension between the cult of
friendship on the one hand and on the other the drive for ascetic withdrawal and
for dedication to a text which promotes self-abnegation and the subsuming of the
individual into the community. But this may only really prove inexplicable if we
take friendship in the sense in which it is most commonly understood in modern
western culture, as an essentially, indeed exclusively, private phenomenon. Such
a framing of friendship reflects a culture which places the highest value on the
distinct and unique personal development of the individual. It is the inherent
interest in, and the importance accorded to, the particular emotional content
of the individual one-to-one bond which, from this perspective, gives friendship
its highest meaning. In this form it is privileged as the most meaningful type of

friendship. A survey of references to friendship in monastic commentaries is a desider-
atum, but the findings may prove scant.

[14] Although by no means exclusively so. The history of the transmission to the Latin West of
ancient theories of friendship is a complex one. For starting points and further references
see e.g. J. McEvoy, 'The Theory of Friendship'; *id.*, '*Philia* and *amicitia*: The Philosophy of
Friendship from Plato to Aquinas', in *Sewanee Mediaeval Colloquium Occasional Papers* 2
(1985), 1–23; White, *Christian Friendship*; E. G. Cassidy, '"He who has friends can have
no friend": Classical and Christian Perspectives on the Limits to Friendship' in *Friendship in Medieval Europe*, ed. Haseldine, pp. 45–67; P. Delhaye, 'Deux adaptations du *De
Amicitia* de Cicéron au xiie siècle', *Recherches de Théologie ancienne et médiévale*, 15 (1948),
304–31.

[15] The question of the adoption of friendship in the context of ascetic revival is also bound
up with the much broader question of the elaboration of a new theology of love in this
intellectual environment. This is a vast subject in itself, and friendship must be treated to
some degree discretely. This is partly because love is more obviously amenable to allegorical interpretation, as love of and for God, than is friendship with its more obvious focus
on human bonds and on equality within the relationship, but more importantly because
of the separate intellectual tradition of friendship. While medieval writers like Aelred of
Rievaulx, for example, followed Cicero (their chief source for ancient ideas of friendship)
in linking friendship to love, the intellectual tradition of friendship obviously predates a
specifically Christian theology of love and is not a derivative aspect of it.

non-sexual relationship and valued for its own sake as a locus of personal development and fulfilment.[16] If on the other hand we can demonstrate that there is a case for understanding monastic friendship as developing from the ancient and medieval traditions of friendship, then the language can be seen to carry a very different set of meanings. As I hope to show, the starting point for monastic writers was a tradition of friendship as a social institution – or more accurately as an integral aspect of human social organisation – which incorporates individual bonds but does not privilege them for themselves as the highest, or the essential, end of friendship. Rather it accords a higher place to the very concept of community which gave the *Rule* its meaning.

Indeed the distinctive characteristic of monastic friendship was its very concern with community. For medieval monastic writers the highest end of friendship was the ascent to God. The particular friend could be the occasion for this, but it was in community where individual friendships could find their true potential and fulfilment. Friendship in this view finds its value not in personal emotional growth within particular relationships but rather in its capacity to extend beyond any such instances and to enrich the community experience and so to lead to God. If the tradition they inherited treated friendship as an aspect of human social organisation, community was the specific form of social organisation with which monastic writers were themselves involved. Furthermore, this type of community was for them not the result of mere historical circumstance but represented the inheritance of a sure path to salvation and the highest human vocation. Monastic friendship does not present us, I would suggest, with a newly individualistic or private conception of friendship in contrast with an old instrumental one. Indeed these distinctions largely emerge from forcing twelfth-century language into the interpretive straightjacket of modern notions of love and friendship. Rather it represents the application of the rich tradition of friendship to the context of monastic community.

New research is suggesting that the friendship practised by monks in the Middle Ages, and the associated networks formed, were not essentially distinctive from the wider political and institutional context. Not only did they share the same inheritance of ideas, but they were fully involved in this wider world, as monks and others were mutually linked by ties and obligations of friendship.[17] By contrast most of those who have studied friendship in its more refined literary manifestations agree, even where otherwise their divergences in approach and conclusions are great, that in the late eleventh and early twelfth centuries, friendship was given a powerful new voice specifically by monastic writers. Two writers in particular, both with strong connections with England, have received special attention in this regard, St Anselm and Aelred of Rievaulx. The politics of the Anglo-Norman realm brought Anselm to Canterbury, while Aelred grew up in the north and in Scotland. Each has been seen as making a revolutionary

---

16 It is important to note that this is not necessarily how friendship functions in the modern world, but how it is conceptualised and valued: see above n. 1.

17 See for example the works cited above, nn. 3 and 9. An example of a recent treatment is P. Dalton, 'Churchmen and the promotion of peace in King Stephen's reign', *Viator*, 31 (2000), 79–119.

contribution to thought on friendship. The question of the nature and distinctiveness of a specifically monastic culture of friendship must turn on our interpretation of the relationship between the ideas of such writers on the one hand and the wider practice of friendship and of network-formation on the other. In other words, can we speak of a revolutionary new approach to friendship, individualistic perhaps or humanist, emerging in this body of erudite texts alongside but separate from the cotidian business of instrumental friendship and the life of the community? Or should we rather see them as sophisticated attempts to approach the particular, very real problems of monastic community – attempts which use the conceptual tool of a well-established tradition of a much more socially and politically located friendship? The remainder of this paper will look at some recent readings of these two key writers (the essential starting points in any such evaluation) in order to suggest some possible approaches to understanding the interaction between these sometimes seemingly discrete spheres of friendship.

In 1963, R.W. Southern characterised St Anselm's letters of friendship as the expression of an intense and passionate experience of God, of the unity of all men, and of the common spiritual endeavour of the monastic community in the ascent to God [for Anselm's letters see also plate 13].[18] The strength of emotion expressed was undoubted, but this was not moved by attraction to the individual friends. Rather it was the result of an 'imaginative projection of his personal ties' into his philosophical vision.[19] For Southern, Anselm's experience of friendship was intellectual not romantic, and was focused on identity of profession and a vision of unity, and hence found its highest expression in community not individuals. It was also clearly distinct from practical activity.[20]

The particular nature of Anselm's friendship is instanced by two types of letter, those in which he expresses the same sentiments to more than one recipient and those in which he extends the same sentiments to strangers as he would to intimates. An example of the former is letter 4, in which Anselm instructs that his friendly message be passed on unchanged to a third party. Importantly, Southern notes of this document: 'This ... was not a private letter.'[21] An example of the second type is letter 120, where Anselm expresses himself in apparently passionate terms to two recipients whom he had probably never met. Southern says of this:

---

18 R. W. Southern, *Saint Anselm and his Biographer: A Study of Monastic Life and Thought 1059–c.1130* (Cambridge, 1963), pp. 67–76.
19 Southern, *Saint Anselm and his Biographer*, p. 74: 'The peculiar ardour of Anselm's imaginative projection of his personal ties no doubt bred misunderstandings in those who did not understand that the fire was primarily intellectual and that it fed an incorporeal ideal. It was a product of philosophy rather than of feeling.'
20 Southern noted a clear division between business and personal correspondence, a division reflected in the structure of the letter collection, which divides at 1093, when he became archbishop: '... the later letters are a business archive ... the earlier letters are personal letters' (Southern, *Saint Anselm and his Biographer*, p. 68).
21 Southern, *Saint Anselm and his Biographer*, p. 70: 'No doubt these words were written under the impulse of a strong emotion. But the nature of the emotion may be judged from a sentence at the end of the letter directing that another of Gundulf's companions, with whom Anselm had much less in common, was to regard everything in it as equally applicable to himself.'

'It cannot be doubted that they [the words of ep. 120] express a personal and passionate longing; but the nature of this longing, and the extent to which it was associated with its ostensible object in the person directly addressed, are not easily distinguished.'[22] Here again the expression of a personal longing which is not directed to an individual intimate indicates a communication which is not private in the normal modern understanding of the term. In both cases, then, Southern is making a distinction between the personal and the private, and one which does not fit with modern notions of friendship: the letters can be both personal and passionate without being private. But nor was this simply a medieval commonplace: it was also probably somewhat disconcerting to Anselm's correspondents.[23] Anselm's friendships, then, 'are the expression of a union of wills, intellectually conceived and passionately expressed. The friend is more of an idea than a person.'[24]

Thus we have, firstly, Anselm as a unique turning point in friendship, and secondly, letters which are personal and passionate but not private. This exposition was elaborated and nuanced in Southern's 1990 reworking of his study of Anselm. Here he linked it even more emphatically to the role of the community in the ascent to God, suggesting in Anselm's case an overriding vision of monastic unity, rooted in community and the ascent to God, which is the occasion of the passion. Thus he concludes, for example: 'For Anselm, human friendship arises entirely from a communion of wills in the service of God, and the supreme expression of this communion in the Church is the monastic community.'[25] For Southern, then, Anselm represents a new direction in friendship which reached its most sublime heights in the shared endeavour of monastic community. The individual friend, we might say, is the instance, not the end, of friendship, and the concern is emphatically not with the individual emotional experience of the relationship between two people.

In 1970 Adele Fiske, in the first book-length study of medieval friendship, also characterised Anselm's friendship as unique, as intensely personal, and as primarily concerned with the ascent to God.[26] However, Fiske's interpretation is fundamentally different: she characterises Anselm's friendship explicitly as a mystical experience.[27] This leads her to a reading of Anselm which, in the tradition of mystical thought, blends rather than distinguishes concepts: friendship is love, friendship is virtue, virtue is in turn love, and so forth, and all such concepts are interdependent. So, for example:

> Anselm's thought here moves in a circle; the cause of love is virtue, but the cause of virtue is love. Love itself is virtue; one cannot love unless one is virtuous; yet

22 Southern, *Saint Anselm and his Biographer*, pp. 72–3.
23 As Southern notes, see above n. 19.
24 Southern, *Saint Anselm and his Biographer*, p. 76.
25 R. W. Southern, *Saint Anselm: A Portrait in a Landscape* (Cambridge, 1990), p. 162.
26 A. M. Fiske, *Friends and Friendship in the Monastic Tradition*, Cidoc Cuaderno no. 51 (Cuernavaca, 1970). Anselm's is a 'very original system of thought' (*ibid*. p. 15/1). His friendships have an intensely personal quality' (*ibid*. p. 15/1), and his early letters show a 'simple familiarity and tenderness' (*ibid*. p. 15/2); '... friendship is for him a means of his ascent to God' (*ibid*. p. 15/4).
27 See below and n. 31.

one must love, and by love make others virtuous. One does not 'merit' love, yet must merit it. It is a circular thought because in the unity and wholeness of his thinking each phrase throws light on the whole. For the circle's centre and circumference is God.[28]

The key to this interpretation of Anselm's view of friendship is the radical identity of the friends, achieved by the interior presence of one to the other. This is associated with the doctrine of the Image, i.e., as Fiske puts this, that 'the soul is a mirror: within it is reflected the Divine Face ...'.[29] As the interior presence of His image is how God is apprehended, so by a similar process are friends fully known to one another and their union achieved, and it is this phenomenon – 'image-likeness' – which for Fiske is the concept central to friendship: 'For union is an interior presence by image-likeness.'[30] Friends are thereby present to one another interiorly, and so are mutually conscious of one another, and this constitutes the essence of their mystical union:

> The 'virtue' by which friendship is 'merited' is, above all, love itself. But friendship, also, essentially *is* love, affectus, a love that is mutual and of which the friends are mutually conscious. These two notes – reciprocity and conscious awareness – indicate an experience that is wholly interior, and that produces an interior presence of the friends to each other, a certainty of love, and a mutual possession of each other, characteristics of mystical experience.[31]

Ultimately, friendship is love, and love is God. This friendship is mystical and eschatological,[32] and this makes the physical presence of the friend effectively irrelevant.[33] For this reason Fiske emphasised, far more than did Southern, Anselm's apparent unconcern with the physical presence of friends – indeed Southern saw this as a traditional idea from which Anselm was moving away, while for Fiske the whole inspiration of Anselm's friendship is absence.[34]

---

28 Fiske, *Friends and Friendship*, p. 15/7. Friendship is also virtue, and virtue is its cause (*ibid.*, p. 15/6, quoted below). Even instances of apparently clearly political friendship are interpreted in a spiritual sense, see e.g. *ibid.*, pp. 15/4–5.

29 *Ibid.*, p. 15/2.

30 *Ibid.*, p. 15/23.

31 *Ibid.*, p. 15/4 (emphasis in original).

32 *Ibid.*, p. 15/17: 'The theology of Anselm inspires both his piety and his friendships, and reveals especially their eschatological character, for the "feeling", the vision, the joy he looks for can be only in heaven.'

33 But separation is not painless, as Fiske points out, *Friends and Friendship*, p. 15/21: 'Anselm thus in theory resolves the conflict [between friendship and separation as a result of God's will] but it remains a painful reality'; cf. also the concluding sentence of the chapter, *ibid.* p. 15/31.

34 Fiske, *Friends and Friendship*, p. 15/4, following immediately from the passage quoted above: 'Therefore Anselm tends to minimize the value of corporal presence, and sees in submission to the will of God, that separates friends, the very means of uniting them, by increasing their likeness to each other in virtue.' For Southern, by contrast, 'The distant realization of the ideal [that identity was the essence of friendship] was not enough. Hence in the realm of friendship Anselm abandoned the time-honoured doctrine that absence was a negligible factor in the union of souls in friendship. His words on this subject have an intensity which it is difficult now to understand' (Southern, *Saint Anselm and his Biographer*, p. 74).

Community, in this view, is still integrally related to friendship but is not so central. Its very purpose may be to foster that friendship which leads to God, but it is not essential to it precisely because that friendship is ultimately an interior experience:

> This concept is central in Anselm's thought, containing all other elements of his ideal of friendship: the aim of friendship is to form one's friend to nobility of character and to love of God. This is the purpose of living together, yet it is a greater joy to know that one's friend is growing in virtue than to have him present, for the spiritual presence of friends within each other is in that similitude of virtue.[35]

Community, however, is given a central place in what is probably the most influential recent book on medieval friendship, Brian Patrick McGuire's 1988 *Friendship and Community: The Monastic Experience, 350–1250*.[36] Both McGuire's characterisation here of Anselm's concept of friendship and his assessment of Anselm's place in the development of friendship resemble those of Southern and Fiske in some important respects. McGuire, like them, sees Anselm's expression of friendship as unique, a revolution in the history of friendship.[37] At the same time he likewise sees Anselm's expression of friendship as emotionally intense but more intellectual than personal, and consequently open to misunderstanding, and disappointing to his friends.[38] And, like Southern again, he sees Anselm's concept of friendship as closely related to monastic community.[39] McGuire also sets this development of the concept of friendship, for all his recognition of Anselm's unique genius, more explicitly in a wider historical context. He identifies a variety of reasons for the flourishing of monastic friendship in the period c.1050–1120, including the influence of the cathedral schools with their interest in classical friendship; an 'interest in deepening the content and quality of spiritual life for the individual'; the Gregorian reform and associated debate literature; the influence of Anselm himself; and the demands of social mobility making greater the need for effective friends.[40] But, crucially and differently for McGuire, the unifying theme in this change in the language of friendship is individualisation. Thus the literary development of the concept of friendship

---

[35] Fiske, *Friends and Friendship*, p. 15/6.
[36] He discusses Anselm at pp. 210–27; for the ideas discussed in this section, see also *ibid.* ch. 5, pp. 180–230.
[37] Although revolutionary in a very different way: e.g. McGuire, *Friendship and Community*, p. 211: 'He [Anselm] appears as the inspirer and promoter of new ways of talking about friendship. Anselm and his followers contributed to a veritable revolution in the expression of human sentiment.'
[38] E.g. McGuire, *Friendship and Community*, p. 214: 'There could often be a gap between what Anselm's correspondents understood him to say and what he really meant. ... Anselm's friends had no firm cultural or linguistic background according to which they could interpret his words. When Anselm wrote to one of them but said that the same expression of love applied to another monk, his friends at Canterbury were unable to see that he was expressing an ideal of friendship rather than his personal feelings for any one of them.'
[39] *Ibid.*, p. 214: 'He [Anselm] looked at friendship as a way to enrich the content of monastic life, which Anselm considered the best and often the only way to reach paradise.'
[40] *Ibid.*, pp. 180–210 and the summary of these points at pp. 227–9.

attests to the individualising of the bond.[41] An earlier, limited, merely political view of friendship is transformed by a concern for individual feelings and an interest in personal relationships.[42] Even the increased need for the instrumental application of friendship, which is important among those reasons for the flourishing of friendship identified by McGuire, leads not towards a more fully articulated instrumental friendship but rather towards the more intense expression of personal sentiment:

> The need to choose sides [in the Gregorian reform] and find allies encouraged communities and individual monks to seek each other out and to define what their bonds involved. Heightened controversy encouraged a heightened statement of tenderness and unity among men in the church.[43]

McGuire's portrayal of this historical context is crucial to his reading of friendship literature: friendship is progressing towards a form of individualism, a development which is presented in positive terms.[44] He sees the development in the concept of friendship as closely linked to the wider social and political context, perhaps more explicitly than did either Southern or Fiske, but at the same time as developing towards a greater awareness of and interest in private feelings and the value of individual bonds for their own sake. Yet Anselm, with his concern for community and his intellectualised friendship (even as characterised by McGuire himself), would seem to stand outside this development. McGuire, however, sees the origin and inspiration of Anselm's friendship wholly differently from either Southern or Fiske. For him, the emotional intensity of Anselm's expression stems rather from a love interpreted in essentially private terms:

> He [Anselm] loved men, and in terms of the human bonds, his world was composed only of men, but there is no evidence that he was a repressed homosexual ... he [Anselm] defies characterization or neat definition. ... I would nevertheless still argue that Anselm had one great love in his life, the young monk Osbern ...[45]

The basis for this conclusion is an interpretation of the letters in terms of degrees of intimacy detectable in the language – specifically in letter 4 where Anselm asks his friends to pray for the soul of his late friend Osbern. McGuire sees this

---

41 e.g. McGuire, *Friendship and Community*, p. 182 [discussing the way in which the successive *Vitae* of St Dunstan exemplify changes in describing friendship]: 'The new formulation individualizes the bond', and *ibid.*, p. 183: 'Holy friendship is much more specific and individualized than holy love', etc.

42 McGuire is quite explicit in this identification of two types of friendship, and in the qualitative distinction between them: e.g. McGuire, *Friendship and Community*, pp. 183–4: 'Just as we saw earlier in the letters of Gerbert of Aurillac, friendship is used as another way of expressing political alliance. There is nothing underhanded about this transaction, but it reduces friendship to a bond with only a very limited religious dimension. ... How could such a one-dimensional view of friendship give way to the rich spectrum of expression that becomes apparent by the early twelfth century?'

43 McGuire, *Friendship and Community*, p. 228.

44 So, for example, from this progressive perspective, Peter Damian can be seen as 'transitional' (*Ibid.*, p. 208), and Anselm as representing the revolution (see n. 37 above).

45 *Ibid.*, p. 211.

relationship with Osbern both as exceptional and as seminal for Anselm's later development:

> The exact nature of Anselm's bond with Osbern cannot be determined, but it seems possible and even likely that Anselm ... did become strongly emotionally attached to this attractive and spirited young man. ... The first letters of friend-ship can be regarded as spreading out to many monks the feelings that Anselm had once reserved for the young Osbern.[46]

The basis for setting apart the relationship with Osbern is the sentence, cited by McGuire: 'Ubicumque Osbernus est, anima eius anima mea est.' This is contrasted with his tone to Gundulf earlier in the same letter: 'Qualiter namque obliviscam tui? Is enim qui cordi meo velut sigillum cerae imprimitur, quomodo memoriae meae subtrahitur?'[47] On these passages McGuire comments: 'The phrases meant for Gundulf convey devotion and loyalty, while those describing Anselm's love for Osbern suggest that the two were bound by a much greater intimacy.'[48] Yet the image of two souls as one is not at all uncommon in friend-ship literature. To take only a few examples from elsewhere in Anselm's own letters, he uses the same phrase (along with more in a similar tone) of the monk Moses of Canterbury in letter 140; he calls Gilbert the other half of his soul in letter 84; and he talks often of the close identity of souls and of love with regard to yet others, in, to take only three examples, letters 41, 115 and 133. More importantly, it is not evident what the basis is for characterising the two expres-sions in letter 4 as dutiful and loving respectively, other than a judgement based on the tone and the vocabulary used. Yet such a judgement would seem to imply a reading of Anselm's language in terms of a register of expression which is, or at least accords closely with, modern conventions for the expression of private emotion. And, as Southern has shown, Anselm's use of language does not fit such a model. Furthermore, the conclusion drawn implies the recognition of degrees of intimacy which reach their highest, or at least most intense, expres-sion in the recollection of particular human love.

To assume that the relationships valued most highly, or at least given priority in terms of literary expression and exploration, by (and consequently the human experiences of greatest interest to) Anselm and his contemporaries were those of private, emotional attachments, may be to import modern priorities and interests. The twin assumptions, firstly that certain terms or figures are more intense, and, secondly and separately, that such intensity relates naturally to private, emotional attachments of an exclusive or unique nature, may only reflect modern, romantic conventions both about the relative importance or interest of 'private' and 'public' relationships and about what terms may appro-priately convey this intensity. This of course can lead to a circular argument: if we want to understand in what contexts, or in regard to what types of relation-ship, Anselm used certain expressions or terms, we cannot begin by assuming

---

[46] *Ibid.*, p. 212, but his conclusion is more complex than this: see below and n. 56.
[47] *Ibid.*, p. 211 and p. 469 n. 83.
[48] *Ibid.*, p. 211.

that certain expressions or terms are more intimate, and that they therefore describe a particular type of relationship.[49]

This approach can also lead to specific problems when we encounter the familiar circumstance, highlighted by Southern, of the use of similar or identical language in very different contexts. In many cases we know, either from external evidence or because it is stated in a letter, that the intimate in question was not actually known personally to the writer, or was known less well than others to whom similar language is directed. Reading Anselm's language in terms of a familiar modern register of expression, we could only conclude that he was using a term 'genuinely' or in a 'real' way in some cases, and 'falsely' or as an analogy to a 'truer' form of affection in others – here an expression of real emotion, there an empty cliché. This may of course be the case, but it cannot be a presumption, and it presents this problem: because it implies a necessarily selective reading of the evidence for the relationships concerned, it must be explicitly justified as selective.[50] On the other hand, we could approach the evidence with alternative questions: can, for example, Anselm's use of the vocabulary of love and friendship be understood as part of a coherent language; what codes and conventions are being used; can we identify an internally consistent use of language whose referents are not necessarily those of modern romantic or individualistic convention (and not decide a priori which instances are 'genuine' and which not)?

McGuire, of course, offers just such an empathetic and culturally sensitive interpretation of many of Anselm's letters of friendship, where others by sharp contrast have produced crude, selective readings based on a simplistic and anachronistic reading of the language. But, differently from either Southern or Fiske, he implies the origin of friendship in a form of private emotional attachment, or at least he relates these other expressions radically to that supposedly more intimate and real expression of feeling. The importance given to private feelings and individual emotion also accords with McGuire's overall aim in the book, to separate feelings from language – as he says in his introduction, to 'get behind the abundant literary commonplaces or topoi about friendship to the people who formed them and to their feelings for each other'.[51] Such a statement might however be taken to imply that topoi are inherently false, rather than effective ways to convey meaning allusively and within shared cultural terms of reference.[52] Moreover, in this view individuality can be seen to be reduced or limited

---

[49] And by implication reflect cultural values by which such relationships are valued more highly as relating to a fuller or more rewarding human experience.

[50] That is not to say again that such a selective reading is unjustifiable (clearly if it was the case that the language was being used variably in such a way, then such a reading would indeed be justified), but rather that such an interpretation must be clearly recognised as selective. It is selective because, as there is no demonstrable correlation between specific language and particular degrees or types of relationship, when (as is frequently the case) there is no conclusive external evidence, the reader can only decide subjectively whether an expression reflects a genuine relationship or is being used 'falsely'.

[51] McGuire, *Friendship and Community*, p. xii.

[52] On reading topos, see e.g. M. Mullett, 'Friendship in Byzantium: Genre, topos and network', in *Friendship in Medieval Europe*, ed. Haseldine, pp. 166–84; see also *Rhetoric and Renewal in the Latin West 1100–1540: Essays in honour of John O. Ward*, ed. C. Mews, C. Nederman, R. M. Thomson (Turnhout, 2003).

by the demands of community: not only is it threatened, but it is marked out as superior to community experience as a basis for the development of human potential.[53] So, for McGuire, Anselm's ideals are expressed or achieved only by subordinating a greater urge to a lesser: 'However much Anselm *subordinated* the subjective desire for the friend to the monastic stability, he *still* thought that the practice and ideal of friendship had a *place within* monasticism.'[54] For Southern and Fiske, by contrast, it could only be defined in terms of monastic community. McGuire talks of a 'doomed' friendship, which seems to imply an individualistic friendship which could not be reconciled with the ascetic ideals of the new monasticism.[55]

Clearly, at one level these interpretations do turn simply on the relationship of language to context. For McGuire, Anselm's letter 4 relates to friendships of differing degrees of emotional intensity, while for Southern it exemplifies one facet of friendship literature, the application of the same sentiments to more than one recipient. But there is also a question here both of the priorities and intellectual interests of the writers, and of the conceptualisation by historians of the relationship between individual and community. For McGuire the emotional content of the relationship with Osbern was seminal, and led Anselm to transfer his emotional energy to others and into monastic life. It was the true underlying feeling. For Southern, as also but somewhat differently for Fiske, the individual friends were the particular instances of a friendship whose true underlying meaning was the ascent to God via monastic community. And this is important because it relates to our first question about the distinctive nature of monastic friendship: is Anselm working within the tradition of friendship, in which individual relations are valued but as an aspect of something more important, and applying this to monastic community, or is he rather focusing primarily on the individual bond as something of higher inherent value, and thus breaking with that tradition?

But the question is in fact more complex with Anselm, at least in McGuire's nuanced reading. McGuire continued his analysis of letter 4, quoted above, with the observation:

> But they [the letters of friendship from the 1070s and early 1080s] are by no means merely the witnesses to the transference of one emotional bond into many. The letters are a monument to a renewed and deepened monastic celebration of friendship.[56]

---

[53] Which it may well be held to be for us, but that may not be the most appropriate basis for interpreting medieval texts.

[54] McGuire, *Friendship and Community*, p. 219 (my emphases). He continues: 'Christ becomes the cornerstone of both community and of friendship, and there can be no implicit conflict between individual and collective bonds,' yet the tone of this passage generally does seem to imply such a conflict at some level.

[55] *Ibid.*, pp. 229–30: 'By its very definition, monastic friendship seems to have been doomed to extinction after a brief moment of acceptance. Anselm's letters had a direct effect on only a few churchmen. The main thrust in the reformed monasticism of the late eleventh and early twelfth centuries was towards greater asceticism, which idealized desert isolation.'

[56] *Ibid.*, p. 212.

Anselm then is doing two things, and the relationship between them is neither obvious nor simple: that is to say, it could be argued that once the emotions inspired in Anselm by Osbern had been transferred to others or to the monastic vocation generally, then his later friendship, as it was developed and expressed over time, was concerned directly and genuinely with this 'monastic celebration of friendship'. We might then ask how important is this original inspiration to our understanding of the development, articulation and reception of his mature ideal of friendship. We cannot, of course, ever know the psychological roots of Anselm's interest in friendship, but that may not be the most important question. While psychological speculation might allow us to guess at why one particular individual engaged with one particular area of interest, be that friendship, ascetic devotion, love, dialectic etc., it cannot explain either the form that engagement takes – the culturally conditioned articulation of that interest – or the reception of the writings so produced in the wider cultural sphere. From this perspective, it is not so important to argue over whether it all started from one intense love or not, but rather to understand the external cultural values which its form of expression reflects.

However the connections between cultural context and shared values on the one hand and individual motivations on the other may be more complex than this. Is it simply that the medieval cultural context determined the specific articulation and reception of Anselm's ideas on friendship, which can then be seen as transferences of what we understand as truer, or underlying, feelings (whether we take these to be sexual or not), which are merely couched in a language overtly concerned with community? Or is it rather that this cultural context itself produced a genuine psychological impulse to experience friendship as fulfilled in community and ultimately in salvation, and not in individual, private experience. In other words, are we applying to Anselm's cultural context our own society's conventional notions of what constitutes the essential area of meaningful experience – primarily individual emotion?[57] If so, then an understanding of the original impulse for Anselm's friendships is important, for two reasons. Firstly, it can determine our reading of Anselm's language of friendship as a whole: are terms and expressions to be taken as evidence of private, affective bonds where this seems to fit the context, and as evidence of the cultivation of monastic *amicitia* where it does not? Or can we read this language more coherently, as reflective (in a wide variety of circumstances) of a monastic culture of friendship, and as rooted in community experience not private loves.[58] Secondly, and consequently, the way in which we interpret this language directly affects our use of the letters as empirical evidence in the detection and analysis of actual relationships and networks.

This is especially pressing when, as seems to be the case, the tone and vocabulary is the same in evidently different contexts, or at least does not seem to

---

57 And possibly thereby also implying that modern psychology simply reveals universal human constants rather than modern, culturally conditioned responses.

58 Assumptions about individualism and community were questioned notably and productively in C. Walker Bynum, *Jesus as Mother: Studies in the Spirituality of the High Middle Ages* (Berkely, 1982), ch. 3 'Did the Twelfth Century Discover the Individual?', pp. 82–109.

divide neatly into such categories as emotive or instrumental, private or business friendship etc. Indeed, a full correlation of Anselm's language to context, as part of a network study, would provide a basis for just such an empathetic understanding of his use of the language of friendship. In the meantime, given the present early state of research on networks, some examples from his letters may illustrate the problem further.

In letter 205 Anselm assures the monks of Bec:

> ... how much and how truly I have always loved you, and how much and how deeply I have longed for you. ... If not all of you know this from experience, for God has increased your numbers since I left you, learn it from those who do know. ... Therefore I beg and beseech all of you equally that the memory and love of me in the hearts of those who have it may not cool down and that it may be enkindled and sustained in the minds of those who do not know me.[59]

Here the language is undoubtedly intense, while the context is clearly not that of an exchange between intimates. Love and memory are treated as transferable commodities, and the implication is that personal acquaintance is not the only context for love. We might also note here that Anselm talks of memory and love – not of feelings.[60] He expects them to gain a real thing not merely to feel. This may not be intended as a metaphor in an age when the reality of divine love was conceived as instrumental in human affairs and in monastic vocation. So the direct extension of friendship to a community seems here to be treated as something real. Can we then dismiss this language as being of a lesser order than similar language used to known intimates, or as false, without running into the problems of selectivity noted above?

This letter exemplifies some of the problems of relating language to context, and indicates something of the value accorded to community. Elsewhere in Anselm's letters we can find the tension between community and individual treated more directly.

In letter 79 he says to the monk Maurice:

> Although the more I love you the more I want to have you with me, yet because I cannot have you I love you even more ... [Y]ou ... should patiently bear our separation as being ordered by Providence, as long as our lord and father the venerable Archbishop Lanfranc commands it, lest by impatience you in any way diminish the very qualities for which I love you most. For although I love you greatly and

---

59 *S. Anselmi Cantuariensis Archiepiscopi Opera Omnia*, ed. F. S. Schmitt, 6 vols. (Edinburgh, 1946–61), vol. 4, p. 98: 'Sed in hac dubietate consolatur me vestra conscientia, qua mihi conscii estis, quantum semper vos et quam veraciter dilexerim, et quid et quantum de vobis desideraverim. ... Et si non omnes hoc experimento, quia deus numerum auxit, postquam a vobis discessi, cognoscitis: ab illis qui sciunt et experti sunt discite. ... Omnes igitur pariter precor et obsecro, ut mei memoria et dilectio in cordibus eorum, qui eam habuerunt, non tepescat, et in mentibus eorum, qui me non noverunt, accendatur et perseveret.' Transl. W. Fröhlich, *The Letters of Saint Anselm of Canterbury*, 3 vols., Cistercian Studies Series 96, 97, 142 (Kalamazoo, 1990–94), vol. 2, p. 144.

60 He does use the word *affectum* earlier in the letter, which in some contexts is rendered 'feelings'.

desire you to cling to me by living in our community with me, yet I desire even more that you cleave inseparably to a good way of life.[61]

Here the obedience which is at the heart of the *Rule* appears to be in conflict with friendship: Maurice should not endanger the friendship by travelling to see his friend. And here again we are confronted with an undeniably intense language. It is interesting, however, that Anselm does not discuss the situation in terms of sacrifice[62] – of sacrificing friendship to obedience. For Anselm, Lanfranc's will is not in opposition to his friendship with Maurice, because only through obedience can Maurice be loveable – it is the key to 'the very qualities for which I love you most'. Again, are we to deduce from this that there is here a weaker or lesser friendship, one which can readily be consoled by a literary conceit. Or should we say that Anselm is rationalising his desires, or their frustration? For there was indeed a real tension here to be resolved, but the point is that Anselm does resolve it, he does not console Maurice.[63] And the resolution may be a genuine one: that monastic vocation creates the conditions for friendship, and if friendship for Anselm is not dependent on private experience, then obedience strengthens friendship by maintaining the vocation which actually is its base. In other words, for Anselm the place of friendship in monastic culture did not have to, nor was it expected to, elicit the sort of tension between the individual and the community which might appear most readily to modern minds.

These examples suggest the sort of ideals of friendship already identified by Southern, to which modern connections between the private and the personal do not apply, and where modern conventions about the appropriateness of certain expressions to particular types of relationship are not relevant. But we might argue that Anselm, on occasion, goes further than Southern's distinction between personal and business letters allows.[64] If we cannot dismiss expressions of love or friendship as insincere, lesser or empty of true meaning on the grounds that they do not fit the sorts of context which seem by our conventions appropriate to such language, then we may need also to go further and to take seriously examples such as this, from letter 165, addressed to Abbot William and the community of Bec:

> Remember too how I always used to gain friends for the church of Bec: following this example, hasten to gain friends for yourselves from all sides by exercising the good deed of hospitality, dispensing generosity to all men, and when you do not have the opportunity of doing good works, by according at least the gift of a kind

---

61 S. *Anselmi ... Opera*, vol. 3, p. 202: 'Licet quo te magis diligo, eo magis mecum velim habere: plus tamen inde te diligo, unde te non possum habere ... et separationem nostram, quamdiu iubebit noster dominus et pater, venerabilis archiepiscopus Lanfrancus, mecum patienter ut divinam dispositionem toleres, nec in aliquo id unde te magis diligo, per impatientiam minuas. Quamvis namque te valde diligam et desiderem, ut mihi mecum conversando cohaereas, plus tamen opto ut bonis moribus indissolubiliter inhaereas.' Transl. Fröhlich, *Letters of Saint Anselm*, vol. 1, p. 210.

62 A theme for which there are abundant Biblical topoi (an obvious example being Luke 23: 42 'But yet not my will, but thine be done,' cf. Matt. 26: 42; Mark 14: 36).

63 Although consolation is one of the most common themes available in the epistolographical tradition.

64 See above, and n. 20.

word. Never consider that you have enough friends, but whether rich or poor, let them all be bound to you by brotherly love. This will be to the advantage of your church and promote the welfare of those you love.[65]

We could of course designate this a lesser, more instrumental type of friendship, and infer from that that 'amor[e] fraternitatis' indicates a lesser experience. But if we recall that, for Anselm, real and intense friendships involve not private feelings but the ascent to God through community, then this friendship, integrally related to the good of the community, although it may not be as intense as those of some of the other letters, yet relates fundamentally to the same goal: the good of the community in which alone friendship can realise its purpose. Without a flourishing community, true friendship cannot be realised, therefore this friendship does not fall into a different category, it is an integral part of the same purpose. If there is less intensity, this is a matter of degree not a qualitative difference.[66] To separate instrumental friendships from more 'real' ones, either on the grounds of separating the political from the emotive or intellectual, or the business from the personal, might be to introduce demarcations of categories where for Anselm there were simply different levels of engagement with one overriding purpose – the community.

While Anselm's voice may still be heard above the alluring whispers of modern romantics, Aelred of Rievaulx's has been more often submerged. His treatises on love and friendship in the context of community life and of the ascent to God have almost routinely been read as personal, even sentimental, autobiography. As, in Père Lachaise cemetery, lovers still place fresh flowers on the memorial to Peter Abelard and Heloise in touching homage to two people whose values and aspirations were so far removed from those of their modern admirers, so has Aelred been embraced by this alien cult. But Aelred set out to produce a Christian version of classical friendship, and his works are, in this sense, even more than Anselm's, crucial to the question of a distinctively monastic culture of friendship. In the remainder of this paper there will only be space to introduce some considerations relevant to one, albeit the most important, of his works on love and friendship, the De Spiritali Amicitia [see also plate 14].[67]

65 S. Anselmi ... Opera, vol. 4, p. 39: 'Memores etiam estote quam ratione semper ecclesiae Beccensi amicos acquirere consuevi; et hoc exemplo amicos vobis undecumque acquirere festinate, hospitalitatis bonum sectando, benignitatem omnibus impendendo, et, ubi facultas operis defuerit, affabilis sermonis gratiam porrigendo. Nec umquam satis vos habere amicos credatis, sed sive divites sive pauperes, omnes vobis in amore fraternitatis conglutinate, quatenus hoc et ad vestrae ecclesiae utilitatem proficere et ad eorum quos diligitis salutem valeat pertingere.' Transl. Fröhlich, Letters of Saint Anselm, vol. 2, pp. 58–9.

66 See also J. P. Haseldine, 'Love, Separation and Male Friendship: Words and Actions in Saint Anselm's letters to his friends', in Masculinity in Medieval Europe, ed. D. M. Hadley (Longman, 1999), pp. 238–55. Fiske makes a related point in Friends and Friendship pp. 15/4–5. The linking of the material and the spiritual welfare of a community is fundamental to monastic culture and a recurrent theme in monastic literature, yet one which is often overlooked, especially with the greater attention normally given to religious poverty.

67 Ed. in Aelredi Rievallensis Opera Omnia I: opera ascetica, ed. A. Hoste and C. H. Talbot, CCCM (Turnhout, 1971), pp. 279–350, hereafter DSA.

Much of the recent interpretation of the *De Spirituali Amicitia* has turned on its Prologue, which is routinely treated, unproblematically, as autobiographical, and almost equally commonly as the autobiographical treatment of sexual experience. There exists a vast literature on Aelred,[68] but Brian Patrick McGuire, once again, is perhaps the most influential recent commentator, as in so many areas of medieval friendship, and he has produced the most balanced critique and summary of the earlier work. His own reading of Aelred, however, built up in a number of books and articles,[69] takes as its starting point precisely the two premises that the Prologue to the *De Spirituali Amicitia* is autobiography and that it treats of sexual experience. Thus, for example, in the chapter devoted to Aelred in *Friendship and Community* he says: 'In Aelred the autobiographical element, present to a greater or lesser degree in Bernard of Clairvaux, William of Saint Thierry and other contemporary writers, becomes explicit and detailed.'[70] He then goes on to make a number of suggestions about Aelred's psychology and sexuality, again based on the premise that this text and the *Speculum Caritatis* were autobiographical, or contain autobiographical passages. So, for example, he states: 'At no point does Aelred say outright: I slept with another man. His autobiographical passage, however, points to a sexual element in the friendship he mentions.'[71] However, by the beginning of the next section, what are at first suggestions and indications have elided into apparently uncontested statements: 'Aelred's transference of sexual energy to spiritual fire came in the aftermath of the conversion to the monastic life …'.[72]

The first question which all such readings raise is the applicability of the term 'autobiography' to this type of writing. Autobiography presents two problems. Firstly, as a recognised genre it is a modern development born of an explicit

---

68 It is barely possible even to begin to introduce the full range of work on Aelred here, but some of the debates referring to sexuality can be approached through, e.g.: D. Roby, 'Early Medieval Attitudes Towards Homosexuality', *Gai Saber*, 1 (1977), 67–71; M. L. Dutton. 'Aelred of Rievaulx on Friendship, Chastity and Sex: the Sources', *CSQ*, 29 (1994), 121–96; K. M. Yohe, 'Sexual attraction and the motivations for love and friendship in Aelred of Rievaulx', *ABR*, 46 (1995), 283–307; see also below n. 72. Fiske, *Friends and Friendship*, pp. 18/1–49, portrays Aelred's friendship in terms of rational love and as eschatological, centred on the ascent to God and related to the doctrine of image-likeness.

69 See e.g. B. P. McGuire, *Brother and Lover: Aelred of Rievaulx* (New York, 1994); id., 'Sexual awareness and identity in Aelred of Rievaulx (1110–67)', *ABR*, 45 (1994), 184–226; and id., *Friendship and Community*, pp. 296–338.

70 McGuire, *Friendship and Community*, p. 299.

71 *Ibid.*, p. 302.

72 *Ibid.*, p. 304, the implication being that the only question here is one of timing. Note that this section of the chapter is entitled: 'Conversion: Dealing with the impulses of sexuality.' (But contrast James McEvoy's comment on Aelred's slow maturation to religious life: J. McEvoy, 'Notes on the Prologue of Saint Aelred of Rievaulx's *De Spirituali Amicitia* with a translation', *Traditio*, 37 (1981), 396–411 at 402.) Marsha Dutton criticised a similar method of argumentation in McGuire's earlier work on Aelred: M. L. Dutton, 'The Invented Sexual History of Aelred of Rievaulx: A Review Article', *ABR*, 47 (1996), 414–32. There is also a sub-debate as to whether Aelred was homosexual, most famously put forward by John Boswell [see e.g. J. Boswell, *Christianity, Social Tolerance and Homosexuality: Gay people in Western Europe from the beginning of the Christian era to the fourteenth century* (Chicago, 1980), pp. 221–6], but this argument is of course logically dependent on that as to whether such texts can be taken to be autobiographical in the first place.

and primary concern for and interest in the development of an individual character, be that development personal, psychological, political or whatever. Along with biography, it arises in a culture which privileges individual uniqueness and personal experience as approaches to exploring the human condition. Medieval forms of writing which bear formal resemblances to biography, including *vitae* and other forms of hagiography, tend rather to present a static picture: signs of sanctity already evident in the young saint-to-be, or pre-conversion indications of spirituality.[73] This is perhaps not directly relevant to all examples of medieval writing about the self. More important however, and more clearly a problem, is the assumption that autobiography as a genre, or writing about the self more generally, in any period actually reflects the truly individual and unique development which it purports to describe. Autobiography and biography are not merely influenced by the distorting effect of memory but are normally constructed with typical or exemplary models and teleological narrative strategies, and incorporate other figures suggestive of a range of future-related conceits such as destiny, fate, inevitability etc. And Aelred is not untypical in this respect. To read medieval texts as autobiographical, and to take autobiography as candid description of individual experience, therefore, presents obvious and immediate problems.

Beyond this, there is the question of the drawing of psychological inferences from such texts. There are some important distinctions to be drawn between, on the one hand, a reading of autobiography as a record of individual or unique developments and, on the other, a psychological or psycho-historical interpretation of such texts. A reading of autobiography could in principle take into account the use of models and narrative strategies when assessing the events or characters portrayed, as part of an empirical study, as indeed many do. Psycho-history is posited on the ability to discern unvoiced meanings or evidence of underlying motivations, often of a sexual nature, which are not expressed overtly in the text. Needless to say, these are not fully distinct approaches: some psychological inference could be brought to bear in the former, and an understanding of models and narrative strategies is essential to the latter. In the case of Aelred's Prologue to the *De Spiritali Amicitia*, as there is no overt reference to sex or sexuality, then to read it not just as autobiography but as revealing of personal sexual history necessarily implies a psycho-historical or psychologically informed reading. This is not to suggest that such an approach is invalid, but merely to clarify the interpretive strategies upon which these readings must rest – whether made explicit or not by their proponents.

The opening section from the Prologue to the *De Spiritali Amicitia*, upon which such interpretations of Aelred have largely been built, is brief indeed:

1. Cum adhuc puer essem in scholis, et sociorum meorum me gratia plurimum delectaret, et inter mores et uitia quibus aetas illa periclitari solet, totam se mea mens dedit affectui, et deuouit amori; ita ut nihil mihi dulcius, nihil iucundius, nihil utilius quam *amari et amare* uideretur. 2. Itaque inter diuersos amores et amicitias fluctuans, rapiebatur animus huc atque illuc; et uerae amicitiae legem ignorans,

---

[73] This also accords with many medieval treatments of friendship as a static relationship, eternal and true, where there is little evident interest in the evolution of personal emotions or the development of a relationship. (But Aelred is more complex in this regard.)

eius saepe similitudine fallebatur. Tandem aliquando mihi uenit in manus, liber ille quem de amicitia Tullius scripsit; qui statim mihi et sententiarum grauitate utilis, et eloquentiae suauitate dulcis apparebat. 3. Et licet nec ad illud amicitiae genus me uiderem idoneum, gratulabar tamen quamdam me amicitiae formulam reperisse, ad quam amorum meorum et affectionum ualerem reuocare discursus. Cum uero placuit bono Domino meo corrigere deuium, elisum erigere, salubri contactu mundare leprosam, relicta spe saeculi, ingressus sum monasterium. 4. Et statim legendis sacris litteris operam dedi; cum prius nec ad ipsam earum superficiem oculus lippiens, et carnalibus tenebris assuetus sufficeret ...[74]

This Prologue is of course modelled closely on Augustine's *Confessions*, and what Aelred seems to be doing is setting up a confession and conversion piece cast in terms of friendship, not composing an autobiography. (Indeed far from revealing deep passions, it has even been read as a tempered rendering of Augustine's theme.[75]) What pleased Aelred was his companions' *gratia*. The effect on him was one of emotional vacillation: 'fluctuans', 'discursus' – a psychological characteristic almost proverbially associated with youth in all contexts, non-sexual as much as sexual.[76] What afflicted him were *affectus*, *amor(es)*, and *amicitia(s)*. The context for this was the unspecified *mores* and *uitia* attendant upon youth. This is what constituted the *similitudo* of friendship for which Aelred accuses himself.[77] What Aelred says he has given up is *spe(s) saeculi*. Finally the term 'carnalibus' here appears to mean, given its context, worldly learning. As this brief passage does not refer literally to sex or sexual activity, then readings of it as revealing of sexuality must imply the interpretive strategies noted above. The basic material upon which such interpretations have been based is an account of a conversion to religious life framed in terms of a transition from youthful vacillation to mature stability. It is the world and the spiritual life, not sexual practice and chastity, with which Aelred seems to be concerned. This is not to say that there is nothing to read 'between the lines', or that we should only take Aelred at face value, but rather to note that we need to be clear about the basis for particular interpretations, especially if the debate is not to be conducted at the level of trading in psychological commonplaces.

The interpretation of the body of the treatise has been guided to a large extent by readings of the Prologue. Aelred's stated aim was to 'draw up for myself rules for a chaste and holy love',[78] and his plan is to examine friendship in three stages: 'the nature of friendship ... its fruition and excellence ... [and] how and

---

[74] *DSA*, p. 287. This is of course not the only text upon which such interpretations have been built, and there is only room here to discuss this one example.

[75] See McEvoy, 'Notes on the Prologue', p. 401.

[76] See McEvoy, 'Notes on the Prologue', on *fluctuans* ('floating', 'drifting' or 'being tossed about'), p. 401, and *discursus*, p. 405.

[77] On *similitudo* here, see McEvoy, 'Notes on the Prologue', p. 402. Note also the similar non-sexual (or not necessarily sexual) friendship described at *DSA*, 3. 85–87.

[78] Prol. 6: '... et regulas mihi castae sanctaeque dilectionis praescribere.' Trans. M. E. Laker, *Aelred of Rievaulx: Spiritual Friendship* (with introduction by D. Roby), *Cistercian Fathers Series* 5 (Kalamazoo, 1977), p. 47. McGuire, *Friendship and Community*, p. 297, emphasises this aspect of Aelred's approach, but relates it in a different way to the question of Aelred's initial inspiration to examine friendship.

among whom it can be preserved …'.[79] In the first two books especially, Aelred outlines a true, spiritual friendship, contrasted with false or lesser forms. This is the core of his Christian version of Ciceronian *amicitia*, whose reward is itself not worldly gain and whose aim is ultimately the ascent to God. The aim of the present paper is not to analyse in detail this construction of friendship,[80] but to make some suggestions about Aelred's initial or underlying motivations for his interest in friendship, which have often been the subject of comment. Of particular relevance here, in addition to the Prologue as already discussed, is his treatment of actual friends, which is especially prominent in the third book of the treatise.

Firstly we might note Aelred's overriding concern with the selection and probation of friends. This is the leitmotif of book three. For example, and summarising earlier sections:

… one should pay attention to the four steps which lead up to the heights of perfect friendship; for a friend ought first to be selected, next tested, then finally admitted, and from then on treated as a friend deserves.[81]

And as he states explicitly: 'But surely a certain impulse of love should be guarded against, which runs ahead of judgement and takes away the power of testing.'[82] That there is more to this than a mere abstraction to justify an underlying interest in 'deeper' or 'truer' friendship is suggested by the amount of detailed advice and space devoted to the practicalities of selection.[83] But how does Aelred treat the actual friendships he describes?[84] One of the longest discussions concerns the angry friend whose lenient treatment by Aelred is questioned by his interlocutors.[85] Aelred discusses this situation in terms not of his personal feelings but rather of the very principles of selection, obligation and honour which apply to friendship. For example:

---

[79] Prol. 7: 'Opusculum igitur istud in tribus distinximus libellis. In primo quid sit amicitia, et quis eius fuerit ortus uel causa commendantes. In secundo eius fructum excellentiamque proponentes. In tertio quomodo et inter quos possit usque in finem indirupta seruari, prout potuimus enodantes.' Transl. Laker, *Spiritual Friendship*, p. 47.

[80] A notable example of this remains P. Delhaye, 'Deux adaptations du De Amicitia de Ciceron au XIIe siècle,' *Recherches de Théologie ancienne et médiévale* 15 (1948), 304–31. I have addressed some aspects of this topic in J. P. Haseldine, 'Friendship, Equality and Universal Harmony: The Universal and the Particular in Aelred of Rievaulx's *De Spiritali Amicitia*', in O. Leaman ed., *Friendship East and West: Philosophical Perspectives* (Curzon, 1996), pp. 192–214.

[81] DSA, 3. 55: 'Quatuor subinde gradus in amicitia, quibus ad eius summam peruenitur, constituendos putauimus; cum amicus primum sit eligendus, deinde probandus, tunc demum admittendus, et sic postea ut decet tractandus.' Trans. Laker, *Spiritual Friendship*, p.104. Note also the obvious parallel to spiritual ascent literature, which goes back to the *Rule of Saint Benedict*.

[82] DSA, 3. 75: 'Cauendus sane est quidam impetus amoris qui *praecurrit iudicium*, et probandi adimit potestatem.' Trans. Laker, *Spiritual Friendship*, p. 109.

[83] See e.g. DSA, ss. 3. 14 ff., 3. 61 ff., 3. 130, etc.

[84] I am concerned here with friends discussed in the treatise, not with the literary personae of the interlocutors of the dialogue and the extent to which they are based on real people.

[85] DSA, 3.16–20 and 33–38.

Certainly that man is very dear to me. Having once received him into my friend-ship, I can never do otherwise than love him. ... And since there was no question of any dishonour being involved, and as confidence was not violated, or virtue lessened, it was right for me to yield to my friend ...[86]

Later it is explained that the friend, however questionable his behaviour, had kept to the laws of friendship, and that it is this that accounts for Aelred's attitude to him.[87] The discussion then turns to general cases and to scriptural *exempla*. Indeed what we have here reads less like a personal sketch than an *exemplum* of dealing with the faults of friends. And notably the lesson to be drawn is not a particularly sympathetic one; it is, rather emphatically, that one should choose friends more carefully in the first place: 'Let us then more carefully consider these five vices, that we may not bind ourselves by the ties of friendship to persons whom either the fury of anger or some other passion is wont to incite to these vices.'[88]

The rest of book three offers little more in the way of personal insight. In a lengthy section just before the end Aelred recalls two dead friends.[89] They are portrayed, naturally, partly through the descriptive tool of allusion, which while never as impersonal as modern naturalistic literary conventions would have it, reflects its own expository priorities, and we get little of their personal charac-ters. They are introduced as an example of the contrast between a friendship based on affection and one based on reason, of which the latter is upheld as the best and described at greatest length. Another character is mentioned briefly as an example of loyalty during a discussion of the various qualities of friend-ship.[90] There is indeed little in the way of personal portraiture, and the, perhaps surprisingly few, recollections of real friends are introduced essentially as exam-ples to illustrate points about the selection and probation of friends and key points about the nature of spiritual friendship, such as the role of reason. Here it is probably worth noting also that the interruptions in the discussion which mark the ends of the first two books, and one other similar passage in book three, serve at least in part to stress the importance of friendship in community: the

---

[86] DSA, 3.20: 'AELREDUS. Homo certe ille mihi carissimus est, et semel a me receptus in amicitiam, a me poterit numquam non amari ... ubi nulla interueniebat inhonestas, nec fides laedebatur, nec minuebatur uirtus, cedendum amico fuit ...' Trans. Laker, *Spiritual Friendship*, p. 95.

[87] DSA, 3.37.

[88] DSA, 3.23: 'Diligentius proinde haec quinque consideremus, ne nos ei amicitiae uinculis constringamus; quos ad haec uitia uel iracundiae furor, uel alia quaelibet passio compellere consueuit.' Trans. Laker, *Spiritual Friendship*, p. 96. Note also that friendship, rather than being seen as a natural sympathy between individuals, is contrasted with nature: 'Now if, instead of friendship, nature prescribed this course of action to him, I would judge him neither so virtuous nor so worthy of praise' (*ibid.*, 3.38: 'Quod si non ei amicitia, sed natura praescriberet, nec ita uirtuosum, nec ita laude dignum iudicarum'). Trans. Laker, *Spiritual Friendship*, p. 100.

[89] DSA, 3.119–27.

[90] DSA, 3.67. There is also the charming picture of the cloister at *ibid.*, 3.82, where all are loved.

discussions of friendship are broken off and the demands of community given due priority.[91]

There is no argument but that Aelred's appreciation of friendship was intensely personal. He says for example:

> ... scarcely any happiness whatever can exist among mankind without friendship, and a man is to be compared to a beast if he has no one to rejoice with him in adversity, no one to whom to unburden his mind if any annoyance crosses his path or with whom to share some unusually sublime or illuminating inspiration.[92]

But we have already seen, in the case of Southern's reading of Anselm, that the personal and the private need not be equated. It is possible, easy even, to make Aelred sound like an individualist, inspired by personal feeling, valuing the inner emotions for their own sake, but his recurrent concerns, illustrated briefly here, at least suggest the possibility of an alternative to the conventional sentimental and sexual readings of his works.

Anselm and Aelred then present us with two related problems: how are we to interpret their concepts of friendship, and how does this intellectual expression of friendship relate to monastic culture more broadly? As we have seen, both had intellectual agendas intimately concerned with the problem of monastic community. Further, both used the language of friendship in ways which do not accord with modern romantic or individualistic conceptions of the value of the relationship. We have also seen that the question of the possible personal motivations and drives which led them to explore friendship is important because it determines not just our understanding of them as personalities but more importantly our reading of their use of the language of friendship, both in its relation to its cultural context and as empirical evidence of actual relationships.[93] These considerations not only caution us against making presumptions about the nature of particular ties, obligations and relationships evidenced in the sources, but also raise the question of whether what we see expressed here is a product of monastic culture or rather evidence of personal feelings or drives, distorted or conditioned by the restrictions imposed by monastic life or contemporary mores. This question takes us to the heart of the problem of attempting to approach friendship in monastic culture.

We can speculate about the reactions of individuals experiencing their lives

---

91 DSA, 1. 71; 2. 71; and more ambiguously 3. 59–60
92 DSA, 2. 10: '... ita ut sine amico inter mortales nihil fere possit esse iucundum; homo bestiae comparetur, non habens qui sibi collaetetur in rebus secundis, in tristibus contristetur; cui euaporet si quid molestum mens conceperit; cui communicaret si quid praeter solitum sublime uel luminosum accesserit.' Trans. Laker, *Spiritual Friendship*, pp. 71–2. See also, for example, his description of love, the origin of friendship, as '... a certain affection of the rational soul whereby it seeks and eagerly strives after some object to possess it and enjoy it. Having attained its object through love, it enjoys it with a certain interior sweetness, embraces it, and preserves it' [I. 19; trans. Laker, *ibid.* pp. 5–6]. Similar excerpts could be picked out from almost the whole treatise.
93 I.e., as argued above (pp. 190–2), it does matter whether we see Anselm as inspired by particular affections or loves which were then transferred into monastic devotion, or as inspired by the vocation of and devotion to monastic community. The same argument applies logically also to Aelred.

within this culture, but that is not the same as treating them as individual-ists struggling against a restrictive, narrow set of institutional impositions. Both Anselm and Aelred have been seen as reconciling friendship to community, but perhaps by approaching the question of monastic friendship thus, assuming as our starting point a necessary and fundamental tension between individual self-expression and community life, we are looking for tensions which are not there – tensions between the *Rule* and our idea of friendship, tensions between the demands of the community and the private emotional or romantic feelings of the individual – rather than the feelings of the member of the community dedicated to and moved by the evidently powerful and stirring doctrine of obedi-ence and humility. This is not to say that there are no tensions at all, as we have seen with Anselm, but rather that we are culturally attuned to expect a different sort.

Nor is this to dismiss the notion that there were preferential emotional attachments in the lives of these monks; while there almost certainly would have been personal affections within some friendship relationships, these were probably seen as only one of a number of ties (others being membership of the same community, kinship etc.) which could lead to and be elevated into *amici-tiae*. Aelred is explicit on this point: '… not all whom we love should be received into friendship, for not all are found worthy of it.'[94] It may indeed be more real-istic to go further and accept that although people did obviously have personal friendships this is not what interested the writers of the letters and treatises which form the bulk of our evidence, nor is it what the classical and medieval traditions of friendship were really about. Indeed, to assume that the language of friendship was used to explore feelings may simply be to miss the point. It may not be enough just to say that we lack evidence for these. If we are looking for the language, the conceptual tools which people used to evaluate their behav-iour, comprehend their world and resolve their personal tensions, we will find it here in the endeavour to realise a fundamentally communal ethical ideal, not in a struggle to resolve an individualistic dilemma.

We can see both Anselm and Aelred, then, as contributing to, or giving defi-nition to, an intellectual agenda, exploring friendship as a fundamental aspect of human relations and setting it in relation to both community and to the ascent to God. How does this relate to the wider monastic world? This is perhaps the most interesting question for current research in this area. Both lived at a time of important reform within monasticism, which went beyond the reform of abuses to a questioning of the nature and essential characteristics of the religious life. The renewed devotion to the literal interpretation of the *Rule* which led among other things to the dramatic rise of the Cistercians as well as sweeping Benedictine reforms, the claims of religious poverty, the air of asceticism in the reformed cloisters – none of this sits easily with a cult of sentimental, intimate or private friendship. It may be that Anselm and Aelred were wholly exceptional and at odds with the monastic culture of their contemporaries, and that their ideas do not in fact reflect anything of mainstream monastic culture. It may be

---

[94] *DSA*, 3.6: 'Nec omnes tamen quos diligimus in amicitiam sunt recipiendi, quia nec omnes ad hoc reperiuntur idonei.' Trans. Laker, *Spiritual Friendship*, p. 92.

that a wider cult of friendship, of which their writings were supreme expressions, was simply in conflict with the idealism of the new monasticism in the midst of which it flourished. Yet a friendship which was in harmony with the *Rule* because it gave expression to the ideals of community must surely make more sense both of the ideas of these two monastic writers and of this historical situation than any concept of friendship which was set against both *Rule* and community. A fuller understanding of this friendship must surely, in turn, form an integral part of our appreciation of monastic culture.

Monastic Time

J. D. NORTH

The Middle Ages might have had no quartz watches, no satellite time signals, no laws of entropy, no relativistic electrodynamics, but they were familiar enough with the numerous shades of meaning that inform our own daily uses of the word 'time' and its cognates, if we allow for slight differences of vocabulary and nuance. 'Time when' and 'time how long', both of them judged on scales of minutes, hours, years, centuries, were distinguished then more or less as now. The finiteness of human life was – then as now – what led ordinary people to wax philosophical on the subject of long periods of time duration. 'The life so short, The task so hard to learn.' It is a short step from thinking about the finiteness of one human life to the finiteness of mankind and the created world as a whole. In the same way our own experience is carved up into intervals of day and night in the way it has always been, give or take a little tampering at the edges of night, using artificial light. The length of a day remains the same. When we come to smaller intervals of time, time as experienced depends largely on what there is to fill it, and it is here that we differ most from those in the monastery. Measuring the hour, rather than the millisecond, was nevertheless something they wanted to do.

Here, then, are the three rough divisions into which I have divided this chapter: time in the longest intervals conceivable, time taken day by day throughout the year, and the hours into which the day is conveniently subdivided.

While the length of human life sets us thinking about the longest intervals of time, that does not mean that we all draw similar conclusions. Eschatology is the hidden variable. Attitudes to the 'four last things' – death, judgement, heaven, and hell – radically affected the medieval Christian outlook on time on the largest scale. While a few daring individuals played with Aristotelian fire, and considered the possibility that the world had no beginning in time, for most Christians the Old Testament account of creation meant that the world had existed for a few thousand years at most. The New Testament led most to suppose that once the second millennium had arrived, the world's history would be quickly over. I need not remind you of the importance accorded to Hexaëmeral literature in the upper reaches of scholarship. Scientific expertise had been called upon even in late antiquity by Basil, Ambrose, Augustine, Dracontius and others, in writing commentaries on the Book of Genesis. This exegetical tradition continued throughout the Middle Ages, with Grosseteste and Aquinas notable contributors to it. But you did not have to be a skilled philosopher or theologian to get the point about the creation of the world as a historical event, or to live in a state of apprehension about its expected end. You could even draw a simple philosophy of time out of the Bible, without struggling with Augustine's famous treatment of the idea that time begins and ends with the created material world. The Book of Revelation hints at much the same idea. As John Wyclif's version has it, the angel

> lifte up his hond ... and swoor bi hym that lyveth in to worldis ... that time schal no more be. (Rev. 10:6)

Time, on this Christian account, would soon be no more, although we are at the beginning of a difficult philosophical road down which I will not venture. It is a road leading to such questions as those of God's timelessness, heavenly timelessness, and eternity.

I want to stay firmly on the monastic hearth, where scholastic subtleties might have been lacking and where the word historiography had not yet appeared. Here, all were meant to see history as simply the working out of God's plan for mankind. The monastic historian was naturally committed to that equivalence, and the theme spilled over into literature too. One illustration of this from a monastic source is Bede's account of Caedmon, the illiterate herdsman who – without any prior training – was inspired to sing the story of Genesis and the unfolding of scriptural history. Caedmon also looked into the future, and to the final judgement, and so in a sense sang the song of all of time.[1]

There is no shortage of examples of history being fitted into the pattern of the six days of creation. Martin of Tours, father of Western monasticism, set the scene when he included a passage on Antichrist – if it is his – in the first *Dialogue*. Quintus Julius Hilarianus, writing in 397, thought that there were just 101 years to go before the six thousand years of history were up.[2] As a variant to the sixfold division there is Joachim of Fiore's tripartite view of history, based on his vision of a ten-stringed psaltery. The third *status* was to be won by the Church only after a great struggle in which would appear two new orders of spirituals, one of mountain-top hermits and one of spiritual meditators. Secular clergy and laymen were also found a place in his vision of the New Jerusalem, with various categories of monks grouped around the seat of God, with secular clergy and tertiaries below.[3] Joachim's theology of history seeped into the Franciscan order,

---

1 *Ecc. Hist.* IV. 24.
2 B. McGinn, *Visions of the End* (New York, 1979), pp. 50–53.
3 B. McGinn, *The Calabrian Abbot Joachim of Fiore in the History of Western Thought* (New York and London, 1985). Abbot Joachim (1130?–1202) founded his own monastic order of St John. The foundations of his teachings were revealed to him in a series of visions, one of which he had on the day of Pentecost, 1183, while visiting the important Cistercian monastery at Casamari. He writes: 'I had entered the church to pray to Almighty God before the Holy altar, there came upon me an uncertainty concerning belief in the Trinity, as though it were hard to understand or to hold that all the Persons [Father, Son, and Holy Spirit] were one God and one God all the Persons. When that happened, I prayed with all my might. I was very frightened and was moved to call on the Holy Spirit, whose feast day it was, to deign to show me the Holy mystery of the Trinity. The Lord has promised us that the whole understanding of truth is to be found in the Trinity. I repeated this and I began to pray the psalms to complete the number I had intended. At this moment without delay, the shape of a ten stringed psaltery appeared in my mind. The mystery of the Holy Trinity

and the fact that the third *status* that had been anticipated in 1260 failed to materialise did not put an end to apocalyptic history. This remained a powerful, often revolutionary, force into the seventeenth century, but one that was more influential within the mendicant orders, and visionary groups generally, than within the monasteries.

There was another, much more subtle, method of dividing up historical time that crept into Western theology from the direction of Islamic astrology, and this was influential wherever scientific learning was valued. The method postulates a pattern in the religious history of the world based on certain conjunctions of the planets Jupiter and Saturn. Drastic changes in the fortunes of religious sects were related to shifts in the triplicity (a set of three signs of the zodiac) in which such conjunctions occur. They remain within a triplicity for about 240 years before changing. Since there are altogether four triplicities, the complete cycle takes about 960 years, which is close on the traditional thousand.

The most famous book on great conjunctions was by Albumasar, but the doctrine was well known from many other writers. It can be used to provide stepping stones, for example from the rise of Islam to the birth of Luther, and much more besides. It became linked with non-astrological millenarianism, and if I were to mention Roger Bacon, Albertus Magnus, John Ashenden, Reginald Lambourne and John Lydgate as scholars who adopted it – a Franciscan, a Dominican, a secular and a couple of Benedictines for good measure – I should be in danger of obscuring the simple fact that almost *all* university men who had passed beyond the elements of astronomy accepted it in some degree. Was it anything more than lip service that they were paying to Arabic sources? A letter from the Benedictine Reginald Lambourne to William Rede of 1367 shows that he, at least, took it very seriously indeed.[4] History, in short, was made to exhibit the rhythm of the heavens, and so was a subject for scientific treatment.

Having drawn attention to some of the most comprehensive of all time divisions, I shall turn to something more familiar. I have no doubt that most historians, when asked about monastic time, would think first and foremost of the ecclesiastical calendar. Here we have a subject to which it is quite impossible to do justice in a short space, but I want to single out just one or two aspects of the long story. The core of the calendar is the list of saint's days, often a martyrology, always movable feasts (such as Easter), and gradually other festivals were added (for the consecration of virgins, for the faithful departed, for purification, for marriage, and so forth). These were simply the events which the Church wishes to commemorate annually, and which are included because some sort of public worship was planned for them. To this extent, the calendar was common

shone so brightly and clearly in it that I was at once impelled to cry out, What God is as Great as our God!'

This was the inspiration for his third main work, *Psalterium decem chordarum* where he expounds his doctrine of the Trinity and attacked the doctrine of 'quaternity' (an overemphasis on the 'one essence' of the Godhead that seems to separate it from the three Persons of the Trinity and so create a fourth), which he attributed to Peter Lombard.

4   Reginald Lambourne was a fellow of Merton who later became a Black Monk at Evesham and later still at St Mary's, York.

Church property, although local custom always shaped the finer detail. Often also included in such calendars was enough astronomical material to make it possible to regulate the variable parts – the movable feasts, the cycle of leap years, and in due course such phenomena as the phases of the moon and lunar and solar eclipses. I could enumerate a long list of astronomical, astrological, and related medical information that such calendars often contained, but the very fact that the calendar repeats after a solar year, and that the Easter cycle repeats after nineteen years, should be enough to make my simple point, which is that timekeeping within the Church, even at the most sacred level – which is to say, the celebration of Easter – was a question of bringing our experience into a relationship with the visible heavens.

For the counting processes by which the priest or clerk settled such questions as the date of Easter there were complex mnemonic schemes that could be applied with no great intellectual effort, and unfortunately no guarantee of understanding. Many of those who tried to apply them, often unsuccessfully, were no doubt under the impression that they were practising high science, but for that one needs to look to tables of a very different sort, namely those for calculating planetary positions. Here there are two Benedictines to be given honorable mention, Walter of Odington of Evesham Abbey and Richard of Wallingford, abbot of St Albans, from the early fourteenth century. I might mention also Thomas Cory of Muchelney Abbey from the mid-fifteenth, if only as a copyist of some of the most advanced tables of the period (Batecomb's, of 1348). Their work is at the very core of a burgeoning Western scientific consciousness, but to consider it would be to wander away from the simpler theme of the ecclesiastical calendar. Richard of Wallingford added to just such a calendar an astrological treatise, for the instruction an unspecified queen – probably Philippa, queen of Edward III. That was the exception. The rule was a commonplace document, intrinsically no more exciting than a pocket diary in which holidays are marked.

There is one aspect of the calendar, however, that does deserve mention in connection with a finer point of timekeeping that is often misrepresented. There was a groundswell of discontent with the underlying Julian calendar that several English scholars voiced, to some effect, at regular intervals between the early thirteenth century and the Gregorian reform of the calendar in the late sixteenth. Grosseteste and Bacon are the best known English complainants, but there were others, some of whom had their own ideas about schemes of improvement. The monastic contribution to this debate was not especially significant; the slip of the calendar was not yet very serious in Bede's day, although he did complain that the full moon was ahead of its date as given in standard lunar tables.[5] Another minorite complainant besides Bacon was Robert of Leicester. The most revolutionary English proposal was one made by Richard Monk, but despite his name he seems to have been no monk. He is described as a 'chaplain of England', and was educated at Oxford, where in 1434 he compiled calendrical tables using the Eyptian year of 365 days. More famous in his day were the conti-

---

[5] J. D. North, 'The Western Calendar', ch. 4, *The Universal Frame: Historical Essays in Astronomy, Natural Philosophy and Scientific Method* (London, 1989), p. 42.

nental contributions made by such activists as Nicholas of Cusa, Paul of Middel-
burg, and later Scaliger and Petavius, but my aim is not to trace the history of this
movement, let alone the astronomical details. I want merely to point out that
the whole question was never one of establishing a coherent calendrical scheme
merely for the sake of its astronomical accuracy. The aim of the movement, from
beginning to end, was to celebrate Easter on the 'correct' day. Several Christian
writers referred to the danger of becoming a laughing stock in the eyes of Muslim
and Jewish astronomers, for failure to agree over what was the most important
date of the Christian year. And as for the ecclesiastical calendar as a whole, that
too was far more than an empty shell into which events were entered in the
way we enter engagements in our diaries. It was nothing less than a script for a
dramatic commemoration of sacred history, from the Fall of mankind to Salvation. And the script, like that for the ages of the world commemorating the
Hexaëmeron, was keyed to the cosmos through the solar and lunar movements
that determined Easter.

My last time division will not be the calendar year with its day divisions, but
the hour, as a subdivision of the day. Ancient Egyptian practices ensured that
we reckon twenty-four of them to each day. The reason, strangely enough, is
a consequence of a certain *calendrical* convention, but this is not the place to
probe that rather complex matter any further.

The Egyptians, and after them the Babylonians, divided night into twelve
hours and daylight likewise. This convention resulted in hours that varied in
length with the season of the year. The astronomers, at least as early as eight
centuries before Christ, had their own rival scheme of 'equal hours', dividing
into twenty-four parts day and night taken together, something which we now
all consider to be self-evident. The common people, however, kept the other
convention of seasonally variable hours until, broadly speaking, the advent of
the mechanical clock.[6] Both regular and secular clergy, for whom the division
of time into hours was an important if not a precise art, followed the home-
spun convention, and not that of the astronomers, until the latter was gradually
forced upon all of society by an astronomical fifth column within the Church,
as I shall explain.

Before doing so, however, I should mention that quite apart from the two
chief conventions as to the lengths of hours, there were various conventions as
to the time from which they were reckoned. The ancient Egyptians commonly
reckoned the hours from dawn; from the late Middle Ages, 'Italian hours' are
often taken to be equal hours counted from half an hour after sunset; by 'Baby-
lonian hours' equal hours counted from sunset were often meant.[7] Writing in
Paris or Montpellier in 1271, Robertus Anglicus collected together some traditional ascriptions. 'Many Latins', he said, begin the day in the most natural way,

6   An ivory prism from Nineveh of perhaps the eighth century BC, now in the British Museum,
     shows that converting between the two systems of time-reckoning ('equal' and 'unequal'
     or 'seasonal' hours) was already clearly regarded as an astronomical problem.
7   Broadly speaking, those who, like the Jews and Muslims, used a lunar calendar began the
     day from sunset.

from sunrise, some however from the first sign of dawn, and the astronomers from noon. 'The Chaldaeans', he said, begin the day from midnight and 'the Jews' from sunset – something he supports from scripture.[8] The Jews had the custom of praying three times a day at the third, sixth and ninth hours, and the early Christians later extended that scheme, adding prayers at midnight (when Paul and Silas sang in prison) and at the beginning of day and night. It was St Benedict himself who added a seventh hour of prayer, compline, so completing this rule of the Church for the times of prayer, although one that was subject to much local variation. I will not even try to explain how matins could move around, as one moved from place to place, how lauds was occasionally combined with it, how sext and none could be joined, or vespers with compline.[9] The important thing is that the canonical hours mattered greatly, and that some means of deciding on the times of service was of crucial importance.

The times stipulated were at first understood to be in unequal hours, and in the monasteries of the Greek Orthodox Church unequal hours are still in general use. In Western Europe, however, with the advent of mechanical clocks, equal hours were generally substituted. Such clocks were neither a necessary nor a sufficient reason of the change. There were earlier methods of timekeeping that did in principle make equal hours a natural thing to record. Water clocks, used long before the advent of Christianity, were not particularly reliable, but once graduated they did in principle record intervals of time having nothing to do with the seasons. Even reciting penitential psalms as a way of timing – something that was not unknown – presumably leads to equal hours, although perhaps one recites more rapidly on a frosty night than a warm one.[10] The real change, however, came only with the invention of a fully mechanical clock in the late thirteenth century, and this was in large part the answer to a monastic need.

There are those who want to present the case differently, for example making the invention of the mechanical timepiece a response to socio-economic demand. The demand for prayer at ordained 'canonical hours' is not the only alternative to this more modish final cause, however. Those who look first to the character of a typical early clock and divide it into four parts – its drive, its

---

8   Here he has difficulty with the astrological notion of planetary hours, which seemed hard to reconcile with astronomers' practice.

9   Matins (*matutinum*) may be at midnight, although in France it was often earlier and in Italy even well after daybreak. Lauds (*laudes*) was in principle at sunrise, but has often been taken together with matins. Prime (*prima*, the first unequal hour, now often 6 a.m.), Terce (*tertia*, the third unequal hour, often 9 a.m.), Sext (*sexta*, the sixth unequal hour, noon) and None (*nona*, the ninth unequal hour, often 3 p.m.) are known as 'little day hours' and were in due course often said together. Vespers (*vesperae*) or evensong belongs to sunset, and is often combined with compline (*completorium*, often 9 p.m.). Early English habits of saying None at midday or of taking a midday meal in preparation for a later service has given the English language its peculiar usage of the word 'noon', since at least the thirteenth century. There are, however, old Dutch and French parallels.

The Church of England reduced the canonical hours to morning and evening prayer (later called 'matins' and 'evensong'). The Roman Catholic Church relaxed its own liturgical rule in several respects in 1971.

10.   *Medieval Lunar Astrology: A Collection of Representative Middle English Texts*, ed. M. Laurel Means (Lewiston, New York, 1993), p. 98.

escapement, its methods of time indication, and its display – have, in doing so, identified four different approaches to the historiographic question, providing four different answers to the question of origins. Tracing the evolution of drives, some will begin with water clocks and the like, others with strictly mechanical controls, and some perhaps with the influence of one on the other. Those who concern themselves chiefly with display will inevitably see in the mechanical clock an answer to the problem of turning a model of the heavens with the regular daily motion of the sky above our heads. There is good evidence that this was an important problem in the minds of the first monastic clockmakers, but it cannot explain away all the evidence. It accords well, however, with the fact that when time was indicated on the outside of the earliest mechanical clocks it was done with the help of an astrolabe dial. Against the importance of display, however, there is the argument that many early clocks – and we know nothing of the very first – had no external display, but indicated the time on the hour by means of a bell. As for the question of the evolution of a suitable escapement mechanism, while a desire to produce such a display might have been the chief motivation, there are those who believe that an accidental discovery of a suitable mechanism came first, and that only afterwards was an application sought for it.

The oldest detailed medieval account of the construction of a water-driven alarm for dividing the day into canonical hours is to be found in an incomplete tenth- or eleventh-century manuscript that was written in the Benedictine monastery of Santa Maria de Ripoll, at the foot of the Pyrenees.[11] The alarm had a simple weight-operated striking mechanism, with a rope and weight turning an axle which acted as a flail on small bells hanging from a rod. There was perhaps nothing more by way of dial-work than was needed to reset the alarm, a task no doubt undertaken by the sacristan, as laid down in the rules of the Cistercian, Cluniac, and Benedictine orders.[12] Another Iberian clock with a very simple bell-striking mechanism, this time driven with mercury, is described in the books of Alfonso X, the astronomer king of Leon and Castile in the late thirteenth century.

The first English payment with reference to a *horologium* that seems likely to have been truly mechanical occurs in Norwich in 1273/4; and when this 'old' clock was mentioned again in 1321 it was in connection with payment for a *chord*. This is not conclusive.[13] The earliest written record presently avail-

---

11 F. Maddison, B. Scott, and A. Kent, 'An Early Medieval Water Clock', *Antiquarian Horology*, 3 (1962), 348–53.

12 J. D. North, 'Monasticism and the First Mechanical Clocks', in *The Study of Time*, vol. 2, ed. J. T. Fraser and N. Lawrence (New York, 1975), pp. 381–98 at 383; J. D. North, *God's Clockmaker: Richard of Wallingford and the Invention of Time* (London, 2005), pp. 98–9.

13 When the new clock of 1322 was mentioned, no distinction was made between new and old in the matter of the word *horologium* used to describe both. C. F. C. Beeson, *English Church Clocks, 1280–1850* (London, 1971), pp. 13–16, collects together many early English references, and G. Brusa, *L'Arte dell'Orologeria in Europa. Sette Secoli di Orologi Meccanici*, Busto Arsizio, 1978, pp. 21–2, gives a well-balanced summary of that and the continental evidence. For the Norwich material see also North, *Richard of Wallingford. An edition of his writings with introduction, English translation and commentary*, 3 vols (Oxford, 1976), vol. 2, pp. 316–17.

able that seems certain to refer to a mechanical clock is one in the annals of Dunstable Priory, a house of Augustinian Canons in Bedfordshire. The date is 1283.[14] This record is one of a cluster of similar records appearing suddenly in English ecclesiastical annals of the last two decades of the thirteenth century and referring to *horologia*.[15] The records are usually cryptic, but taken in aggregate they seem to suggest that some new form of timepiece had become available, something costing much more than a sundial, for example. We are told, for instance, that at St Paul's, London, Bartholomew the *orologiarius* drew 281 rations for three quarters and eight days, early in 1286, and more later in the same year, after he was joined by William of Pikewell.

Such records as these lead us to suspect that we are in the presence of a new historical situation by the 1270s or 1280s, and we are fortunate in having two or three fragments of evidence of a very different sort, suggesting that the key invention had not been found at least by the year 1271 – if Robertus Anglicus is a reliable witness. Discussing equal and unequal hours, Robert made a remark to the effect that makers of clocks (*artifices horologiarum*) were trying to make a wheel that would complete one revolution for every revolution of the celestial sphere, that is, once a day.[16] They had not yet managed to perfect their work, he said. It is quite remarkable that out first English cluster of references comes from the next two decades.[17]

The first church clocks rang bells at the hours, and some, if not all, had simple displays. Once the one problem was solved, the other would have been straightforward, but unfortunately we cannot say which came first, display or bell-ringing. The first dials were fairly certainly complex affairs, based on an astrolabe design: a representation, that is, of the celestial sphere of fixed stars. There were other types of display on early clocks. Villard d'Honnecourt draws a device to ensure that the angel on the roof of the church always points towards the sun. There is still an angel of the sort that Villard seems to have had in mind surmounting the bell-tower of San Gottardo in Milan (1330–6), while St Paul's in London, and the cathedrals of Canterbury and Chartres, had similar angels.

The key English records from the 1280s are strangely laconic, and give no sign of local pride. Half a century later, Richard of Wallingford, abbot of St Albans and the foremost Oxford astronomer of his time, built for his abbey a clock in which all traditions came together: bell ringing, celestial display, solar

---

14   There are two arguments for reading the terse statement in this way. First, we are told that a clock was set up above the rood screen (*pulpitum*), a most inconvenient place for a water clock.

15   There are records from Exeter (1284), London (Old St Paul's, 1286), Norwich (1290), Ely (1291), and Christchurch (1292). There follow records for Salisbury (1306), and outside England for San Eustorgio, Milan (1309), Cambrai (1308 or 1318), and one or two more dubious instances.

16   North, 'Monasticism', p. 384.

17   Robert went on to make it clear that a weight-driven clock was at issue, for he mentioned in very general terms a uniformly balanced wheel with a lead weight hung from its axle. It is quite conceivable that he was here prompted by the words of Roger Bacon, written four years earlier, to much the same effect. Roger Bacon, *The 'Opus maius' of Roger Bacon*, ed. J. H. Bridges, 2 vols. (London, 1900). See also the Supplementary Volume, containing a revised text of the first three parts, etc. (London, 1900), vol. 2, pp. 202–3.

and lunar motions, including an eclipse mechanism, with a little astrology and a wheel showing the tides at London Bridge thrown in [see plate 15]. It was driven by a mechanism that had no equal in subtlety before the late sixteenth century. We know all this because he wrote a series of drafts for a treatise on the subject, although he did not live long enough to complete either the book or the clock. Son of a blacksmith though he was, he did not work alone on what was a truly massive enterprise. He was able to make use of the services of professional clock-makers, with the surname Stoke, presumably members of the same family, if they were not simply from the village of that name. Roger and Laurence of Stoke both go under the name of 'clockmaker' (*horologiarius*). The name of Roger of Stoke occurs in the obedientiary rolls of Norwich Cathedral in connection with the building of a new clock there from 1321 onwards. Consider just one detail from the financial records: the iron plate for the dial weighed 87 lbs and was probably five or six feet across. The St Albans clock was on the same grand scale. No matter what the sequence of events leading up to this phenomenon might have been, the end result, measuring out time in hours and minutes though it did, was in two respects an embodiment of monastic ideals. It paid homage to the work of the Creator of the world, and it summoned members of the convent to those services in which the Creator could be worshipped.

Index